Occupied St John's

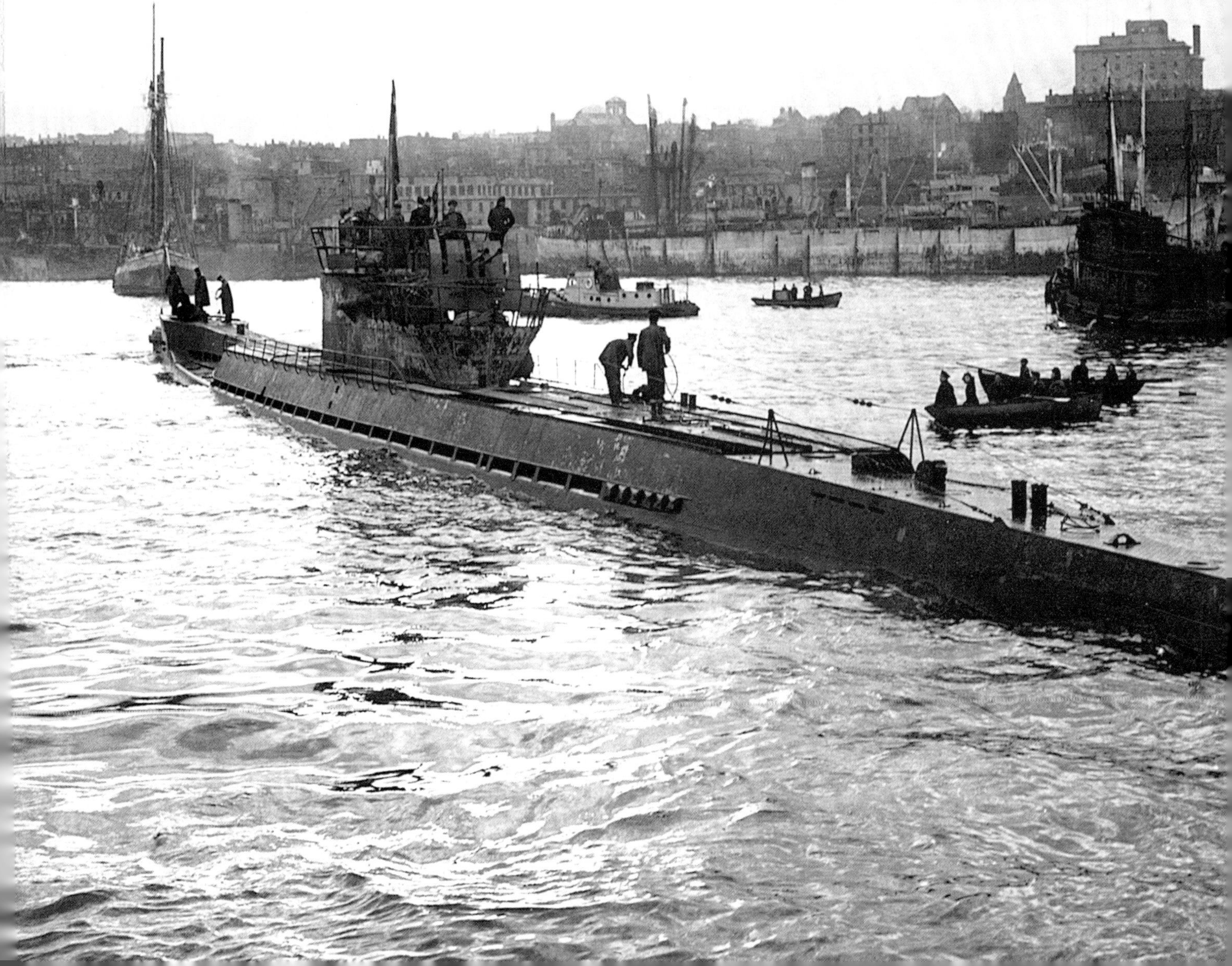

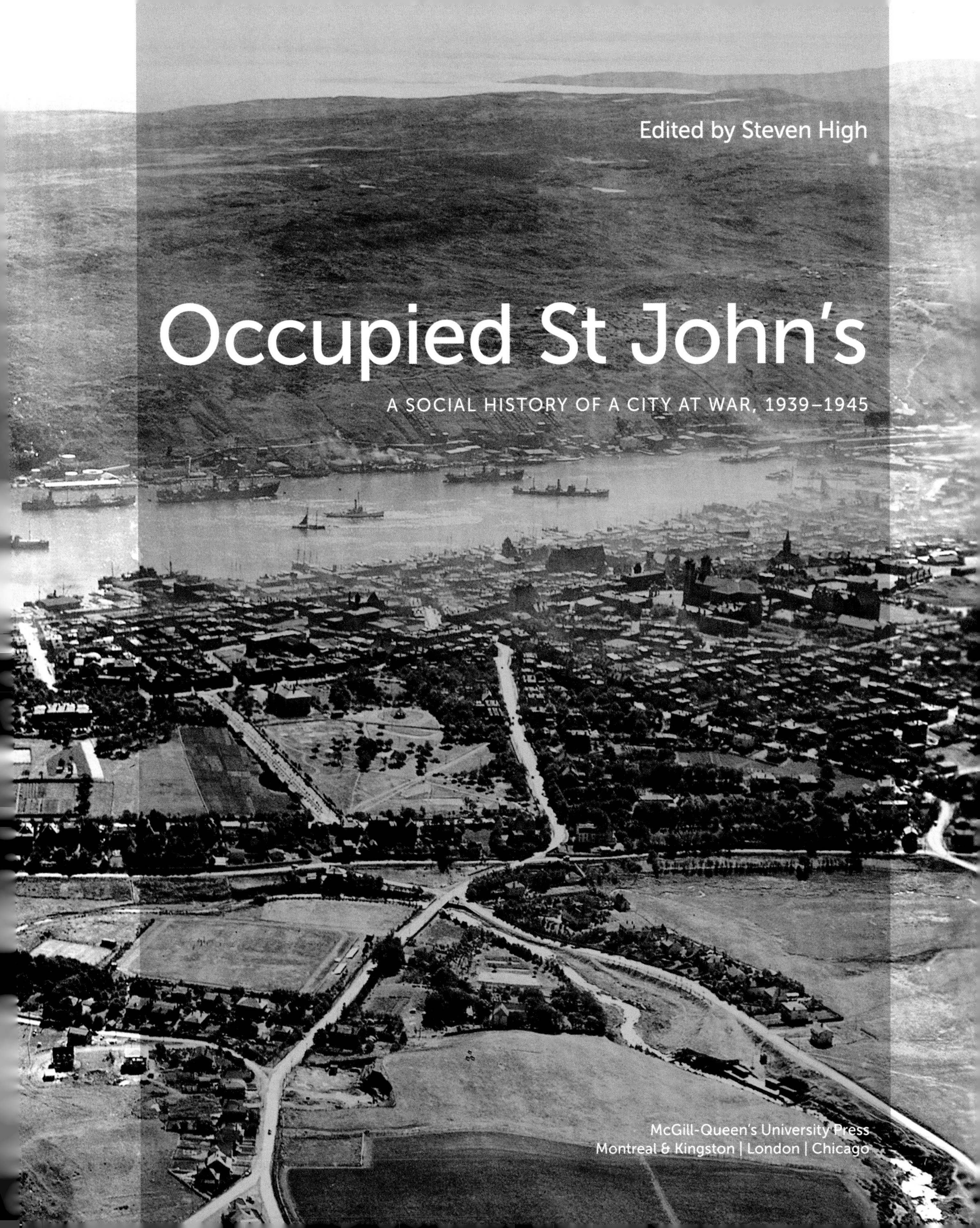

Edited by Steven High

Occupied St John's

A SOCIAL HISTORY OF A CITY AT WAR, 1939–1945

McGill-Queen's University Press
Montreal & Kingston | London | Chicago

ISBN 978-0-7735-3750-7 (cloth)
ISBN 978-0-7735-4817-6 (paper)
ISBN 978-0-7735-8110-4 (ePDF)

Legal deposit third quarter 2010
Bibliothèque nationale du Québec

First paperback edition 2016

Printed in China on acid-free paper

This book has been published with the help of a grant from the Canadian Federation for the Humanities and Social Sciences, through the Awards to Scholarly Publications Programme, using funds provided by the Social Sciences and Humanities Research Council of Canada. A generous subsidy from the Johnson Family Foundation made it possible to greatly increase the number of photographs.

McGill-Queen's University Press acknowledges the support of the Canada Council for the Arts for our publishing program. We also acknowledge the financial support of the Government of Canada through the Canada Book Fund for our publishing activities.

LIBRARY AND ARCHIVES CANADA CATALOGUING IN PUBLICATION

Occupied St John's : a social history of a city at war, 1939–1945 / edited by Steven High.

Includes bibliographical references and index.
ISBN 978-0-7735-3750-7 (cloth)
ISBN 978-0-7735-4817-6 (paper)
ISBN 978-0-7735-8110-4 (ePDF)

1. World War, 1939–1945 – Newfoundland and Labrador – St. John's. 2. St. John's (N.L.) – History, Military. 3. St. John's (N.L.) – History. 4. St. John's (N.L.) – Strategic aspects – History. 5. Civil-military relations – Newfoundland and Labrador – St. John's – History – 20th century. I. High, Steven C.

FC2196.3.O33 2010 971.8'103 C2010-902704-3

Set in 10/13 Calluna with Museo Sans 500
Book design & typesetting by Garet Markvoort, zijn digital

Contents

Illustrations and Tables vii

Acknowledgments xiii

Introduction 3

PART 1 NORTH AMERICA'S FIRST LINE OF DEFENCE

1 | Building a Wartime Landscape 21
Christopher A. Sharpe and A.J. Shawyer

2 | From Defended Harbour to Transatlantic Base 81
Paul Collins

PART 2 REMEMBERING WARTIME ST JOHN'S

3 | The Children's War 113
Barbara Lorenzkowski

4 | Rethinking the Friendly Invasion 151
Steven High

5 | Gate Keeping and Newfoundland Popular Culture 191
Jeff A. Webb

6 | Mona Wilson and the Canadian Red Cross 220
Gillian Poulter and Douglas O. Baldwin

PART 3 CONCLUSION

7 | The Occupation of St John's in Global Perspective 251
Ken Coates and William R. Morrison

Notes 271

Bibliography 303

Contributors 311

Index 313

Illustrations and Tables

ILLUSTRATIONS

HMCS *Wetaskiwin* gun shield art 3
HMCS *Wetaskiwin* gun shield art 3
U.S. transport ship *Edmund B. Alexander,* 1941 4
Aerial view of St John's Harbour 5
Aerial view of St John's Harbour 6
Funeral for those who died in the Knights of Columbus fire 9
Servicemen standing on a wharf on the South Side 10
Depth-charge explosion 11
Convoy in the North Atlantic 12
Norton-class tug HMS *Riverton* (W-47) at HMC Dockyard 14
Bill White and Harold Lake at the observation post in Italy 15
Newfoundland constable on traffic duty 15
YMCA "Red Triangle" hostel on Water Street 16
Horse-and-sleigh races on Quidi Vidi Lake 17
HMCS *Skeena* gun shield art 21
St John's, the harbour and the city, 1940 22
Sergeants of the Lincoln and Welland Regiment 25
The city and harbour looking east, 1940 28
Plan of the Shamrock Field Camp of the Newfoundland Militia 29

Canadian Army Lester's Field Camp, 1942 30
Plan of Lester's Field Camp 31
Lester's Field Camp, 1942 32
Barracks, Lester's Field Camp, 1942 32
Fort Amherst and the RCN Port War Signal Station 33
Two unidentified soldiers and the Canadian Army buildings at Fort Amherst 34
Fort Chain Rock and the Narrows 34
One of the 75-mm field guns at Fort Chain Rock 34
Fort Chain Rock and one of the anti-torpedo baffles 35
One of the ten-inch guns at Cape Spear, c. 1942 36
Cape Spear from the east, 1941 36
The sentry box at Fort Chain Rock 37
25th Regiment, RCA, Heavy Anti-Aircraft Battery, 1941 38
The Light Anti-Aircraft Battery on Hill O'Chips 38
The Light Anti-Aircraft Battery on the South Side Hills 39
An unidentified Canadian soldier manning the Hill O'Chips battery 39
Calver's Field and Shamrock Field camps, 1942 40
Requisitioned property on the site of Fort Pepperrell, 1943 45
Plan of Camp Alexander 47
Camp Alexander 48
Fort Pepperrell and Signal Hill, 1941 49
Fort Pepperrell from the north, c. 1948 50
U.S. Army Barracks on Signal Hill, 1941 51
The American eight-inch coastal defence guns on Signal Hill, 1941 52
Requisitioned buildings on the site of the U.S. Army Supply Dock, 1942 53
Plan of RCN and RCAF Headquarters 54
Combined RCN/RCAF Operations Room, 1942 55
RCAF No. 1 Group Barracks on Kenna's Hill 56
St John's, December 1941 59
Typical wharves and buildings on the South Side of St John's Harbour 60
St John's Harbour and HMC Dockyard, 1942 61
HMC Dockyard, the city, and HMCS Avalon, c. 1942 63
Plan of HMCS Avalon 64
Two unidentified nursing sisters and Surgeon Lieutenant Riddell 65
A bunch of "Flowers" on the South Side of St John's Harbour 66

Construction work on the South Side of St John's Harbour, 1943 67
RCN Barracks on the South Side Hills, 1945 67
Flower-class corvette HMCS *Saskatoon* on the slipway at Bay Bulls, 1944 69
American M3 Stuart tanks on Military Road, All Nations Day Parade, 1943 71
One of the ten-inch gun barrels at Cape Spear in 2009 74
The ruined gun emplacements at Fort Chain Rock in 2009 75
Fort Amherst in 2009 76
Still serving: the city and one of the 4.7" guns at Fort Amherst 77
Graves of forty of the victims of the Knights of Columbus fire 78
The American army dock in 2008 79
Maps of military sites in the St John's area (foldout) *following 80*
HMCS *Moose Jaw* gun shield art 81
St John's Harbour from the South Side, 1944 82
Corvettes moored alongside the South Side wharf 83
Major-General W.H.P. Elkins, Atlantic Command, inspecting a Sergeants' Mess 85
Downtime on a Canadian corvette 87
Depth charges on HMCS *Matapedia* 87
Rough water 88
HMCS *Matapedia* outside the Narrows 89
Battery Village 90
HMCS *Matapedia* in the North Atlantic in winter 92
"The BL 4" gun on the foc'sle of HMCS *Midland* 92
River-class destroyer HMCS *St Laurent* leaving port 93
Friendship 95
Horsing around 96
HMS *Smiter* near the American dock 98
Picking up survivors from a sunken U-boat 99
Looking out over St John's Harbour 103
Sailors in port 104
More sailors 106
HMCS *Trillium* gun shield art 113
HMCS *Saskatoon* gun shield art 113
St John's Harbour entrance 114
St John's, from harbour 115
St John's street scene 118

Sterling Restaurant at 348 Water Street 120
Streetcars travelling east on Water Street 121
Winter street scene in St John's 123
Running child 125
Aerial view of St John's Harbour, c. 1940 127
An American soldier standing with a young boy on Long's Hill 128
Soldier on a bicycle in front of the Tractor and Equipment Company building on Water Street 128
Looking down Power Street towards the RCN Barracks on the South Side Hills 129
Bowring Park, 1942 130
A soldier and child, possibly outside the sanatorium on Topsail Road 131
Winter conditions at sea 132
View of the Knights of Columbus building at the corner of Harvey Road and Parade Street 133
View of the ruins of the Knights of Columbus hostel after the fire 136
Funeral procession for the victims of the Knights of Columbus fire 137
The severely damaged ship remembered by people interviewed 139
Canadian Army convoy leaves Lester's Field Camp, 1941 140
St John's at night, after the blackout 142
RCAF Church Parade on Military Road 144
HMCS *Dauphin* gun shield art 151
Gun shield art on board the HMCS *Dolphin* 151
American troops leaving for Newfoundland, c. 1941 152
The *Edmund B. Alexander* 153
Church Parade of the RCAF Women's Division 154
Shipwrights gun shield art 157
A Red Cross vehicle with blackout blinders 157
"Two of the 'O' boats at HMC Dockyard" 159
Guarding the gate 161
Newfoundland Constabulary, c. 1941 162
The York Theatre 164
Inside the Knights of Columbus building/hostel on Harvey Road 167
Able Seaman Levis Leboeuf, RCN Volunteer Reserve, 1942 167
Unidentified merchant seamen, 1942 169
Survivors, 1942 169
Civilian workers at Fort Pepperrell 170

"British submarine P554" 173
Posted to Newfie 174
Royal Navy anti-submarine escort carrier HMS *Smiter* in St John's 177
Gun play 178
Blacked-out headlights, c. 1942 183
Avalon taxi 184
South Side barracks 186
HMS *Burwell* gun shield art 191
Aerial photograph of Fort Pepperrell and Quidi Vidi Lake 195
Presentation by U.S. Army officers to civilian workers at the Fort Pepperrell base 196
Edgar Bergen and Charlie McCarthy on stage 196
Couples dancing 198
Audience sitting at band concert 199
Civilian employees at Fort Pepperrell 200
Early construction of the Fort Pepperrell army base in St John's, 1941 201
U.S. soldiers going for a walk 203
American soldiers embarking on a troopship bound for home, 1945 205
American troopship departing for home, 1945 209
HMCS *Transcona* gun shield art 220
Surrendered German U-boat in St John's Harbour 221
Mona Wilson, assistant Red Cross commissioner, Newfoundland 222
Harbour viewed from gun emplacement at Cabot Tower 224
A party at the Caribou Hut 227
A spot of tea or coffee for all callers at the Canadian Red Cross office 228
Mona Wilson in front of the Red Cross office 229
Naval officers' wives filling comfort bags for survivors 230
Mona Wilson and volunteers with ditty bags 231
Mona Wilson welcoming survivors at Canadian Red Cross headquarters 233
Lascars from India – merchant seamen survivors landed in St John's 234
Delivering mail to ships 235
Country drive and picnic for hospital patients 236
Mona Wilson with Major Moore and Major Klock 237
Sorting fish, 1945 239
"Taken from my window in the Newfoundland Hotel, 1945" 240
Mona Wilson in the Red Cross station wagon 242

Blackout announcement, *Evening Telegram,* 22 May 1940 243
Civil Defence Information Memorandum No. 13, *Evening Telegram,* 11 April 1942 243
Miss Maud Krumm and the Red Cross truck 245
Canadian Red Cross staff 247
HMS *Dianthus* gun shield art 251
Surrendered German submarine U-190, 1945 253
"Newfy V.E. Day" 257
HMCS *Burlington* victory party, 1945 260

TABLES

Table 4.1 Employment on Canadian and American bases in Newfoundland 187
Table 7.1 U.S. armed forces, global distribution, April 1945 262

Acknowledgments

Occupied St John's is the product of a three-year-long collaboration among ten contributors, fifty interviewees, and the Johnson Family Foundation. The project was initiated by Paul Johnson, who envisioned a book on 1940s St John's, Newfoundland. The war years have largely escaped the attention of historians, and Mr Johnson wanted the city's social history told. To that end, James Hiller was brought on as an advisor and managing editor. He then approached me. For years, I had been researching the U.S. military presence in Newfoundland, Bermuda, and the British Caribbean and so I had a head start. As my book *Base Colonies in the Western Hemisphere* was already coming out, I agreed to edit an anthology that would delve deeply into the experience of the city, its residents, and visiting servicemen and servicewomen. Mr Johnson flew me to St John's for a meeting, where we agreed on an anthology that would speak to academics and to the larger public. It would be an anthology with a difference, as the contributors who answered our 2006 "Call for Proposals" would benefit from a shared research base. The Johnson Family Foundation generously funded the newspaper research and allowed us to employ students to conduct fifty interviews with those who remembered the wartime city. The interviewees were tremendously generous with their time, answering our many questions. Everyone seemed to be as excited with the project as we were. The Johnson Family Foundation provided office space and telephone service for the interview team, which consisted of myself, Kenny Hammond, Stefan Jensen, Nancy Rebelo, Stephen MacPherson, and Kristen O'Hare. The bulk of the interviewing was done by Kenny, a Memorial University student. We would like to thank the many people who assisted with the logistics of this phase of the project, especially Heddy Peddle, Dale Russell Fitzpatrick, and Judy Rudofsky from the Johnson Family

Foundation. The recording equipment came from the Centre for Oral History and Digital Storytelling at Concordia University.

The Johnson Family Foundation has also provided a generous publication subsidy to McGill-Queen's University Press, allowing us to include far more photographs than would otherwise be possible. *Occupied St John's* therefore offers a visual record of the war years. These evocative photographs were found in a variety of places in Newfoundland, such as the St John's City Archives, the Maritime History Archives, the Centre for Newfoundland Studies, and the Public Archives of Newfoundland and Labrador. We would like to thank the many archivists for all of their assistance. Special thanks go out to Helen Miller at the St John's City Archives and to Gary Green of the Crow's Nest Military Artefacts Association, who went "above and beyond." Gary, for example, contacted a number of private individuals who donated wartime photographs to the splendid "Battle of the Atlantic" online exhibition, part of the Virtual Museum of Canada. We would like to thank these donors for giving us permission to reproduce their images here. When told of our idea to open each chapter with a photograph of one of the gun shields that decorate the walls of the Crow's Nest Officers' Club, Gary offered to share his speaker's notes for visitors. They include remarkable stories, and we have included them as captions. Thanks, Gary! Other photographs were found at the Public Archives and Records Office of Prince Edward Island and Library and Archives Canada in Ottawa, as well as at the Canadian War Museum. Still others were scanned from the photo albums of the Canadian sailors that Barbara Lorenzkowski interviewed in Halifax for another project. The two maps included here were created by Charlie Conway of the Memorial University of Newfoundland Cartographic Laboratory. He also painstakingly pieced together a mosaic of more than 200 aerial photographs, available online. We therefore see St John's from a variety of angles.

As editor, I would like to offer a special thank you to the contributors to the book. I could not have hoped for a better group of historians and historical geographers to respond to our initial call for proposals. They have been tremendously supportive throughout the process and generous in providing feedback to me and to one another. Every contributor had the opportunity to read multiple drafts of each chapter. Douglas Baldwin even proofread the entire manuscript as it neared completion. Most of all, however, I would like to thank James Hiller, who has been a rock during this long process. He invested many hours in the project, as did Heddy Peddle. Both believed deeply in the project and helped push it to completion. I would also like to thank Gary Browne for his words of encouragement along the way. And it has been a privilege to work with Paul Johnson, whose love of Newfoundland and its history made this project possible. Thank you!

We also benefited from positive feedback from the anonymous reviewers at McGill-Queen's University Press as well as from those who attended the "Occupied St. John's" session at the 2009 meeting of the Canadian Historical Association, where four contributors shared their findings. From the moment we approached John Zucchi, the press has been fully behind the project. I would also like to thank Joan McGilvray, Kyla Madden, and Judith Turnbull for their constructive feedback. Additional funding from the Canada Research Chairs program paid for some editorial support as the manuscript neared completion. I want to thank Matthew MacDonald and Anna Sheftel for their assistance in this regard.

Last but not least, I would like to acknowledge the many people who agreed to be interviewed for this project and whose stories appear in the chapters that follow. Their willingness to share their wartime memories with strangers has enriched this book, bringing it to life. While limited space has meant that only a small fraction of these war stories have made it into the book, the recordings will soon be available to other researchers and the public. These interview recordings are yet another contribution to Newfoundland history as well as to the history of the Second World War.

Occupied St John's

Introduction

STEVEN HIGH

Left HMCS *Wetaskiwin* gun shield art. "Wetaskiwin is probably the most famous of the gun shields. The Queen sitting in a puddle of water is known as 'The Wet Ass Queen,' an obvious play on the ship's name. Note that the puddle resembles the map of Newfoundland. The date (May 1941) refers to the ship's arrival in St. John's to establish the Newfoundland Escort Force (NEF). It is the first gun shield ever painted and the second to be hung in the Nest. The painting originally hung in Wetaskiwin's wardroom." Gary Green, *A Guide for Some of the Gun Shield Art and Ship's Badges of the Crow's Nest Officer's Club* (St John's: Crow's Nest Military Artifacts Association, Newfoundland).

Right HMCS *Wetaskiwin* gun shield art. From photograph album of Marjorie Ferguson, Halifax.

> The city of St John's looks like the slum district of Chicago. They have streetcars and automobiles. The people drive on the opposite side of the road, I can't tell if I'm in an alley or a street. The people talk a little different than we do but not much. After each statement they say, "You know." We will live on ship until June 1st. We eat in the mess hall. It takes about forty-five minutes for us to be served and eat. There are 1,000 men eating at once ... There is not much snow here. It rains about every other day, seems to be warmer here. I climb up into a mountain some and go ice skating. I skate up above the clouds.
>
> Cecil Hutchens, 1 March 1941[1]

Cecil Hutchens, a nineteen-year-old soldier from Iowa, wrote these words to his parents soon after arriving in St John's on board the giant troopship *Edmund B. Alexander.* He was one of a thousand American soldiers sent to garrison Newfoundland against a possible German attack. France had fallen and Great Britain was fighting for its very survival. Fearing the worst, President Franklin D. Roosevelt sought to secure the Panama Canal and the Atlantic and Caribbean approaches to North America. In exchange for fifty old destroyers, Great Britain agreed to lease army and navy base locations for ninety-nine years in Newfoundland, Bermuda, and the British Caribbean.[2] Roosevelt repeatedly called the Anglo-American destroyers-for-bases deal of 2 September 1940 the single most important act in the defence of the United States since Thomas Jefferson purchased Louisiana from Napoleon Bonaparte.[3] Newfoundland's proximity to the North Atlantic shipping lanes and its emerging role as a stepping stone in the "Great Circle Route" for transatlantic aviation gave it tremendous stra-

U.S. transport ship *Edmund B. Alexander*, 1941. Donated by Captain Harry Stone. PF-306.749, box 03, Maritime History Archive.

tegic value in 1940–41. The nagging fear that German air power might somehow establish a toehold in the Western Hemisphere likewise made it imperative that the United States and Canada secure the virtually undefended dominion.[4] In the memorable words of historian Peter Neary, the large-scale deployment of Canadian and American troops quickly transformed the island into a "garrison country."[5]

Soldiers, sailors, and airmen flooded into Newfoundland. Cecil Hutchens's Minnesota-based unit was part of the first wave of American servicemen to be deployed in and around St John's. This unit had gone by train to New York City, a journey that took three days. "There were two train loads of us," Hutchens wrote to his parents. "Each train had eight coaches and one baggage car." Upon their arrival in New York, the servicemen immediately boarded the troopship the SS *Edmund B. Alexander*. "The U.S. captured this ship from the Germans in the [First] World War," he continued. "It was rebuilt in 1928 and is the S.S. American ship now. It hasn't been used for nine years. It is a very nice ship, seems just like a hotel only it rocks."[6] And rock it did. The troopship sailed for seven days, catching a "light storm" on the way. "The waves got as high as 50 feet," Hutchens reported. Living arrangements on the vessel were so cramped that four men were assigned to each cabin, which measured just nine square feet. Hutchens later recalled that "there was only enough room for one of us to get up and get dressed. When he moved out, the next would get up and so on."[7]

When the *Edmund B. Alexander* finally entered St John's Harbour on 29 January 1941, the arriving soldiers were warmly welcomed with a "big parade." The ship, said to be the largest to enter the Narrows up to that point, acted as a floating barracks until the spring time. Everyone we interviewed for this project recalled the gleaming white ship berthed on the South Side and the excitement that accompanied its arrival. Like many of his compatriots, Cecil Hutchens fell in love with a Newfoundland woman, and they married in 1942. Unlike most newlyweds, the couple settled in St John's after the war. Hutchens's story and that of the *Edmund B. Alexander* have been joined ever since. In 1996, at the age of seventy-five, Hutchens was featured in a full-page story in the *Evening Telegram;* the article pictured him holding a giant Stars and Stripes flag and featured several historic photographs of the ship. "He's the last in the province of those American soldiers who came here 55 years ago," wrote journalist Bob Benson.[8] In our 2007 oral history interview, Cecil Hutchens indicated that he had always been known in St John's as one of the boys who came over on the great ship.[9] As we will see, the vessel's arrival looms large in Newfoundland's public memory of the war, marking for many the beginning of the "friendly invasion" of the country. In consequence, it has largely overshadowed the arrival of Canadian servicemen to the city.

There is little doubt that the war years had a profound effect on St John's and its inhabitants, yet the social history of the wartime city has been largely overlooked. In part, this startling absence is due to the continuing enmity between military and social historians in Canada and the United States. Political differences between the two fields have served to exaggerate the divide between "home front" (social history) and "battle front" (military history). This division of scholarly labour is plainly evident in the historical writing about wartime St John's.[10] For their part, Newfoundland historians such as Peter Neary have examined the impact of the war from the vantage point of the Newfoundland

Aerial view of St John's Harbour. Control no. 19900192-018-1, Canadian War Museum.

state, the six-person, appointed Commission of Government that ruled the country from 1934 to 1949.[11] The global economic crisis of the 1930s had a devastating impact on Newfoundlanders and nearly bankrupted their government. British financial support came with a heavy price – the end of democratic self-government. With all six commissioners (three Newfoundlanders and three British civil servants) appointed by the British government, Newfoundlanders had no say in the decision to lease land to the United States for army and navy bases. The 99-year-leased bases loom large in Neary's wartime "home front" narrative, overshadowing the city's important role as a naval base. By contrast, Canadian naval historians such as Marc Milner and Bernard Ransom have documented the central role of "Newfyjohn" as a naval base in the Second World War, but have done so with little or no reference to the impact of the base on the town itself.[12] We therefore get little sense of the everyday realities of living in a city at war or the impact of the war on the city's 40,000 inhabitants.[13]

Yet, as we will see, port cities like St John's defy easy categorization. Old distinctions between "home front" and "war front" were erased as the city's residents were thrown into the thick of it. "We all felt we were in the front lines because of the ships and the convoys," recalled Paul O'Neill.[14] So numerous were the soldiers, airmen, and sailors from Canada and the United States that the residents of St John's took to calling their arrival a "friendly invasion." The *Evening Telegram*, for example, ran an editorial on 3 February 1941, shortly after the

Aerial view of St John's Harbour. Control no. 19900192-018-1, Canadian War Museum.

arrival of Cecil Hutchens on the *Edmund B. Alexander*, succinctly entitled "Occupation of St. John's."[15] This reference and others like it convinced us that *Occupied St John's* was an appropriate title for this book.

The dozens of images that appear in these pages provide further evidence of the profound impact of the American and Canadian "invasion" of St John's. We see aerial photographs of the wartime city, the bustling harbour, military installations under construction, marching servicemen and women, and the aftermath of the devastating Knights of Columbus fire. We also catch glimpses of everyday life. From the vantage point of visiting servicemen and women, we see the camaraderie and cramped conditions on board the convoy escorts and the hard conditions at sea. These photographs are an integral part of the chapters that follow.

Each chapter begins with a photograph of gun shield art that has been on display since the war in the Crow's Nest Officers' Club – perched on the top floor of a four-storey warehouse downtown. According to Gary E.H. Green, who regularly gives tours of the club on behalf of the Crow's Nest Military Artifacts Association, painted gun shield art "bear[s] testament to the many naval ships and officers which have visited the port of St John's and the Nest since it opened in 1942," and is a living memorial to the navy crews who fought and died in the North Atlantic during the Second World War. Green suggests that gun shield art first appeared at the Crow's Nest soon after it opened: "Ships' officers following Captain (D) Mainguy's directive not to deface the Nest's walls with graffiti, but to leave a memento no larger than two feet by two feet, created cartoons depicting some attribute of the ship or its company. These designs were subsequently copied on the ships' forward gun shield." The first gun shield to be placed in the Nest, according to Green, was the "Wet Ass Queen" (HMCS *Wetaskiwin*). We therefore placed it at the outset of the introduction. The captions provided for the painted gun shields come from Green's tour pamphlet, which he so generously shared with us.

This book also features several maps of the wartime city, locating military installations and providing further orientation to readers unfamiliar with St John's. A special mosaic map, painstakingly pieced together using aerial photographs, by Charlie Conway of the Department of Geography at Memorial University, allows you to zoom in to the wartime city and explore its nooks and crannies. It works much like Google Earth, but circa 1942. We have arranged to upload it onto the website of the Centre for Oral History and Digital Storytelling at Concordia University (http://storytelling.concordia.ca/occupied/).

Those expecting a complete history of St John's during the Second World War may be disappointed, however, as an anthology cannot cover all the ground. Still, while each author has approached the city in his or her own way, they have also read and commented on one another's chapters. We also benefited from the fifty oral history interviews conducted for this project. The life stories of the interviewees surface in multiple chapters, further connecting the seven chapters together. *Occupied St John's* consists of six thematic chapters divided into two sections of equal length as well as a concluding chapter.

PART I: NORTH AMERICA'S FIRST LINE OF DEFENCE

> It is a matter of historical fact that the rock-bound east coast of this rugged island is just about the most strategic piece of ground in the world, with Gibraltar the probable exception. As far as the Battle of the Atlantic is concerned, nothing can touch it ... It is in every sense of the word, a garrison town. Newfoundland itself is a garrison island, the most important in the North Atlantic.
>
> Trent Frayne, *Globe and Mail* (Toronto), 11 June 1943

Part I of this anthology, "North America's First Line of Defence," comprises two chapters that examine the rapid militarization of the city and its harbour. Photographs and maps are integral to the story being told here. In chapter 1, "Building a Wartime Landscape," historical geographers Christopher A. Sharpe and A.J. Shawyer, both at Memorial University, challenge the view that the "friendly invasion" came in one big wave that inundated the city. Rather, they claim, the occupation of St John's came in four waves. The Canadian Army ("W" force) arrived first, in 1940, establishing itself at Lester's Field and at Fort Amherst, guarding the mouth of the Narrows. The Americans followed with the arrival of the *Edmund B. Alexander* in January 1941. The U.S. Army (Newfoundland Base Command) selected a tract of farmland alongside Quidi Vidi Lake, known as Pleasantville, for the site of Fort Pepperrell. From there, U.S. servicemen quickly spread out to other sites in and around the city, including Signal Hill. The Royal Canadian Air Force, which built a new aerodrome at Torbay, on the outskirts of the city, constituted the third wave. The final wave came from the sea in the form of the Royal Canadian Navy. St John's, or "Newfyjohn" as it was fondly called by Canadian sailors, became a major naval base for convoy escorts and a port of refuge for stricken ships and survivors plucked out of the North Atlantic. The presence of the "sheepdog" navy was perhaps most obvious of all, dominating as it did the harbour and the South Side. The authors remind us that the "harbour was the city's lifeblood, its window on the world." Yet wartime restrictions prohibited any photographs being taken of the harbour, and much of the Canadian military infrastructure, built on land leased only for the duration of the war, was demolished at war's end.

Sharpe and Shawyer reveal how each new wave established a base of operations in or around the city and then spread out to occupy a dense web of restricted areas in the city and its environs. In each instance, the authors identify the social and economic consequence of this occupation and draw comparisons between them. "Squeezing military installations into the fabric of an established town like St John's often led to conflict," they write. The expropriation of homes and businesses to make way for the American and Canadian bases, for example, resulted in the displacement of dozens of families. Occupation became much more than a metaphor, but an accurate description of the scale and scope of the growing military presence in the city.

In chapter 2, Paul Collins, a Newfoundland-based naval historian, examines the transformation of the harbour itself from defended port to naval base. St

Funeral for those who died in the Knights of Columbus fire of 12 December 1942. View taken looking southeast, overlooking the Fort Townshend barracks, St Bon's, and the Basilica. Photo #01-11-22, City of St John's Archives.

John's played a key role as an escort base and port of refuge during the war. Until recently, most of the historical scholarship on the Battle of the Atlantic has been written by American or British historians. This fact served to minimize Canada's role and to denigrate it. It was only with the publication of Marc Milner's *North Atlantic Run* that the Royal Canadian Navy began to get the attention that it richly deserves. Building on Milner's lead, Collins shows us how St John's went from being a defended port to "one of the most important escort bases in the Battle of the Atlantic." In the process, we learn that St John's was an important site of refuge for stricken ships and survivors. Evidence suggests that fully 6,000 survivors were cared for in the city, and the city's cemeteries provide ample proof that many others did not make it.

Newfoundlanders were by no means bystanders to the warfare raging around them. With the outbreak of war in Europe in 1939, Newfoundland men enlisted in large numbers. In all, 3,419 served in the Royal Navy; 713 in the Royal Air Force; 3,600 in the overseas forestry unit; 1,668 in the Newfoundland Militia; 1,160 in the Canadian forces; and as many as 10,000 in the merchant marine.[16] Even the traumatic memory of the first war, when the Newfoundland Regiment was all but decimated in a single day, did not deter them from enlisting. This patriotism could be found in the unlikeliest of places. The general manager of the Newfoundland Railway, for example, exhorted his employees to greater effort in his bulletin of 1 November 1939: "Our contribution is that of loyalty and patriotism first. The war demands on the British Treasury suggest that we, as loyal and patriotic British, have a special job to do to save society for [*sic*] Nazism and Bolshevism, which means Cannibalism. Therefore we must do our bit. Let us do it together and attack the enemy man-fashion."[17]

Servicemen standing on a wharf on the South Side, looking towards numerous warships docked at St John's Harbour during World War II. Photo #01-045-025, City of St John's Archives.

It might seem far-fetched today, but many North Americans feared the worst in the months that followed the fall of France. Great Britain stood virtually alone against the German war machine. What would happen should the Royal Navy fall into German hands? Would North America be safe behind its oceanic moat? The United States had long depended on British control of the Atlantic Ocean, as its one-ocean navy was concentrated almost entirely in the Pacific. A prominent story that ran in the *New York Times* in August 1940 warned that Germany might attack Canada and other parts of the British Empire should Great Britain succumb.[18] This news story was accompanied by several photos, including one of a picturesque Newfoundland outport "near St John's." In the crisis atmosphere that then prevailed, even this innocuous tourist photograph seemed designed to tell readers that the island stood defenceless.

Much the same point was raised in letters to the editor to North American newspapers, including the Toronto *Globe and Mail*. Alfred B. Morine, a former member of the Newfoundland House of Assembly, for example, warned in July 1940 that should Britain fall, "Newfoundland is the danger point, and its defense from invasion is vital for the Empire, to Canada, and to the whole American continent." Indeed, the "seawalls of St. John's should forth with be adequately protected by forts and soldiers. The hour to occupy them has come."[19] Soon thereafter, Morine got his wish when Canada announced that it would spend a million dollars fortifying Newfoundland. The island was "regarded as one of the Dominion's most important outer defences," reported the *Toronto Daily Star.* The Newfoundland airport at Gander was now deemed "as significant as Singapore, the Suez Canal or Gibraltar."[20]

At 42,000 square miles, Newfoundland is the tenth-largest island in the world, and it stands just 1,640 miles from the Irish coast, flanking sea and air routes.[21] To shore up the defence of North America after the fall of France, the United States and Canada formed the Permanent Joint Board of Defence in August 1940.[22] Not a party to the agreement, Newfoundland was certainly on the agenda. "Newfoundland ports," the *New York Times* reported soon thereafter, "may soon be converted into fortified naval bases."[23] Two weeks later, with the Anglo-American destroyers-for-bases deal signed, readers of the *New York Times* were shown a panoramic view of St John's taken from Signal Hill. The caption read: "The Newfoundland base is of major importance to protect any northeastern approach of the United States."[24]

Newfoundland's strategic value was subject to hundreds of news stories in North American newspapers.[25] Sometimes these articles were accompanied by a map locating the island and its new bases. In January 1941, the *New York Times*

Depth-charge explosion. Photo 0042 from photograph album of John Cecil Stevens, Halifax.

Convoy in the North Atlantic. Photo 0047 from photograph album of John Cecil Stevens, Halifax.

published photographs of Newfoundland-bound U.S. soldiers clad in parkas and fur hats on board the *Edmund B. Alexander*.[26] "The Newfoundland base is ideally placed to defend this hemisphere from any attack by way of northern waters," wrote Harold Denny a few days later. He then explained that "these bases are our eyes, set far out from our vital spots."[27] Other journalists wrote much the same thing. Stanley Truman Brooks, for example, emphasized Newfoundland's relative proximity to Europe "as the bomber flies" in a series of articles published in the *St Louis Post-Dispatch* and the *Christian Science Monitor*.[28] In one article, immodestly entitled "Newfoundland – Gibraltar of the North," Brooks told his readers that "[w]ith Newfoundland as the pivot, American defense will swing north to within a few hundred miles of Greenland, dominating any future bases there. Eastward the air eyes of America will be pushed some 1,600 miles closer to Europe than is New York ... Were this base in the hands of invading powers, then America and Canada would be in dire peril from Halifax, west to Detroit, and South to the shipyards of Virginia."[29]

Newfoundland's status as North America's first line of defence went largely undisputed in 1940–41 as Canada and the United States dug in to defend the continent should Britain fall. These first two chapters offer us a bird's-eye view of the resulting transformation of the wartime city and harbour. Part I thus sets the stage for the accounts of everyday life and wartime encounters with foreign servicemen that follow.

PART II: REMEMBERING WARTIME ST JOHN'S

St. John's, where British, American, Canadian and Newfoundland armed forces were stationed and where ships constantly brought crews of all nationalities, was for four years a very cosmopolitan place. Add to this the effect of the blackout and darkened streets and the propensity of soldiers and sailors to carouse and quarrel, and it is not surprising that there were from time to time outbursts of rowdyism, small epidemics of window smashing and so on.

Humphrey Walwyn, governor of Newfoundland, 1945[30]

Historian Sonya Rose once wrote that war, "especially total war, transforms the everyday in unparalleled ways."[31] This was certainly true of wartime St John's, which experienced a dual invasion of Canadian and American servicemen. In Part II of the book, "Remembering Wartime St John's," the contributors focus on the stories told by wartime residents and visitors alike. To listen to men and women of a certain age recount their wartime experiences is to be transported back to that time, if only for a moment. The decades melt away as memories of childhood or young adulthood are remembered in vivid detail.

Fifty residents of St John's were interviewed by the project team about the war. They recalled the darkness of the wartime streets during the blackout and told of families gathered around radio sets listening to the latest war news. Everyone we spoke to remembered where they were when the Knights of Columbus Hostel burned. By making these interviews central to the collective story being told, the second part of *Occupied St John's* reveals aspects of the war years in St John's that were never recorded in the archives or reported in the newspapers. While these wartime accounts were shaped by class and religion, gender proved to be particularly significant. As we discovered, Newfoundland men and women experienced the wartime city differently.[32]

What do people remember about the war? Are there any surprises? For the purposes of this project, we adopted a "life history" approach to oral history interviewing. Interviewees were asked a series of questions that followed the life course from childhood to old age. The wartime questions were grouped under several headings, such as "1939–40" (where we asked about enlistment, the memory of Beaumont Hamel, and the coming of the Canadians) and "the friendly invasion" (where we turned our sights on the Americans). Was the U.S. occupation always friendly? How did it compare to the Canadian invasion? We then asked about the removal of families from the Lower Battery and Pleasantville, the building of the bases, social interaction with servicemen, nightlife, and issues of gender, culture, and politics. As this was a group project, the interviews were carried out by five students (one Memorial University student did the bulk of the interviewing) and me. While each contributing author examines the city's social history from a different angle, the life stories that were collected tie chapters 3 to 5 together.

Because of the passage of time, we were too late to record the stories of the generation who had been middle-aged during the war.[33] Most of our interviewees had been young adults, teenagers, or children during the 1940s.[34] Taking this

Norton-class tug HMS *Riverton* (W-47) at HMC Dockyard. Photo by William A. Ramsay, control no. 20030014-073-2, Canadian War Museum.

as her starting point, social historian Barbara Lorenzkowski examines the wartime city as seen through the eyes of a child. To discover their childhood worlds, she listened closely to the twenty-five interviews conducted with residents who were children or teenagers during the war years. While most historians have focused on the experience of childhood in the context of school, Lorenzkowski shifts our attention to children's gendered lives outside of school. Girls recalled home or school, whereas boys remembered going down to the harbour, hanging out at the rifle range, witnessing fights, and playing with live ammunition. In fact, only boys recalled interactions with foreign servicemen outside the family home. The military occupation brought a sharp increase in vehicular traffic, and city roads, which were once the playgrounds of children, became dangerous. Several devastating accidents involving children sparked a public debate about adult supervision and adequate playgrounds. "The new 'geography of danger,'" Lorenzkowski writes, "emphasized the threat posed by speeding vehicles and sought to regulate and limit children's access to public space for the sake of their own protection."

The next two chapters revisit the friendly invasion. My contribution, chapter 4, explores how interviewees compare and contrast American and Canadian servicemen and their bases. The popularity of the American GI in wartime Newfoundland is legendary. GIs have long been associated with prosperity and good times, and Newfoundland women are often said to have favoured the Yanks. The Canadian servicemen, by contrast, have been blamed for everything – from public drunkenness to overcrowding. Historian John Edward FitzGerald even claimed that the Canadians were despised during the war.[35] Our in-depth interviews with fifty men and women do not support this position. To the contrary,

Left Bill White and Harold Lake at the observation post in Italy, 1944. Donated by Mrs Robin Lake. PF-312.586, Maritime History Archive.

Right A member of the Newfoundland Constabulary on traffic duty at the intersection of Water and Adelaide streets. The man talking to the constable is carrying a large codfish, *Scenes of St. John's*. Photo by Lieut. Alice Ducile Talman, control no. 20010159-002-15, Canadian War Museum.

almost everyone warmly remembered the courage and sacrifice of the Canadian sailors who were fighting and dying in the North Atlantic. We heard about a harbour crowded with warships, battle damaged vessels, exhausted survivors, the blackout, the hostels, and about families having Canadian servicemen over for supper. In fact, the Canadians were often at the centre of the war stories being told. The Americans were well liked, but so too were the Canadians.

Rarely has the risk of war "transformed a country so dramatically for the better," wrote Kevin Major in his popular history of Newfoundland and Labrador.[36] The building of the foreign bases brought full employment and higher wages. At the peak of employment in June 1942, the Canadians employed 7,000 men, the U.S. Army another 10,000, and the U.S. Navy an additional 3,500.[37] Hundreds of women also found employment on the bases. This sudden prosperity was bolstered further by the purchasing power of Canadian and American servicemen. American diplomats reported, for example, that the prosperity of 1942 was "without precedent in the history of the island."[38] The total savings deposited in the Royal Bank in St John's increased from $29,463,000 in 1941 to

$39,368,000 in 1942. In the meantime, imports shifted dramatically from Great Britain to the United States – hardly surprising given the war.

With the wartime boom, however, came inflation and overcrowding. By year's end, the cost of living was fully 50 per cent higher than the prices prevailing in St John's in October 1938. There was not much in the way of price control, save for a rough sort of price ceiling for milk, eggs, and margarine. Molasses was virtually unobtainable in the city. The housing shortage was acute. The 1942 Commission of Enquiry into Housing and Town Planning in St John's, for example, found that 27 per cent of housing in the city was substandard.[39] Rent control only existed for occupied places, as landlords could hike rents whenever tenants moved out.[40] One American diplomat noted that "extortionate rents are being charged in numerous cases."

So great was the economic impact of the base building boom that one American workman concluded that Newfoundlanders "like us now for our money, let us hope that by the time we leave they will like us for other reasons."[41] There was no need to worry. Newfoundland residents found plenty of other reasons to like their Yankee visitors. In St John's, the U.S. Army and Navy acquired a stellar reputation for good discipline. This widely held belief took on significance when the government claimed that the behaviour of American personnel was "exceedingly good, particularly compared to the Canadians." According to the archival evidence available, the total number of serious criminal cases involving American servicemen was small: only forty-three American soldiers and sailors served time in HM Penitentiary during the war.[42] The governor of Newfoundland at the time, Humphrey Walwyn, declared that the general attitude of the visiting forces "was one of friendliness; the American took the Newfoundlander as he found him and the Newfoundlander did the same with the American."[43]

Before long, the U.S. bases became powerful symbols of progress. In its October 1945 assessment of the war's impact, the Newfoundland government

YMCA "Red Triangle" hostel on Water Street, near the railway station, *Scenes of St. John's.* Photo by Lieut. Alice Ducile Talman, control no. 20010159-002-5, Canadian War Museum.

acknowledged the cultural power of the American bases at St John's, Argentia, and Stephenville. To the government, these bases served as models in modernity to be aspired to and copied: "Already the effect upon Newfoundland building and architecture, heretofore stereotyped and ugly, is discernible in new civilian buildings and housing schemes. Up to date methods in heating and plumbing, applied on the Bases are being adopted widely; for example central heating by oil burners is spreading rapidly."[44] For individuals intent on "modernizing" Newfoundland, the coming of the Americans brought about needed changes. Even in landscape gardening and town planning, the U.S. bases provided Newfoundlanders with "good object lessons." As a matter of fact, "they have probably done, and will continue to do, much towards the 'modernization' of Newfoundland building, architecture, communication systems and the art of better and more comfortable living generally."[45] By contrast, the Canadians, at war since 1939, built quickly and cheaply. Nearly all the temporary buildings occupied by the Canadian armed services were well within the city limits, and most of them in congested areas.[46]

Horse-and-sleigh races on the frozen surface of Quidi Vidi Lake during World War II. The buildings of Fort Pepperrell are shown in the background. Photo #01-045-013, City of St John's Archives.

The wartime changes were many and varied. For example, the rules of the road were rewritten and automobile drivers had to swerve from the left side of the road to the right by war's end.[47] Yet, as Jeff Webb cautions in his contribution to this book, there is a danger in rushing to the conclusion that Newfoundland only became modern as a result of the friendly invasion. In chapter 5, Webb emphasizes continuity over change. In doing so, he argues that the cultural impact of the U.S. bases has been overstated by Peter Neary, Kevin Major, and others. For Webb, the war did not "abruptly thrust a significant portion of Newfoundland into America's version of the twentieth century."[48] Newfoundland was already modern and had a long-standing connection to the U.S. mainland. Though fondly remembered as a "vibrant period" in the cultural history of the country, the war did not introduce residents to new forms of popular culture. According to Webb, "The transition of a hypothetical, tradition-bound backward area of the world into a secular, capitalist and innovative place through the actions of American business and military is a common trope. That impression is not accurate. Long before the *Edmund B. Alexander* docked in St John's, phonographs, movies, live concerts, travellers, and radio had all provided jazz, the early variants of country music, and other musical forms to Newfoundlanders." If Newfoundland had reached a cultural cross-road of sorts in the 1940s, it was between a "modern culture of Britishness [and] American values."

Part II concludes with the contribution of Acadia University professors Gillian Poulter and Douglas Baldwin. In "Mona Wilson and the Canadian Red Cross," they investigate the activities and perceptions of Mona Wilson, who was seconded from Prince Edward Island to establish the Canadian Red Cross in Newfoundland. With a volunteer force of local Canadian and Newfoundland women, Wilson supplied clothing, hospital equipment, and recreational activities for Canadian servicemen in St John's. She also provided care and comfort to hundreds of survivors of ships sunk or damaged in the North Atlantic. Drawing from Wilson's diaries, letters, and official reports, Poulter and Baldwin describe the wartime city and its people through the eyes of this remarkable woman.

In the concluding chapter, Part III, historians Ken Coates and William Morrison ask us to place wartime St John's in global perspective. The arrival of thousands of soldiers in Tonga and Trinidad, in the Yukon and Newfoundland, "seriously disrupted the existing economic order, challenged the status quo, and often resulted in a major reorganization of the local social and economic structure."[49] In most of these cases, the biggest "headaches" for military and civilian authorities involved sex and race. For many people, "the GI was the man from the movies."[50] Yet, as the contributors to *Occupied St John's* make clear, there is also a danger in assuming a universalized experience. Not all friendly invasions resulted in the rapid Americanization of local cultures.

CONCLUSION

All the contributors to *Occupied St John's: A Social History of a City at War, 1939–1945* arrive at the same conclusion: that the usual distinction between "home front" and "battle front" in North America is largely irrelevant in wartime St John's. The city was on the front line in the Battle of the Atlantic; yet it was still home to its 40,000 residents. With this shifting perspective, the harbour rather than the U.S. army base occupies centre stage. Following the lead of our interviewees, most of whom warmly recalled their wartime encounters with Canadian sailors, *Occupied St John's* reconsiders the central place of the U.S. friendly invasion. In the essays that follow, the Canadians take their rightful place alongside Cecil Hutchens and his countrymen in the wartime narrative. The social history of the wartime city was thus a triangular encounter, as Newfoundland civilians interacted with foreign servicemen of two allied countries as well as with merchant seamen from around the world.[51]

Part 1 | North America's First Line of Defence

SECRET

1

Building a Wartime Landscape

CHRISTOPHER A. SHARPE
AND A.J. SHAWYER

HMCS *Skeena* gun shield art. "Skeena, named for a salmon river in British Columbia, has a jumping salmon as her badge. Her gun shield depicts a rather seductive salmon luring a U-boat while holding a depth charge under her fin. Presumably they are in for a fatal encounter." Gary Green, *A Guide for Some of the Gun Shield Art and Ship's Badges of the Crow's Nest Officer's Club* (St John's: Crow's Nest Military Artifacts Association, Newfoundland).

In some respects, Newfoundland's greatest contribution to the war effort lay in simply being there.

Don Jamieson[1]

Newfoundland's history and geography made it inevitable that the province would play a role in World War II. Lying off the eastern seaboard, far out into the Atlantic, it was the first line of defence should a European war cross the ocean. Canada and the United States were acutely aware of its strategic position and anxious to harness Newfoundland for their own defence. Canada declared that "the integrity of Newfoundland and Labrador is essential to the security of Canada,"[2] and the United States looked toward using Newfoundland as part of a hemispheric defence scheme. But Newfoundland, caught in the crossfire of other nations' defence plans, was bereft of a diplomatic voice. It had lost its sovereign independence in 1934 when Britain suspended its nationally elected government because of Newfoundland's financial difficulties and replaced it with an appointed commission of six members (three British and three Newfoundlander), chaired by the governor. These strategic and political considerations provide the background for the story we tell here: the changes in the landscape that resulted from the transformation of St John's into a garrison town, to become the "Gibraltar of the West."[3]

In 1939 St John's was the capital of the country of Newfoundland. It was a compact city of about 40,000 people. You could walk across it in half an hour. The harbour was the city's lifeblood, its window on the world. Historically, the

St John's, the harbour and the city, 1940. Quidi Vidi Lake is on the right of the image. Image H027, Newfoundland and Labrador Air Photo and Map Library, Department of the Environment.

city had international trade connections through the fishery and furs and, more recently, through forestry and mining. It had developed a manufacturing base, producing clothing, housewares, foundry products, and foodstuffs, although most of the raw materials were imported. The Newfoundland Railway connected St John's with the ferry to Canada. The city had no airport, although the British had recently constructed a new international airport at Gander in the expectation that it would play a major role in the rapidly developing transatlantic commercial airline business.

Squeezed between the harbour and the surrounding hills, the houses in St John's were tightly packed, often in ranges along narrow streets. Years of economic difficulty had resulted in few new houses being built, and many of the existing houses sheltered too many people: family, extended family members, and boarders. Beyond the city limits were well established farms that supplied the city with fresh food. And fishermen from the Battery, at the north end of the harbour, supplied the city with fish.

Beginning in 1940 this modest city of 40,000 was overrun with visiting military personnel from two foreign countries – Canada and the United States.[4] It is likely that on any one day there were 1,600 Canadian Army personnel, 2,400 Royal Canadian Air Force (RCAF), and 3,600 Royal Canadian Navy (RCN): a total of about 7,600 Canadians.[5] There were probably about 5,500 American troops at Fort Pepperrell, although on occasion there may have been as many as 7,000.[6] This overall estimate of 13,300 does not include transient naval person-

nel (at least 80 men per ship) but still represents about 30 per cent of the prewar population of St John's. Canada and the United States had different strategic interests and different legal rights in Newfoundland, and this caused an unnecessary duplication of defence facilities and the posting of more garrison troops than necessary.[7] Furthermore, the development of the military facilities was conceived and carried out in haste and without precedent, and was often surprisingly haphazard. Because there was no nationally elected parliament to which the capital city could turn for help – St John's City Council being the only representative government in the country (see High, chapter 4, this volume) – the city had to deal with the problems of accommodating both civilian and military needs on its own.

INITIAL DEFENCE ARRANGEMENTS IN ST JOHN'S

Newfoundland had made a magnificent contribution to the Allied cause in World War I.[8] The decimation of the Newfoundland Regiment in the battle of Beaumont Hamel on 1 July 1916 is an iconic event in the collective memory of Newfoundlanders. However, in 1939 Newfoundland's financial situation was so precarious that there was no possibility that it could establish its own military force as it had done in the Great War. But the government was willing to do what it could, within its limited means.

The 1936 Newfoundland Defence Scheme identified five strategically significant resources: the Newfoundland Airport (Gander), the Botwood harbour and seaplane base, the city of St John's, the Bell Island iron mines, and the termini of nine transatlantic cables. The scheme also noted that the country was entirely undefended: "[N]o plan of any sort exists for the active defence of Newfoundland, and … the only armed forces consist of 255 Constabulary and 50 Rangers, armed with obsolete and inefficient weapons."[9]

As war approached, both the Newfoundland and Canadian governments asked the British government what defence measures it would be prepared to offer in the event of war. The answer was none, other than the general protection of the Royal Navy (RN). Fortunately for Newfoundland, it had as its governor Vice-Admiral Sir Humphrey Walwyn. With his career experience in the RN, the governor appreciated the strategic importance of the country entrusted to his care. He lobbied aggressively, and successfully, for Canadian involvement in local defence. And Canada did come. The Canadians provided weapons and training for the Newfoundland Militia, and their presence provided security for the major military and economic assets of the country.

The government put the country on a war footing on 1 September 1939 with the passage of the Act for the Defence of Newfoundland, giving it the power to make war regulations.[10] Two days later Newfoundland declared war and Governor Walwyn arranged for the installation of an anti-submarine net across the Narrows, between Chain and Pancake Rocks.[11] A recruiting office was set up for volunteers to serve with the British Army, navy, and air force;[12] a civilian Newfoundland Forestry Unit was established to serve in the United Kingdom;[13] and an internment camp was built on the north shore of Quidi Vidi Lake to accommodate enemy aliens.[14]

In the absence of a trained military force, the Newfoundland Constabulary was required, quite literally, to hold the fort for the first several months of the war. It provided security for the internment camp,[15] and fifty men were dispatched to Bell Island to guard the iron mines against sabotage. Meanwhile, the government created the Newfoundland Militia to serve as a local defence force,[16] although the commencement of training was delayed because of the lack of uniforms, equipment, and a training officer. The government had asked the U.K. Dominions Office to lend it the services of an experienced training officer,[17] and the man to carry out this assignment arrived shortly after the outbreak of war with a hundred rifles and 54,000 rounds of ammunition in his luggage.[18] Secretary of Defence Brian Dunfield's visit to Ottawa in September resulted in the Canadian government providing a hundred more rifles, as well as bayonets, scabbards, slings, and eight Lewis guns.[19] With this equipment in hand, recruitment of two companies – each of ninety-one officers and men, for service to last the duration of the war – could begin.

The first task of the Newfoundland Militia was to support the anti-sabotage work of the Newfoundland Constabulary. Teams consisting of a police constable and a militiaman were posted at the Windsor Lake water supply, the termini of the four transatlantic cables in Cuckold's Cove, the Newfoundland Broad-

Sergeants of the Lincoln and Welland Regiment on motorcycles, Lester's Field, 1942. The regiment was based at the Newfoundland Airport from June 1941 to 18 March 1942 and then at Lester's Field until 11 May 1943. Lincoln and Welland Regiment Museum.

casting Company's radio station in Mount Pearl, the St John's dry dock, and the Imperial Oil storage tanks on the south side of the harbour.[20] By April 1940 the police were able to return to normal duties, as there were now enough trained militiamen to take over.[21]

At this early stage of the war, the threat of sabotage was the primary concern. When the Lincoln and Welland Regiment arrived in St John's in March 1942, they patrolled the roads on motorcycles, checking potential landing sites and other strategic locations.[22]

Defending Bell Island

As early as 1937 the Canadian chiefs of staff had written a memorandum entitled "The Defence of Sydney and Its Steel Industry."[23] At least 30 per cent of Canada's steel came from the Dominion Steel and Coal Company's (DOSCO) smelter in Sydney, and all the iron ore to supply it came from the mines at Wabana on

Bell Island. Looking ahead to the production of munitions and the defence of the mines, the chiefs argued that Bell Island was a matter of imperial concern. Indeed, Germany had been one of the mine's best customers – the last German ore boat had departed less than a week before the outbreak of the war. The Germans knew the location intimately.[24]

By early 1940 all involved parties agreed that the threat to the Wabana mines was attack from the sea, not sabotage. At Britain's request,[25] and with some lobbying by L.E. Emerson, commissioner for justice and defence, Canada agreed that because of a mutual direct interest "the responsibility for providing a measure of protection in Bell Island is ... one that the Canadian government is prepared to share with the Newfoundland government."[26] On 26 March 1940 the British high commissioner wrote to Prime Minister Mackenzie King to inform him that the Newfoundland government had approved the Canadian proposal to install two 4.7-inch guns and two searchlights to defend the Bell Island loading piers, and to train members of the Newfoundland Militia in their use.[27] The Battery was constructed in June and manned by Royal Canadian Artillery personnel until 27 August 1940, when it was taken over by the newly trained men of the Newfoundland Militia's 1st Coastal Defence Battery.[28]

The fifty-man Bell Island detachment of the Newfoundland Constabulary was housed in the Star of the Sea Hall, which was rented by DOSCO. These makeshift premises were taken over by the militiamen, who occupied them until April 1941, when purpose-built barracks, also paid for by the company, were ready for them.[29]

Defending the Newfoundland Airport

When he heard Prime Minister Mackenzie King's statement to the House of Commons on September 8 regarding the relationship between Newfoundland and the security of Canada, Governor Walwyn wrote to the Dominions Office suggesting that the Canadian government be invited to take over the Newfoundland Airport and the Botwood Seaplane Base for the duration of the war. But Britain had plans beyond the immediacy of war. The secretary of state for dominion affairs replied that "there are strong reasons against handing over airports to the Royal Canadian Air Force. Newfoundland is destined to play an important part in post-war trans-Atlantic services and it is considered it would be undesirable to allow these airports which are such an important factor in our bargaining position vis-à-vis Pan American airways and the United States to pass out of our control, even temporarily."[30] A member of the Civil Air Administration War Group was more blunt: "It is one thing to let them in, but it would be another thing to get them out."[31] But the crisis in France in June 1940 quickly led to changed priorities, and the following year Britain agreed that Canadian air units be allowed not only to operate from the two Newfoundland air bases but to take over their control and maintenance.[32]

But this decision did not sit easily with Newfoundland. Canadian aviation authorities argued that the two facilities needed ground defence. Emerson opined that "it would ... be a grave mistake to import troops for this purpose [because] it would be resented, and I think properly so, by the public."[33] But military necessity overrode his concerns. On 14 June 1940 the Canadian government offered to station a flight of bomber/reconnaissance aircraft and a flight of fighters, as well as troops, to defend Gander. The Newfoundland government agreed. Nine hundred men of the Black Watch (Royal Highland Regiment) of Canada arrived on 20 June 1940 "to protect the Newfoundland Airport and Botwood Seaplane Base against sabotage and/or ground attack by enemy armed forces."[34] Their arrival marked the beginning of the friendly invasion of Newfoundland by foreign troops. It would not be long before Canadian troops arrived in St John's.

The Newfoundland Militia and Shamrock Field

By the end of 1939, 189 men had joined the militia, but there were no barracks to accommodate them anywhere in the city and the East and West End Fire Stations had been pressed into service as a stop-gap measure.[35] But the decision to expand the militia to 500 men in 1940 in order to man the Bell Island battery meant that permanent barracks were needed. A site was acquired through an informal arrangement between Emerson and the president of St Bonaventure's College. Emerson informed his colleagues that he had "taken over a field to the north-west of the Christian Brothers' Monastery on Newtown Road, which I think is the best site in St John's for training. It is a large field, well fenced and overlooked only on one end by private houses. There is ample space for a large number of tents or huts and room to drill and manoeuvre as well. My present arrangement with ... Brother O'Connell, is that we shall not be liable for any rent but shall compensate them for any damage done to the field."[36] Shamrock Field thereby became the first World War II military encampment in St John's.

The men were originally housed under canvas, because it was intended that they would remain on the site for only three or four months while the permanent barracks were being built elsewhere.[37] However, by the end of October 1940 it had been decided that this was to be the location of the permanent establishment. The tents were replaced by blocks of barracks that accommodated 250 men as well as messes, a cookhouse, an ablution and latrines block, a lecture hall, an administration block, a canteen, quartermaster stores, an infirmary, a guardhouse, a workshop, and a garage.[38] The camp at Shamrock Field gave the citizens of St John's their first close-up view of military activity: soldiers drilling on the parade grounds of the Newfoundland Constabulary at Fort Townshend[39] and marching daily to the Sand Pits north of the city to practise marksmanship on the rifle range.[40] They were soon to have many more reminders that the country was at war.

DEFENCE AGREEMENTS

Within a two-week period in the fall of 1940 two formal agreements (Canada with the United States, and the United States with Britain) and an informal

The city and harbour looking east, 1940. The tents and buildings of the Newfoundland Militia Camp on Shamrock Field are at right centre. Image H028, Newfoundland and Labrador Air Photo and Map Library, Department of the Environment.

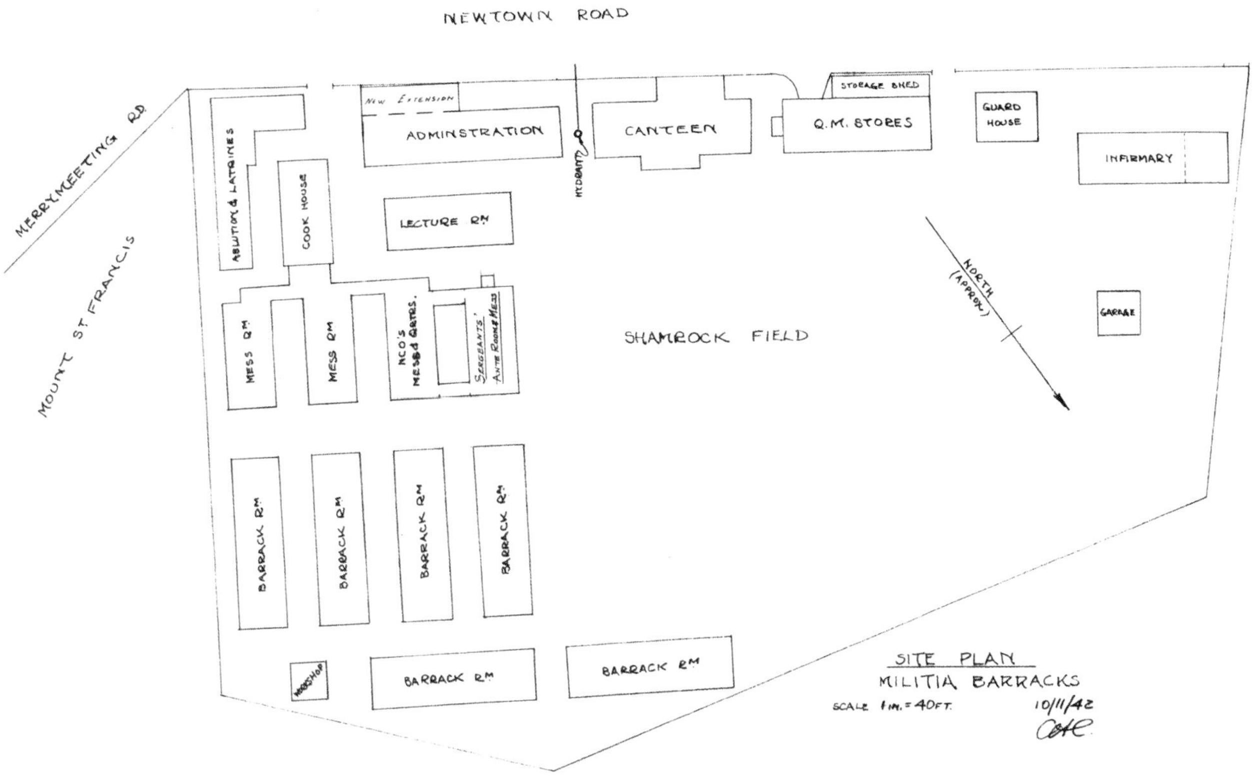

Plan of the Shamrock Field Camp of the Newfoundland Militia. Plan 1242, 10 November 1942. RG 4.3 41/83, Rooms Provincial Archives.

understanding between Newfoundland and Canada changed the face and history of Newfoundland. The Ogdensburg Agreement between President Roosevelt and Prime Minister King resulted in the creation of the Permanent Joint Board on Defence (PJBD), which made several recommendations regarding Newfoundland. The so-called Destroyers for Bases deal between Britain and the United States had significant impacts on Newfoundland. These are discussed below.

In August, while Prime Minister King was chatting with President Roosevelt on his train in Ogdensburg, New York, the Canadian minister of national defence for air (C.G. Power) was in St John's discussing joint defence arrangements with Newfoundland's Commission of Government. Canadian aircraft and troops had been stationed at the Newfoundland Airport since June. Now the Canadians seemed to be thinking of a formal agreement that would give them control over the defence of the whole country. The commission wasn't prepared to accept this and its reluctance led to the unusual situation whereby Canada stationed troops, aircraft, and, eventually, a large part of its navy in Newfoundland, a foreign country, with nothing more than the informal agreements worked out at three bilateral meetings – the meeting with Power and two conferences, one in November 1940 and a second in April 1941. A Canadian high

Canadian Army Lester's Field Camp, 26 September 1942. REA 260-2. Reproduced with the permission of the Minister of Public Works and Government Services, 2008.

commissioner was appointed in the summer of 1941, and bilateral discussions gave way to diplomacy.

The agreements reached at these three meetings are generally referred to collectively as the Canada/Newfoundland Defence Accord and assumed a partnership of equals, "despite the profound differences in size, power and wealth and the degree of self-government enjoyed."[41] Power's visit led to the immediate decision to strengthen the defences of St John's.[42] Canada agreed to station an infantry battalion "in the vicinity of St. John's," construct coastal artillery batteries to defend the harbour, and build a naval base; it also confirmed its intention of building an airport for fighter aircraft. All of these new facilities were to be paid for by Canada.[43] Power's view of the discussions was that Newfoundland and Canada should help each other. Cognizant of Newfoundland's sensibilities, he commented: "[I]t was to be understood that there would be no encroachment whatever on the autonomous rights of Newfoundland."[44]

THE CANADIAN ARMY ARRIVES IN ST JOHN'S

The Canadian Army command authorized for Newfoundland ("W" Force) became operational on 16 October 1940 under the command of Major-General L.F. Page. The men of the advance party of the Montreal-based Victoria Rifles who arrived on 14 November were the first foreign troops to take up residence in the city.[45] But how and where were they to be accommodated? The governor

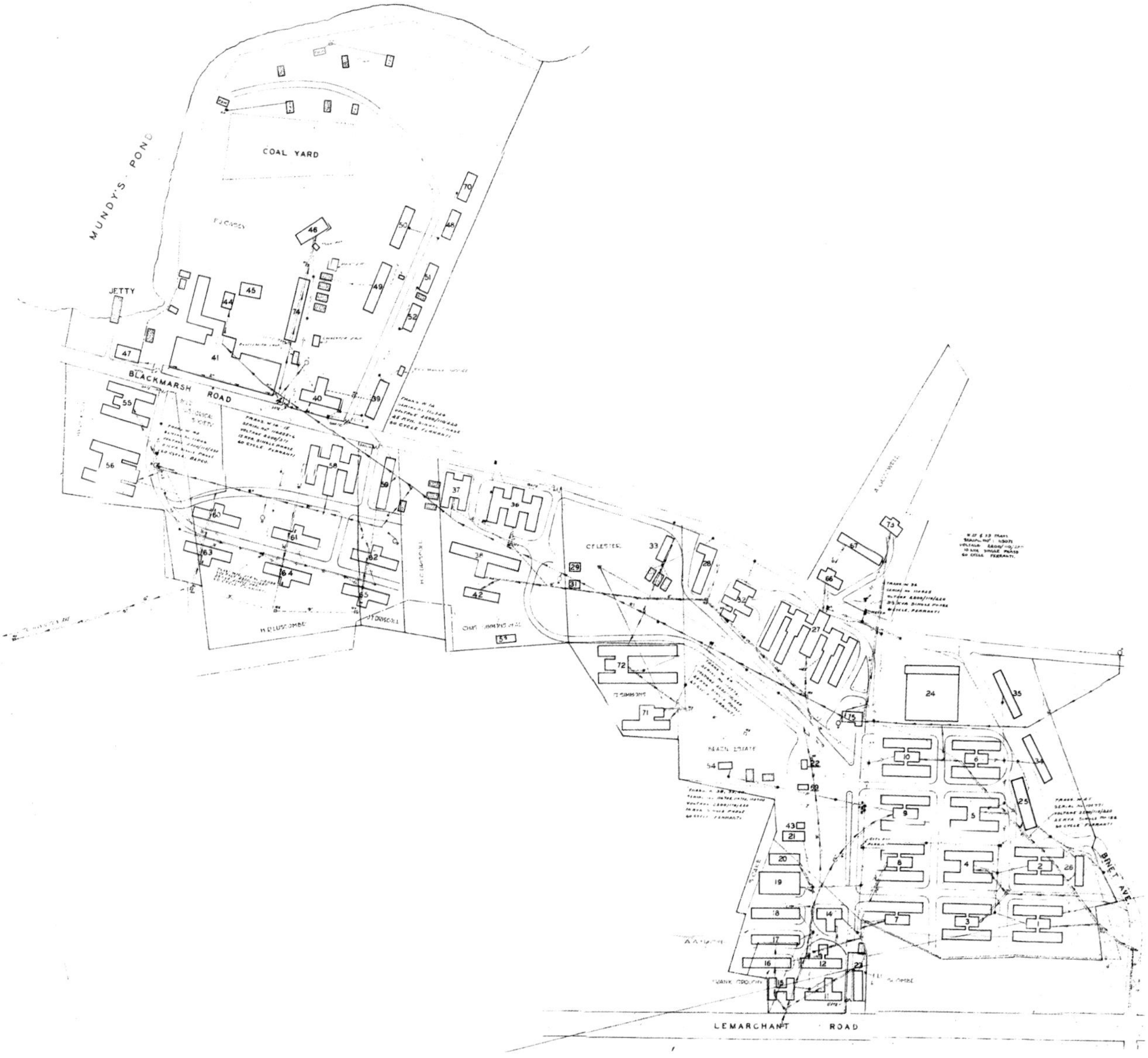

Plan of Lester's Field Camp. DND NMC 91826. Courtesy of the Map Library, Queen Elizabeth II Library, Memorial University of Newfoundland.

offered to evict the 170 university students and 100 teachers-in-training from Memorial University College to provide temporary accommodation. The offer was declined. The Canadians decided to start work on a permanent camp immediately and to move men in by company as quickly as the barracks were ready.[46] They chose to build on Lester's Field, a rise of land between LeMarchant Road and Mundy's Pond, west of Beaumont Street. They wasted no time. Leases with a number of private owners were signed on 1 October, "for the duration of the war plus six months," which appears to have been the normal Canadian practice.[47] By mid-December all 775 men of the Victoria Rifles had moved in.[48]

Left Lester's Field Camp, 1942. Lincoln and Welland Regiment Museum.

Right Barracks, Lester's Field Camp, 1942, looking south to the backs of houses on the north side of LeMarchant Road. Lincoln and Welland Regiment Museum.

The Canadian base was built to defend St John's. It was never officially named, and signalmen answered the telephone saying, "St John's Defences."[49] Locally it was always referred to as Lester's Field Camp, taking its name from Charles Lester, one of several carters, butchers, and cabmen who had traditionally used these open fields for grazing their animals.[50]

Lester's Field Camp became a self-contained town of about eighty buildings.[51] There was a dense concentration of barracks, mess buildings, canteens, and warehouses, as well as a laundry, carpenter shop, paint shop, ammunition storage, drill hall, chapel, dental clinic, No. 26 Military Hospital, a nurses' residence, and a fire hall. Blackmarsh Road remained open to civilian traffic but ran like a tunnel between the fences that surrounded the two parts of the camp north and south of the road.

The St John's City Council criticized the quality of the Canadian buildings, wishing that they were better-quality permanent structures, like those being erected on the other side of town by the Americans.[52] Typically the Canadian buildings were very basic structures, covered only with tarpaper, but this criticism was unfair. Canada was already at war, and the camp at Lester's Field was built and occupied in less than three months – with no intention that the buildings would remain after the war. The Americans were not at war. They were simply hedging their bets against the possible collapse of Britain and the end of British naval control of the Atlantic. By the summer of 1940 American military planners had recognized that the security of the United States and the Western Hemisphere were inextricably linked and that the bases in Newfoundland were the northern linchpin in the network of bases designed for hemispheric defence in the case of global conflict. The Americans had 99-year leases on all their sites, and they built accordingly.[53] The Canadians had leases that would expire six months after the end of the war, and they, too, built accordingly.

Canadian soldiers established a number of defensive sites across the city. The major concern was defence of the harbour. The governor informed the Canadian government that "on December 26th [1940] there were 46 merchant ships in the harbour, aggregating 118,948 tons ... Most of these ships need repair due to heavy weather, enemy action and machinery defects, and others are loading and unloading ... during the winter months it is expected that approximately 100,000 tons of shipping will be daily in this port and open to destruction with impunity by a raider."[54] But the lack of equipment permitted only stop-gap measures. In November 1940 the hastily authorized "Q" Battery, Royal Canadian Artillery (RCA), manned a temporary examination battery (for the identification of incoming ships) equipped with two 75-mm field guns at Fort Amherst, on the

Fort Amherst and the RCN Port War Signal Station (right centre). PA-136970, Canada, Department of National Defence/Library and Archives Canada.

Above left Two unidentified soldiers and the Canadian Army buildings at Fort Amherst. Photo #01-045-129, City of St John's Archives.

Above right Fort Chain Rock and the Narrows. VA147-214, The Rooms Provincial Archives.

Left One of the 75-mm field guns at Fort Chain Rock. Courtesy of Parks Canada.

south side of the Narrows.[55] In June of 1941 these were replaced by two quick-firing 4.7-inch guns, and the 75-mm field guns moved to permanent mountings at Fort Chain Rock on the opposite side of the Narrows. Two 60-inch, 800-million candlepower searchlights provided illumination.[56]

The buildings of the Fort Amherst Battery were tightly clustered around the lighthouse. Two of the existing buildings were converted to a canteen and a depot, and new buildings were erected to house officers, sergeants, 150 other ranks, a washroom, a guard house, and a battery office.[57]

The Royal Canadian Navy built a two-storey barracks squeezed between the road and the cliff, just west of the army buildings to house the three officers and twenty-four ratings who manned the Port War Signal Station and operated the controlled minefield.[58] Water for all the military establishments at Fort Amherst initially came from a new pond created by a series of dams built on top of the

South Side Hills in 1942. Unfortunately the water was of poor quality, and a new pipeline had to be laid from the Imperial Oil facility on the south side of the harbour. However, the original dams and cisterns were maintained as a source of water for firefighting.[59]

The harbour defences were completed in June 1941[60] when a counter-bombardment battery consisting of two 10-inch guns on loan from the United States was installed at Cape Spear.[61] A sprawling complex of twenty-two buildings provided accommodation and mess facilities for the Canadian artillerymen.[62]

Just as the farmers, carters, butchers, and cabmen had to accommodate the creation of the camp in the Lester's Field area, so the fishermen had to step aside when Fort Chain Rock was built. Acquisition of the site should not have been a problem because most of it was crown land. However, many of the residents were long-term squatter families who "had always lived here." Inevitably there were conflicts between these residents and the military authorities. The residents were not tempted by offers to sell up: "These civilians have been offered a certain sum for their property but are holding out for a larger amount and are, perhaps, trying to be as disagreeable as possible."[63]

Fort Chain Rock and one of the anti-torpedo baffles. PA-135878, Canada, Department of National Defence/Library and Archives Canada.

Facing page, above One of the ten-inch guns at Cape Spear, c. 1942. Murrin/Hunt fonds, Newfoundland Collection, Provincial Reference Library.

Facing page, below Cape Spear from the east, 1941. The lighthouse and U.S. Army aircraft warning station are to the left, the Canadian Army buildings to the right. The Narrows is at top left. Reproduced with the permission of the Minister of Public Works and Government Services.

This page The sentry box at Fort Chain Rock. Edgecombe's stores are to the left and the army recreation building is behind. VA 147-349, The Rooms Provincial Archives.

The solution to this impasse at Chain Rock illustrates the dilemma of the Commission of Government. It was faced with the military's legitimate demands, but it was also concerned with protecting the personal lives of the citizens from intrusion. The solution lay in the 1943 designation of Fort Chain Rock as a restricted area. This allowed the fishermen to continue to live and fish there alongside the military activities. The residents were issued passes and given permits to place on the windshield of their vehicles. "There remains the question of entry to the area from ... the harbour ... it would be unreasonable to expect the men to wait around the harbour until a Sentry turned up to examine their credentials ... this might be overcome if a sentry post was established on the wharf."[64] This was done.

The Canadian Army also established a number of anti-aircraft (A/A) and searchlight[65] batteries in and around St John's. In retrospect this was an unneces-

Left 25th Regiment, RCA, Heavy Anti-Aircraft Battery (probably on Blackhead Road), 20 September 1941. PA-209687, Canada, Department of National Defence/Library and Archives Canada.

Right The Light Anti-Aircraft Battery on Hill O'Chips. VA 147-422, The Rooms Provincial Archives.

sary precaution, since Germany never developed the capability to attack North America from the air, but this could not have been known in 1939. The batteries were of two types. A Light (LAA) Battery, designed for low-level defence, was equipped with a 40-mm Bofors gun.[66] It could easily be accommodated in an urban area because it usually required only one hut. A Heavy (HAA) Battery, normally equipped with four 3.7-inch guns capable of firing a shell to 39,000 feet, required several buildings and could not be so easily accommodated.[67]

Squeezing military installations into the urban fabric of St John's wasn't easy. Construction of the LAA Battery on the Hill O'Chips illustrated the difficulties in requisitioning property for the military. The owner of a house on the Hill O'Chips was invited to lease or sell the property to the military, but she refused to do either. Standard negotiations having failed, the government swung into action with dizzying speed. General Page phoned Sir Wilfrid Woods, commissioner of public utilities, at 4:30 PM requesting that the site be requisitioned.[68] Woods signed the notice of expropriation, which was then delivered to the owner's solicitor at 5:10 PM and to the owner, at her home in Topsail, at 6:05. The property now belonged to Newfoundland. The owner later received $15,000 in compensation.

The military did not always get its way. In May 1941 General Page negotiated with the Misses Calver to lease half their field as the temporary site for about thirty tents needed to house the 126 men of an anti-aircraft searchlight troop scheduled to arrive on 2 June. The army sought permission from the city to put up a temporary cookhouse and ablutions tables and to connect the site to the city water supply. The period of occupancy was to be "not more than three months" because permanent huts were to be built elsewhere.[69] But then the following year they asked for and gained permission from the city to erect permanent buildings in the field to house a Bofors gun troop headquarters. By March 1943 they had put fourteen buildings on the site, at which point the Calvers' neighbours, the Roman Catholic Sisters of Mercy, protested. The Sisters' convent and orphanage adjoined the field, and their lawyer argued that the military buildings were too close to the orphanage and were a fire hazard, "which was a source of considerable disquiet to the sisters."[70] General Page wondered whether the military necessity for the buildings "outweighed the dangers to which the Sisters and children of this large institution were exposed." He argued that the field was the most advantageous site for the A/A defences, being "a nerve centre controlling the whole of the Canadian portion of the A/A defences, not only in St John's but of the Torbay aerodrome as well."[71] His plea fell on deaf ears. The city passed a demolition order for all the camp's buildings within 300 feet of the orphanage.[72]

The efforts of the Canadian Army to plan for the defence of the city were under constant surveillance by the residents of St John's, who were not afraid to speak out if they felt the military was becoming too intrusive. The result was sometimes a refusal by the city to grant a building permit. In one case a neighbourhood petition successfully thwarted a plan to build a wet canteen on a well-to-do residential street. In another case the city council declined to issue a building permit for some buildings because "it was felt that too much space

Left The Light Anti-Aircraft Battery on the South Side Hills. VA 147-459, The Rooms Provincial Archives.

Right An unidentified Canadian soldier manning the Hill O'Chips battery. Photo #1-45-003, City of St John's Archives.

had already been taken up in the city by similar buildings and another location would have to be found outside the limits."[73] The detention barracks in Rennie's Meadow on Carpasian Road was a different matter. City council approved a permit for this facility but a few days later wrote to General Page expressing concern that perhaps "it may have acted too hastily in granting the permit without being better acquainted with the details as to the general use and purpose of the building." The concern was that it would be located adjacent to a residential area and in close proximity to the children's swimming pool in the Rennie's River. However, the councillors were mollified by the explanation that the inmates would be soldiers who had transgressed military regulations, not criminal laws, that a detention barracks was "the most orderly of military installations," that the site would be fenced, and that the only thing to be seen in the barracks yard would be soldiers drilling, and so the building permit was not revoked.[74]

It was much easier for the military to requisition sites outside the city. The HAA Battery at the Torbay aerodrome was sited on land leased from the owners of Field Farm with the promise that the army would remove its buildings and restore the property at the end of the war. The army did this and more: the soldiers even helped to harvest the potatoes![75] The experience of the Field family graphically illustrates the small-scale interconnections between peace and war. Mr Field remembered that "land near the house was taken over ... They had an

Calver's Field and Shamrock Field camps, 26 September 1942. REA 260-9. Reproduced with the permission of the Minister of Public Works and Government Services.

anti-aircraft gun compound, sodded in and a gun crew of about 20 soldiers. Right in the yard where our house is they built a barrack block, and they put an anti-aircraft gun in our field ... So we grew up ... with these servicemen right in the yard. And, to get into the house night time, say after midnight, you would be challenged by the military, and the same way we couldn't go into the wooded area where the ammunition dump was unless we had passes. We all had passes to get to the field where we used to graze our cattle ... the gun was never fired in our field. Any time for practice, they would take it away."[76]

The Canadian Army needed to requisition large tracts of land for rifle-, mortar-, and battle-training ranges – more than 2,000 acres along the Cape Spear Road and 500 acres northeast of Windsor Lake. Each of these ranges required the acquisition of a mix of crown and private property. Reading between the lines of the official documents, one senses an unfailing courtesy and empathy towards those property owners affected by the exigencies of war.[77] But the citizens of St John's soon had more than the Canadian Army to contend with. In January 1941 the American army arrived in town.

Newfoundland and the "Bases for Destroyers" Deal

On 15 May 1940 a harassed Winston Churchill cabled Franklin Roosevelt, president of a carefully neutral United States. Churchill asked for "the loan of 40 to 50 of your older destroyers to bridge the gap between what we have now and the large new construction we put in hand at the beginning of the war."[78] This cable, and the complex discussions that flowed from it, led directly to the American invasion of Newfoundland. It is important to consider how this came about.

In May 1940 the war was going badly for Britain, and Churchill was convinced that he desperately needed those destroyers. At the same time the Americans, increasingly concerned about the possibility of the war crossing the Atlantic, made the establishment of advanced defensive bases offshore a high priority. These two needs came together to produce the Anglo-American Leased Bases Agreement.[79] President Roosevelt recognized that Congress would agree to lending the destroyers only if doing so made the United States safer. To convince Congress, he needed "molasses" – some concession – from Britain. The Leased Bases Agreement, "an arrangement whereby the UK Government would give air and naval facilities to the US for hemispheric defence,"[80] and Churchill's assurance that the British fleet would not be allowed to fall into enemy hands provided Roosevelt with his molasses.

The agreement gave the United States 99-year leases on base sites in the Caribbean in exchange for the fifty World War I–vintage destroyers. However, the base sites in Newfoundland and Bermuda were leased to the United States "freely and without consideration."[81] Thus, a neutral United States came to Newfoundland to preserve its own security by stationing "mobile reserves held in readiness to meet and repel the first signs of aggression anywhere in the Western Hemisphere," not to defend Newfoundland.[82]

The agreement was essentially a private deal initiated by Churchill and Roosevelt. Newfoundland and the other colonies were presented with a *fait accompli*, to the astonishment and annoyance of most senior British and Canadian military authorities.[83] The Commission of Government was caught between the needs of the old European nation fighting for its very survival and a young North American juggernaut obsessed with protecting both its neutrality and its security. Churchill appealed to Newfoundland's loyalty in a published letter: "I can readily appreciate the feelings which ... might arise that Newfoundland was being asked in this Agreement to give up much which she holds of value ... we ask her to accept this Agreement. It will be yet one more example of what she is ready to do for the sake of the Empire, of liberty and of the welfare for all mankind." The commission loyally and dutifully replied: "We ... feel confident that the personal commendation of acceptance of the Agreement by the Empire's leaders in this crisis will not fail to impress [Newfoundlanders] with the importance of the part they are playing in strengthening co-operation between the two great democracies in the struggle for the freedom of mankind."[84]

But the agreement had profound diplomatic implications. To this end, Emerson and the commissioner for finance, J.H. Penson, spent two months in London trying to impress upon the authorities the seriousness of the situation, to no avail. Emerson characterized the agreement as "one-sided throughout and often extremely harsh,"[85] commenting, "[W]e cannot impress too forcefully upon the Dominions and Foreign Offices our astonishment and alarm at the idea that our sovereignty should be invaded in this manner."[86] He was particularly concerned about the extraterritorial rights granted to the Americans and the excessive general powers they demanded – and got – outside the leased areas. He was most incensed by the fact that the Americans were granted immunity from taxes and duties on all materials imported into the country.[87] To make matters worse, the commission did not even have the comfort of a formal document to consult. The famous exchange of notes took place on 2 September 1940, but the Leased Bases Agreement was not signed until 27 March 1941. In June the commission passed the necessary enabling legislation,[88] but by then the Americans had already arrived.

The Americans Choose Their Sites

The Leased Bases Agreement gave the United States the right to choose sites for bases that they would then have to build at their own expense.[89] The Americans wasted no time. On 16 September 1940, only two weeks after the agreement was finalized, a Board of Experts, under the command of Admiral John W. Greenslade, arrived aboard the cruiser USS *St Louis* to select the sites.[90] The board met with the Commission of Government that morning. It is difficult to imagine how stressful this meeting must have been. The seven men of the commission were determined to do what they could to protect the commercial viability of the harbour and mitigate the inevitable impact the Americans were going to have on the city. But they knew that neither they nor the city council had any bargaining power.

In the St John's area, the Americans had the immediate need of operating facilities for a light naval force and a base from which army units could defend these facilities.[91] The governor reminded the Americans that St John's Harbour was already seriously congested and that the Canadians, too, wanted to use it, though without acquiring frontage. Greenslade, however, insisted that he wanted to use the harbour for berthing, repairs, and supplies and that he wanted frontage. As for the army base, in answer to a query from Commissioner Woods, he replied that in peacetime the base would have to accommodate about 2,200 men, but in wartime it would have to house up to 30,000. The scale of this was astonishing. The city itself had only 40,000 souls.

Emerson expressed great concern at the prospect of having both Canadian and American forces stationed in the city. He said that if even 1,000 men were brought in immediately "they would probably have to sleep in the streets." He suggested that the Americans consider the possibility of using a barrack ship as an interim solution to the problem of accommodation.

After this first meeting, the American officers reconnoitred various sites in St John's as well as sites in Argentia and Stephenville. On 21 September 1940 the American Board of Experts and the commission reconvened at Government House. During the next four hours the face of St John's was dramatically and irrevocably changed. General Greenslade reiterated that he wanted a naval base on the south side of the harbour, with at least a 1,200-foot frontage, and 160 acres for an army camp south of St John's in the vicinity of the junction of Bay Bulls Road and the old Petty Harbour Road. This site would be conveniently near roads and the railway and appeared to be a better airfield site than the one the Canadians had chosen at Torbay. Discussion continued until the meeting was interrupted by the handing in of a note from a member of the American board who was still out looking at sites. Greenslade read the note to the meeting: "By all means ask for 160 acres more or less generally along north side of Quidi Vidi Lake, extending back to, but not including golf course. Many advantages, for houses only affected and little farmed."

This was a surprise. The Quidi Vidi site had not previously been discussed as a possible site. Even more surprising, once the possibility of Quidi Vidi was introduced, there was no further discussion of it and the conversation returned to other matters. However, later in the meeting Greenslade said, completely out of context, "I would like to ask if the substitution of the Quidi Vidi Area would be acceptable in place of the original site recommended." The governor replied, "Yes, and we will change your memorandum to that extent." And in this casual way Fort Pepperrell was created in Pleasantville, on the north side of Quidi Vidi Lake, beyond the city limits. The American Bases Act 1941 authorized the granting of leases for 198 acres upslope from the lake for the base itself; 28 acres in the White Hills to accommodate a water supply reservoir, dog kennels, and a radio tower site; and 2.5 acres on Signal Hill as an anti-aircraft battery site. The Americans showed no concern for the fact that the area north of the lake was occupied by a number of established farms.

The Americans later abandoned their plans for a naval base in St John's Harbour,[92] which would have severely compromised both physical space and the

Newfoundland maritime economy, instead choosing to build a large supply dock at the northeastern end of the harbour, below the fishing community known as "the Battery." The fishermen of the lower Battery now joined the farmers of Pleasantville in having their lives changed forever.

Clearing the Way for Fort Pepperrell

About fifty property owners along the north side of Quidi Vidi Lake received requisition notices even while construction of the new American base got underway. The properties ranged from large prosperous farms to suburban lots, and the owners from smallholders to institutional owners like the Bally Haly Golf and Country Club and Mount Cashel Orphanage.

The note from Lord Lothian to the American secretary of state stipulated that compensation would be paid, but the method of arriving at the value of the property was not defined.[93] This was an issue over which the commissioners and the American officials fought bitterly. The Americans said that they would pay compensation only for the appraised market value of a property. Governor Walwyn reminded them that the agreement stipulated that the compensation process be mutually agreed upon and that the American position was unsatisfactory to Newfoundland. He also pleaded his case to London: "[C]ompensation should be based on something more than, or different from, a mere appraisement of the market price of the property, and should include something by way of compensation for disturbance and re-establishment."[94] In other words, there should be an allowance for "disturbance" – loss of livelihood and "goodwill" in business affairs. If the Americans refused to accept this, he warned that "the extra cost will have to be found somewhere otherwise we should have the sorry spectacle of some people who are now decently housed and in reasonably good circumstances being reduced to the position of impoverished shack dwellers."[95]

The governor also wrote to the British ambassador in Washington, urging him to plead Newfoundland's case: "[M]any of these people [whose property is being requisitioned], by the exercise of inherited aptitudes, have wrestled a living out of extremely unpromising physical conditions but they cannot be expected to re-establish themselves in a short time in a new undeveloped area at approximately the same economic level as that on which they are now living without financial assistance in excess of the normal appraisement of their existing lands and buildings, and we ask your assistance in bringing this home to the United States Government."[96]

The Americans, however, never accepted the idea of compensation for disturbance, as it was not standard practice in the United States. Newfoundland went ahead and created a Board of Arbitration, presided over by Supreme Court Justice W.J. Higgins, who was assisted by two appraisal experts.[97] Every person whose property was requisitioned had the opportunity to speak before the board. The board in turn would "make full examination into all questions of values ... would advise the Government as to the amounts to be paid." Britain agreed to pay the difference between the American appraisal and the one recommended by the board.[98]

David had beaten Goliath, but only by making – and paying for – an accommodation in the face of American intransigence.

Requisitioned property (parcel no. 34) on the site of Fort Pepperrell, 1943. A60-87, The Rooms Provincial Archives.

The assessment by the American Board of Experts that the land in Pleasantville was "little farmed" demonstrates either that the board members didn't appreciate the subtleties of the cultivated landscape in Newfoundland or that, in this physical environment, land was more intensively and imaginatively cultivated than in the United States. In either case, the issue led to further complications. The farmers argued that "pasture" was not always pasture but was part of a crop rotation and should be compensated as cropland; that "bogland" was not wasteland but instead provided compost to enrich the fields; that "woods" had a value for the timber that was taken from them for fuel, buildings, and fencing. Newfoundland revised the scheme, valuing cultivated land (crops and pasture in rotation) at $400/acre, permanent pasture at $250/acre, woods at $150/acre, and scrub at $60/acre. For the nine suburban lots fronting on the Boulevard, the compensation was $9/frontage foot.[99] All buildings of any kind were valued by cubic foot, with the amount of compensation determined by the quality of construction. The additional compensation for disturbance – that is, the cost of removal and loss of profits – was calculated at either 10 per cent or 20 per cent of the total value for land and buildings. Only an owner could be compensated for land, but a tenant could be compensated for disturbance.

Because every person whose land was requisitioned was given the opportunity to speak before the Board of Arbitration, we have a complete record of the heartfelt arguments that were advanced in support of individual appeals. Farmers explained to the board that it was not a simple thing to move to another farm. One said, "I would not go on [to] strange land; it takes a long time to establish a farm." Another complained, "There is not a place to get. Prices are going up. Property we buy is gone up twice as much. It is taking a mean advantage of the people being evacuated from their homes." None of the farmers were optimistic about getting another farm close to the city where their children went to school and where they carted their milk and produce to sell. The younger ones looked for work on the base. The older ones expressed more distress: "I cannot see how I can make a living at my stage of life ... I do not know where I can go. I am 59 ... I am right out of business as a farmer. At my age, tell me what I can do."

Faced with a complete loss of livelihood, most farmers were not shy about pressing their case. They sought compensation for their livestock if they could not continue to farm elsewhere: "Unless I can get pasture land [for dairy cattle] – and there is none to get anywhere – I will have to go out of business." Some sought compensation for the value of fencing destroyed or the value of stones in a defunct stone wall. In one case, a farmer was awarded the $70 he requested to compensate him for the value of a manure pile "rendered useless" because the Americans had disposed of it before he could cart it away and sell it.

The process of expropriation took three to six months. Meanwhile, the Americans got on with the business of constructing Fort Pepperrell, sometimes with alarming consequences: "The rifle range is right in front of my place. They fire up right over it. You cannot do anything ... you cannot get in our road"; and "The boundary [of the farm] was right along side my house; bullets comes in and strikes the house. I was feeding the pigs one day and one [bullet] came and struck the can I was feeding in."

THE AMERICANS ARRIVE IN ST JOHN'S

One thousand American troops arrived in St John's on 29 January 1941 aboard the *Edmund B. Alexander*.[100] They remained billeted on the ship until May, when they moved into temporary accommodations under canvas at Camp Alexander, located on fifteen acres of leased land north of the city on Carpasian Road.[101] They remained there until November, when they began to move into Fort Pepperrell. The medical needs of the troops were served by a temporary hospital fitted up in the leased property at Northbank, a gracious home on the north shore of Long Pond, and the headquarters of Newfoundland Base Command was temporarily located in a rented house.[102]

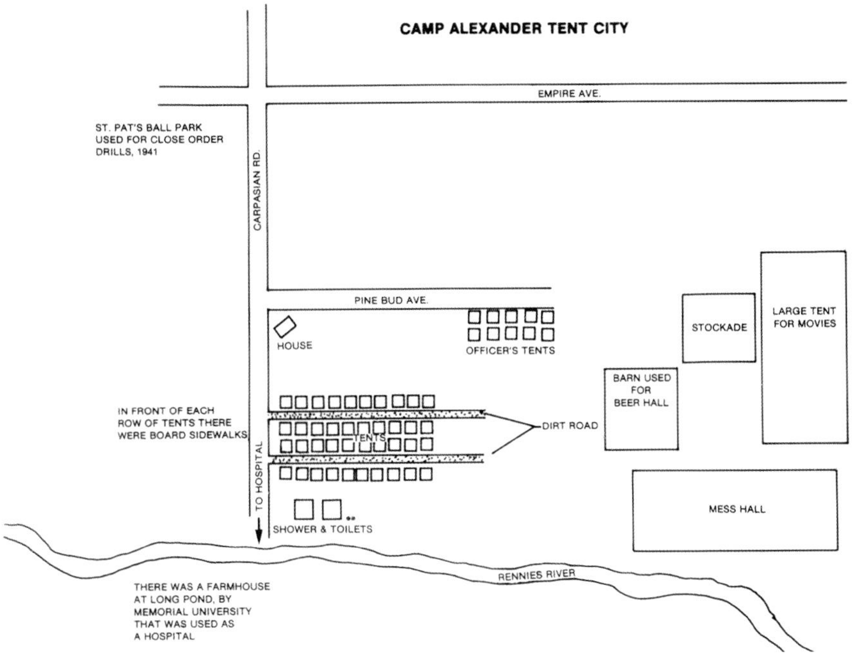

Plan of Camp Alexander. John Cardoulis Fonds, PF 306.230, Maritime History Archive.

Building Fort Pepperrell

Construction of the American base at Quidi Vidi, which was soon named Fort Pepperrell,[103] had been underway since October 1940, long before the details of the Leased Bases Agreement had been finalized in London. Non-American firms were ineligible to bid on any of the base construction contracts,[104] and American Base Contractors, a consortium of three American companies, was contracted in February 1941 to do the work.[105] This does not seem to have ever been an issue in St John's. Newfoundland labourers were probably more interested in the opportunities for employment than with principles of sovereignty,[106] and the government more interested in dealing with problems relating to customs and excise concessions, wage rates, and the extension of American jurisdiction outside the boundaries of the leased areas. During November/December 1941, as the camp neared completion, there may have been as many as 5,000 Newfoundland civilians employed at the site.[107] The migration of men to St John's in search of base employment was hampered by bottlenecks in the transportation system, and their arrival in the city added to the shortage of rental accommodation, which remained a critical problem all through the war. The shortage was so severe that as the American soldiers vacated the tents at Camp Alexander and moved into the newly constructed barracks at Pepperrell, the tents were lined with wallboard and fitted as sleeping quarters for workmen employed at the base.[108]

The government had initially been told that the base would accommodate 1,350 officers and men, but in light of the changing military situation, the cap-

Camp Alexander. John Cardoulis Fonds, PF-306.183, Maritime History Archive.

acity was increased to 3,200 by March 1941[109] and finally to 5,500.[110] The magnitude of this project must have amazed everyone – commissioners, members of city council, and citizens. Fort Pepperrell eventually contained more than 200 buildings laid out on a road pattern shaped like a cowboy hat. Dozens of barrack blocks were supported by a complete suite of service buildings – for power, security, laundry, a hospital, a fire station, a movie theatre – making the base a complete American city within the city of St John's.

The Americans Expand Their Footprint

The Americans, like the Canadians, quickly expanded their footprint because they were concerned about the vulnerability of St John's, and especially the harbour, to enemy attack.[111] Although the reality was that "enemy action in Newfoundland never exceeded nuisance proportions,"[112] this concern was not unfounded.[113] The Canadians had already considered, and rejected, Signal Hill as the site for the 4.7-inch guns that ended up in Fort Amherst because the commanding officer felt that the hill was too often obscured by low-lying cloud. This was a peculiar observation, given that the hill had been an important signal station since at least 1704. The Americans, though, decided that Signal Hill was the logical place from which to defend both the harbour and the *Alexander.* By the end of February 1941 they had installed a mobile four-gun, 155-mm battery plus an anti-aircraft battery consisting of four 3-inch and sixteen .50-calibre machine guns. In May this had been augmented by the addition of two 8-inch coastal defence guns.[114] By the time construction had ceased, the American position on Signal Hill contained eighty-six buildings. The gun positions were of reinforced concrete, but the other structures were of wood-frame construction. These included eighteen barracks capable of accommodating 478 men, a dispensary and post exchange, machine and carpenter shops, two mess halls, and two recreation buildings.[115]

To ensure the adequate defence of their St John's base, the Americans built a number of prepared positions around St John's and Conception Bay to which mobile guns and searchlights could be rapidly moved if necessary.[116] And, con-

Fort Pepperrell and Signal Hill, 1941. U.S. Army Air Corps Photo Section, Newfoundland Air Base, Declassified NWD 745022, NARA, 1974.

Fort Pepperrell from the north, c. 1948. John Cardoulis Fonds, PF 306.179, Maritime History Archive.

cerned about the security of the Torbay aerodrome, they posted guards on the beaches at Logy Bay, Outer Cove, Middle Cove, Torbay Bight, and Flatrock.[117]

The commission constantly faced the kinds of problems that inevitably arise when one sovereign state has the right, given by a third party, to operate inside another. On more than one occasion the governor vented his frustration to the dominions secretary in London about the lack of consultation by the Americans.[118] A particularly annoying problem was the Americans' use of land outside the official leased area without consultation with, or permission from, the Newfoundland government. A weary Emerson, faced with a request for approval of yet another *fait accompli* – a lease on twenty-six acres, involving nine property owners, for an ammunition storage area, several miles from Fort Pepperrell on Portugal Cove Road, a lease negotiated without benefit of consultation with the government – commented to his fellow commissioners: "[W]e have accepted the presence of the U.S. armed forces in St John's, we are allowing U.S. guns to be placed on Signal Hill ... we have acquiesced ... in the use of a wharf leased ... for the berthing of the [troopship] *Edmund B. Alexander.* Having successfully swallowed these fairly large camels, I do not think we need strain unduly at the small gnat which ... [this] proposal ... represents."[119]

The American expansion beyond the original leased areas was considerable. It was retroactively authorized by the American Bases (Supplementary Bases) Act 1942,[120] which approved the lease for the 26-acre ammunition storage site and expanded it by 210 acres to create a restricted area around it.[121] It also added 860 acres to the target range in the White Hills and added 6 acres in the Battery, where the army supply dock had been under construction for some months.[122]

U.S. Army Barracks on Signal Hill, 10 October 1941. PA-135879, Canada, Department of National Defence/Library and Archives Canada.

The American eight-inch coastal defence guns on Signal Hill, 10 October 1941. Murrin/Hunt Fonds, Newfoundland Collection, Provincial Reference Library.

The Army Supply Dock

After abandoning the plan to build a naval base on the south side of the harbour, the Americans built a 605-foot-long $1-million dock below the Middle Battery to facilitate the supply chain to all their sites in the country.[123] Its size and modern mechanized equipment provided a stark contrast to the traditional finger piers that lined the harbour perimeter. The property of more than eighty residents of the Battery was requisitioned, and many of these residents came before the Board of Arbitration during the winter of 1941–42.[124] Some earned only a few hundred dollars a year in the fishery and worked as longshoremen as well. A few were high flyers and earned thousands. But all were treated fairly, although in many cases the compensation could not repair the damage done to their lives. There was a four-part compensation scheme. The rate for land was $30/foot for waterfront and $5/foot for inland frontage. Following normal practice, the buildings were surveyed so that their cubic capacity could be estimated, and compensation was paid by the cubic foot at rates reflecting quality of construction. There was also compensation for fishing gear. Because there was nowhere else in the harbour where the fishermen could continue fishing, their gear was rendered useless, but they were given compensation for its replacement value nonetheless. Finally, property owners received compensation for disturbance at the rate of 20 per cent of the total value of their land and buildings.

A jumble of houses, wharves, stores, and flakes stood on the land requisitioned for the dock. As in Pleasantville there was confusion about property ownership. Some people had documents; many did not: "I took in the property. The property was lying there, idle." Sometimes the Americans just tore down or burned buildings for which there was no listed owner: "I fished to the last of August last year. It was only since they burned down the place I had to give it up. I handed it all over to the Government. I even gave them my splitting knife." Only property owners were given notice. Tenants came to know about it only if their landlord thought to tell them: "We had premises from Smith's ... we bought a store and built on Smith's property ... we lost our fit-out. It was burned when Smith's stuff was taken." One property owner on the waterfront permitted six others who didn't live in the battery to "tie on" to his place. When the property was requisitioned, all the tenants lost their access to the fishery.

So, by the summer of 1941, the Canadian Army was settled into Lester's Field Camp and the Americans were constructing Fort Pepperrell and the army supply dock. Then the Royal Canadian Air Force arrived.

Requisitioned buildings on the site of the U.S. Army Supply Dock, 1942. A60-45, The Rooms Provincial Archives.

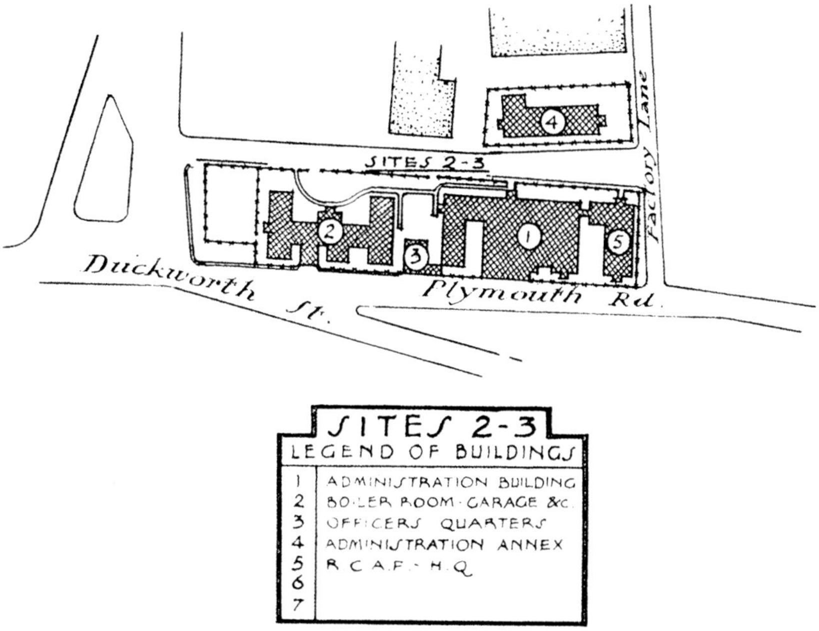

Plan of RCN and RCAF Headquarters. Detail from Map 819, RG 4.3 41/83, The Rooms Provincial Archives.

THE RCAF COMES TO ST JOHN'S

The fall of France in June 1940 led to Britain's acceptance of Canada's offer to supply aircraft and military defences for Gander and Botwood, from which, it was thought, the whole island could be defended.[125] By October, however, it was obvious that fighter aircraft needed to be located closer to St John's, and the Permanent Joint Board on Defence recommended that a new aerodrome be built. Newfoundland agreed, on the understanding that Canada would pay for it but would not use it for civil aviation.[126]

The site, several miles northeast of the city, was selected by a survey party in November 1940. Most of the property required was crown land, but about a dozen farmers had some or all of their lands expropriated, the title passing to Canada.[127] Newfoundland could not afford to purchase private land, but even had the resources been available, this would not have been contemplated because "on political grounds, difficulty would be seen in making contributions for the purchase of property required for Canada."[128] The perennial suspicion of Canadian motives meant that Canada's having title to land in Newfoundland was to become a sore point in discussions between the two countries at the end of the war, despite the size of the Canadian investment. The original estimate was that construction would cost almost $2 million but the final tally was $11,709,431.[129] The hangars, control tower, barracks, and drill hall were clustered on the eastern side of the original main runway, and ancillary communication and radar sites were scattered over the Avalon Peninsula.[130] Aviation fuel was stored at a newly constructed depot far to the west of the city, and a third runway was completed in 1943.[131]

Airport construction had hardly begun when its principal role changed from that of local defence to convoy protection. In March 1941 the British Admiralty alerted Canadian authorities that German U-boats were almost certainly going to move into the western Atlantic now that they had access to French ports.[132] It was now urgent to provide air and sea protection for convoys across the whole expanse of the Atlantic, even if the aircraft only acted as scarecrows.[133] This required the expansion of the new aerodrome and the addition of bomber/reconnaissance aircraft to the Hurricane fighters already allocated to it.[134] It also required a new administrative structure, and on 10 July 1941, No. 1 Group, Eastern Air Command, took over tactical control of all RCAF units in Newfoundland.

In its early days, No. 1 Group worked out of the Newfoundland Hotel at the east end of the downtown, and most of the personnel were billeted in rented accommodation scattered across the city.[135] By the summer of 1942 a headquarters building had been erected near the Hotel, adjoining RCN headquarters, to permit coordination of air support for convoy operations in a combined operations room.[136] In August, barracks to house the headquarters personnel were built on Kenna's Hill, west of Fort Pepperrell, on land purchased by the Canadian government from the estate of one of the city's leading merchant families for the princely sum of $58,000.[137] The city was initially asked to permit the construction of nine temporary buildings to provide "domestic accommodation for about

Combined RCN/RCAF Operations Room, 24 September 1942. PA-180609, Lt Gerald Moses/Canada, Department of National Defence/Library and Archives Canada.

RCAF No. 1 Group Barracks on Kenna's Hill. Photo #11-01-680, City of St John's Archives.

400 men," but as so often happened, the establishment grew beyond the original request, in this case to incorporate twenty-one buildings. They included barrack accommodation and messes for officers, non-commissioned officers (NCOs), and other ranks, both women and men, a canteen, and a garage.[138]

The Kenna's Hill facility was on the outskirts of the town, and the Torbay aerodrome, where as many as 2,000 flying and support personnel were based, nearly three miles beyond that.[139] Consequently, RCAF activity was not as visible to the people of the city as that of the Canadian Army or the RCN. Thus the RCAF's vital role in defending North Atlantic convoys was not fully appreciated. The airmen deserved better. Until modern aircraft finally began to arrive in 1944, they fought at a great disadvantage: "Challenged by some of the worst flying conditions in the world, plagued by fog and ice, they coaxed their underpowered, poorly-equipped machines to exceed all normal limits of performance, knowing too well that the prevailing westerly winds would often make the return flight the most hazardous part of each mission."[140]

It must have been exciting to live in St John's that summer of 1941. There was so much military construction, so many job opportunities, so much money in people's pockets. Anti-aircraft batteries, searchlights, and military encampments were springing up all over town, and aircraft were constantly droning overhead. And then, to add to the already high level of activity, the navy came to town.

THE RCN COMES TO "NEWFYJOHN"

Perhaps because of the country's maritime heritage, the citizens of St John's developed a greater affinity for the sailors than for the other Canadian servicemen. And for the sailors, Newfyjohn was their favourite port of call.[141]

When the Newfoundland Defence Scheme was prepared for the Dominions Office in London in 1936, St John's was referred to as a possible port of refuge in the event of war.[142] As it turned out, St John's was rapidly transformed from an undefended port into the major Canadian base for transatlantic escort vessels.[143] The men of the Royal Canadian Navy had not dreamed of spending the war in little ships, acting as sheepdogs to plodding merchantmen. But the Royal Navy did not have enough ships to protect the vital convoys, and the Americans, though initially willing to help, withdrew from the Atlantic after the Japanese attack on Pearl Harbor on 7 December 1941. Canada stepped into the breach.[144]

The Newfoundland Escort Force

The war at sea was going badly for the Allies in the spring of 1941. Three merchant ships were being sunk for every new one built, and eight U-boats were being launched for every one sunk.[145] Amazingly, the pivotal events that were to have such profound effects on St John's were arranged in a quick, brief exchange of telegrams. On 20 May the First Sea Lord wrote to the naval officer in charge (NOIC) at St John's saying that because U-boats based in captured French ports were now able to operate much farther afield, a base on the western side of the Atlantic was now an urgent necessity. St John's was the obvious choice because of its location, but the Admiralty wanted to know whether fog conditions were tolerable.[146] The NOIC optimistically replied that "St. John's is defended and has the best facilities in Newfoundland. Average fog not more than two or three days per month."[147] That same day the Admiralty asked Canadian Naval Service Headquarters (NSHQ) how many Canadian corvettes were available for local escort duties in Newfoundland waters. The reply was seven, but that fifteen more would be available within a month and a total of forty-eight within six months. Furthermore, NSHQ said, "[W]e should be glad to undertake the task of anti-submarine convoy escort."[148] And thus the Newfoundland Escort Force (NEF) was born. Twenty-four hours later, seven new Canadian-built corvettes had departed from Halifax for St John's,[149] and three of them sailed on the NEF's first escort mission on 2 June 1941.

The RCN's commitment to open-ocean convoy protection and the creation of the NEF came before any thought had been given to whether St John's could provide the necessary facilities and services. It could not: "St. John's ... had almost every disadvantage except that of geography. Everything required for the construction of a large naval base would have to come from outside the island. Communications were inadequate; skilled labour was scarce; docking facilities, billeting facilities, fuel and fuel storage were all lacking."[150] However, in spite of it all, the NEF swung into operation, a naval base was built, and the RCN participated fully in the Battle of the Atlantic. This experience allowed the navy to come of age and provided its "self-defining mythology and lore."[151]

Building the Canadian Naval Base

Four days after the first three corvettes sailed to join their convoy, the governor, Vice-Admiral Walwyn, wrote to the secretary of state for dominion affairs to express his concerns about the difficulty of sharing the already-cramped commercial space in St John's Harbour with operational naval forces:[152]

> We are of the opinion that it will be just possible to provide the base requirements of the force ... but this will involve extensive requisitioning of commercial premises on the waterfront, considerable dredging, building or rebuilding of approximately 3,200 lineal feet of wharfage and a building programme covering about 50,000 square feet of floor space on the waterfront apart altogether from magazines, recreational and hospital facilities and housing ... After dredging, construction of new jetties and laying of trots[153] ... 55 naval vessels can be accommodated in the harbour[154] ... The result will be to reduce drastically the number of merchant vessels which can be sheltered in St John's harbour and ... repaired.[155] You will have realized, of course, the great cost which will be involved in compensating owners of waterfront properties for damages which will be caused to them by requisitioning of their premises.

Transformation of a mercantile harbour into an operational naval base began in the summer of 1941 and continued until 1945. It was fortunate that the Americans had abandoned their plan to build a naval base on the south side of the harbour because three sites of the Canadian naval base were to be located in precisely the area originally earmarked by Admiral Greenslade. The Admiralty agreed to pay for the acquisition of the necessary property, the title of which would be vested either in the Admiralty or Newfoundland, and for the construction of the base facilities. Canada agreed to operate both the base and the Newfoundland Escort Force. [156]

St John's, December 1941. Note the number of merchant ships in the harbour. HMCS Avalon is under construction at centre right. PA-192-822, Canada, Department of National Defence/Library and Archives Canada.

Having to build the base from scratch meant that, during the desperate battle against increasingly aggressive and very successful U-boats through the winter of 1941–42, the NEF had to make do with support facilities that were less than ideal. As one veteran put it, "Although Newfyjohn was a naval base of world significance, it wore a curiously impermanent air, like a travelling tent show ... there were no naval shore facilities at St John's ... Unlike the army and air force, both with big, permanent installations, the navy at St John's seemed to operate out of its hat."[157] However, "Newfyjohn lives on in the memory of thousands of corvette sailors as a warm and outgoing place, the home of hospitable and friendly people, and of the finest, most efficient escort base in all of North America."[158]

The south side of the harbour was occupied by a number of houses, fishing sheds, and stages, as well as by many large commercial enterprises vital to Newfoundland's economy.[159] To minimize the disruption, the navy built a continuous twenty- to thirty-foot-wide wharf along a portion of the south side in front of the existing mercantile premises. The property owners were to receive a monthly rent for the duration of the war plus twelve months, and would then take possession of the new wharf. For many, the naval wharf was of better quality than their own and the compensation paid by the Admiralty was so highly valued that at the end of the war some owners declined early termination of the rental.[160]

Typical wharves and buildings on the South Side of St John's Harbour. A61-59, The Rooms Provincial Archives.

His Majesty's Canadian Dockyard

An entirely new dockyard was built in the northwest corner of the harbour to provide space for naval stores, torpedo and ordnance depots, repair shops, and the fleet mail office. This was an active commercial area filled with finger wharves and flakes owned or tenanted by merchants who needed water access and with shops along Water Street, where one could find everything from fish and lumber to a barber shop and a draper. Some buildings also had residential space on their upper floors. Enormous quantities of goods and equipment had to be moved from the requisitioned premises, but there was little available storage space in town. One claimant described how he "moved hastily, all the [engine] parts were lumped together. It would take weeks to sort out. I had no place to put them ... I had a telephone call from someone who said if I was not out by noon they would be down to put me out."[161]

Property acquisition began in June 1941. The first approach to the owners entailed negotiating a lump sum. Those who declined to accept were given requisition notices in August. The government could then enter upon the property at any time. Major Lyons of the Canadian Army acted as agent for the Admiralty. Like the Americans, he argued for assessing properties only for market value.

But Justice Higgins, chairman of the Board of Arbitration, was adamant that the practice established in Argentia, Marquise, Quidi Vidi, and the Battery would be followed here: "[T]he Government has put in ... the replacement value of the buildings; that was the basis on which we started our Arbitration ... That is the decision of the Board; that is our principle and we have never varied." When Major Lyons protested, Justice Higgins said to him, "I would suggest that you get a local man [to do your valuations]. It is different here than it is in Canada."

Disturbance was included in the compensation. This acknowledged that the relocation of a business would cause a hiatus in the operation, some expense, and loss of customer goodwill, all expressed in loss of profits. Up to three years' anticipated future profits, calculated on the basis of the previous three years' activity, was the rule of thumb. But these Water Street businessmen were astute. They wanted the calculation to be based on 1941 alone because the rise in profits

St John's Harbour and HMC Dockyard, 26 September 1942. PMR 84-731. Reproduced with the permission of the Minister of Public Works and Government Services, 2008.

since 1940 had been phenomenal. Take, for example, the profits of the draper ($4,441 in 1939, $6,061 in 1940, and $9,484 up to August 1941) and of the barber ($85.45 for August 1940 and $175.80 for August 1941). According to various claimants, "Business is not 'as usual' but very much better than usual"; "Shopping crowds positively throng the streets in fine weather"; and "Every day is like Christmas Eve on Water Street now."

The astute businessmen claimed compensation for damage to goods being removed; in one instance, for example, "enamelware was chipped and sold at reduced prices." They claimed the cost of furniture storage while they were between places, and some asked to be compensated for all the expenses entailed in setting up their business elsewhere. Several claimed money for long-time employees: "Your petitioner has been compelled to dispense with the services of four old employees of the Company through its being compelled to discontinue business [requisitioned]. The said servants have been unable to obtain employment and will be a charge on the Company. What I did do I gave them six weeks salary." Justice Higgins replied, "I say we should give consideration to claims of this character."

The ripple effect of the requisitioning of property was far-reaching. One property owner, whose property had been requisitioned by the Admiralty, informed his tenant that he was required to "vacate the premises forthwith ... at the earliest possible moment ... We are in the unfortunate position of not being able to treat you along the lines we would wish." The tenant, in turn, telegraphed a business contact in New York to say, "[A]s my warehouse, etc. being taken over immediately for Admiralty requirements regret unable to accept ... any further business until can arrange re-establishment elsewhere."

Residential tenants had difficulty too, as accommodation was at a premium in town: "We have not got a place to live yet ... furniture is stored ... moved at 10:00 PM in the rain, dark, no lights [on account of the blackout]. A lot of things got broken ... They had to have this house down the next morning."

HMCS Avalon

Buckmaster's Field, north of LeMarchant Road, was acquired as the site for the barracks complex that would become HMCS Avalon, originally planned to accommodate about 1,000 officers and men.[162] The field was initially leased from the Royal Trust Company but was later purchased by the Canadian government.[163] The forty-one buildings included barracks and officers' accommodations, canteens and messes, a chapel, a sick bay and a dentist's office, a drill hall, a bakery, a laundry, storehouses, classrooms, a cinema, and a recreation hall. Provision was made for the accommodation of 575 members of the WRCNS, the first naval women to be drafted for duty outside Canada.

In Newfoundland, the men of the navy, like those of the army, had to make do with facilities that lacked the glamour of the long-established bases in Canada. One officer described Avalon as "a collection of raw wood two-storey buildings high up on the bald blanched hills surrounding the busy little harbour."[164] It

may not have been glamorous, but HMCS Avalon was vital to "the … unending work of convoy escort and U-boat warfare."[165]

HMC Dockyard, the city, and HMCS Avalon, c. 1942, looking north. RE 93-2412, 763-IMG005. Reproduced with the permission of the Minister of Government Works and Services, 2008.

By the end of 1942 the footprint of the RCN had been extended well beyond the confines of Buckmaster's Field. In addition to the wharves, warehouses, training buildings, and machine shop established on the south side of the harbour, there were ammunition storage facilities carved out of the cliffs along South Side Road, the new naval dockyard, and the headquarters building on Plymouth Road. There was a wireless station some miles south of the city in the Goulds, a controlled mining station[166] and Port War Signal Station at Fort Amherst, and another Port War Signal Station at Cape Spear.

The navy also built a 250-bed hospital. The existing civilian hospital capacity could not possibly accommodate the huge increase in demand created by the addition of naval personnel to the city's population. Thus a naval hospital and nurses' residence were built in the grounds of the existing Fever Hospital, located south of Quidi Vidi Lake. The new hospital opened in April 1942.[167]

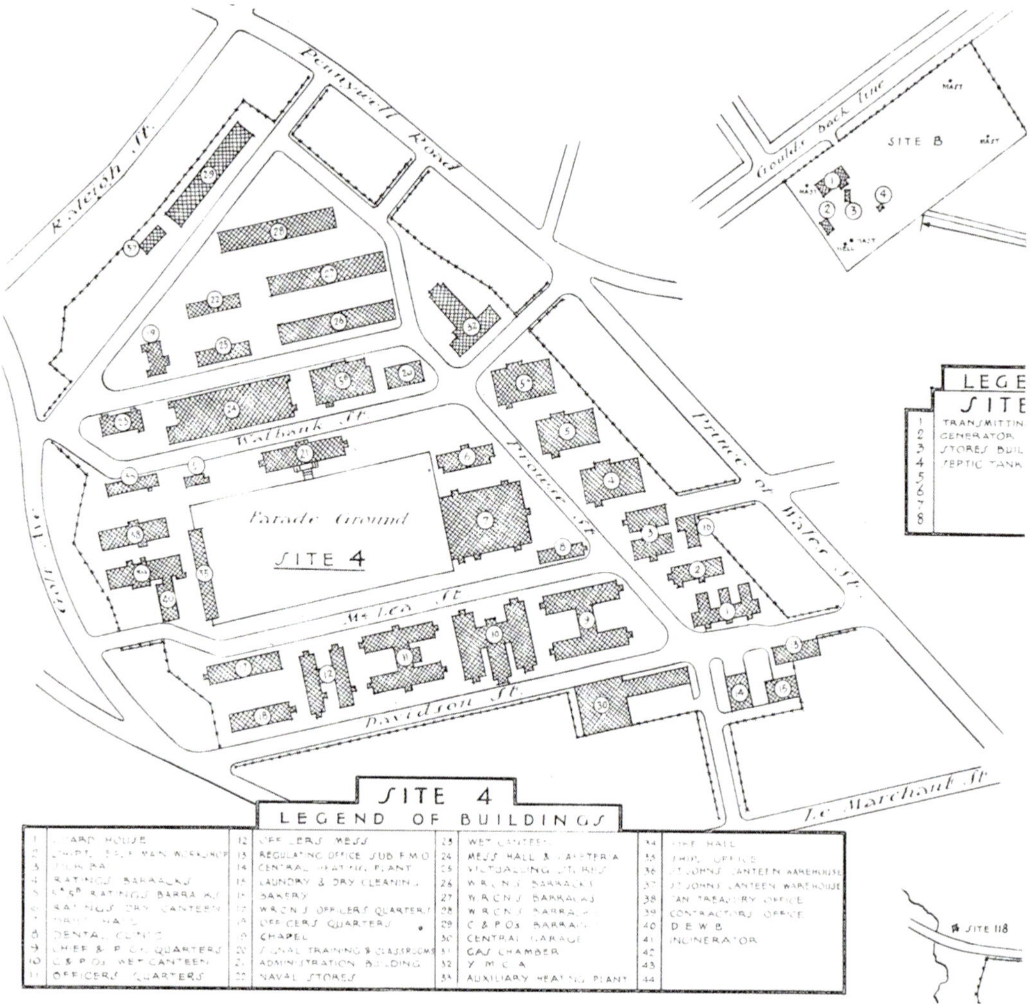

Plan of HMCS Avalon. Detail from Map 819, RG 4.3 41/83, The Rooms Provincial Archives.

THE MID-OCEAN ESCORT FORCE AND BASE EXPANSION

In January 1942 the ships of the Newfoundland Escort Force amalgamated with some Britain-based Royal Navy vessels to form the Mid-Ocean Escort Force (MOEF) and began to escort convoys between Ireland and the Grand Banks.[168] The British ships used Argentia as their Newfoundland base, but the RCN continued to operate out of St John's, and by the summer of 1943 it was obvious that a major expansion of the base was desperately needed. Seventy warships were now using the harbour, more than twice the number originally planned for.[169] The harbour was simply too small to accommodate the combined needs of the Merchant Marine and the expanded naval force. The congestion became intolerable.[170] There was a shortage of wharf and storage space, heavy-lift cranes, and repair facilities, and this led to such significant delays in the turnaround of damaged ships that some escort vessels missed their convoys. Moreover, the supply chain to the island was frequently interrupted. The situation was so serious that in the spring of 1942 the Montreal-based representative of the Ministry of War Transport issued a dire warning to the Newfoundland government: "[U]nless prompt and drastic action is taken I am absolutely convinced that the colony will not get in sufficient coal and supplies to put them [*sic*] through the winter."[171]

But it was not until the spring of 1943 that it was decided that the navy's repair and support facilities should be expanded.[172] The navy's immediate need was

Two unidentified nursing sisters and Surgeon Lieutenant Riddell leaving RCN Hospital No. 1, St John's, Newfoundland, 27 July 1942. PA-137827, Canada, Department of National Defence/Library and Archives Canada.

A bunch of "Flowers" on the South Side of St John's Harbour: HMS *Dianthus* (K-95), HMS *Trillium* (K-172), and an unidentified corvette framed by another corvette's minesweeping davits. Photo #1-45-008, City of St John's Archives.

a new barrack complex to house as many as 1,500 men and 850 women. There was no room at Buckmaster's Field, so the barracks were built on a very difficult, steeply sloping site overlooking the existing naval buildings on the south side of the harbour.[173] The expansion plans also included more warehouses, a tactical training centre, an upgraded machine shop, a harbour craft repair shop, a new cafeteria, and a second 250-bed naval hospital. Fuel storage capacity had became a critical problem, and a tank farm, the largest built anywhere by the RCN, was built on the South Side.

Naval base expansion meant more intrusion into the lives of the people who lived and worked near the sites, particularly on the South Side.[174] This was a long-settled community,[175] and many of the people in the forty or so displaced families had been living on property that had been handed down through several generations. Few were fishermen. They worked in a variety of employment, some downtown, others locally in the commercial premises on the South Side. Some operated small businesses in their homes. The requisitioning of property cost a few people their livelihood, but the incidence was not as high as it had been in Pleasantville and the Battery. Some lost their homes, demolished for naval construction; others lost only a portion of their land, taken for the con-

Above Construction work on the South Side of St John's Harbour, 3 December 1943. PA-166490, Harold L. Scott/Library and Archives Canada.

Below RCN Barracks on the South Side Hills, 1945. PA-209678, Canada, Department of National Defence/Library and Archives Canada.

struction of a switchback road up the South Side Hills to the site of the new barracks.

Compensation was set at $65/foot for waterfront land and $20/foot for road frontage, values considerably higher than those paid for property in the Battery. Buildings were valued per cubic foot but with variation depending on the quality of construction. A well-built house with good plumbing and a good cellar might be valued as high as 80 cents/cubic foot; a house built on shores (posts) with no plumbing might be valued as low as 33 cents/cubic foot. Compensation for disturbance was calculated at 20 per cent of the value of the land and buildings. For many of those who took their claims before the Board of Arbitration the sticking point was the value placed on the buildings. It was now 1943 and the war's effect on the local construction trade was being felt. A shortage of materials, owing in part to a lack of shipping space, had sent the price of construction materials sky high. According to one expert witness, "building cost is up 125 percent since the war. Labour is up 100 percent." In another case, the government valued a house at 37 cents a cubic foot, but the expert witness, who had been a carpenter for fifty years, testified: "I cubed up the house [in question] … I made it up on a cube of 52 cents. Four or five years ago an ordinary house would have cost 32 cents to 43 cents [per cubic foot] but today the stock has doubled [in price]. Some hardware has trebled. I thought 52 cents was pretty fair."

It was very difficult to value a house in poor repair. How do you arrive at a replacement value for a house that is not fit to live in even though someone does indeed live there? One expert witness opined, "Unfortunately this man [the claimant] has been living there his life time through hard times and the house has gone back. He has not kept it in good repair. To look at the house and start to figure on a poor man's house, a builder has a problem. He is looking for nothing, and then he has to figure on building something for a man fit to live in." In other words, he cannot build an old and dilapidated house.

For those who lost land at the back of their property to permit construction of the new road up the slope to the new barracks, there were further problems. Construction of the road had destabilized the drainage, and a flash flood in December 1944 caused considerable damage. One claimant who had lived in his home for thirty-six years told the board: "I blame the [Naval] road. I blame it [the flood damage] on the new road at the back of the house … it is a menace to the safety of the house. The safety of life … I wouldn't buy the house where it is today, sir, under any condition." The tragedy for the families affected by the building of the access road and the barracks was that by the time the project was completed, the war was over. The barracks were never occupied and were demolished in 1947.

The rule of thumb for the naval hospital was that it had to have the capacity to accommodate 5 per cent of base complement and 50 per cent of ship-based complement. The 250 beds of Naval Hospital No. 1 were insufficient to handle the projected increase in Avalon's complement, yet the site was too small to permit an expansion of the existing building. No other nearby site was available in the centre of the city, so the new hospital was built in the west end of the

Flower-class corvette HMCS *Saskatoon* (K-158) on the slipway at Bay Bulls, 17 July 1944. Panorama of photos CWM 20030014#2 and CWM 20030014#3, George Metcalf Archival Collection © Canadian War Museum.

city beside the government tuberculosis and mental hospitals. The government agreed to acquire and service the site on condition that at the end of the war it would be given the hospital, so that the existing, inadequate TB facilities could be expanded.[176]

The problem of inadequate space and repair facilities in the harbour could only be solved if a dockyard were built somewhere else. In August 1942 it was decided that a marine railway should be installed at Bay Bulls, twenty miles south of St John's.[177] In the interim, since it would take at least a year for the railway to be built, the Americans loaned Newfoundland an 1,800-ton floating wooden drydock, which was towed from Perth Amboy, New Jersey, to the harbour in August 1943.[178] Newfoundland offered to contribute $300,000 towards the cost of acquiring the necessary property in Bay Bulls and then to lease it to the Canadian government.[179] Canada agreed to assume the construction and operation costs. More than $3 million was spent on the marine railway itself, the barracks and officers' quarters, administration facilities, a sick bay, a machine shop, miscellaneous service facilities, and an anti-torpedo net across the harbour mouth.[180] However, the documentary record suggests that the benefits were never commensurate with the effort and expense involved in building the railway because it was completed so late in the war.

We have described the flurry of activity caused by the arrival of Canadian and American forces in the city – dozens of construction sites, thousands of military personnel, fenced-off restricted areas, anti-aircraft installations dotted around the city, and merchant ships vying for space in the harbour. How did the city cope with this invasion?

THE CITY OF ST JOHN'S: COPING WITH THE OCCUPATION

During the first year of the war the citizens of St John's watched as the Newfoundland Militia set up camp in Shamrock Field and then assumed guard duties at various sites around the city. Initially, the impact on the city's landscape was negligible, but the second year of the war was unimaginably different. In the space of ten months, from October 1940 to July 1941, the Canadian Army, the U.S. Army, the RCAF, and the RCN all arrived to set up shop in St John's. There was no part of the city that was not affected by the camps enclosed within perimeter fences,[181] the military vehicles in the streets, the sentries at gun batteries, and the demarcation of restricted areas. St John's City Council had to cope with this difficult situation, all the while attempting to provide normal municipal services. It is all too easy to forget, as many who record wartime activities do, that "ordinary life goes on, insisting that it, too, be heard in the midst of great public drama."[182]

It fell upon the city to provide water and sewer services to the military. The city fathers worried about both the quantity and the quality of the water at the city's water reservoir, Windsor Lake. A 1941 editorial noted: "[A]rrangements were being made by the Municipal Council to supply about one million gallons of water daily to an airport which will be established. Plans are already proceeding to provide the US bases at Quidi Vidi ... from Windsor Lake ... The Canadian Army barracks and the American troopship are already drawing heavily upon the Windsor Lake reserve ... A question which must be determined is whether the reserve is capable of providing, possibly, an additional three million gallons daily without risking a shortage. War or no war, there can be no such thing as taking chances with the water supply of St John's."[183]

The city council watched helplessly as military vehicles tore up the city's streets. At a 1941 meeting with Commissioner of Public Utilities Sir Wilfrid Woods, the city produced a list of eleven miles of road surface that needed repair, at an estimated cost of $114,000. But neither the Canadian nor the American military was prepared to recognize any responsibility in the matter.[184] Moreover, the council was not permitted to levy taxes on the military. Canada declared that all the property that it had acquired was owned by His Majesty and was therefore not taxable by a municipal government,[185] and the Leased Bases Agreement exempted the Americans from payment of local taxes.

However, the Canadian high commissioner considered the city's claims to be a serious matter: "The local situation has reached a point where, unless we do something substantial to meet the city's wishes, an ugly situation may well develop" because "local feeling is stronger against Canada than against the United States."[186] Well aware of Newfoundland's sensitivities, he recognized the "need to employ every counter we have to gain good-will for Canada, or rather

American M3 Stuart tanks on Military Road, All Nations Day Parade, 1943. Photo #1-45-020, City of St John's Archives.

to help remove the feeling of coolness and suspicion with which Canada is, and has long been, regarded."[187] He recommended that the Canadian government provide financial assistance to the city. The Canadian War Cabinet accepted his recommendation of a voluntary payment of $10,000, but the city council refused to accept it. It wanted a payment of taxes at the same rate (5 per cent of appraised rental value) as the Admiralty was paying. In the end Canada reluctantly agreed and paid $11,260 on behalf of the RCAF and the Canadian Army.[188]

The Americans built permanent buildings at Fort Pepperrell, but the Canadians built temporary buildings, more than 250 of them,[189] on the understanding that they would be demolished at the end of the war.[190] In this city of wooden buildings, the risk of fire was ever-present, and the local press continued to remind council of its responsibility to minimize the chance of a major conflagration caused by accident or sabotage.[191] The harbour itself constituted a serious fire hazard because of the concentration of fuel and ammunition storage facilities.[192]

RCAF bombing and training areas in Conception Bay and Witless Bay, south of St John's, were not used constantly, but when they were in use, normal activity was interrupted. When Commissioner Woods heard that Gull Pond, in the Witless Bay area, was to be enclosed within a bombing range, he wistfully lamented the inevitable loss of good trout fishing there.[193] The navy rifle range on the South Side Hills had to have a highly visible system of warning flags to indicate when the range was in use "because the area is frequented by berry pickers."[194]

The Housing Shortage

There had been a housing shortage in St John's for many years before the war, and the military occupation exacerbated it. Rapid rent inflation led to the imposition of rent restrictions as early as December 1941.[195] One of the reasons for the increased stress on accommodation was believed to be the influx into the city of those seeking employment during the base-construction boom. However, evidence for the number of these job-seekers is fragmentary and often conflicting. At the end of 1943 about 10,000 men were on defence-related jobs in Newfoundland as a whole, but it is impossible to determine how many of them worked in St John's, although one press report put the number working at Fort Pepperrell at 600 in the winter of 1941.[196] However, a 1942 survey of housing conditions in St John's[197] provides a fragment of data: an estimate of the number of residents in military or non-military employment who had moved into the city within the previous two years – the years of the rapid mobilization of labour for base construction. Of 1,968 persons in non-military employment, only 63 (3.2 per cent) had lived in St John's for two years or less. Of the 533 persons with military employment and/or who worked for the various base contractors, 76 (14.2 per cent) had moved into the city within the previous two years.

A second reason given for the increased stress on accommodation was the number of military personnel, particularly RCN, living off-base. In 1943, 1,650 naval men were reported to be living in civilian accommodation, many of them with dependants.[198] The following story illustrates an all-too-common situation. Paul Meschino, a Toronto architect, was taken on as a civilian employee of the Works and Services Building Division of the Naval Service and posted to St John's to work on the South Side barracks and Bay Bulls marine railway projects. He lived in barracks at Buckmaster's Field until his fiancée arrived from Canada. He then moved off-base. The only accommodation they were able to find was one unheated room in a downtown house. There they had no access to a kitchen and shared the single bathroom with the household, which consisted of two families totalling nine adults.[199]

Local public opinion put the blame for the city's accommodation problems squarely on the military. The Americans sent all dependants, between 700 and 1,000 of them, back to the United States immediately after the attack on Pearl

Harbor.[200] The Canadians, who were already at war, did not do the same for the Canadian dependants.[201] Rather, they agreed to a quota on the number of dependants permitted to live in the city. Both they and the commission were roundly criticized for this decision. One editorial put it this way: "The Government allowed the servicemen to bring their wives here without making certain that suitable accommodation was available, and has done nothing to help alleviate the present overcrowding. It is an odd twist of circumstances that citizens of St. John's now find they cannot obtain living quarters in their own city at any price."[202]

The Social Clubs

The presence in St John's of thousands of young men and women, far from home, some of them living in grave danger much of the time, others enduring the tedium of garrison duty, made the provision of recreational facilities imperative. Both the Canadian and the American bases provided some sports facilities, but most of the social interaction between military personnel and civilians occurred in off-base facilities.[203] They were built by institutions such as the Salvation Army, the YMCA, the YWCA, religious dominations, and patriotic groups. Their physical impact on the townscape was limited, but the services they provided – including dances, movies, letter-writing facilities, meals, and beds – were welcome distractions for the servicemen and women and for the hundreds of local residents who gave up thousands of hours of volunteer time to run these facilities and organize the events. (See Collins, chapter 2, this volume.)

AFTER THE WAR: THE OCCUPATION ENDS

When the war in Europe ended in May 1945, the military personnel left as quickly as they had come. The strength of the Canadian Army in Newfoundland peaked at 5,692 in mid-December 1943.[204] By November 1945, this number had been reduced to 660,[205] and by the end of June 1946 they were all gone.[206] The RCAF, too, left without delay. In mid-August 1945 the last operational squadron departed from Torbay and returned to Dartmouth, Nova Scotia. No. 1 Group was disbanded and its headquarters closed down.

At times there had been as many as 8,000 Canadian seamen in St John's.[207] In mid-July 1945 the ships of the MOEF returned to their bases in Britain and Canada, and by August the shore-based RCN complement was down to 2,000. At the end of September the status of the base was reduced to "care and maintenance," leaving "nothing to mark its passing but a tradition and a few genes in the Newfoundland bloodstream."[208] St John's was left to adjust to these new circumstances but without all the excitement that had accompanied the new arrivals in 1940 and 1941. The party was over and it was time to pick up the debris and tidy things away.

What happened to the hundreds of temporary military buildings, many of which did not comply with the fire code? Now that the exigency of the war was over, the city council insisted that they be demolished. The buildings on Shamrock Field that had housed the Newfoundland Militia (later Regiment) were cleared away and the site returned to the Christian Brothers, as promised. The fate of the Canadian camp at Calver's Field is described in a newspaper ad: "For sale at Calver's Field. Large amount lumber, doors, sashes complete with frames; wallboard, jacket heaters, stoves, 2 large kitchen ranges suitable for hotel or restaurant. We would also sell buildings as they stand to anyone who would wish to take them down."[209] The Canadians offered their Lester's Field buildings for sale and removal from the site,[210] although Purity Factories was given permission to take over two warehouses to expand their biscuit manufacturing business, thereby creating 250 new jobs.[211] They are still in use today. All the other buildings were demolished and the sites returned to their owners.[212]

Canada owned the land and buildings at the RCAF Kenna's Hill site and retained them for use after the war, initially by the RCAF and then, after 1949, for the RCMP. The unresolved confusion about land title at Torbay Airport was resolved by Newfoundland's entry into the Canadian confederation on 1 April 1949.

The Admiralty offered many of its buildings to the Newfoundland government. The two naval hospitals were gratefully accepted,[213] and the tactical training centre on the South Side became a trades college. Canada purchased

One of the ten-inch gun barrels at Cape Spear in 2009. C.A. Sharpe.

The ruined gun emplacements at Fort Chain Rock in 2009. C.A. Sharpe.

Buckmaster's Field and demolished most of the buildings, leaving the Drill Hall, which remains as a municipal recreational facility today. The marine railway at Bay Bulls came to a sad end. It had never been commissioned, it had no official name, and the government's refusal to relax its prohibition against any commercial use of the facility, either by Canada or anybody else, led to the railway's being listed as surplus to requirements by the War Assets Corporation in 1946 and abandoned.[214]

The Americans reduced the size of the garrison at Fort Pepperrell after Pearl Harbor and again at the end of the war in 1945, but they retained the facility until August 1961.[215] Then they departed, after only twenty-one years of their 99-year lease had expired, and the site reverted to its traditional name of Pleasantville. The well-made buildings were then occupied by the Newfoundland and Canadian governments.

THE LEGACY IN THE LANDSCAPE

Our focus in this chapter has been to comment upon the different ways the occupation of St John's affected the physical landscape of the city. The war had brought some major changes, among them the conversion of farmland or open land to other uses, a conversion that was immediate and irreversible. In the case of Fort Pepperrell, HMCS Avalon, the RCAF base, and the RCN dockyard, the land changed from private to public ownership. Upwards of 200 properties were requisitioned, leaving owners and tenants displaced and their livelihoods disrupted. Hundreds of military buildings were constructed. Military installations and training grounds created restricted areas both inside and outside the city. But much of the military landscape was quickly dismantled at the end of the war or the buildings put to non-military uses.

There is only scattered evidence of the military occupation today – rusted coastal guns in their crumbling bunkers on Bell Island and at Cape Spear, other bunker debris at Fort Chain Rock and Fort Amherst, and row upon row of military gravestones in the Joint Services Cemetery, opened by the Canadian government in 1941,[216] and other cemeteries throughout the city.

A small plaque on a road bridge near the mouth of Rennie's River serves as a reminder of the complex interaction between nations: "King's Bridge constructed

Fort Amherst in 2009. C.A. Sharpe.

Still serving: the city and one of the 4.7-inch guns at Fort Amherst. C.A. Sharpe.

by City of St John's, Newfoundland Government, Canada, United States Army. Contractors McNamara Construction Co. Ltd., Toronto, Canada. Designed by J.W. Beretta Engineers Inc., San Antonio, Texas, September 1943."

Elsewhere in this volume, the social and economic effects of the occupation are commented upon. And there were political impacts, too. The collective experience of the war set the wheels in motion for Newfoundland to return – somehow – to an elected and responsible government. And other, intangible effects of the military occupation played a role in the postwar planning of the city's landscape. H.A. Winter, who had replaced the indefatigable Emerson as commissioner for justice and defence in 1944, commented to the dominions secretary that "the Bases may have a greater effect than is at present imagined ... Already the effect upon

Graves of forty of the victims of the Knights of Columbus fire (12 December 1943) in Mount Pleasant Cemetery, 2009. C.A. Sharpe.

... building and architecture, heretofore stereotyped and ugly, is discernable in new building and housing schemes. Up to date methods ... adopted on the Bases are being adopted widely ... Altogether the Bases have probably done much toward the 'modernization' of Newfoundland building, architecture ... and the art of better and more comfortable living."[217]

More "comfortable living" was certainly included in the design of houses built by the St John's Housing Corporation.[218] Created by the government in 1944, the corporation was given the task of developing the new suburb of Churchill Park on 800 acres at the northern edge of St John's. Central heating, generous plumbing, efficiently designed kitchens, and allowances for natural light were features of these houses, and thus they represented the first large-scale example of domestic modern architecture in the city.[219] The subdivision itself was described as "laid out in modern style, so that every future street will be broad, and lined with grass and trees, as in American and Canadian cities."[220]

The American army dock in 2008. A.J. Shawyer.

During the war a large portion of the harbour was upgraded with new wharves, buildings, and facilities to meet wartime needs. After the war this upgrading continued as the old finger piers of the north side were cleared away and replaced by a modern harbour apron that echoed the design of the U.S. Army supply dock.

The overall impact of these changes was profound. One sympathetic observer wrote: "The war has wrought strange changes in the life of North America's outer bastion. You can't drop a couple of armies, plus the Canadian navy and Uncle Sam's flotillas on an easy-going country and not have earthquakes happen ... even though the contribution may be the result of a geographical accident which dropped the island smack in the middle of the gateway to North America and made it the primary defence post of Canada."[221]

ACKNOWLEDGMENTS

We would like to thank Charles Conway, cartographer, Department of Geography, Memorial University of Newfoundland, creator of the maps and the photo mosaic – and cheerful provider of help and advice. We would also like to extend thanks to the Memorial University of Newfoundland Career Enhancement Programme and our MUCEP students: Dawn Adams, Kimberley Fitzpatrick, Kayla Boyd, Stephanie Avery, and Jill Baker. Thanks also go out to Kevin Aucoin, Steven High, Daphne King, Len Murphy, Wanda Murrin-Davis, William C. Parrott, Bill Rompkey, Hazen Scarth, Suzanne Sexty; Brenda Conway, Provincial Reference Library; Larry Dohey, Archives of the Roman Catholic Archdiocese of St John's; Janet Lacroix, Canadian Forces Joint Imagery Centre; Helen Miller and Neachel Keeping, City of St John's Archives; Don Parsons, Marilyn Dawe, David Taylor, and Margo Page, Parks Canada; Paul Power, corporate secretary, Newfoundland and Labrador Housing Corporation; Craig Wm Smith, Lincoln and Welland Regiment Museum; Melanie Tucker and Craig Tucker, Provincial Archives of Newfoundland and Labrador; Government of Newfoundland and Labrador, Registry of Deeds; Newfoundland and Labrador Air Photo and Map Library; Memorial University Centre for Newfoundland Studies; Memorial University Folklore and Language Archives; and the Royal Newfoundland Regiment Museum, St John's.

2

From Defended Harbour to Transatlantic Base

PAUL COLLINS

HMCS *Moose Jaw* gun shield art. "Here a large moose has his jaws wrapped around a protesting Hitler. The ever popular V-for-victory is very pronounced and if you look closely, you will see a U-boat in the antlers. While on a training exercise after just arriving in St. John's, *Moose Jaw* was diverted to assist convoy SC42 which was under heavy attack. In her first battle, *Moose Jaw* rammed and sank U-501, the first U-boat sunk by a Canadian warship." Gary Green, *A Guide for Some of the Gun Shield Art and Ship's Badges of the Crow's Nest Officer's Club* (St John's: Crow's Nest Military Artifacts Association, Newfoundland).

Canada's naval heritage, particularly its Second World War record, has experienced something of a renaissance over the past twenty-five years. Until the mid-1980s, few Canadians really knew just how important the Royal Canadian Navy's contribution had been to the winning of the Battle of the Atlantic. Much of the history of the Atlantic trade war is written by the two major Western powers involved – Britain and the United States. Both tend to offer vivid descriptions of their own national efforts to the exclusion of those of the lesser powers, such as Canada.[1] Things changed in 1985, thanks in large measure to two relatively unknown historians at the time – Marc Milner and Michael Hadley. Milner's *North Atlantic Run* disputed the popular perception, perpetrated by mainly British historians, that the Royal Canadian Navy (RCN) was poorly trained and incompetently led – more of a danger to itself than the enemy.[2] He demonstrated that, despite tremendous challenges, the RCN held the line during the darkest days of the Battle of the Atlantic, allowing the Allies to marshal their forces for their successful assault on Hitler's U-boats in the spring of 1943. Hadley's *U-Boats against Canada* explores Canada's inshore war, whereby the RCN endured losses in its own waters rather than pull forces out of the more important battle against the U-boats being waged further east in the North Atlantic.[3]

In the twenty-odd years since Milner's and Hadley's books were published, numerous anthologies, histories, memoirs, and articles on Canada's Second World War naval experience have appeared. Newfoundland and the Newfoundland Escort Force/Mid-Ocean Escort Force are continually referenced in almost all of these works. This is because the history of the RCN during the Second

World War and that of St John's, Newfoundland – or "Newfyjohn" as it was affectionately known – are inextricably linked. Canada's main Second World War escort base was not located at Halifax, Nova Scotia, as is normally thought, but at St John's.[4] What makes the base at St John's even more interesting is that, not only was it Canada's largest "overseas" commitment, but the Royal Canadian Navy managed to create a major naval base from scratch in the heart of a capital city with a civilian population of 40,000 when American and Canadian army forces already occupied most of the available vacant land.[5]

Milner suggests that the establishment of the Newfoundland Escort Force (NEF) in May 1941 was a milestone in Canadian naval history.[6] Hadley points out that the creation of the NEF elevated the RCN from a minor player in coastal defence to a major participant in ocean operations.[7] The RCN's two official historians, Gilbert Tucker and Joseph Schull, argue respectively that St John's importance as a naval base "can hardly be exaggerated" and was actually "the key to the western defence system."[8] On the other hand, some historians are less glowing in their assessments. Tony German observes that in 1942, "apart from its natural shelter and the friendship that Newfoundlanders always extend to men of the sea, [St John's] had little to offer the Escort Force."[9] He contends that, for what became a major naval base almost overnight, St John's had the leanest of facilities.[10] James Lamb opines that HMCS Avalon, as the St John's base was commissioned, was almost "more a state of mind than actual substance."[11]

Regardless of the varying opinions, all recognize St John's' central role in the Battle of the Atlantic. Relatively little has been written, however, about how the port developed from merely a defended harbour into an escort base of strategic importance. This is not really that surprising. While much has been writ-

St John's Harbour from the South Side in 1944, showing the RCN barracks under construction. Photo by William A. Ramsay, control no. 20030014-088-2, Canadian War Museum.

Corvettes moored alongside the South Side wharf. Photo by (Able Seaman) John Peterson, 1923–2008, control no. 20000224-008-2, Canadian War Museum.

ten about all aspects of the Battle of the Atlantic, the various hostilities-only bases from which naval assets operated have received scant attention.[12] Even in St John's, both the historiography and popular memory recall the American army presence more so than that of the Royal Canadian Navy, despite the fact that thousands of sailors and hundreds of warships were stationed here during the war. Noted Newfoundland historians Sean Cadigan, Peter Neary, and Paul O'Neill provide very little coverage of HMCS *Avalon* in their works.[13] In fact, until recently, the most thorough examination of the base at St John's was a 1994 *Acadiensis* article by Bernard Ransom.[14] Interestingly, Jo Shawyer and Chris Sharpe make a similar complaint as to the lack of attention given the large Canadian army base at Lester's Field in the west end of St John's.[15] Possibly this myopic view of the Canadian presence is the result of the longevity of the American residency, or maybe it was the haste with which the Canadian facilities were dismantled at the end of hostilities. Perhaps, as Steven High suggests, it is a by-product of the lingering hangover from Newfoundland's still contentious decision to join Canada in 1949.[16] Regardless, as is pointed out elsewhere, St John's was as much a battle front as a home front, and the presence of battle-scarred warships and merchantmen and the pathetic sight of survivors coming ashore to be taken in hand by Mona Wilson and her Red Cross volunteers brought this dichotomy home on a daily basis.[17] Consequently, while the other chapters in this collection examine the overall militarization of St John's and its social repercussions, this chapter, in an attempt to properly recognize the city's importance as a naval base during the Battle of the Atlantic, specifically traces the naval development of St John's from a defended harbour to one of the most important naval bases in the North Atlantic.

By the time the first ships of the newly created Newfoundland Escort Force arrived at St John's in May 1941, the city was already an armed camp. Blackout regulations had been passed, censorship was in force, air raid drills had been held, and everyone expected an enemy attack at any time. Indeed, Barbara Lorenzkowski points out that even local children feared that a German attack was imminent.[18] However, it was the sight of thousands of military uniforms and vehicles that confirmed the impression that St John's really was a city under siege. As discussed elsewhere, through an August 1940 agreement (signed in March 1941), Britain gave the United States the right to construct bases on British territory in the Western Hemisphere in return for fifty surplus destroyers, five of which went to the Royal Canadian Navy. As an attachment to this agreement, Britain also offered the United States bases in Bermuda and Newfoundland, "freely and without consideration."[19] By war's end, tens of thousands of American servicemen had been stationed in Newfoundland and Labrador, and hundreds of thousands of U.S. military personnel and passengers had passed through the various U.S. facilities throughout the colony.[20]

The Canadians, on the other hand, arrived earlier – in 1940 – and set up camp in Lester's Field, the departure point of Alcock and Brown's famous June 1919 transatlantic flight. Ottawa made the commitment to defend Newfoundland even before Canada entered the war against Germany.[21] Where once Ottawa considered Newfoundland to be a liability, now it saw its neighbour as an "essential Canadian interest" and an important part of the "Canadian orbit." But despite these high-minded words of fraternity, the reality was that Newfoundland presented a number of potential targets important to Canada: the airport at Gander; the transatlantic seaplane base at Botwood; the iron ore mines on Bell Island, which provided one-third of the ore for the steel mills of Cape Breton; the numerous cable and wireless stations along the coast; and of course, the city of St John's, the economic and political centre of Newfoundland. Furthermore, thanks to its geographical position, Newfoundland was the "key to the gulf of Canada" and "in many ways [its] first line of defence."[22] Indeed, Governor Walwyn lamented that it was "quite apparent that Newfoundland [was] being considered only in so far as the defence of Canada is concerned."[23] During the "Phoney War" in Europe, the Canadian government did not act upon its commitment. In fact, after visiting Ottawa to discuss Canada's defence plans for Newfoundland, Commissioner L.E. Emerson complained that no preparations at all had been made.[24] However, this state of affairs changed as the German *Blitzkrieg* swept through France and the Low Countries a few months later,

Major-General W.H.P. Elkins, GOC-in-C Atlantic Command (extreme right), inspecting a Sergeants' Mess in St John's in February 1941. Control no. 19920076-011, Canadian War Museum.

and Ottawa dispatched the first battalion of the Black Watch of Canada to Newfoundland and stationed five Digby bombers from RCAF (Royal Canadian Air Force) No. 10 Squadron at Gander.

During the rest of 1940 and the first half of 1941, what Churchill christened "the Battle of the Atlantic" grew in ferocity as German submarines pursued the vital convoys connecting Britain with North America further into the Atlantic. Initially, the Royal Navy (RN) escorted convoys to longitude 22° west, but as U-boat attacks progressed into the mid-Atlantic, Britain pushed this to 35° west and occupied Iceland, both to deny it to the Germans and to use it as a refuelling point.[25] The RCN, based out of Halifax, could only provide convoy escort as far as the Grand Banks, thus leaving a distance of approximately 2,000 kilometres in which the convoys travelled with little or no protection. This area became known as "The Pit" because it was this stretch of ocean where the U-boats attacked with impunity.[26] It soon became clear that establishing a forward base at St John's, as had been done in Iceland, extended coverage more than 1,000 kilometres further east into the Atlantic.[27]

When Naval Services Headquarters (NSHQ) in Ottawa received the Admiralty's query in May 1941 as to the number of new corvettes that it could contribute to a base in the "Newfoundland focal area," it surprised London by offering to establish the base itself.[28] The Canadians had a number of reasons for their enthusiasm. First and foremost, the protection of the transatlantic convoys against U-boat attack was the single most important responsibility in the Battle of the Atlantic. Without the safe and timely arrival of the convoys in the United Kingdom, the war in Europe would be lost. The Royal Navy had been derelict in its preparations in this area. The Admiralty thought that the menace to trade would come from surface raiders and that any submarine threat was nullified by the development of ASDIC (an underwater detection device developed by the Allied Submarine Detection Investigation Committee), now called SONAR. Nonetheless, within the first few months of the war, it was evident that Germany's U-boats were more than just a nuisance, and the RN was woefully short of escort craft.[29] The government of Prime Minister Mackenzie King saw trade protection as an area where Canada could make a major contribution to the war effort without suffering the horrendous casualties of the First World War. However, a navy needs warships and Canada only had a few, and these were already committed. British shipyards could not help – they were hard-pressed to outfit the Royal Navy. With ease and speed of construction in mind, NSHQ decided on the corvette – or more particularly the "patrol vessel–whaler type" – which could be built to mercantile standards in Canadian shipyards.

The Flower-class corvette, as it was named, developed from the *Southern Pride*, a whale-catcher built by Smith's Dock in Yorkshire, England. The Royal Navy placed its first order with Smith's in July 1939 and considered the ship suitable because certain characteristics required for whale catching also applied to anti-submarine warfare – "seaworthiness, manoeuvrability, and rapid acceleration."[30] A mission from the Canadian Manufacturers Association returned from the United Kingdom at the end of August 1939 with the plans, which they gave to the National Research Council. The NRC in turn provided these to Naval Headquarters, which quickly compared the corvette to the Halcyon-class patrol vessel or "bramble sloop," a design that they had initially wanted the British to build. Neither the corvette's speed, endurance, nor armament equalled that of the sloop, but in typical Canadian fashion, it was considered good enough. It was also easy to build and could be constructed at a fast rate. Even more important, at least to Mackenzie King, corvettes could be built in Canadian yards. Churchill referred to the little warships as "cheap and nasties." The "nasty" was debatable, at least in the Canadian case, but the cheap part was certainly on the mark. Contract prices for this program varied to some degree, depending on the location of the building yard and adjustments to specifications, but it never exceeded $606,000 per vessel.[31] Regardless, in the first program, twenty-eight corvettes were to be built by twelve shipyards from the Maritimes to the West Coast, all deliverable by the end of the 1940 navigation season. Another order of thirty-six quickly followed, bringing the total to sixty-four.[32] With such a rapid production of vessels, manning became a problem.

When war was declared on 10 September 1939, the Royal Canadian Navy consisted of 145 officers and 1,674 men, plus approximately 40 retired officers and 3,684 reserves. However, with the dispatch of the last of the reserves to the east coast upon the declaration of war, the RCN just about exhausted its supply of trained men. Naval Headquarters adopted a set of mobilization plans; the first called for 5,472 individuals in all ranks by the end of 1940 and a further 7,000 by the end of the following year. In short order, NSHQ revised this estimate to 1,500 officers and 15,000 men after three years. By the end of 1940, the ships of

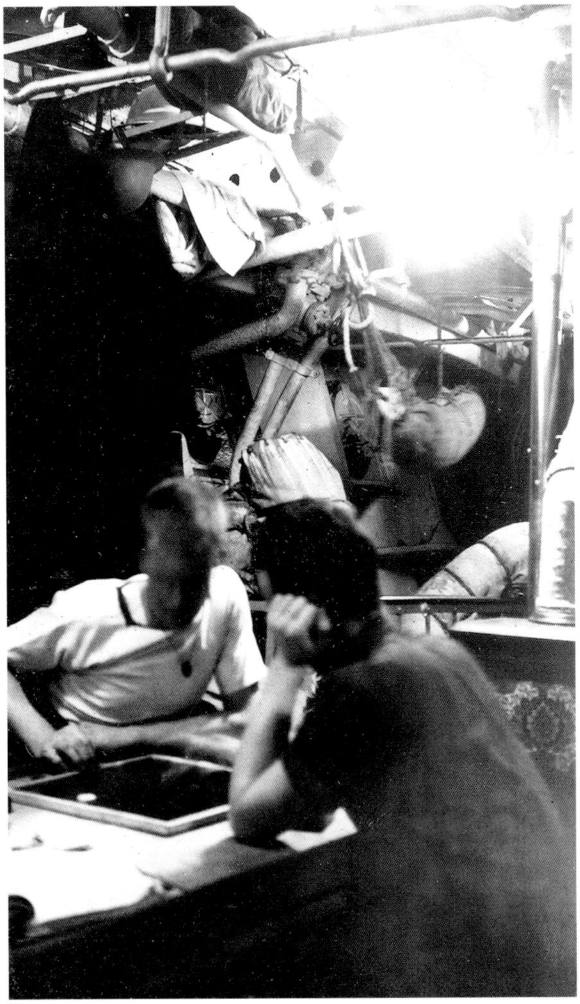

Left Downtime on a Canadian corvette. Photo 0045 from photograph album of John Cecil Stevens, Halifax.

Right Depth charges on HMCS *Matapedia*. Photo 0002-2 from photograph album of Marjorie Ferguson, Halifax.

the first building program were coming off the ways in rapid succession, and the RCN was seeking to crew fifty-four corvettes, twenty-five minesweepers, six vintage American destroyers, and an assortment of motor launches requiring in total approximately 7,000 officers and men. Canada had its navy, now it needed a mission.

In response to the westward advance of German U-boats into the mid-Atlantic, the Admiralty requested that the RCN establish the Newfoundland Escort Force at St John's.[33] This was to be a temporary measure, in force only until the Americans entered the war and took over all convoy escort in the western Atlantic per the ABC1 (American British Conversations) agreement, signed without Canadian participation in early 1941.[34] Once the United States Navy (USN) did so, most Canadian naval forces would be moved to the eastern Atlantic. However, by this point, the Americans were a significant presence in Newfoundland, and the Canadian government grew uneasy as they watched U.S. force levels steadily increase.[35] It further grated the Canadians that the ABC1 agreement granted strategic control of the Northwest Atlantic to the United States. Canadian authorities not only were concerned over the prospect of a permanent American presence at their front doorstep but also bristled that Canada's more experienced naval forces would be under American direction.[36] Canada wished

Rough water. Photo 0010 from family photograph album of John Cecil Stevens, Halifax.

HMCS *Matapedia* outside the Narrows. Photo 0005 from family photograph album of Marjorie Ferguson, Halifax.

both to impress upon its allies the "vital nature" of its interest in Newfoundland and to project itself onto the world scene.[37] A large naval facility at St John's was "just the ticket."

From the beginning of the war, Canada resisted any British attempt to subordinate its sovereignty and the autonomy of its armed forces. Unlike the governments of the other Commonwealth and occupied nations, the King government rejected the suggestion that Canada's navy should simply operate as part of the Royal Navy. The country's small fleet had been built to protect its extensive coastline, and it was only the imminent threat of invasion and the personal plea of Prime Minister Winston Churchill in 1940 that persuaded Prime Minister King to send Canada's small destroyer force to the eastern Atlantic. The creation of the NEF and the establishment of an RCN base at St John's could be seen as moves directly related to the defence of Canada and highlight the country's contribution to the Allied war effort.[38] Canadian Minister of Defence J.L. Ralston suggested at a meeting of the War Cabinet that the Newfoundland Escort Force offered the RCN the opportunity to play "an important and vital role in the Western Atlantic."[39] Furthermore, by establishing a major escort base in St John's, Canada could both reassert its presence in Newfoundland and retain control over its own forces in its traditional waters. It appeared to be a win-win situation all around for Canada and the RCN. Consequently, the actual operational performance of the NEF was "less important in 1941 than the mere fact of its existence."[40] The Newfoundland Commission of Government, however, was hesitant about having another foreign country – especially Canada – occupy its territory. This hesitation was not without cause.

Battery Village, seen from HMCS *Matapedia*. Photo 0002 from family photograph album of Marjorie Ferguson, Halifax.

In August 1940 Prime Minister King and President Roosevelt met in Ogdensburg, New York, and agreed to form the Permanent Joint Board on Defence. One of the board's first duties was to produce a worst-case plan, code-named "Black," in the event that Britain fell and North America lay open to Nazi attack. This plan included the occupation of Newfoundland.[41] The Newfoundland government, only learning of this after the fact from the Americans, complained to London that the Canadians were making plans for Newfoundland without consulting them.[42]

Another reason the Newfoundland Commission of Government was hesitant about allowing the RCN to set up an escort base at St John's was that it felt that Newfoundland had not been fairly treated in the Anglo-American Leased Bases Agreement of 27 March 1941. The deal had been negotiated at the same time that President Roosevelt was pushing his Lend-Lease Bill (passed 11 March 1941) through Congress, and its outcome had as a consequence been seriously affected.[43] It was obvious from the start that the Americans had definite ideas about what they wanted out of any agreement. Knowing Britain's desperate need for war materials, they pressed their advantage in sometimes not so subtle terms.[44] Of particular concern to the Newfoundland government representatives were the "general powers" insisted upon by the Americans. These essentially granted the United States full autonomy over the areas to be leased, giving it unprecedented authority over the property and inhabitants of a sovereign country.[45] Furthermore, the Newfoundland government had also hoped to acquire economic considerations from the United States as compensation for its contribution to the deal, but it was sadly disappointed. The best that was offered was the promise to "consider sympathetically" the development of mutual trade between the two countries.[46]

Newfoundland's representatives at the negotiations, L.E. Emerson and J.G. Penson, recognized that the terms of the agreement were "one-sided throughout and often extremely harsh" and might not be well received when made public.[47] Acting on Governor Walwyn's suggestion, they requested that Prime Minister Churchill address a personal letter to the people of Newfoundland acknowledging "the considerable sacrifices" that the American plan represented, and portraying acceptance of the agreement as a matter of patriotic duty.[48] In public, the Newfoundland government presented the agreement as fair and equitable, and the accord was accepted without serious objection once it was made public. Regardless, Newfoundland had taken "some hard diplomatic knocks" and this experience coloured the commission's attitude when it came to negotiating the establishment of the RCN base at St John's.[49]

Initially, the Admiralty's plan was to base thirty-six warships at St John's, of which about a quarter would be in port at any one time.[50] Overall command would rest with the Americas and West Indies Command based in Bermuda, although this was soon changed to the Western Approaches Command in Liverpool. The Newfoundland government would act as agents for London and acquire the necessary land, either through lease or purchase, and supply what manpower and materials it could.[51] As previously mentioned, Ottawa at first offered to set up the base using its own resources, and consequently, because the majority of the vessels would be Canadian, an RCN commodore was appointed flag officer, Newfoundland Force. However, the scope of the operation soon expanded, with the projected size of the force increasing to sixty-three ships, of which sixteen would be expected to be in harbour at any one time.[52]

At about the same time, the estimates on the cost of establishing the base were presented. The cost of the land and the construction of the facilities for the base came in at approximately $10 million. Ottawa began to have second thoughts about shouldering financial responsibility for the base and reconsidered its initial offer.[53] This caused considerable embarrassment to all parties, and faced with the prospect of serious delays, the Admiralty diplomatically renewed its original proposal to underwrite the base while welcoming any financial contribution from Canada.[54] Ottawa agreed but expected Canada "to be given some interest in the new base for her outlay" and insisted that no decision on the base after the war would be made without Canadian consultation.[55]

For its part, the Newfoundland government felt that from "the point of view of the future of Newfoundland and the sentiment of the people," it was best for the base to be Admiralty owned and operated.[56] In fact, London suspected that

Left HMCS *Matapedia* in the North Atlantic in winter. Photo 0003 from family photograph album of Marjorie Ferguson, Halifax.

Right "The BL 4" gun on the foc'sle of the Flower-class corvette HMCS *Midland* (K-220), moored at Bowring's Wharf. HMCS *Napanee* (K-118) and HMCS *Timmins* (K-223) are moored ahead. Photo by (Able Seaman) John Peterson, 1923–2008, control no. 20000224-008-1, Canadian War Museum.

the estimates provided by the Newfoundland government probably reflected this local preference.[57] The Admiralty accepted that the financial burden properly belonged to it, and took solace in the thought that some of the material and equipment needed could be obtained from the Americans through Lend-Lease.[58] Consequently, the various parties agreed that the Admiralty would establish and retain ownership of the base but that the RCN would maintain and administer it. As Gilbert Tucker observes in *The Naval Service of Canada*, "The RCN in St John's was something like a tenant living free of rent in a house which he himself designed, of which he paid for upkeep, and in which members of the landlord's family were welcome to take shelter."[59]

By the spring of 1941, St John's was already a defended harbour as well as the base for the Newfoundland Defence Force, which comprised five corvettes, two minesweepers, and four Fairmile patrol boats.[60] The naval officer in charge (NOIC), Captain C.M.R. Schwerdt, RN, former secretary to the governor, was making arrangements to install an anti-torpedo baffle at the entrance to the harbour and develop an examination service using two former Newfoundland Customs cutters, the *Marvita* and the *Shulamite*, complete with their crews.[61] A 4,000-tonne Admiralty fuel tank was being constructed, and plans were underway to erect a Port War Signal Station, as well as a "High Frequency Direction Finding" (HF/DF) station and a radio beacon at Cape Spear.[62] In addition, Cabot Tower was manned as a Port War Signal Station by one RCN leading signalman and five ratings, and Fort Amherst was employed as an examination battery and was manned by four RCN signalmen.[63] By the time the NEF arrived in May, new fixed coastal and anti-aircraft defences were being installed in St John's and vicinity. In the interim, four mobile 155-millimetre guns and two 8-inch railway guns, manned by American troops, were set up in and around the city.[64]

In any event, on 20 May 1941, the Admiralty formally requested that Canada base its burgeoning fleet of corvettes at St John's. Seven days later the HMC ships *Agassiz, Alberni, Chambly, Cobalt, Collingwood, Orillia,* and *Wetaskiwin*, under the command of Commander J.D. "Chummy" Prentice, sailed into St John's harbour. The Newfoundland Escort Force had arrived. When Commodore L.W. Murray assumed his appointment in June as commodore commanding, Newfoundland Force (CCNF), all the ships originally allocated for the NEF had arrived – six

River-class destroyer HMCS *St Laurent* leaving port. Photo by William A. Ramsay, control no. 20030014-073-4, Canadian War Museum.

RCN destroyers and seventeen RCN corvettes, and seven RN destroyers and four RN corvettes.[65] Convoys now assembled at Bedford Basin in Halifax Harbour, and the Western Local Escort Force (WLEF) based there escorted them to the Western Ocean Meeting Point (WESTOMP) just east of the Grand Banks. The NEF took the convoy through "The Pit" to the Mid-Ocean Meeting Point (MOMP) off Iceland. There the Royal Navy assumed responsibility, and the NEF left to refuel in Iceland. The NEF subsequently picked up a westbound convoy from Britain and proceeded to the WESTOMP, where the WLEF took the convoy to Halifax for dispersal. The ships of the NEF then proceeded to St John's for rest and resupply.

In June 1941 Captain G.L. Stephens, the engineer-in-chief of the RCN, inspected the facilities at St John's and concluded that he was being asked to "match urgent need with unpromising circumstance." He felt that the port could not be "considered as normally suitable as a base for a large naval force."[66] The harbour was small, just 700 metres wide and roughly 2 kilometres long, and it would have to be shared with Newfoundland's substantial mercantile fleet.[67] Support facilities were minimal, despite the fuel tanks on the South Side and the Newfoundland Dockyard situated at the head of the harbour. The harbour front itself was a tangle of fishing stages, ships' storehouses, and finger piers, most of which were in decay, and the Americans had already leased a large portion of what space was available. At the same time, a joint Admiralty/Ministry of War Transportation mission headed by E.A. Seal, senior official of the British Admiralty Delegation (BAD) in Washington, visited St John's to examine the legal and technical details involved in coordinating escort group operations with mercantile repairs. Seal and his colleagues concluded that St John's Harbour could not accommodate any more than twenty-four escort and auxiliary craft.[68] Nevertheless, Stephens came up with a plan that provided over 7,000 linear feet of jetty space, suggesting that at least fifty-five vessels could be provided for in St John's Harbour.[69] The plan eventually proposed additional fuel tanks and an underground magazine on the South Side, a 1,000-man barracks, a 250-bed hospital, two Port War Signal Stations at Fort Amherst and Cape Spear, and a radio station in Mount Pearl.[70]

During July the NEF was organized into twelve escort groups – eleven for convoy escort and one comprised of fast warships for special convoy escort – and an operational schedule was set out based on a 110-day cycle.[71] Even so, while twenty-one convoys were escorted during August without losses, Admiral Murray felt that the forces assigned to each convoy (no fewer than four escorts) were insufficient.[72] He also pointed out in his monthly report that many changes were made within the groups as a result of casualties and refits. On the positive side, joint RCN/RCAF operations commenced, with RCAF patrols extended to include convoy reconnaissance. An RCAF operations room was set up next to RCN Operations with a telephone system consisting of a direct line to the telegraph room of the Department of Posts and Telegraphs and two city lines.

Up to this point, all Allied convoys and their protection were under Admiralty control. This changed in August when Churchill arrived in Placentia Bay aboard

Friendship. Photo 0055 from family photograph album of John Cecil Stevens, Halifax.

the *Prince of Wales* to meet with Roosevelt to plan war objectives. The meeting ultimately produced the Atlantic Charter. As a result of this conference, the U.S. Navy assumed strategic control over the western Atlantic and took over the escort of all HX convoys and fast westbound convoys, leaving the slow SC convoys for the Royal Canadian Navy.[73] To facilitate this, meetings were held

Horsing around. Photo 0005 from family photograph album of John Cecil Stevens, Halifax.

between Admiral Murray and his staff and Admiral Bristol, commander Task Force Group 4, Argentia, and his staff. It soon became evident that the NEF did not have the forces, most particularly the destroyers, to protect the SC convoys properly. As a result, the Admiralty agreed to cancel the planned withdrawal of RN ships from the NEF and detailed five more RN destroyers and seven corvettes to assist.[74]

In October 1941 Murray ventured the opinion that the reputation of the RCN rested on the "success or failure of the NEF."[75] By then, initial shoreline developments were underway and the seventy-odd warships of the NEF were fully operational. Murray directed operations from the upper floors of the Newfoundland Hotel, and the ships of the NEF were tied up on the South Side or in the middle of the harbour, being serviced by the depot ship HMS *Greenwich*, the fleet supply ship *City of Dieppe*, and the oilers *Teakwood* and *Clam*. All the same, this was considered only a temporary measure until the United States assumed its full responsibilities in the western Atlantic according to the ABC1 agreement. As it turned out, this did not happen, and after 7 December 1941 the base at St John's was transformed from being merely a stop-gap measure to being an escort base of strategic importance.

After the Japanese attack on Pearl Harbor, the USN pulled most of its escort forces out of the Atlantic for duty in the Pacific.[76] In one fell swoop, Admiral

Murray's command was forced to supply all the transatlantic escort forces in the western Atlantic.[77] The NEF was renamed the Mid-Ocean Escort Force (MOEF) in February 1942, and in addition to supplying ships for oceanic escort, Murray also had to release escorts for convoy duty further south to contend with the slaughter of ships along the American eastern seaboard.[78]

With the United States now an official belligerent, local commanders became very concerned about a German raid on Newfoundland. Indeed, the American commander, Major-General G.C. Brant, felt that such an attack was "not only possible ... but very probable."[79] From early in the war, the authorities feared some sort of assault on Newfoundland. Roosevelt expressed his concerns to Churchill in April 1941 and proposed sending additional American forces comprising a half battery of eight-inch guns, one squadron of three medium and three heavy bombers, and 57 officers and 575 men to bolster defences.[80] All feared that, should the Germans get a foothold in Newfoundland, the whole east coast of Canada and the United States would be open to attack. In fact, a 1944 newspaper article reported that evidence given before a U.S. congressional hearing suggested that Hitler had once planned to attack Newfoundland as part of a campaign against the United States.[81] Indeed, at approximately 5:30 PM, 3 March 1942, three tremendous explosions rocked the city. It was later determined that three torpedoes had detonated on the cliffs at the entrance to St John's Harbour – one under Fort Amherst and the other two under Cabot Tower. Parts were recovered, but Admiral Murray and his staff could see no reason why a U-boat commander would fire torpedoes into the harbour or why all three missed their targets.[82] No organized assault was ever launched against Newfoundland, but the RCN did develop a denial plan for the facilities at St John's just in case.[83]

In the meantime, in order to maintain the required convoy schedule with his overstretched resources, Murray had to adhere to the more direct Great Circle Route, which prevented significant detours around known U-boat concentrations. The tighter schedule affected not only crew morale and training, because of the shorter layover time between crossings, but also team cohesion and continuity as a result of ship substitution within escort groups.[84] Breakdowns became more frequent, as the greater wear and tear in the harsh North Atlantic was exacerbated by a much higher incidence of repair defects from the seriously overstretched facilities in St John's.[85] Dockyard space, or lack thereof, was a real problem.

Newfoundland required a fairly large mercantile fleet to serve the many towns and communities spread out along its considerable shoreline. As the main port on the island, St John's was the assembly point for these local convoys, as well as those travelling to Halifax, Sydney, and Labrador. During the first five months of 1942, 298 ships were convoyed between St John's and various ports.[86] St John's was also the natural port of refuge for many weather- and battle-damaged merchant vessels. According to a report produced by the RCN, on one day alone – 31 January 1941 – fifty-three merchant ships took shelter in St John's Harbour.[87] Canada's high commissioner to Newfoundland observed in April 1943 that during the eighteen months he had been in Newfoundland, there had not

HMS *Smiter* near the American dock. Photo by William A. Ramsay, control no. 20030014-073-1, Canadian War Museum.

been "a single day in which not one, but a number of merchant ships [had] been waiting to get in to the drydock."[88] As a port of refuge, St John's was also a safe haven for survivors.[89] Between June 1942 and May 1943, as many as 2,976 survivors arrived at St John's. Evidence suggests that upwards of 6,000 survivors were cared for in St John's during the Second World War.[90]

With the pressure for merchant ship repair, docking facilities for escort vessels caused concern among naval planners. The Americans agreed to allow RCN forces to use their floating dock at Argentia, but even though the repair/refit facilities were only operating at 75 per cent workload, the Admiralty reserved them for the exclusive use of British escort groups. RCN had access to the facilities only for those ships that "require[d] assistance in an Emergency."[91] RCN escorts did have priority at the Newfoundland Dockyard, and from November 1941 to March 1942 the RCN occupied an average of fourteen days out of the twenty-four worked each month. However, as 1942 progressed, it became clear that the drydock situation placed serious constraints on St John's utility as an escort base. During the fall, use of the dock increased dramatically, accounting for 75 per cent of total docking time, compared to 26 per cent during the same period in 1941.[92] It is interesting that the drydock crisis occurred when the forces at St John's were actually decreasing as a result of the redeployment of sixteen MOEF escorts for the Torch landings in North Africa. From a peak of seventy vessels in January 1942, the MOEF fell to about sixty by mid-year, levelling out at fifty in January 1943.[93] Two expedients were investigated to relieve the situation. The first was the acquisition of a floating dock, and the second was the development of an overflow facility at Bay Bulls, located approximately thirty kilometres south of St John's.

The British Admiralty Delegation tried to find a floating dock in Canada throughout 1942, but with little luck. The closest it came was the smaller section of the Vickers Montreal dock, which was sixty-one metres long and had a lifting capacity of 7,100 tonnes.[94] This request was turned down by NSHQ, as new construction was considered the overriding priority and the dock could not be spared.[95] By the fall/winter of 1942–43, the docking problem had reached crisis proportions, manifested by unacceptably long delays in repairs and the corresponding incidence of missed sailings. In the end, it was not until September 1943 that the U.S. Navy was able to provide a floating dock with 1,800-tonne lifting capacity from Perth Amboy, New Jersey. In the meantime, other remedies were considered. High Commissioner Burchell complained that the dockyard was only operating for one shift per day and was closed on Sundays and holidays. He pointed out that, despite the extreme pressure on repair facilities at St John's, the dockyard was actually "idle" for a total of ninety-five days per year. Burchell argued that it should operate two, if not three, shifts per day year-round and on all but a few holidays.[96] Unfortunately, Burchell's plan did not take into account the severe shortage of skilled labour in Newfoundland, despite the fact that 170 apprentice mechanics had been hired in the summer of 1941.[97] This situation was further exacerbated by the development of Bay Bulls as an overflow facility.

Engineer-in-Chief Captain G.L. Stephens's original nominee for an overflow site, Harbour Grace, was rejected by NSHQ as being too costly to develop.[98] In its stead, Bay Bulls was chosen, and in July 1942 the Canadian War Cabinet approved the project at a total cost of $3 million ($2 million for the haul-out and support facilities and $1 million for harbour protection).[99] The Newfoundland Commission of Government committed to a contribution of $300,000, part of which was the acquisition cost of the site itself. General construction contracts

Picking up survivors from a sunken U-boat. Photo 0045 from family photograph album of John Cecil Stevens, Halifax.

were let in the fall of 1942, but completion was not anticipated before the end of 1943.[100] Paradoxically, disaster at sea brought some relief on shore.

The Admiralty's *Monthly Anti-Submarine Report* of January 1943 pointed out that for the previous six months the RCN had borne the brunt of attacks in the Atlantic. RCN forces accounted for 48 per cent of North Atlantic escorts, but RCN-escorted convoys suffered 80 per cent of the losses in this theatre.[101] The Admiralty was very concerned and requested that the Canadian ("C") escort groups be transferred to British command. Ostensibly, this was to fill the vacuum left by the deployment of RN escorts to the newly formed tanker convoys in the central Atlantic, but it also afforded Canadian escorts the opportunity to use the modern training facilities at RN bases. NSHQ initially baulked but acquiesced following a couple of disastrous convoys battles. Consequently, starting in January 1943, the four C groups were transferred to the eastern Atlantic. This effectively reduced the force at St John's to two destroyers and nine corvettes, most of which were employed on local convoys.[102]

Unfortunately, the respite was short-lived. Most of C groups returned by midwinter, and the average number of escorts at St John's at any one time rose to twenty-five. In March, 143 escorts were serviced, of which eleven required docking, and 2,300 repairs were completed at the base facilities. HMCS Avalon was again seriously overstretched. Even after being in operation for almost two years, the base was still deficient in conventional machine tooling and light engineering plants. Workshops lacked the necessary lathes to effect engineering repairs, and basic foundry work could not be done onshore owing to the absence of such essential equipment as power hammers.[103] The machine shop, smithy, and foundry facilities on the South Side were considered "a fire hazard," and the electrical shop was "poorly equipped ... and working under adverse conditions." The RCN dockyard suffered similar deficiencies. Some machinery still had to rely on a temporary power supply, as the main switch panel was incomplete; the welding equipment and stand-by generators were lacking rectifiers; and while needed motor compressors had arrived, there was no power supply available to operate them.[104] Furthermore, in the high-tech aspects of anti-submarine warfare, HMCS Avalon was deficient in facilities to repair and upgrade advanced electronic equipment such as radar, HF/DF, and ASDIC.[105]

In April 1943 the British Admiralty Delegation – still led by E.A. Seal – once again travelled to St John's and met with senior NSHQ officials to plan improvements to the base.[106] To maintain the buildup of forces in Britain for an invasion of Fortress Europe, St John's needed to be able to service the maximum number of escorts with minimal turnaround time. This figure was set at fifty and required "major new construction and reorganization of the base repair capacity." In his report, Seal recommended that a new machine shop complex be constructed on the South Side to provide heavy engineering plant, smithy, and foundry facilities, and that a new naval stores building be installed on an adjacent piece of land. The current dockyard storehouse would then be converted to a light engineering/electronic shop to handle electronic navigational and ASW (Anti-Submarine Warfare) equipment repairs. The plan also called for a new 1,000-square-metre harbour craft/boat repair shop with haul-out, plus an eighty-vehicle garage for the existing barracks complex. Harbour defences were also beefed up, with the controlled minefield in the Narrows upgraded and enlarged and a fully equipped boom defence depot built at the Admiralty's wharfage on the South Side. As well, a new 250-bed hospital would be built in the city's West End.[107] Training was also on the agenda.

HMCS Avalon provided for the working up and refresher training of many of the RCN's recently commissioned ships.[108] From the summer of 1941, Mobile Anti-Submarine Training Unit No. 11 under the direction of Commander G.A. Harrison, RN, provided almost all onshore training. In the unit's first year of operation, 120 ships received 496 periods of training totalling 1,144 hours and 45 minutes.[109] The 1943 expansion plans envisioned a considerable expansion of training facilities, including Defensively Equipped Merchant Ship (DEMS) training at Cape Spear and anti-submarine and signal training in space provided by an annex to the South Side barracks. As well, elaborate simulator trainers, including an anti-aircraft dome teacher and a tactical anti-submarine attack teacher, would be installed on an adjacent site.[110] By the end of hostilities, the Tactical Training Centre (TTC) in St John's contained an anti-submarine school, a gunnery school, a radar school, and a Loran[111] School, plus a Night Escort Teacher (NET). A report issued in mid-1945 indicates that, on 6 April 1945 alone, fifty-one classes were taught between 0900 and 1730. These consisted of thirty-five gunnery, eleven anti-submarine, one radar, two Loran, and two NET classes, which included the use of the Depth Charge Driller.[112] The DEMS training range on the cliffs at Cape Spear mounted both anti-aircraft and larger-calibre practice artillery pieces. Seal's report estimates that the new facilities necessitated an increase in personnel at St John's of 1,500 ratings (mainly tradesmen) and 850 servicewomen.[113] (The cost of the expansion program was $7 million, which brought the total Canadian investment in the base at St John's to $16 million, albeit to the Admiralty's account.)[114]

April 1943 also saw Malcolm MacDonald, the British high commissioner to Ottawa, suggest that a combined Canadian, British, and American committee be established "to examine repair problems for warships and merchant ships" in the Northwest Atlantic. Recognizing Newfoundland's importance in this area, MacDonald recommended that representatives of the government of Newfoundland be included in this committee.[115] On 12 August 1943 the committee met in Ottawa under the chairmanship of (now) Rear-Admiral G.L. Stephens, with Sir Wilfrid Woods representing the government of Newfoundland. During the discussions, Woods stressed the necessity of reserving the Newfoundland Dockyard for the repair of merchant ships, as because of its close proximity to the convoy routes it was "the natural port of refuge for damaged and defective ships." The committee recognized this fact, but also stressed that there were times when naval vessels had to take precedence. As it was, only running repairs could be completed, and refits of warships had to be undertaken in British or American ports. The committee recommended that a new floating dock of no less than 3,000 tonnes and capable of handling the largest escort vessel replace the recently acquired 1,800-tonne dock as soon as possible. At the same time, planned improvements to the naval facilities at St John's needed to be "completed and manned as quickly as possible," and the labour force at the Newfoundland Dockyard augmented with skilled labour from Britain "without delay."[116]

However, by the summer of 1943, the tide of battle had changed in the Atlantic. In May, when forty-one U-boats were sunk and Admiral Karl Dönitz, commander-in-chief of the *Kiegesmarine*, pulled all but a few of his boats out of the Atlantic, the initiative passed to the Allies. While the U-boats did return to the battle with heavier air defences and new weapons and sensors, losses soared as successes plunged. Finally, in January 1944, Dönitz abandoned his patrol lines, and boats once again became lone wolves, attacking victims as opportunity allowed. With the introduction of the *Schnorkel* – a retractable, valved tube that reached the surface when a U-boat was at periscope depth, and supplied the sub's engines with air – sightings of U-boats dropped drastically. Furthermore, U-boat captains, knowing that the Allies could detect their signals, only contacted U-Boat Command when absolutely necessary. These factors combined to make the lone-wolf U-boat very hard to track until it attacked. Consequently, the battle was not over, and convoys still needed protection against this increasingly wily and unpredictable enemy. By 1944, the RCN assumed almost complete responsibility for transatlantic trade protection, and an average of seventy warships remained based at St John's for the balance of the Second World War – a force roughly the same as the original NEF at its peak in January 1942. This time, however, the force consisted primarily of the newer River-class anti-submarine frigates and increased-endurance corvettes, plus a fair representation of Canada's destroyer fleet. In total, between January 1942 and May 1945, 545 escorts were stationed at St John's, not including motor launches. Under trying circumstances, "Newfyjohn" provided a reasonably organized and relatively well-equipped maintenance, training, and support base until the end of the war.

But what of the men of the RCN? By war's end, 5,000 naval personnel were stationed in St John's, and thousands more had passed through the port, posted on the various warships.[117] How were their needs met while in port, and what impact did all these young sailors have on the already overstretched hospitality of the residents of St John's?

War is a young man's game, and this was certainly true of the Royal Canadian Navy during the Second World War. The average ages of RCN and RCNVR (Volunteer Reserve) officers during the war were twenty-nine and twenty-eight years respectively. The average lower-deck age was even less at twenty-two years, with many being just over eighteen years old.[118] With such youthful personnel, recreation and entertainment were major factors in crew morale. Whereas the Americans provided facilities for their personnel on the various bases themselves, the Canadian services relied heavily on local facilities.[119] While barely more than a good-sized town, St John's did its utmost to meet this challenge.[120]

Sports, of course, were a major feature of any recreation program, and there was no shortage of competitive and recreational opportunities in the city, all available to RCN personnel. Rugby, soccer, baseball, softball, and cricket were

Looking out over St John's Harbour. Photo by Lieut. Alice Ducile Talman, control no. 20010159-002-3, Canadian War Museum.

played at the Feildian and Ayre Athletic Grounds and at the St George's and Memorial Fields, and aside from the various service and open leagues, hockey was played at the St Bon's Forum and the Prince of Wales Arena almost daily. Tennis was offered at Government House (officers only) and at Bowring Park and the Riverdale Tennis Club. Swimming, golf, squash, and bowling were available to officers and men alike at various facilities throughout the city, and bicycles could be rented at Martin's Cycle Shop, Duckworth Street. The navy provided badminton and gymnasium facilities at the naval barracks at Buckmaster's Field, and hunting, fishing, and "spending a few days under canvas" were all attractions of the RCN's St John's Naval Camp at Donovan's, just outside St John's.

Of course, "liquid refreshment" was a requirement for any successful run ashore, and officers had the pick of the more "civilized" establishments, including their own Seagoing Officers' Club, better known as "The Crow's Nest." Officers were also expected to attend Captain (D)'s cocktail party every Friday. While the young officers were charged a one-dollar cover, the invitation guaranteed that their female companions were "admitted free of charge." From there, the happy couples could proceed to the City Club, the Bally Haly Golf Club, or the Bella Vista Country Club. Both officers and men frequented the Old Colony Club and the Terra Nova Club. Ships' crews had naval canteens at the naval dockyard on Water Street and at the naval barracks. In addition, those of the lower deck had their pick of dozens of cafes and taverns that catered to the ordinary soldier and sailor. Some of these were considered less than respectable. Two of the most notorious were the Green Lantern on Water Street and the Queen Tavern on Queen Street, both of which caused the chief of police concern because they were often "frequented by disorderly persons."[121]

Neither was there a shortage of places to eat, although the military had to put a number of them "off limits" due to health concerns. Two that were approved

Sailors in port. Photo 31 from family photograph album of Marjorie Ferguson, Halifax.

were the dining room and restaurant at the Newfoundland Hotel. However, officers and ratings alike had to be on their best behaviour, as the flag officer Newfoundland Force and his staff occupied the top floors of the hotel. Officers could also get a meal for forty cents at the Fort William Officers Mess and the Naval Barracks Officers Mess, and both officers and men were welcome at the United Service Organization (USO) club on Merrymeeting Road. There were a variety of restaurants and lunch counters on Water and Duckworth streets, and tearooms on Henry Street and Rawlins Cross. For a town of just over 40,000 civilians, St John's boasted a total of five cinemas – the Paramount, Capitol, Nickel, Star, and York – all of which featured the latest Hollywood films.

To get to the various attractions, the men of the Royal Canadian Navy could choose a number of forms of transportation, all at reasonable prices. Streetcars cost twenty cents, buses ten. Taxis charged seventy cents during the daytime and one dollar at night, but as the 1942 *Naval Guide Book* points out, most were "very loathe to carry passengers to and from the South Side." Transportation to and from one's ship by way of "bum boats" cost twenty cents "if obtainable," and authorities had to bring in regulations governing these harbour craft after a couple of near disasters.[122] The more studious could avail themselves of reading material from a number of places, including the Gosling Memorial Library on Duckworth Street, the RCN's Magazine Exchange, and the Canadian Legion at the corner of Bannerman Street and Military Road, which offered material to "officers, ratings and their families."

Shopping was offered by four department stores, all located on Water Street – Bowring Brothers, Ayre and Sons, James Baird, and the Royal Stores, and there were no less than six drycleaners, including Soon Lee's near Rawlins Cross, the site of the only traffic lights in the city. The Commercial Cable Company, at two locations, and the Water Street office of the Anglo-American Cable Company ("Just Ask for 'Anglo'") provided telegraph facilities, and the Avalon Telephone Company was responsible for the telephone service.

Sailors' religious needs were also well met in St John's. The Church of England cathedral on Church Hill and St Mary's, St Michael's, and the historic St Thomas's churches held services for the men of that faith every Sunday at 11 AM and 6:30 PM. The Gower Street, Cochrane Street, George Street, and Wesley United churches also held services at those times. Roman Catholics could attend mass every hour from 7 to 11 AM on Sundays, and at 7:30 and 8:30 AM on Wednesdays, and Confession at convenient times every Wednesday, Friday, and Saturday. Presbyterians were welcomed at St Andrew's Church on Queen's Road, and the Salvation Army held services at their halls on Springdale, Adelaide, and Duckworth streets every Sunday at 11 AM and 6:30 PM. Those who were Christian Scientists gathered at the Crosbie Hotel on Sunday mornings and Wednesday evenings.

Possibly the most well remembered service facilities in St John's during the Second World War were the three hostels. The Caribou Hut might be the most famous of the three. During the 1,637 days it operated, "The Hut" rented 253,551 beds, served 1,545,766 meals, and hosted 1,518 movies, 459 dances, 395 shows, and 205 Sunday-night sing-songs with a total attendance in excess of 700,000 people.[123] Canada's high commissioner to Newfoundland Charles Burchell officially opened the Red Triangle, the YMCA hostel on Water Street West, on 8 January 1942. Built at a cost of $100,000, the facility boasted a social hall for dances and concerts, a lounge, an 1,100-person dining room, and sleeping accommodation for 50 men.[124] The Knights of Columbus hostel on Harvey Road opened in December 1941. The horseshoe-shaped building featured an auditorium, recreation room, restaurant, and dormitories, and could accommodate approximately 400 men. All of the hostels were famous for their hospitality, but unfortunately, the last named became infamous for a tragedy.

On 12 December 1942 a fire broke out in the attic of the Knights of Columbus hostel. The building had been built to provide a recreational facility for military and merchant marine personnel, and consequently dances, concerts, and other entertainments were frequently held. All were well attended, and the event held that cold December night was no different. Uncle Tom's Barn Dance played to a packed audience, and the show was broadcast over radio station VOCM. Suddenly there was a cry of "Fire!" and the broadcast ended. Within forty-five minutes ninety-nine people were dead, including twenty-five naval personnel, and one hundred injured. The inquiry into the fire, headed by retired Chief Justice Sir Brian Dunfield, concluded that many of the victims died from smoke inhalation, not from the fire itself. Most had been trapped in the auditorium because the exits opened inward and did not have panic bars and the windows were shuttered because of blackout regulations. In his February 1943 report, Justice Dunfield also concluded that while the fire was the work of an arsonist, there was no evidence that enemy agents had started it.

More sailors. Photo 32 from family photograph album of Marjorie Ferguson, Halifax.

Regardless, suspicion of enemy action persisted, and not without some justification. There had been other fires in buildings frequented by military personnel during the same period. The Old Colony Club had burned with the loss of four lives, and fires had been set at the USO club and at the Red Triangle hostel. Much was made of the fact that someone had torched the Knights of Columbus hostel in Halifax shortly before. However, what really fuelled alarm was the rumour that only ninety-eight bodies of the ninety-nine people reported killed were recovered. No one was ever charged with the crime.

Of course with so many young men in St John's, many of them away from home for the first time and with money in their pockets, it was inevitable that some would end up in trouble with the police at least once. Statistics indicate that during 1941, a year since the arrival of the Americans and six months since the creation of the Newfoundland Escort Force, there were 3,417 criminal prosecutions, an increase of 1,203 from 1940 and almost double the number from 1939.[125] By 1943, there were 8,000 criminal cases, 1,000 more than 1942.[126] A large portion of these were liquor related, and a great many involved the men of the Royal Canadian Navy. Possibly the most notorious incident occurred on Christmas Night in 1941 when 150 naval ratings destroyed the Imperial Café on Water Street.[127] Popular memory has it that the Americans were much better behaved than the Canadians, and a review of the Magistrate's Court section of the *Evening Telegram* during the war seems to bear this out. [128] Seldom did a day go by that a Canadian naval rating or soldier did not appear before the magistrate. However, in truth, the infrequency with which American servicemen appeared before the bench resulted more from an agreement between the Newfoundland government and the American authorities than from the Americans' better behaviour. While some American military personnel did appear before local courts, the majority were transferred to the U.S. military. While often the punishments handed out by military courts were harsher than those of civilian courts, this special treatment did cause some ire within the community.[129]

As mentioned elsewhere, a substantial number of women were also directly involved in the war effort in St John's. However, one group that has received little attention over the years is the Women in Royal Canadian Naval Service (WRCNS), commonly referred to by their British moniker – the Wrens. Formed in July 1942 and fashioned after their British counterpart, the WRCNS were the oil that kept Canadian naval operations moving. With most of the men involved with operations at sea, Wrens took over the everyday duties that allowed the navy to function smoothly under trying conditions. This was especially true at HMCS Avalon. Wrens drove staff cars and lorries through St John's narrow streets; coded, decoded, or sent messages; made sure sailors were paid as soon as they docked; and ran most of the training equipment. By the end of the war, Wrens were working in forty-eight trades and the WRCNS establishment at HMCS Avalon was second in size only to HMCS Stadacona.[130]

Newfoundland was considered an "overseas posting" for these women, and indeed, the hardships that many endured just getting there certainly brought this point home. However, the conditions they found when they arrived were really what made them realize that they were on the front lines of the Battle of the Atlantic. Former Wren Ruth Gray recalls that "being in Newfoundland was just like being in Britain. We felt under fire. We weren't really being shot at, but we could hear gunfire outside." German U-boats were also an acknowledged menace, and Gray remembers convoys being delayed in St John's Harbour for weeks because U-boats were reported just outside.[131]

In addition to rationing, blackouts, air raid drills, and censorship, Wrens also had to endure the very tight security of a naval facility at war. Former coder Tish Herbert remembers that whenever she and her fellow Wrens reported for their shifts at Fort William, "Navy guards carrying rifles, with fixed bayonets, checked [their] passes and credentials several times" as they made their way to their work areas.[132] If she needed a further reminder that she was in a shooting war, the almost daily arrival of survivors, or worse – casualties – further exposed her to the stark realities of war. One particularly vivid event, Gray recalls, was the loss of HMCS *Valleyfield* off the south coast. She says it made a lasting impression on her because she had attended high school with two of the "boys" on the ship.[133]

Despite the contributions, not to mention the sacrifices, these women and their counterparts in the army and air force made to the war effort, they were still subject to a malicious whispering campaign as the war dragged on. Supposedly, women in uniform were promiscuous and just interested in sex and snagging a man. The rumours had such a detrimental impact on recruiting and thus the war effort, that the National Film Board produced two shorts, *Proudly She Marches* and *Wings on Her Shoulders*, to dispel them. A pay increase also helped restore morale and recruiting, and the various armed forces never lacked for female volunteers.[134] By the end of the war, 568 WRCNS had served with HMCS Avalon.[135]

At the start of the Second World War, St John's, Newfoundland, was merely a defended port, similar to hundreds of other ports that ringed the North Atlantic. Over the span of the war, however, it evolved into one of the most important escort bases in the Battle of the Atlantic. Mirroring the experience of the Royal Canadian Navy, under whose care the base was administered, this development was not a smooth, well-planned progression, but an ad hoc process ordained by events at sea and politics on shore. Hundreds of warships and thousands of naval personnel were posted at HMCS Avalon during the war, and the RCN relied heavily on the city of St John's to provide for them. The citizens of St John's rose to the challenges, supplying land, labour, and materials, and, just as important, recreational and entertainment facilities. Hostels were established; sports leagues were started up; dances, concerts, and suppers were held; and homes were opened to servicemen, many of whom were away from home for the first time. While the people of St John's went above and beyond, it was not solely for altruistic reasons. Because of the presence of the various armed forces, St John's and Newfoundlanders in general experienced a prosperity previously unknown to them. It was a mutually beneficial experience and a remarkable accomplishment for both the people of Canada and their Newfoundland hosts.

Visit our website at http://storytelling.concordia.ca/occupied/ to zoom in on the wartime city. It works much like Google Earth, c. 1942.

Visit our website at http://storytelling.concordia.ca/occupied/ to zoom in on the wartime city. It works much like Google Earth, c. 1942.

Part 2 | Remembering Wartime St John's

55
BRITISH CONSOLS Cigarettes
Extra Mild
LIFEBUOY
HEALTH SOAP
SAVON DE SANTE
MASSO
DENTAL TYPE
THE NEW HUTAX
TOOTH POWDER
SCIENTIFICALLY CORRECT
Guaranteed
COLGATE'S SHAVE STICK
POCKET COMBS

3

The Children's War

BARBARA LORENZKOWSKI

Left HMCS *Trillium* gun shield art. "Presumably because of his sailor outfit, Donald Duck was a favourite subject for gun shields. This one depicts Donald scooping up a U-boat with a fish dip net. It is the second gun shield to be painted but the first to be hung in the Nest. Upon seeing the 'Wet Ass Queen' in the Nest but not mounted on the wall, winger Larry Mofford told his CO Skinny Hayes he could do one better. He immediately returned to the Trillium, spent the night painting the picture, returned to the Nest the next day and secured it to the wall before the Queen was up." Gary Green, *A Guide for Some of the Gun Shield Art and Ship's Badges of the Crow's Nest Officer's Club* (St John's: Crow's Nest Military Artifacts Association, Newfoundland).

Right HMCS *Saskatoon* gun shield art. This gun shield is almost identical to the one on the HMCS *Trillium*. From family photograph album of Marjorie Ferguson, Halifax.

In examining the social history of the Second World War, historians have begun to rediscover age as a category of historical analysis.[1] The story they tell, in remarkably similar terms, revolves around the mobilization of Canadian school-aged children and youth for the war effort and the moral panic that ensued when some children became latchkey "orphans," their soldier fathers fighting abroad, their mothers working long hours in war industries. "Juvenile delinquency" and "youth run wild" emerged as catchwords of a public discourse that juxtaposed the "good" children and the "bad," thereby reinforcing both a sense of patriotic duty and the importance of traditional gender roles, for only in traditional families could the "youth problem" presumably be contained.[2] While these studies have much to teach us about public perceptions of childhood, they reveal little about children's wartime experiences. Children's own voices remain muted, taking public stage only in the carefully crafted cadences of high school yearbooks or the children's pages of national newspapers.[3]

Yet, if we listen to the "winds of childhood" – as they rustle in childhood memoirs, echo in letters, and ring through oral history interviews – the history of the children's war unfolds along very different narrative lines.[4] As the Canadian writer Janet Lunn notes in her memoir, "Those war years are a very long time ago now and my wartime memories are jumbled in my mind like photographs in a box." Her memories of "newspaper pictures of battles and heroes" mingle with "stories of terrible deprivations in Britain." Memories that taste of adventure – "the ration books, songs, movies, radio programs, the sailors who came to us for home-cooked meals, and the air raid drills" – are "all mixed up"

St John's Harbour entrance, seen from the city. From family photograph album of James Nicol Walkey, Halifax.

with the haunted thoughts of "our neighbour who died on 'The Death March from Bataan,' my cousin Paul, and the boy who came home without his legs."[5] Wartime memories, in other words, do not come packaged in a tidy, linear narrative, and nor do these memories linger in the social space that historians have probed most extensively, the schools. More typically, the story of the children's war, as it is remembered from the vantage point of adulthood, reveals itself in a series of vivid images and vignettes.[6] Just as young Paul O'Neill and his brother were "copying around" in Bay de Verde one winter afternoon, jumping from one ice block to the next, so, too, did the women and men who shared their wartime memories of growing up in St John's "jump" from one memory to the next in a fluid movement that was not bound by the straightjacket of historical chronology.[7]

This chapter draws upon twenty-five life-course interviews conducted by a team of research assistants in St John's in the late summer and fall of 2007.[8] If the past is a foreign country, as the historian David Lowenthal surmised over two decades ago, so, too, is the land of childhood whose inhabitants have left few written sources behind.[9] "In retrieving the experience of childhood," Jean

Barman has mused, "we are almost inevitably forced to resort to memory – in other words, to retrieve the experience as it has been remembered by adults." As oral historians and historians of childhood have reminded us, memories of childhood are produced in a dialogue between interviewer and interviewee, with "each individual's perceptions of past experience ... filtered through a contemporary lens."[10] We thus need to be cognizant of the many pasts that echo in personal reminiscences and the intricate interplay between history and memory. At the same time, however, the lives of our interviewees overlapped in what still felt like a "small town." The tapestries of their memories share common patterns and highlight certain narrative threads that serve as a corrective against the fallibility of individual memories.

The chorus of voices that emanates from these interviews is moving not only for its individual "melodies," which were modulated by the storyteller's age, gender, class, and religion, but also for its collective evocation of growing up in a city at war. Elsewhere, as Neil Sutherland has suggested, the war "merely formed the background to the day-to-day immediacy of [children's] lives." But for children in St John's – as in the seaports of "Montreal, Halifax, Sydney, ...

St John's, from harbour. From family photograph album of James Nicol Walkey, Halifax.

and, later, Prince Rupert and Vancouver" – the line between home front and battlefront became increasingly blurred as they watched warships lining up in the harbour,[11] as they encountered soldiers, sailors, and airmen "walking back and forth in the streets, with their rifles on their shoulders,"[12] as they received word of ships torpedoed in the Battle of the Atlantic, with sailors on board who had joined their family for Sunday dinner just weeks earlier, and as they heard explosions echoing across Conception Bay when German submarines attacked the ore ships off Bell Island in two separate raids on 5 September 1942 and 9 November 1942.[13] When George Ledrew stated that "we were part of the war zone in the western hemisphere," he spoke for many of our interview partners for whom memories of the war loomed large – so large indeed that the immediacy of the war in children's lives is tangible even across a temporal divide of more than six decades.

In order to disentangle the many strands of childhood that were so tightly interwoven with larger threads of religion, class, and gender, this chapter charts the maps of childhood in ever-widening concentric circles.[14] After probing children's geographies in the 1930s and 1940s, it turns to the social spaces inhabited jointly by boys and girls as they witnessed the coming of the war and the subsequent transformation of "small-town" St John's into a city that seemed to be in perpetual motion, with warships crowding the harbour, soldiers parading in the streets, and servicemen "invading" family homes as boarders and frequent dinner guests. The study then maps the gendered worlds of childhood, for gender sharply demarcated the ways in which children experienced the war and interacted with the servicemen stationed in town. Although girls and boys alike marvelled at the novel dinner guests who read teacups after dinner, helped them with their French homework, and took them out to the movies or sliding on the hills, only boys regularly interacted with sailors, soldiers, and airmen beyond the realm of the family home.

Their maps of childhood in wartime St John's encompassed a far greater territory than the ones recalled by women of the same age cohort. Women's childhood stories of home-based leisure and school-centred entertainment contrast with men's tales of going "down to Water Street," gazing at ships at the harbour, hanging out at the rifle range, witnessing fights – both orderly and wild – in the boxing ring and or at Bannerman Park, piling onto excursion trucks to Bowring Park, and lurking around the "outside perimeters" of "Camp Alexander," where American servicemen freely dispensed chocolate bars and Coke.

The final part of this study examines how local maps of childhood were reshaped by the invasion of the city by motor vehicles. Soaring rates of traffic accidents prompted a public debate on which public spaces were appropriate for children and which were not. In foreshadowing later-century debates on the reformulation of public space into an adult space, within which children's movements would be tightly regulated, the stories of children's lives in wartime St John's tell both of the remarkable freedom that children (and particularly boys) enjoyed in the city and of subsequent attempts to curtail this freedom in the name of public safety. The new "geography of danger" emphasized the threat posed by speeding vehicles and sought to regulate and limit children's access to public space.[15]

CHILDREN'S GEOGRAPHIES

"The town," remembers Ann Abraham, "was so small before the war."[16] Small, too, was the harbour that would soon be crowded with corvettes and destroyers, making the "few outport schooners that still came in" look "out of place now, small and unimportant," as Helen Porter recalls in her childhood memoirs.[17] Barely 2 kilometres long and 700 metres wide, the "snug, almost land-locked St. John's harbour" was the heart of a city of 40,000 people whose principal stores clustered along Water Street.[18] From here, the cobblestone streets climbed the steep hills that surrounded the bay, each lined with "endless rows" of houses, as Mona Wilson, Canada's Red Cross assistant commissioner, wrote to her sister Jane in September 1940.[19] To Wilson, who had just arrived in St John's to tend to the needs of Canadian servicemen, the rhythms of town seemed reminiscent of an earlier time. The clatter of horseshoes echoed in the roads as horse-drawn carriages delivered groceries and coals around town.[20] In the winter months, the horses strained to pull the carts, laden with coal, over the hills. When the horses slipped on the icy streets, the drivers "would be beating and driving up the horses, and it was terrible," Ann Abraham recalls.[21] In the summer, the iceman made his rounds once a week, and when he came, Eileen Collins remembers, "the kids would crowd around to ask for a chip of ice. That was your treat."[22] Cars were a rare sight on the streets, which were ruled by groups of youngsters from the neighbourhood who played until darkness fell.[23]

As Helen Porter recalls in her memoirs, religion served as an important point of identification for the city's youngsters. On the first day of Lent, the children of her South Side neighbourhood "made a practice of counting Catholics" by looking for an ashen mark "dabbed on their foreheads. Cousin Dot would gasp, 'Oh, My God, I never thought she was a Catholic, did you?' ... [A]s we rushed out of Goodie's Store after having seen the tell-tale mark on the salesgirl who always served us." Living in a predominantly Anglican neighbourhood, young Helen, a Methodist, found the services in the local Anglican church, St Mary's, both intriguing and disorienting: "I never knew the proper responses to make to the readings, and it seemed strange to kneel for prayer in church, though I always did it for my bedside prayers at home."[24] The public school system reinforced such divisions by streaming children of the Roman Catholic, Anglican, and United churches into schools of their own religious affiliation.

Many of our women interviewees recall rhythms of childhood that revolved around home, school, and church. Their younger selves did not question the strictures of religion that formed a "natural" part of their week. "You woke up at six in the morning," Ann Abraham remembers, "and your Sunday clothes were at the bottom of your bed, and you put them on, and you went to church."[25] Religion circumscribed their lives, curtailing both physical movement and vocal expression. "Being a Protestant, you were not allowed to skate or slide on Sun-

St John's street scene. Photo by Lieut. Alice Ducile Talman, control no. 20010159-002-8, Canadian War Museum.

days," Patricia Winsor remembers, whereas Eileen Collins, who was educated by nuns, recalls the annual retreats of her youth. For an entire week, she and her sisters "couldn't speak, either at school or at home. And we listened to lectures, and read holy books, and went to the first mass of the day at 6:30 in the mornings. There were four girls in our family. Mum must have thought she was in heaven!"[26]

But since class, not religion, determined residency patterns in much of the city, children played with youngsters of different denominations on their neighbourhood streets. "Even though half the street was Roman Catholic and half was Anglican," recalls Tom Goodyear, "they were fairly close-knit." Once, as a boy, he walked into the neighbour's home next door to find the entire family kneeling on the kitchen floor. "And I didn't know what to do ... and I closed the door, and I went home, and I told my mother." He learned that his neighbours were saying the rosary. Later, his mother gently admonished him: "'My son, it wouldn't have done you any harm if you had knelt down beside them.' So, that's the type of woman that she was."[27] Joe Prim's best friend "went to a different school because he was not the same religion," while David Edwards took a Roman Catholic girl to the school dance, despite his mother's persistent admonitions: "Dave, don't you think you could find a nice Spencer girl to take to the dance?"[28]

The oral history interviews at the core of this study provide tantalizing evidence that the stark denominational boundaries in St John's could be subtly subverted, for children did not necessarily abide by the rules of the adult world. As David Nasaw found in his study on nineteenth-century New York, the children in tenement districts blithely disregarded the boundaries of ethnicity that structured their parents' lives. Their sense of belonging was shaped, first and foremost, by territory. Living in ethnically mixed city blocks, they "played with kids who at home spoke different languages, ate different foods, and worshipped different gods. Kids whose parents would not have dreamed of socializing became best friends."[29] In creating communities of childhood, the children of St John's, too, forged friendships across denominational boundaries.

Chasms of wealth separated the Water Street merchants and the city's educated elites from "the average Newfoundland worker, for whom life was a perpetual struggle against geography, the weather and mounting debts," as historian David MacKenzie has written.[30] Children were well versed in reading markers of social class, be it an affluent neighbourhood address or the clothes worn by passersby that projected either respectability or poverty. The most inescapable sign of social status was occupation. Working-class children whose parents had scrambled to send their first-born to one of the city's private colleges dreaded the first day of each school year when they had to reveal their father's occupation. Forty years later, Helen Porter still remembers "the way everybody giggled, or nearly everybody, when someone like Vera or Freddie Smity replied, in a very low voice, a cook or a longshoreman." Her well-to-do classmates who came from families of wholesalers, manufacturer's agents, doctors, or general merchants also chuckled when Porter identified her father as "Chief Rater at the Freight Office." Each year, Helen's mother emphasized her husband's formal title: "*Chief Rater*, don't forget. I'm not going to have them laughing at you." Each year, with the careless cruelty of children, Helen's classmates laughed anyway, although the girl never told her mother.[31]

In middle- and upper-class homes, children were barred from the front parlour when their parents entertained visitors. They quietly served tea or sat on the stairs, watching their parents hosting "Navy people" or the officers of the Quebec Rifles. Only the very young were admitted into this adult world, as was five-year-old Frankie O'Neil in her great-uncle's mansion. She sat in her school uniform "on some officer's knees with my white bloomers just showing ... passing out peanuts" to the guests.[32] More modest homes did not allow for such a clear delineation of adult and children's spaces. Here, domestic life revolved around the kitchen, often the only heated room in the house, where the family's radio set brought news and entertainment.

Class determined the outer limits of children's worlds. Youngsters from affluent backgrounds enjoyed trips to the countryside in the family car, travelled to Britain on family holidays, and pictured their older selves pursuing higher education or professional training outside the country, thereby following in the footsteps of family members and friends who had studied at Bishop's University (Quebec) or trained as nurses at St Vincent's Hospital in New York.

Sterling Restaurant at 348 Water Street. Photo by Lieut. Alice Ducile Talman, control no. 20010159-002-10, Canadian War Museum.

Regardless of their social class, girls "knew" that their working years represented merely an interlude between school and marriage. As Helen Porter reminiscences, "We knew that, somewhere in the world, some married women worked at jobs outside the home, but we were all quite convinced that such a catastrophe would never happen anywhere near where we lived, and that if it did it would spell disaster for the family and all it stood for."[33] Without exception, the women and men who lived through the war years as children and youths describe mothers who worked as full-time homemakers. When children ambled home from school in little groups for their ninety-minute lunch break, "mother was there with dinner cooked."[34] To run a household with several youngsters was a time-consuming operation that invested mothers with great parental authority. In a recurrent theme, our interviewees describe their mothers as "efficient and organized," as the family's financial manager and "dominant decision-maker." As Joe Prim succinctly puts it, "Mother was devoted to us, and she called the shots."[35] With mothers being bound to the home by either custom or necessity, the traditional family remained intact throughout the war years. As a result, the moral panic over "eight-hour orphans" whose mothers had found work in lucrative war industries never entered the public discourse in Newfoundland. In six years of wartime coverage, the St John's *Evening Telegram* did not once evoke fears of an "epidemic" of juvenile delinquency owing to motherless and fatherless homes – a common refrain in Canadian and American newspapers.[36]

When children built obstacle courses on dirt roads for their games of marbles, the wind blew up dust from the roads and carried it into family homes, thereby adding to the never-ending round of family and housework chores. On the eve of the Second World War, even middle-class households in St John's could rarely afford modern household technology and only the wealthy could hire young girls from the outports to work as maids.[37] In 1935, census enumerators counted 1,329 women in domestic service, which amounted to over one-third of the city's

Streetcars travelling east on Water Street, passing the Marshall Building, *Scenes of St. John's*. Photo by Lieut. Alice Ducile Talman, control no. 20010159-002-6, Canadian War Museum.

female labour force.[38] Working-class families had to do without such help.[39] Children relished the "taste of toast ... held to the embers of the coal stove," but it was their mothers who had to tend to the wood- or coal-burning stove, who mended clothes, knitted socks, mittens, and hats, prepared meals for their families, and, in the city's rural outskirts, which did not yet have running water, hauled water from a nearby water tab.[40]

"My mother was a great person to make a dollar go around a long way," Norman Crane remembers. In his family, as in many others, such frugality and ingenuity meant the difference between comfort and deprivation.[41] Although the department stores on Water Streets offered glimpses of North American consumer culture, as did the accounts of friends and relatives who had found work in the Maritimes and the eastern seaboard, most households made do without prefabricated and brand-name goods.[42] In Patricia Winsor's family, "they made their own bread and their cookies and biscuits. You brought a barrel of apples and put it down in the basement. And you picked your own berries and made your wine out of the berries. The meat-man came to the door; the milk-man came to the door; the vegetable-man came to the door."[43] Some working-class women found respite in the early mass they attended each morning at the Basilica, thus carving out a space – however fleeting – of their own. "My mother," remembers R.J. Gallagher, the youngest of thirteen children, "she'd be given sainthood ... She would get up at six in the morning, go to seven o'clock mass, went to mass and communion, walked back, took off her coat and put on her apron and went in the kitchen. And that's where she stayed until seven at night until we had our supper. She cooked all our meals."[44]

With memories of the Great Depression still vivid in their minds, working-class children and youth in St John's measured their family's well-being in neither money nor consumer goods, but in food and occupational stability. "I often heard my mother saying that there were times before the war when father brought home fifty cents a week," recalls Gilbert Oakley, whose father worked as a sail-maker on Water Street. And yet "we always had plenty to eat." In the fall, when the schooners returned from Labrador, "people would bring salted salmon, salt cod fish, peach-berries. And they paid when they got their money."[45] In Joe Prim's family, whose breadwinner had gone to sea with an English merchant company, the pangs of hunger were held at bay by the vegetables grown and animals raised on his grandmother's farm in the West End. "We never had too much, but we always had enough to eat," Joe Prim says in a tribute to his "pioneer" grandmother who "taught me the fundamentals of farming and rearing animals and hard work."[46] Much like their contemporaries in British Columbia, whose childhood Neil Sutherland has probed so perceptively, our interviewees – most of them born in the 1920s and 1930s – "focused on the immediate aspects of their lives" and "took their circumstances, no matter how harsh, as a given in life."[47] They took pride in their families' self-sufficiency and described the casual back and forth in close-knit neighbourhoods.

It was in the home that the lives of adults and children intersected in patterns that were unique to each family. Given the young age of our interview-

Winter street, *Scenes of St. John's*. Photo by Lieut. Alice Ducile Talman, control no. 20010159-002-7, Canadian War Museum.

ees during the war years, it is not surprising that both women and men situated their younger selves firmly within family networks. Women described how they turned to their mothers for advice and affection, while men fondly evoked father-son outings in which close bonds were forged. "Father," reminiscences Paul O'Neill, "was the kindest man I ever came across." Only once did he chastise his two young boys, hitting them with his slipper after their wild jumping destroyed the bed's spring box. "But this was the only time he ever raised his hands, and afterwards, he was full of remorse," Paul O'Neill smiles. "Mother, on the other hand, she did not spare the rod." By contrast, other male interviewees characterized their fathers as distant, aloof, and taciturn, but paid tribute to their warm and joyous mothers.[48]

Within the family home, bonds of love and affection cut across gender lines. Helen Porter's father regularly took his daughter, a ferocious reader, to the local lending library "over" on the city's north side, and he celebrated her thirteenth birthday by inviting her along to Toronto, where he was attending a railway convention. Patricia Winsor remembers her father, a police officer, as "a gentle giant" who treated the family to humorous stories about disorderly servicemen.[49] Indeed, whether children gravitated towards the collective "we" of their family or towards their peer group seemed to be a question more of class than of gender. In large working-class families, which could afford neither housemaids nor nursemaids to alleviate the burdens of home care, men and women stated matter-of-factly that "with a big family, the attention has to be spread around. You made your own way generally." Or, as Eileen Collins put it, as a middle child in a family of five children, "You are really ignored because mom and dad have been busy with the first two and take you for granted, but it is benign neglect, which is nice." Importantly, such benign neglect did not preclude regular and affectionate interaction between parents and children.[50]

Age determined how far children were allowed to venture from the family home. When Eileen Collins and her siblings "stayed out after dark when we were small, mother would have – now, this sounds barbaric – but she would meet us at the door with a cord of the electric iron in her hand, and it was folded up, and as we each came in after dark we got a whack on the leg as we ran past her and up the stairs." As children grew older, the territory which they could explore on their own expanded, yet its outer limits remained defined by parental edicts so clearly understood that they rarely needed spelling out. James Walsh, for one, who freely roamed the farmlands that surrounded his family home, knew that he was not expected to "spend much time in the east end of the city at my age."[51] The constraints that governed children's access to public space derived from the dictates of parental authority that sought to instil in children this "inextricable mix of morality, on the one hand, and politeness and gentility, on the other."[52] When a member of our interview team lightheartedly inquired whether his respondent ever "got into trouble" (a question designed to elicit memories of mischievous childhood adventures), the answer illuminated the strictures of an earlier era that placed a high stake in personal reputation. As Joe Prim firmly stated, transgressions carried social repercussions. "When I was growing up, I never had any trouble and my friends never had any trouble. When somebody got into trouble with the police, they were marked. Very rarely did you hear of anybody getting in trouble with the police."[53]

Consumed by the rhythms of their own world, children paid little attention to the growing international tensions in Europe in the mid-1930s. Their fathers, in turn, were reluctant to share stories of their own battlefield experiences in the First World War. David Edwards muses, "I don't remember my father talking much about the war," although his father's friends could sometimes be enticed to share carefully edited stories: "They never told you stories about death or injuries or fellows being dismembered. Stories that they told were happy memories, little parties."[54] As the horrors of the battlefields did not lend themselves to "tales of heroism and danger," many First World War veterans lapsed into silence or sought out the company of fellow veterans.[55] Despite their fathers' reticence, the children who walked the city's streets encountered reminders of war's horrific toll. To this day, James Walsh can picture First World War veterans in St John's "with legs missing and arms missing" and their wooden legs painted green. One veteran, still in his forties, lived in his neighbourhood. "His arm was

Running child. Photo by Lieut. Alice Ducile Talman, control no. 20010159-002-11, Canadian War Museum.

gone and he had his sleeve tucked in," James Walsh recalls. "And I can remember when his comrades were parading by, all of a sudden the sleeve came out of his pocket and the stump stood straight out. And I figured even at that time that he was saluting his comrades." Little wonder that the young boy feared for his father when war was declared: "I thought I am going to lose my dad."[56] It turned out that his father was spared from serving in active duty. Age, poor health, or their status as married men with dependants prevented the fathers of most of our interviewees from enlisting. Indeed, nearly half of the male volunteers in Newfoundland were declared medically unfit to serve during the Second World War.[57] While their fathers supported the war effort by volunteering for public duty as air-raid wardens, children witnessed their brothers, uncles, cousins, and the neighbourhood boys marching off to war, their absence a painful reminder of the all-encompassing nature of the conflict.[58]

A CITY AT WAR

It is the voices they remember. When Britain declared war on Germany on 3 September 1939, Neville Chamberlain's radio address to the British nation was carried into homes across Newfoundland. Eight-year-old David Baird listened "to the voice coming out of the radio," its solemnity lending a personal air to the abstraction that was war. "When the war was declared, it was a speech by Winston Churchill that I recall," remembers James Walsh, who was only six at the time. "I didn't exactly recall what he had said but it was his voice that we heard."[59] Elsewhere on the continent, twelve-year-old Christopher Chapman in Toronto, Ontario, listened to "King George's halting speeches with long pauses between words as he struggled with a crippling stutter," as did young Priscilla Galloway in Victoria, British Columbia.[60]

Whether it was the novelty of the medium or the fact that news travelled quickly over airwaves, the radio loomed large in childhood memories. The immediacy of the spoken word that emanated from radio sets captivated youngsters, who also recall the grave countenance of adults. Eileen Collins remembers staying at a teacher's summer house for a dance rehearsal when she was fourteen. One evening she and her classmates "were all shooed out of the house and told not to come in until after the news was over. Her husband was listening intently to the news bulletin. This was when Poland was being invaded. That was my recognition that something was wrong with the world." For nine-year-old Helen Porter, it was the invasion of Czechoslovakia – described by "chocolate-voiced" radio announcers – that brought home the war abroad. "This was the first time the war touched me," she recalls, "just thinking about the children in Czechoslovakia." Margaret Kearney, in turn, learned of the war from her father, a radio aficionado who had set up a short-wave system in the family's dining room: "Dad came in and said: 'There is war.'" Eight-year-old Paul O'Neill never had a chance to perform the play he was staging with friends on 3 September 1939, as "Dad came down and said: 'There will be no audience there tonight. There is war in Europe. Newfoundlanders will be involved.' And we went down and listened to the radio."[61]

Listening to the radio was a communal act. Families gathered in kitchens and dining rooms, and neighbours dropped by to listen to the news.[62] "I think we were glued to the radio all the time. It was your contact with the world," remembers Vicki Cheeseman, who was eleven years old when war was declared.[63] As the twelve o'clock news from London came on, children were hushed as their parents listened. "Once the news came on, there was no talking," Gilbert Oakley says. "You were not allowed to say a word."[64] In a similar vein, Patricia Winsor describes how "everything went quiet" once the radio was turned on. "The children were given a book to sit down and read so you didn't ask questions" while radio announcers analysed troop movements and discussed the fickle fortunes of war.[65]

The radio also enlivened the sombre mood. Children listened to *Superman* and *The Inner Sanctum* and, together with their parents, tuned in to *The House of Peter McGregor.* "It was marvellous," Stuart Fraser says of the shows that brought American popular culture into St John's households. "Every Sunday, these shows would be on and every Sunday in our house, we sat at the fire on a winter evening, and Mother did her knitting, and Dad did some woodcarving, and I played or read, and we listened to these shows."[66]

The American radio station "Voice of the United States" (VOUS) at Fort Pepperrell carried popular tunes into Newfoundland homes, offering an alternative to the Sunday hymns that had previously aired on the "Voice of Newfoundland" (VONF). "Music would cheer you up," says George Ledrew, who, like other St John's youngsters, regularly tuned into VOUS. Children quickly memorized the patriotic tunes broadcast on the radio and sang the songs of victory – "Keep the Home Fires Burning" and the war's unofficial anthem "There'll Always Be an England." They also hummed songs like "Kiss me good-night, Sergeant Taylor. Tuck me in my little wooden bed," much to the chagrin of local teaching orders. Twelve-year-old R.J. Gallagher, who performed on a local radio program once a week, was stopped on the streets by a priest from the Basilica who indignantly inquired, "What was the song you sang last night? The dirty love song?"[67] With mounting concern over unruly men and disorderly women, even the sweet, high-soaring voice of a twelve-year-old sounded suspicious to the guardians of

Aerial view of St John's Harbour, c. 1940. Control no. 19900192-018-5, Canadian War Museum.

Left An American soldier standing with a young boy on Long's Hill, looking southeast. The Methodist College is to the left, and Gower Street United Church is in the background. Note the white "blackout stripes" on the bumper and fender of the car. Photo #01-11-006, City of St John's Archives.

Right Soldier on a bicycle in front of the Tractor and Equipment Company building on Water Street. Cash's Indian is shown in front of the store. Photo #01-11-10, City of St John's Archives.

public morality. To them, the overt sensuality of the music seemed to signal a decline in traditional mores.

Probably the most painful social change wrought by the war was the departure of the city's young men. Some grade 11 students marched straight from their high school graduation to the recruitment office, at the tender age of seventeen.[68] Before they left, "those slick-haired, eager-faced boys" had their photographs taken, which later graced the pages of the *Evening Telegram*. In the scrapbooks that Helen Blundon lovingly assembled during the war, the faces of her brother, her cousin, her future husband and his two brothers, and "boys from practically all over Newfoundland" gaze at the observer, their youthfulness as yet unmarred by the war. "Even those who came back," Helen Porter contemplates, "never wore quite the same expression on their faces again."[69] Pride and heartbreak mingled as brothers, cousins, uncles, and boys from "our street" enlisted in the armed forces. "I was twelve years old, and I had four brothers, and it was such a traumatic time," remembers Vicki Cheeseman, the youngest of eight siblings. Two of her brothers went overseas, one of whom went "missing for quite a while in Africa," while an older sister worked as a nurse in London, England, as the city was reeling under sustained German bombing attacks.[70] Patricia Winsor's beloved grandmother, partly paralyzed after a stroke, was seated on a chair on the sidewalk near Harvey's Pier to see off her son. When her uncle saw his mother, Patricia Winsor recalls, "he broke away from the ranks to say good-bye to his mother and the sergeant in charge got really angry. And I got angry at the sergeant. Boy, was he shouting at Uncle Frank. I can remember this day, and all the people, and losing my shoe, and this man shouting."

The war retained its glamour only if it remained at a safe emotional distance. When some of the older girls at Bishop Feild School joined the navy and air force, "we were so proud of them," remembers Ann Abraham. "When they left, we had a special prayer for their safe return." While young Ann marvelled at the transformation of her former schoolmates as they proudly donned their uniforms, Helen Porter fell apart when her cousin Harold joined the Royal Navy, clinging "to him like a baby" when the time came to bid goodbye. "Harold and two of his brothers and just about every eligible man on the South Side ... joined up," she remembers, "most of them in the Royal Navy, a few in the Merchant Marine. Growing up near the sea as they had done, ships were second nature to them; it seemed more natural to fight on the water than on a grubby battlefield."[71] Just as the city's young men departed, "sailors of every allied nation" began to line the streets of St John's – "everyone it seemed, but our own boys," as Helen Porter wrote wistfully in her memoirs.[72]

The Royal Canadian Navy quietly entered town in 1941 to make final preparations for the Newfoundland Escort Force, which would soon shepherd large

Looking down Power Street towards the RCN Barracks on the South Side Hills. Photo #01-045-019, City of St John's Archives.

Bowring Park, 1942. Herbert Roberts Collection, 2007-8 Album, Crow's Nest Military Artifacts Association.

convoys of ships across the North Atlantic. It was the far more dramatic arrival of the American troopship the *Edmund B. Alexander* on 29 January 1941 that captured the public imagination.[73] Mothers, fathers, and uncles took youngsters down to the South Side to admire the "big spectacle," one that was only enhanced when the sailors gave a band concert on the wharf and then marched through town, handing out chocolate bars. In the minds of the children, the muscular American servicemen, with their strong white teeth, soon became associated with the taste of Coke and chocolate bars "the likes of which we had never seen in our lives."[74] For the next four years, the harbour would remain "a magnet for us kids," Paul O'Neill recalls. "We all felt we were in the front lines because of the ships and the convoys."[75]

Local boys who dreamed of making a living from the sea had always gazed longingly at the outport schooners bobbing on the harbour's waters. On the eve of the war, twelve-year-old Joe Prim earned fifty cents a week taking his grandmother's nine cows to graze on the hills of the South Side, and "all the time," he reminiscences, "I'll be looking down at the harbour," watching the boats and the seamen from the Merchant Marine, "and I figured, some day I was doing this myself."[76] Just two years later, corvettes and destroyers, alongside Portuguese and Spanish trawlers, crowded into the harbour. Newfoundland coastal boats no longer sported the vivid colours of the pre-war years. They too were painted grey, "just like the warships," to help shield them from attacks by the German submarines that roamed the waters of the Atlantic. The sheer number of ships that lay anchor during the war years awed the city's children. Young George Ledrew often walked down one of the old wooden piers to look at the fifty or sixty ships sitting in the harbour, as did David Baird, whose father owned a provision store on Water Street. "After school," he remembers, "we came here and would get a lift home with our father at five or six o'clock and we used to hang around and see around."[77]

Whereas men's memories of the harbour are laced with a sense of adventure, women recall the harbour as a site of social occasions. So closely are memories of the war intertwined with the harbour that Eileen Collins took members of our interview team on an extended harbour tour, painting vivid pictures of wooden wharves – "rickety in many cases" – where, today, only concrete structures stand.[78] After mass on Sundays, Collins remembers, "Mom and Dad would take us all for a walk" around the finger wharfs. "Dad had lived the first few years of his life on the south coast, so he loved the water and the ships. And he always had a little chat with one of the skippers."[79] For Helen Porter, who grew up on the South Side of St John's, the harbour was a place both poetic and prosaic. Her "memories of a clock-calm harbour, cloudless skies and thick clusters of blueberries on the Hill" mingle with recollections of "the smells of fish and oil and fat that drifted upward on certain winds" and the day her cousin "Dot and I watched some boys throwing stones at a plain, thick-lipped girl from the Battery because she, according to them, 'did it' with sailors."[80]

Most men on the South Side worked for merchant companies, made barrels in small cooperages, or lined up at the wharves each morning, "unloading coal or salt boats at Morey's or Wyatt's." Their children made the harbour their playground, transforming it into "a skating rink, a swimming pool, a place to catch tomcods, a place to skip stones." In the war years, South Side boys too young to enlist made a fortune selling Coke bottles to American servicemen, while South Side girls skipped on the smooth surface of the wharves, regularly inviting "one of the free French fellows to come over and run into the ropes and skip a bit."

Parents placed few strictures on their children's play at the harbour, which they regarded as an extension of the neighbourhood. There were limits, of course, to parental indulgence. When Helen Porter and her cousin Dot took a ride on "a weatherbeaten old waterboat ... our families feared we must be neophyte scarlet women to trust ourselves to a bunch of merchant seamen way outside the narrows where nobody would be able to hear you yell for help."[81] Wartime censorship prevented the local papers from evoking the sights and sounds of the harbour that figure so prominently in childhood memories of the war.

When the first American servicemen stepped off their troopship, the *Edmund B. Alexander*, in January 1941, the city's children marvelled at the newcomers' strange attire. "They had these huge, hooded jackets," chuckles Eileen Collins, and "socks that were half an inch thick. We didn't know what to make of them." But, she continues, "as soon as they discovered that our climate, even in wintertime, was much milder than many had expected back home," they left their parkas in the closet and did not even put on overshoes in the slushy St John's winters.[82]

A soldier and child, possibly outside the sanatorium on Topsail Road. The sanitorium opened its doors in March 1917 and closed in 1972. Photo #01-44-005, City of St John's Archives.

Children and adults alike judged servicemen according to the clothes they wore, contrasting American style with the baggy, shabby uniforms worn by Canadian soldiers. As women and men remember, the Americans were "dressed to kill," looked "very sharp," and impressed with their "lovely caps" and "jazzy uniforms."[83] "These guys were polite, beautifully dressed, well dressed," recalls Margaret Kearney, while young Helen Porter noted, with the sharp eyes of a twelve-year-old, the closely cropped hair of the American soldiers and their strong white teeth.[84] By contrast, Canadian uniforms attracted unflattering commentary. Children – well versed in reading clothes as a marker of social status – would later remember "baggy khaki pants brought in tight around the ankles, badly fitting tunics ... and huge clumsy boots."[85] Such categorizing was a popular pastime in wartime St John's. Canada's Red Cross assistant commissioner, Mona Wilson, charged with outfitting survivors of German submarine attacks, "always tried to find out in advance the nationality of the men who were coming in. If they were Norwegians, the largest sizes in clothes were laid out for the burly Scandinavian, if they were Chinese, the very smallest, and the brightest colored shirts for the negroes."[86]

In public conversations about servicemen, the badge of glamour was bestowed only on American soldiers. "Their drill, their marching was snappy," Stuart Fraser remembers. "It was precise. It was a lot more disciplined than the Canadian troops," whose marching rarely prompted the "cheers," "claps" and "exclamations of joy" that greeted American soldiers as they paraded through town.[87] Not only did Americans wear clothes that fit, they also "fitted in," as several of our

Winter conditions at sea. From family photograph album of James Nicol Walkey, Halifax.

interview partners remarked in almost identical terms.[88] In their friendly, brash, easygoing manner, "the Americans just came in and relaxed and had a good time and took part in all the things we had going," Paul O'Neill recalls.[89] Although prone to brag loudly about "how superior 'back home' was to 'Newfy'" – a practice so common that Newfoundlanders awarded it its own moniker ("we called this 'gatching'") – the Americans "weren't especially rowdy and they seemed more interested in sex than violence."[90] As children soon discovered, however, it was difficult to maintain such broad generalizations in personal encounters, for neither the Canadian sailors who helped children cut down a Christmas tree nor the boarder who lovingly sewed a raincoat for his four-year-old boy "somewhere in Canada" fit the stereotype of the ugly Canadian.[91]

Six decades after the war, former Canadian navy officer Don McClure still recalls the legendary Newfoundland hospitality that made the harbour so popular with seamen of every nationality.[92] In 1941 the *Evening Telegram* told of a taxi driver who, "after hauling two crippled British seamen all over town for a couple of hours, flatly refused to accept his fee for the drive. Seemed to feel that the men had already done their bit." Other local car owners stopped at the city's servicemen hostels and clubs "to pick up soldiers and sailors for trips into the surrounding country."[93] Young David Baird and his brother accompanied their father when he picked up four sailors at the Caribou Hut to take them out for a swim. "Four guys off a destroyer," Baird muses, "and I can still remember their names: Hobs, Dobs, Philip and Herb."[94] If men did the driving, it was women who extended the invitations. Ann Abraham's mother spontaneously invited over young servicemen who had attended Sunday services at her church. When family friends cautioned the widowed mother against opening her home to unknown strangers, she remained unconvinced. "No, no, no, no, they must be nice boys, or they wouldn't be going to church." The parents of David Edwards also approached soldiers and sailors after church services to invite them home for dinner. The mother of Vicki Cheeseman invited two French-Canadian soldiers over for Sunday dinner every weekend as a tribute to her own two boys serving overseas. Stuart Fraser's mother, in turn, picked up the phone and called the commanding officer at the Canadian air base at Torbay, reminding him, "If anybody wants to eat, just come to the house!" "She just felt," her son says, that "these guys deserved a home-cooked meal." In such informal encounters, many enduring friendships were forged. "Some of them spent quite a few meals in our house," Stuart Fraser recounts. "Some of them kept in touch long after the war. Some of them became friends."[95]

View of the Knights of Columbus building at the corner of Harvey Road and Parade Street, looking east. Also visible is an army truck and the Dooley's Dry Cleaning building. Photo #01-11-020, City of St John's Archives.

At Christmastime the local press encouraged the "[m]others of lads who are now abroad ... to fill in the empty chair at the dinner table on Christmas Day" with "some other mother's boys," couching its appeal for wartime solidarity in the language of universal motherhood, replete with the slogan "Let us invite a Service man."[96] Each year, on Christmas day, as Patricia Winsor remembers, "my father and I and my brother would walk down to Caribou Hut" to "take these gentlemen" home for Christmas dinner. In the privacy of their homes, children caught intimate glimpses of the sailors and soldiers stationed in town. In meeting servicemen up close, children were impressed with gestures and appearances. As adults, they would recall the politeness of a British officer who, even "in the stormiest days ... always took off his hat before he came in through the door," or the hairy chest of the Canadian soldier who boarded with Patricia Winsor's family and stitched together a raincoat for his own little boy back home.[97]

Visiting servicemen acted as surrogate brothers for the young, cutting down a Christmas tree in the woods, pulling it home on a sled, and stuffing the children's Christmas stockings with forbidden treats. When young Ann Abraham found chewing gum in her stocking on Christmas morning, it confirmed her belief in Santa Claus, since her mother would never have bought her chewing gum. "My mother did hate chewing gum ... It was like a cow, chewing gum. It was a terrible thing." "It never entered my mind," she adds, that the "six burly sailors" who had walked into the house on Christmas Eve "had brought a whole lot of stuff for our stockings."

The servicemen whom children encountered in their homes were not the "unruly men" described in reams of newsprint, but young fellows who "missed family and children," took joy in taking the children out sliding on a brisk winter afternoon, and assisted Vicki Cheeseman with her French-language homework. That June, the young girl brought home a 98 in French.[98]

Children's frequent, if casual, encounters with servicemen put a personal face on the battles of war. Ann Abraham and David Edwards both remark on the haunting absence of young sailors who "had been at the house and they never came back. And you know that their ship had been sunk, whereas others would come back again."[99] For Margaret Kearney, the Battle of the Atlantic wore the face of Ted, a young sailor from Quebec her mother had met at the Knights of Columbus. Whenever his Corvette lay anchor in the harbour, Ted visited the Kearney's home. "The last time Ted came in," Margaret Kearney remembers, "he must have come through the front door – it must have been evening – and he sat right down in the den and did not speak to anybody. He just sat there. And mother stayed in the den with him (there was a fire in the den) and somebody made him a cup of tea, and he still did not speak. We learned later that there had been a terrible battle out in the Atlantic and that the Corvette had picked up as many survivors as it could. But it couldn't take any more and they had to leave servicemen in the water." The memory of the distraught young man stayed with Margaret Kearney, who had begun to volunteer at a servicemen's hostel. "The men," she recalls, "always seemed to be lonely. It was something in their eyes, and I could never forget what happened to Ted that night he walked into our house. It gave us an insight of what it was like on the water."[100]

Gliding through the dark waters of the Atlantic and attacking both civilian and military vessels, German submarines became synonymous with death and destruction. In keeping with the tenet of secrecy, sailors on shore leave in St John's had to cover up the names of their ships (though the names were proudly displayed on little rosettes they used to carry), for "you weren't supposed to know what ship was in port," as Ann Abraham remembers. Far more difficult to conceal was the destruction wrought by the Battle of the Atlantic as the wounded ships floated into the harbour. When ten-year-old James Walsh visited the harbour in the early 1940s, he saw "ships in various states of destruction." Gilbert Oakley was also struck by the sight of the damaged boats in the harbour: "There was one that had a lot of paper on it, and there was a torpedo that went right through it. And the fishermen used to call them bomb-boats and they would bring sailors to the boats, tied in the middle of the harbour," for a fee of twenty cents so that they could inspect the damaged boats.

What historian William Tuttle has called a "flashbulb memory, the freeze-framing of an exceptionally emotional event down to the most incidental detail," captures some of the iconic moments that burned themselves into the memory of St John's youngsters, irrespective of their gender, class, or religion.[101] When disaster struck twice in 1942, the victims included not only neighbourhood boys but also the servicemen who had read teacups or pulled sleds up snowy hills. On 14 October 1942, the ferry *Caribou* was torpedoed on its regular run between North Sydney, Nova Scotia, and Port aux Basques, Newfoundland, and sank in the Cabot Strait. Among the 130 victims were family, friends, neighbours, and acquaintances, including the "really good friend" of Helen Porter's cousin Harold, the brother of one of Ann Abraham's classmates, and a family friend of David Edwards's. The son of a widow, living across the street of James Walsh and his family, survived with only a broken arm, one among about a hundred survivors who were pulled to safety from the frigid waters of the Atlantic. "He was in the Royal Navy and he was coming home when the *Caribou* was torpedoed," James Walsh remembers.[102] Stories quickly spread of men, women, and children "clinging to life rafts, pieces of wreckage, and the one lifeboat that managed to stay afloat. Some were crying, others were dying. Still others were shouting the names of loved ones, hoping to hear the reply 'I'm here!' Some did."[103] Only six months after the sinking of the *Caribou*, thirteen-year-old Helen Porter accompanied her father to a railway convention in Toronto, a celebratory occasion that turned into "the most frightening experience of my life." To guarantee the safety of the ferry they took from Newfoundland, a destroyer and a corvette sailed alongside while a plane flew overhead. The journey took thirteen hours in a raging storm. Porter begged her father to let them fly home after the convention, an impossible proposition given the family's tight finances.[104]

On 13 December 1942, one hundred people perished in the devastating fire that destroyed a local servicemen's haunt, the Knights of Columbus hostel. Across

View of the ruins of the Knights of Columbus hostel after the fire of 12 December 1942. Photo #01-11-022, City of St John's Archives.

town on this winter evening, children and adults were listening to *The Barn Dance,* a popular radio show broadcast every Saturday live from the servicemen's hostel. "We were listening to it that night," Helen Porter recalls. "Everybody listened to it, and suddenly you heard screams." James Walsh, too, remembers, "All of a sudden there was screams, and then we lost radio contact." As eleven-year-old Paul O'Neill pulled away the heavy blackout curtains to peer out of a window of his home, other children across town stepped outside onto the streets or "ran to the back of the house" to look at the sky. In strikingly similar terms, eyewitnesses describe "that red glow … in the sky" and recount apocalyptic scenes: "flames, smoke going up," "flames coming out of the sky," and flames so fiery that they "scorched all the houses on the other side of the road." Twenty-year-old Kathleen Williams, who loved attending the barn dance at the Knights of Columbus every Saturday, looked at the rosy glowing sky with great worry. Only her mother's premonition had prevented her from going to the dance that night.

"We did lose a maid," Margaret Kearney states, "and one of my mother's friends was on duty there." Helen Porter recalls the two brothers who been at the barn dance that fateful evening: "One of the fellows in the barn dance – he was only sixteen – he died. His brother got out, but was never the same." Gilbert Oakley's account reflects the greater freedom boys had to roam the city: "We went over the next morning and looked around, and they were taking the bodies out and I was only seven or eight years. My oldest brother was almost eleven years, and all the houses all blistered." Paul O'Neill and his brother also went up to the site of the fire the next morning, "and all the corpses were laid out on the floor [of the Armoury] in rows and people were going in, trying to identify relatives. And we just went in with them. Nobody ever stopped us. They were too upset, trying to identify relatives."[105] Just as American children would remember, with sharp clarity, their whereabouts during the attack on Pearl Harbor, St John's youngsters would be able to recount, over six decades later, the sight, sound, and smell of the Knights of Columbus fire. More than even the arrival of the *Edmund B. Fitzgerald* or the sinking of the *Caribou*, the fire acted as a "flashbulb memory" that encapsulated the emotional intensity of the war years.

Across North America, children believed fervently in the righteousness of the "good war," wanted to "pitch in" and "do their bit" by buying war savings stamps

Funeral procession for the victims of the Knights of Columbus fire. The photograph shows at least seven trucks with soldiers along each side heading towards Mount Pleasant Cemetery. The image was taken on Hamilton Avenue near the top of Shaw Street, with part of Elton's Esso service station shown at the right. Photo #01-38-001, City of St John's Archives.

and war savings bonds, witnessed the despair of classmates whose brothers perished in the hostilities, practised air-raid drills, and dreaded hearing news of the London blitz – much like St John's youngsters did.[106] Yet, in this eastern-most city of the continent, which served as an important Allied naval base, children felt the ripples of the war particularly keenly. As Allied servicemen guarded the skies and waters surrounding the city, children feared that "it would only be a matter of time before the German bombers were hovering over St. John's."[107] Torpedoed ships that floated in the harbour told of the Battle of the Atlantic more vividly than any news reports could. The screams from the burning Knights of Columbus hostel, abruptly silenced as the radio transmission faltered, echoed in children's ears and fuelled fears of enemy sabotage. These children grew up in a city at war where the line between the home front and the battlefront grew less distinct every day.

GENDERED SPACES

In the early 1990s, William Tuttle examined 2,500 letters in which American women and men shared their childhood memories of the Second World War. "Their letters," Tuttle writes, "strongly reinforced my belief that gender is the most important variable in children's life."[108] In mapping the gendered worlds of childhood in wartime St John's, this study has encountered boys who freely roamed the city and revelled in "the male world of adventure."[109] Boys, as historian E. Anthony Rotundo has so memorably said, were "inhabitants of an alternate world" that "flourished in backyards, streets, parks, playgrounds, and vacant lots, all of which compose 'a series of city states to play in.'"[110] The childhood memories of our male interviewees seem at their most vivid when men tell of their own youthful exploits in wartime St John's. Although both boys and girls regularly interacted with servicemen in the family home, only boys carried these interactions – which ranged from fleeting encounters to sustained friendships – into public space.

Not for boys was the home-based leisure and school-centred world that several of our women interviewees so fondly remember. Ann Abraham, who would continue a long family tradition of entering the teaching profession, recalls her years at Spencer College in glowing terms: "It was second to none. It was our home, and it was made to feel like our home. This is your home. You are not here for visiting. We come in the morning and sit down on the floor and play jackstone ... We had dancing in the afternoon at the school, and we had our Guides and Brownies [meetings] in the school in the afternoon." Patricia Winsor, who attended Bishop Feild School and later Spencer College, similarly remembers how "everything revolved around the school." The young girl thrived in a social space that offered room for athletic pursuits – "basketball, field hockey, gymnastics, folk dancing" – and close-knit circles of friendship. "It was an all-girl world," Patricia Winsor recalls. "I enjoyed school. We only had one grade on each level so you know girls from the very start. My mother went to the same school. I was involved. I was a prefect."[111]

This photograph shows the severely damaged ship remembered by so many of the people interviewed. Photo 003, from family photograph album of Marjorie Ferguson, Halifax.

By contrast, only one of our male interviewees remembers teachers as friendly or inspirational."[112] More typically, if they touch upon memories of schooling at all, men remember schools as an alien, often repelling space.[113] Norman Crane disliked the British teachers at Bishop Feild: "[They] weren't the most understanding people. But I survived. I got through it ... I didn't like the English. I didn't like them at all. I had no affinity for them at all. They were condescending." R.J. Gallagher, in turn, remarks, "I wasn't a very good student. I didn't like school. The Brothers were very strict." Joe Prim attended Holy Cross School "because it was the only Catholic school in the area, and the Christian Brothers really were tough ... It was the Christian Brothers and they were tough." So "tough" and "strict" were his teachers that the youth decided to join the Merchant Marine at the age of sixteen, preferring the company of men on the submarine-infested waters of the Atlantic to the oppressive atmosphere at Holy Cross. "I left school at an early age," Joe Prim says. "I had the choice to face the Germans or face the Christian Brothers."[114]

The campaign to mobilize children and youth for the war effort reached youngsters of either gender. Schoolchildren listened to principals who provided daily reports on the latest battles;[115] they prepared their very own "little diary of the war" by copying newspaper headlines into scrapbooks;[116] and they traced the movement of Allied troops. "They used to have war maps," James Walsh recalls, "and every evening we used to sit around the living room with the war map on the floor and listening to the radio and hear the reports of the advance and sticking the flags in the area. We had this war map with flags plastered all over to indicate the advances made by the Allies."[117] In predictably gendered ways, schools called upon girls to knit socks, make fruitcakes, and, after the war brides arrived in mid-1945, assist the young mothers with children in tow. "I remember these poor creatures getting off the boat," Ann Abraham says, "and that was before the days of disposable diapers, and most of them had one or two babies with them. The smell of urine, it was terrible."[118] Meanwhile boys were called upon to join the cadets or collect aluminum and scrap metal for the war effort.[119]

Yet such organized mobilization was not what fired boys' imagination. In keeping with the tenets of boy culture, boys were drawn to public spaces where they could play and explore beyond the watchful eyes of adults. While teachers and principals dissected the fortunes of war, boys pictured – in colourful fashion – the fate of the German foe should he happen to fall into their hands. "On the way home from school, during wartime, we argued the war," Paul O'Neill remembers. "'What would you do with Hitler?' 'I'd put him into a hand-slicer and slice him slowly to pieces.'" He and four other boys from the neighbourhood sold candies and drinks and brought the proceedings to a local radio station

Canadian Army convoy leaves Lester's Field Camp, February 1941. Control no. 19920076-004, Canadian War Museum.

that awarded each donor with a brief appearance on air: "'And now the Cochrane Street gang, what do you boys got?' 'We've got $5.23.' 'Wonderful, wonderful, that's for the boys overseas. We are buying smokes for the boys overseas.'" The time in the spotlight was short – "just long enough to say who you were and where you were from and how much money you made" – but satisfying nonetheless. "We felt we were doing a great job for the war effort. We had one sale every couple of weeks," Paul O'Neill recounts.[120]

Nothing excited boys more than the enforcement of blackout orders and the staging of air-raid drills. "Every night," Stuart Fraser recalls, "I had to put up shades on the window – beaverboard – so that no light would show." Girls, as well, were "going around [the house] every night, putting up shutters and making sure drapes were closed," but only boys appear to have accompanied their fathers on their nightly rounds as wardens.[121] David Edwards describes "going out with [my father] in the neighbourhood, checking on the windows of our neighbours to see whether there was no light shining through ... And I remember the next day, my father saying: 'Now I have to go to Mrs Brown and I have to go to Mrs Whoever, tell her that last night, her lights were shining." Gilbert Oakley, in turn, who was only twelve years old at war's end, needed no formal appointment as warden: "When we were children and we saw lights coming out of somebody's window, we knock at the door and tell them. We are on the door telling them, there is light shining out."[122] The utter darkness into which the city was plunged each night was punctuated only by air-raid drills that simulated a German bombing attack. "During those air-raid drills," Paul O'Neill remembers, "they sent trucks around with bundles of splits and they'd pour kerosene over the splits and light them and throw them onto the sidewalk, and then you had to run out, get the stirrup pump out, fill it with water and go: pump, pump, pump. I was too young, but the men on my street would do it. It was pretty exciting for us."[123] The drama of fire, even of the pretend variety, stirred the hearts of boys as they breathlessly observed how "people would run with a bucket of water and a stirrup pump, in case anything happened. And every week, they go out and throw them at different places and people would run and put them out, just in case of an air raid."[124] Paul O'Neill envied the older boys who acted as bike messengers during these drills, carrying messages back and forth through the darkened streets, whereas six-year-old Stuart Fraser observed his father's air-raid duties with much apprehension:

> My dad was involved in the air-raid protection. His job was to instruct people on how to use a stirrup pump, how to distinguish incendiary bombs, and how to tell the difference between one that goes bang and [one] that just burns. So, on Wednesday afternoon, he would pick me up [from school] and we would go home and have our dinner, and it was out in the field to practise how to put out a bomb. As a youngster, I was not too impressed with this bomb thing because I had seen movies of London burning. And the first time my father came to set this thing off, I was petrified. But it didn't do anything – it just burst into flames. And my

St John's at night, after the blackout. Photo by William A. Ramsay, control no. 20030014-088-1, Canadian War Museum.

> two cousins and myself and mother and everybody in the family was out there with buckets of water and the stirrup pump was used. You put a bit of water in the bucket and pump and my mother would direct the hose ... The other type of bomb blew an aching hole in the middle of the field.[125]

The drama of civil defence drew boys out onto darkened public streets and the wide-open spaces of the countryside. By contrast, women's stories of blackouts and air-raid drills unfold in the domestic setting of family homes or home-like schools, where "the whole school would go down to the basement and have a concert" during an air-raid practice.[126] The boundary between "private" and "public," which a generation of historians has called into question, held more than rhetorical significance for children and youth in wartime St John's.[127] In the sheltered space of the schools – themselves an extension of the world of domesticity – girls assumed warden duties of a kind by ringing the bells that signalled their classmates to head for the basement.[128] Yet they still moved and acted within a space built for children but regulated by adults. The freedoms to wander, to explore, and to experiment that boys so confidently claimed as their own were denied to girls or, in the very least, severely circumscribed.

This is not to say that girls preferred to play indoors, for both girls and boys roamed the city's open spaces. On the eve of the Second World War, the rural outskirts of the city had not yet been swallowed by suburban developments and local children found nature just a stone's throw away. Eileen Collins encountered goats grazing on the hills of the South Side when her father took the family for Sunday walks, while Ann Abraham remembers "running through thistle-fields" with her friends and hiking and cooking meals over camp fires with her fellow Girl Guides: "It was so easy. You were near enough to the country that you could do these activities."[129] When Vicki Cheeseman spent the summers on her grandparents' farm in Topsail, she "could ride the horse down the street to get a drink" after she had performed her household chores. At home in Bishop's Falls, she muses, "There was no such thing as indoors. Summer or winter, you played outdoors." Stuart Fraser, whose father ran a successful farm in the west end of the city, recalls a solitary childhood: "I was very much alone. Not many people around to play with. But I like open spaces and I loved the farm." James Walsh, by contrast, remembers "lots of kids around" in the city's northern outskirts, where land was cheap and children played softball, baseball, football ("they call it soccer now"), and skated in the winter months.[130] Cars were few, everybody walked, and children roamed the streets and explored the rural outskirts far away from the watchful eyes of adults, but usually in groups of friends or, in the very least, with a sibling. Then, as now, there was safety in numbers.

In her moving childhood memoir, *Below the Bridge: Memories of the South Side of St John's*, Helen Porter makes an eloquent case for a world of play that was inhabited jointly by girls and boys. "Here, then, is another way in which the South Side did not conform to the North American standard," she writes, describing how "most of the games we played were totally integrated ... One's status as a player depended more on skill and prowess than on sex." Mostly, however, our interviewees describe worlds of childhood in which the other gender played a marginal role at best. "Girls!" laughs James Walsh. "They were a nuisance, early on. Especially, a buddy of mine who had a sister and she persisted in following us around. I recall he used to throw stones at her, trying to drive her away." "We never had much to do with girls," concurs Norman Crane. "They never went fishing with us. They used to screw up their faces when we'd put a worm on a hook. We were always out in the woods or up the South Side Hills and we were active outdoors."[131]

In the social world of boys, athletic prowess was held in high esteem. As a member of the Church Lads Brigade, David Edwards "was trained for a lot of things – sports, military aspects of drill, games" – all construed as "naturally" boyish activities. "I don't remember girls being quite as active as that," he adds.[132] Joe Prim's world of childhood, as well, revolved around athletic pursuits in which girls did not participate: "I played soccer and baseball, and in the winter I played hockey. Girls did not play any sports. They swim in the summer. I don't know what girls did. I wasn't interested in women then."[133] At home, siblings rubbed shoulders at the dinner table, but even here boys needed to be reintroduced to the world of civility at times, as Margaret Kearney remembers with a smile: "When brother came back from Scout camp, Mother would have to teach him to behave again."[134] Once boys and girls stepped over the threshold of the

RCAF Church Parade on Military Road, heading for the Cathedral of St John the Baptist. Control no. 19790310-316, Canadian War Museum.

family home into the culture of their peers, their social worlds diverged, reconnecting only at the onset of adolescence.

The arrival of thousands of sailors and soldiers in wartime St John's provided boys with a stage on which to enact the rough-and-tumble world of boy culture. Stories of unruly servicemen reached the ears of Patricia Winsor in the tranquility of her home, where her father, a policeman, regaled his family with tales of drunken sailors and soldiers who, once sobered up, began fighting with one another in overcrowded cells "because one was a navy and one a soldier" and "they were loyal to their uniforms." In the social world of boyhood, these figures of lore – and the material traces they left behind – assumed a tangible presence that spoke of danger, physical prowess, and naughty allure. Young Gilbert Oakley walked over to the site of an airplane crash and sifted through the broken pieces: "There were parts of the airplane everywhere, and I picked up a part of an aluminum pipe that had broken off." The boy painted his wartime souvenir yellow and held on to it "for years" afterwards. Meanwhile, in the city's northern outskirts, James Walsh marvelled at the soldiers practising manoeuvres in the countryside nearby his home. "You see them going through the farmland, and going with their rifles, and there was live ammunition all over the place. It's a wonder we weren't killed." Happily ignoring the danger, James Walsh and his friends picked up live ammunition, placed it in tree-holes, and "discharged the bullets" with a nail placed atop a lengthy stick. Both boys began smoking during the war, a "manly" vice facilitated by the platoons of soldiers who littered the streets with cigarette buds. "You could pick them up on the streets," James Walsh recalls. "They were so cheap. They tossed them all over the place." Gilbert Oakley recalls asking an American soldier coming down the hill "for a cigarette and he gave us a cigarette each ... We used to go down to Water Street to pick up cigarette buds and my logic was: if anybody's got TB, they'd be out in the hospital, the sanatorium. And I had two boxes – one with matches, the other one for the big cigarette buds." As recent research has suggested, smoking remained a manly habit well into the 1940s, its puffs of white smoke and distinctive odour demarcating men's and women's spaces and, by extension, the social worlds of boys and girls.[135]

In wartime St John's, boys and men shared social spaces from which girls were excluded. Paul O'Neill and his brother spent hours at the American rifle range in St John's, where the boys collected "the shells that had fallen down. So everybody had a little collection of things from the rifle range." Yet, above all, it was the washrooms that beckoned the youngsters. "They had toilets there," recounts Paul O'Neill, "and we'd love to go in there and read what was written on the walls. As kids, we thought it was marvellous because all these poems were written on the walls by naughty Americans." Thomas Doyal, in turn, "being of an inquisitive age," loved to lurk around the outside perimeters of Camp Alexander to befriend American servicemen stationed in town. "Soldiers being soldiers," he says, "we would be passed chocolate bars the likes of which we had never seen in our lives – O'Henry, Hershey Bars, and Coke in bottles. And, of course, we'd be in seventh heaven and we'd go back day after day." One young soldier grew so fond of the boy that he kept in touch by correspondence, his three letters to Thomas Doyal – dated 30 July 1945, 1 October 1946, and 5 January 1947 – lovingly preserved to this day.[136]

In a self-described "garrison town" in which Canadian and American servicemen peopled the streets, as did Allied sailors of every conceivable nationality, the men in uniform were not construed as dangerous. On the contrary, if we are to believe the indignant writings in the *Evening Telegram*, it was the servicemen who required protection from "children carrying out a persistent campaign of cadging for coppers, cigarettes or various other things. Strangers, in particular the sailors and soldiers, are almost exclusively the objects of these attentions."[137] In his characteristic bluntness, "Spike" – whose pointed columns in the *Evening Telegram* gave a public voice to the American servicemen in town – observed that "there are, definitely too, too many ragamuffins, rascals and pests in general, in the form of small boys, who spoil the time with their everlasting begging. If you don't 'give' you're stuck with them for the afternoon – and if you do – well – you're still stuck." Spoiling otherwise pleasurable outings to St John's Bowring Park, the young lads deserved "a darned good licking," Spike recommended.[138]

The city's young women solicited much favourable social commentary by servicemen stationed in St John's. Kathleen Williams liked to "go along the streets with the girls, two or three girls, and the sailors would be walking on the other side: Hi Red! And the Americans loved their red hair. And I said to my mother, 'I want to dye my hair.' And she said to me, 'What's the trouble?' And I said, 'They call out to me too much.'"[139] Our women interviewees who came of age during the war years recall social outings with Canadian and American servicemen that were sanctioned by both parents and the community. "They were *always* polite, always," says Margaret Kearney. "We used to go to dances at the Royal Canadian Air Force. They put you in a truck and they cart you down there and you dance with the guys and then come home." Eileen Collins recalls that her sister's American boyfriends invited their dancing partners onto the American base, Fort Pepperrell, where "there was fine dining for a very reasonable price ... And the girls who went out with them had silk stockings. They were happy." Vicki Cheeseman, as well, was invited to the base by "a couple of American chaps." "I was always partial to the Americans," she confesses. "It was fun and they were fun. The music was always good. Generally, they had live bands."[140]

Unlike the boys, who had carefree interactions with servicemen, young women internalized the rules of propriety that governed their behaviour at movie theatres, dancing halls, and servicemen's hostels. "My older sister, Mary, worked as a volunteer hostess at the U.S.O.," Frank Kennedy writes in his memoirs, "and every night after work a different serviceman walked her home in the blackout. They never got inside the house, though, my mother saw to that."[141] To guard female virtue, parents and employers enforced curfews meant to shield young women from the moral dangers of the night.[142] Despite these restrictions, women recall a freedom of movement that was palpable. "We had a freedom in the city," marvels Margaret Kearney. "We could walk anywhere in town. We could walk on Water Street in the evening at Christmastime and I never remember any aberrations. As young girls – grade 8 or 9 – we would go to each other's houses and we would walk home, and we would leave their house at eleven o'clock in the evening and walk home and feel safe and not be frightened."[143] Eileen Collins, in turn, recalls the evening she "walked home in the dark with a flashlight," accompanied by two girlfriends. "So we were walking home, the three of us from a later movie. We dropped off Alice and when we got to Rawlins Cross, all the troops were coming out from the airport, the party-goers. They were noisy. And we were scared and we started to run. When we stopped, there was this little sailor ... and he said: 'Girls, if it made you feel any better, I would walk with you.' And he did. And Peg lived on Circular Road – her father was a judge – and there was a dark corner at the end of Circular Road, and we walked down and walked up, and we stood on the street talking for a few moments, and I thanked him ... He walked me home for protection, a little Canadian sailor. He was just so nice."[144]

Much like their younger brothers and cousins, young women knew the city's geography intimately. But while the city's public spaces spelled "excitement" for boys, young women were keenly aware of the threats that might lurk in "dark corners" after nightfall and would apprehensively observe the drunken exuberance of partying servicemen. Even in adolescence, women's freedom of movement differed in kind from the freewheeling exploits of the city's boys. Whereas boys enjoyed the freedom to roam, women cherished freedom from sexual assault.[145]

THE "TRAFFIC PROBLEM"

Prior to the war, children in the country's capital were far more likely to spot horse-drawn carriages or trolleys, making their downtown loop, than automobiles.[146] At a time when the automobile revolution had transformed North American towns, cities, and countrysides, most Newfoundlanders continued to rely on horses, streetcars, boats, and the railway to get around.[147] Cars were owned by taxi drivers or the wealthy, both of whom felt a communal obligation to ferry around their neighbours, a courtesy that local car owners later extended to servicemen stationed in St John's.[148] The streets, rough as they were, seemed safe to the city's children, who did not yet have to compete for public space with trucks or military vehicles. "Most of the streets were unpaved," Norman Crane remembers. He still recalls the "trucks going around, sprinkling the streets to keep the dust down." But, he adds, "There weren't very many cars."[149]

The arrival of American and Canadian servicemen heralded a transformation of public space that youngsters watched in awe. As Patricia Winsor marvelled, the Americans "had all these big tractors, pushing all this earth around. We had never seen anything like it in St John's." Joe Prim, too, recalled the "big, heavy trucks" that transformed previously quiet streets into busy thoroughfares, with motorized "Americans and Canadians going back and forth all the time."[150] Viewed through children's eyes, the American servicemen who marched on the streets, handed out cigarettes, chocolate, and Coke, and cut dashing figures at the boxing ring seemed to be in perpetual motion. "We had the Americans walking around and marching around and driving around," remembers David Baird. "They must have brought in trucks and cars and jeeps, and they all had big, white stars on."[151] The city's children, used to playing on the streets until darkness fell, found themselves jostling for space with motorized vehicles.

Suddenly, St John's, too, had a "traffic problem," as the *Evening Telegram* wrote in August 1941. Neither drivers nor pedestrians seemed inclined to pay much heed to each other. In a series of opinion pieces, "Spike," the American newspaper columnist, dropped his usually lighthearted tone to warn "drivers of motor vehicles, especially of military transportation, that in a few days, driving will be even more hazardous – due to the fact that school will be out. Children, even more than usual, playing in the streets. And children at play are apt to dash thoughtlessly out in the front of your machine – from nowhere in particular."[152] In the months to come, Spike repeatedly admonished drivers to slow down and exert caution, an appeal that fell on deaf ears. As he observed in June 1941, "drivers of military vehicles, both American and Canadian, are still running wild. Too fast, and seemingly without regard for the rights of others."[153] By the end of the year, the "traffic situation in town" remained as perilous as ever. As Spike noted in his column, "There are still more careless and thoughtless drivers around here than we've seen in many months. And not all of 'em are Newfoundlanders either. Some of our own drivers are far too reckless – drive much in excess of speed limits and risk other people's lives too freely."[154]

It was pedestrians who paid dearly as drivers sped over cobblestone streets, and the number of fatal traffic accidents soared. In June 1941, eleven-year-old Maud Bragg "was killed instantly on Saturday afternoon on Quidi Vidi road, east of the General Hospital, when she was hit by a bluish green motor car which sped westward at a fast clip ... the motor car hit the child and hurled her at a distance of twenty or thirty feet in front of her mother. The car proceeded without stopping."[155] A year later, a truck overturned off the street nearby Waterford Bridge, smashing down on two brothers, aged seven and thirteen, who had been drinking from a well near the roadside. The younger boy died instantly; the older later succumbed to his injuries in St Clare's Hospital.[156] In December 1942, seven-year-old Edna Stevens was hit by a car "going at a terrific speed" while walking with her aunt, Stella Kirby, on the sidewalk. The little girl, the *Evening Telegram* reported, was found dead underneath the car.[157] The fact that each accident was chronicled, as were the many near misses, suggests how quickly and dramatically the rules of the streets had changed. Within the brief span of six years, St John's was dragged from the age of horse and carriage into the automobile era.

In response to these new hazards, local opinion-makers sought to regulate and limit children's access to public space for the sake of their own safety. The new "geography of danger," to quote the human geographer Gill Valentine, emphasized the threat posed by speeding vehicles, the need for social and legal sanctions to rein in reckless drivers, and the importance of banning children from the city's streets.[158] In the summer of 1941, a "Traffic Safety Campaign" instructed drivers in proper traffic etiquette and lobbied for stop signs at dangerous intersections in the vicinity of the Newfoundland Hotel.[159] Newspaper reports lauded a courteous female driver who showed the good sense of letting a child and a dog pass on a street where "[t]oo many of the drivers we've seen would have simply blown their horns and dashed madly past, letting the kiddie fend for itself."[160] Meanwhile, the *Evening Telegram* published children's ditties that encouraged safe road practices, such as the entry submitted by Freddy Pike on 3 Pleasant Street: "Stop! Look! And Listen! Before you cross the street! Use your ears and then your eyes, and then use your feet!" Yet such tame measures proved insufficient, as vehicles continued to crowd formerly quiet streets and drivers stubbornly refused to slow down. In exasperation, Spike recounted "several narrow escapes of school children, going to and from school, where drivers of motor vehicles simply ignored the kiddies and drove merrily on their way."[161] However, newspaper reports also reveal the reluctance of pedestrians and children to yield the public space of the streets to motorized vehicles.[162] Just as drivers routinely ignored red lights or traffic signals by uniformed traffic-control officers, so, too, did pedestrians.[163]

By 1942, public discussion shifted to the creation of new, sheltered spaces in which children could play safely. Newspaper editorials now encouraged youngsters to restrict their play to the spatial confines of parks and playgrounds. "So imminent are the risks run by children sliding over streets and roads used by motor vehicles," wrote the *Evening Telegram* in January 1942, "that the practice should be prohibited." In condemning one of the most popular winter pastimes of the city's children, the paper pointed out that "[n]ot an incline in the city is any longer safe for sliding. Winter traffic has become general and the number of vehicles in use has very considerably increased as the result of the various defence activities. For a child to shoot down over a hill intersected by thoroughfares along which conveyances of various kinds are constantly moving is nothing short of courting disaster." As the *Evening Telegram* advised, parents, police, and municipal authorities should work towards an "arrangement" by which the "healthy and invigorating pastime" of sliding could be enjoyed without incurring "unnecessary risks."[164] Foreshadowing the public rhetoric of later decades, streets were declared dangerous and the city's children invited to play in "proper" children's spaces that were carefully supervised by adults. The *Evening Telegram* warmly endorsed the efforts of the Children's Playground Association, which, for over twenty years, had sought to "provide the children with recreation in safety." As the writer reasoned, "With the immensely increased use made of the streets by motor vehicles, the risks of accidents to children are greater than ever before, and this is likely to be more apparent after the schools close. Further, the streets are too dirty to be used as playgrounds. A hand or knee grazed by a fall on such a surface might mean blood poisoning or lockjaw, complaints with which no chances should be taken. Those dangers are far less likely in the grass-covered parks."[165] Yet, we may add, the "grass-covered parks" provided none of the excitement offered by the city's unregulated public spaces. As the oral history interviews at the core of this study vividly attest, St John's children were not easily dissuaded from using the city itself as a playground. They preferred the allure of "tent city" at Camp Alexander, the bustle of the harbour, and their public interactions with servicemen to the formal "recreation facilities" that the Children's Playground Association so valiantly promoted.[166]

CONCLUSION

Focusing on childhood memories of the war, this chapter has examined what human geographers call "the child's 'ecology,' that is, the physical environment and 'social space' in which children grow up."[167] Put simply, place mattered in the shaping of the social worlds of childhood. In the seaport city of St John's, children came of age in a "war zone," where the Battle of the Atlantic left visible scars – both in the haunting absence of sailors whose ships had been torpedoed by German submarines and the damaged boats that floated in the harbour, having narrowly survived an encounter with the enemy. The submarine attack on Bell Island, the sinking of the *Caribou,* and the sirens that called through the night during air-raid drills reminded children of the reality of the war. "Almost nothing surprised because we expected anything to happen at any time," James Walsh recalls.[168] In a society stratified by class and an education system organized along denominational lines, the shared social experience of the war provided common narrative ground. Regardless of their family's social status or religious affiliation, children marvelled at the convoys assembling in the harbour, looked with trepidation at the red sky that signalled the burning of the Knights of Columbus servicemen's hostel, or shifted uneasily in their seats as they watched newsreels about the Battle of Britain, for "these were actual pictures of people being killed, buildings collapsing, the air-raid police running around in Britain with the stretchers – not for young eyes," as Stuart Fraser muses.[169]

Laced with emotion, childhood memories of the war are striking for their sense of immediacy. For Helen Porter, the feeling of pure joy is forever tied to the moment her cousin Harold "put down his duffle bag" in the lower hall, "looked up and grinned," having been missing for weeks after his ship, the HMS *Firedrake*, was torpedoed by German submarines. "I won't attempt to describe what happened next," Porter has written. "Sometimes, when I'm trying to define happiness, joy, bliss, relief, I remember that night. But there are no words."[170] Over six decades later, our interviewees still recall the tastes, smells, sounds, and sights of wartime St John's, the senses acting as agents of memory.

The recollections of our interviewees evoke the gendered worlds of childhood, allowing us to reconstruct how girls and boys moved through the city's public spaces. The culture of boyhood that saw boys freely roaming through streets and over fields sharply contrasted with the spaces that girls identified as their own, namely the home and the school. It was in the family home that the worlds of childhood and the ordinary adult world connected – fleetingly so for children who flourished in the culture of their peers, intimately so for others who were embedded in the rhythms of family life.[171]

Most tragically did the two worlds connect when speeding automobiles – driven by the urgency of wartime – struck children walking on sidewalks, drinking from roadside wells, or riding their sleds on the city's steep streets in wintertime. In contemplating the social costs of the traffic problem, local opinion makers recommended restricting children's play to parks and playgrounds. In merging with adult-regulated spaces, children's spaces were to be stripped of their freewheeling, experimental and daring characteristics – safer, yes, but also infinitely more boring. Not incidentally, this vision of public order remained elusive during the war years. And yet these early attempts to shield children from the dangers inherent in public spaces resonate with contemporary debates on children's uses of public space. As Gill Valentine has stated, since the 1970s, children in much of the Western World have been "losing their freedom to be in public space both during the day as well as at night," with "traffic squeezing children out of public space."[172] Here, then, is an unlikely cost of the friendly invasion. In accelerating the automobile revolution in wartime St John's, the trucks, tractors, and military vehicles that invaded the city between 1939 and 1945 irrevocably altered children's geographies, making it ever more costly to roam the city's streets and, over time, gradually curtailing children's "freedom in the city."[173]

4

Rethinking the Friendly Invasion

STEVEN HIGH

Left HMCS *Dauphin* gun shield art. "The RCMP officer riding the U-boat is her Commanding Officer, Lt. Cdr. R.A.S. McNeil, who was a former member of the RCMP Marine Division." Gary Green, *A Guide for Some of the Gun Shield Art and Ship's Badges of the Crow's Nest Officer's Club* (St John's: Crow's Nest Military Artifacts Association, Newfoundland).

Right Gun shield art on board the HMCS *Dolphin*. Photo 006-2 from family photograph album of Marjorie Ferguson, Halifax.

Wartime was looked back on by Newfoundlanders as the American era, years when they saw first hand the swaggering largesses of the country to which thousands of their relatives had gone in search of jobs.

Wayne Johnston, *Baltimore's Mansion*

To almost everyone, then, compared with America the Beautiful, the Canadians were like vichyssoise: cold, half French, and difficult to stir.

John FitzGerald, *Newfoundland Quarterly*

The popularity of the American soldiers and sailors stationed in wartime St John's was genuine and long-lasting. Virtually everyone we interviewed remembers the morning of 29 January 1941 when the *Edmund B. Alexander* squeezed through the Narrows into St John's Harbour and docked on the South Side. Despite the cloudy and cool weather, turning to heavy rain, it was a big event.[1] Cecil Hutchens, a young soldier from Iowa, was on the troopship. What he remembers most was the strangeness of the Newfoundland landscape. He had called it the "last place in Hell," but like so many others, he soon fell in love with a Newfoundland woman and came to call St John's his home.

The arrival of the giant troopship marked the supposed beginning of the "friendly invasion" of Newfoundland and Labrador in the Second World War. Its basic storyline has been told and retold so many times that it is familiar to most Newfoundlanders. The construction of U.S. army and navy bases at Argentia, Stephenville, and St John's brought jobs and prosperity to the island. Wages at the bases were good and the hours steady. Business boomed on Water Street. Yet Newfoundland's love affair with "the Yanks" is perhaps best symbolized by the large number of marriages that resulted. Estimates range widely, but some say 25,000 Newfoundland women married Americans over the time that the bases were operational (two of the three U.S. bases closed in the 1960s).[2] All of our interviewees spoke of sisters, cousins, and friends who moved away with their new husbands.

By contrast, the *other* wartime invasion of Newfoundland has received little attention and almost no fanfare. Nobody remembers when the Canadians arrived in St John's. There was no *Edmund B.* to mark their arrival. No plush bases. No celebrity system. Until recently, no one has tallied up the number of Newfoundland women who married Canadian soldiers, sailors, and airmen during the war. The wartime prosperity is rarely associated with the Canadians. Yet they were on the island in comparable numbers. They seemed to slip in undetected during the night. "I don't remember them arriving," recalled Louise Lambiase. "I remember them being here." Many of the interviewees had difficulty telling us where the Canadians were stationed in the city. They seemed to be all over. In effect, the American impact on the country has been measured in social, economic, and cultural terms, whereas the Canadian presence has been understood in political or strategic terms or as a negative counterpoint to the American.[3]

If nationalist historians like John FitzGerald are to be believed, the streets were filled with drunken Canadian soldiers and sailors who destroyed property and behaved badly. While Newfoundlanders "instantly accepted the handsome, well-dressed young Americans, all boasting their own teeth, much to the cha-

American troops leaving for Newfoundland, c. 1941. PF-306.752, Maritime History Archive.

The *Edmund B. Alexander*. PF-306.749, Maritime History Archive.

grin of the jealous Canadian troops already stationed in St. John's," the Canadians were "despised."[4] We are told that Canadian military vehicles tore up city streets and that their dependants contributed to the housing shortage. Canadians erected tarpaper shacks, while the Americans built modern buildings in a pleasant suburban environment. For some, Canadian actions during the war appear anything but altruistic. From its "lair" on Circular Road (Canada House), FitzGerald writes, the "Canadian wolf" sought to devour the Newfoundland lamb for its resources and strategic location.[5] The other invasion has thus been cast as an unfriendly one by Newfoundland nationalists, who believe that the country was railroaded into Confederation in 1949.

As a mainlander, I enter the fray with some trepidation. There are of course many reasons why Newfoundlanders would have preferred the coming of the Americans, reasons relating to the fishery and out-migration to New England. But there is little doubt that the bitter aftermath of the Confederation debates has provided the lens through which many Newfoundlanders look back on the war.[6] After 1949 every wartime move by the Canadians has been read for signs that Canada sought to annex Newfoundland and Labrador. My purpose for writing this chapter is not to ascertain whether union with Canada was a good thing

Church Parade of the RCAF Women's Division, 3 June 1945. Control no. 19790310-136, Canadian War Museum.

or not, or even whether it was fairly arrived at. The nationalist critique of Britain's failure to restore responsible government during the war, or immediately thereafter, resonates with me. What interests me here is that nationalist anxiety during the war and thereafter has profoundly shaped how the war is publicly remembered in Newfoundland. Anti-Confederates have a stake in depicting the Americans alone as the friendly ones. As a result, the social and economic dimensions of the Canadian invasion have never been fully explored. "No one knows what the Canadians have done," lamented Joe Prim in his interview.

This chapter argues that the myth of the "drunken Canadian," like the "poverty myth"[7] of the 1930s, was a product of Newfoundland nationalism and the different legal regimes governing the servicemen and servicewomen of the two countries. Were the Americans that much more popular than the Canadians? Did Newfoundland women favour the Yanks in love and marriage? Not so long ago, I would have answered yes to both questions. I have spent ten years studying the 99-year-leased bases in Newfoundland, Bermuda, and the British Caribbean and have found considerable evidence that the Americans were well-liked, at least in Newfoundland (race complicated the American occupation of the other "base colonies").[8] Our oral history interviews, however, have forced me to reconsider the deeply ingrained assumption that American servicemen were more popular than the Canadians.

The interviews reveal a wartime story that has been overshadowed by all the attention given to the American friendly invasion, one that is centred on the visiting Canadian forces. The project's interview guide was heavily weighted towards the Americans, yet many of our interviewees shifted the conversation to the Canadians. One person after another told us how their families invited Canadian servicemen into their homes for a meal or a hot bath. Older women spoke of their volunteer work at the Caribou Hut, the Knights of Columbus Hall, and the Red Triangle. Younger women told us how they liked to dance the jitterbug with Canadian sailors in these locally run hostels. Life-long friendships were forged in these encounters. It may be counter-intuitive but Newfoundland women proved just as likely to marry Canadian servicemen as to marry American ones. In fact, almost everywhere we went we discovered a deep reservoir of respect and goodwill for the Canadian sailors who were fighting and dying in the cold waters of the North Atlantic. What is particularly interesting about the interviews is that even those people who expressed the most hostility towards "the Canadians" as a group would, a few moments later, tell us that their families invited Canadian servicemen home for dinner. The ugly Canadian was always an abstraction in these interviews; it was nothing personal.

How, then, is wartime St John's remembered? What do people remember most, and why? In trying to answer these questions, we find that people's memories linger in the everyday realities of living in a city at war: a harbour crowded with warships, battle-damaged merchant vessels lying idle, the exhausted survivors of torpedoed ships, the blackout, searchlights piercing the night skies, volunteer work, entertaining the troops, and bases under construction. While enlistment and the civil defence measures imposed on the city loomed large in the pages of the St John's *Evening Telegram*, the newspaper was silent on the subject of ships in the harbour. Wartime restrictions required that this be so. This wartime precaution has contributed, I think, to a tendency by historians to emphasize the bases on land rather than the ships at sea. This chapter reminds us that the usual distinction made by North American historians between the home front and the war front is largely irrelevant in wartime St John's. The city and its residents were in the thick of it. St John's was both home front and war zone.

A CITY AT WAR

The sacrifices made in the first war were on everyone's mind in 1939. Newfoundland had lost "the cream of the crop" at Beaumont Hamel and was left a devastating legacy of absent fathers and broken men.[9] Ann Abraham's mother once told her that "there wasn't a day that would go by when she was still a girl at school [in the first war] when somebody would come and need to go home because her brother had been killed. So there wasn't a family that wasn't touched then." Nurse A. Maude Brown's father came back from the war on crutches. His leg never fully healed, making it difficult for him to farm. He "spent his life doing what he could around the yard." Others encountered this legacy while walking down Church Hill in the 1930s and seeing veterans with wooden legs – the wood in those days was painted an ugly green.

Thousands of Newfoundlanders nonetheless volunteered to fight. In an effort to avoid what happened to the Newfoundland Regiment in the First World War, the Commission of Government dispersed recruits in the Royal Navy, Royal Artillery, Royal Air Force, and in the Canadian armed forces. Thousands of others joined the Merchant Marine and the forestry unit. One interviewee after another listed the family members who went off to war and paid tribute to the ones who never came back. Ann Abraham described the familiar pattern: "The boys, the men, when they got to grade 11 would all go down and volunteer right away, at seventeen, as soon as they got out of school. It was felt: This is your duty, to fight for your country and to preserve freedom for your children and grandchildren." Helen Porter observed that her cousin Harold and two of his brothers joined up, as did "just about every eligible man on the South Side." This patriotism was not universal, as several interviewees told us that they never gave enlistment a moment's thought. This opinion was expressed most forcefully by lawyer James J. Halley: "I wasn't so God damn fool to get involved in one of England's wars. I was too Irish."

The departure of the various contingents of volunteers was accompanied by a great deal of fanfare. Interviewees described the crowd-lined streets as the first contingent of volunteers marched down Long's Hill to the waiting ship. After waving goodbye to loved ones, residents relied on the BBC (rebroadcast on VONF radio) for their news. "Everyone was around the radio," recalled Daisy Hiscock. "Once the news came on," Gilbert Oakley added, "there was no talking. You were not allowed to say a word." The radio connected St John's to the world.[10] Families with fathers or sons overseas were particularly hungry for information. Care packages were sent and letters trickled back. Louise Lambiase remembers sending a package to her brother each month. It was stuffed with food tins, bottles of whisky, and other treasured items. She was always amazed when she heard that the package had arrived safe and sound.

The oral narratives contain clear evidence of the war at sea. Submarines prowled nearby waters, and one fired several torpedoes towards the mouth of the harbour. Daisy Hiscock, who lived alongside the Narrows at Fort Amherst, remembers the roar of the explosions. The Canadian soldiers stationed near her home made commemorative rings out of the metal salvaged from one of the torpedoes. The war hit home in late 1942 with the loss of two ore carriers on 5 September and another two on 9 November, off Bell Island in nearby Conception Bay. The *Caribou*, a passenger ship that plied the waters between Sydney, Nova Scotia, and Port-aux-Basques, Newfoundland, was lost on 14 October 1942 with great loss of life. This difficult period was capped in December with the

Left "Shipwrights gun shield art." The painting hung in the Crow's Nest Officers' Club. Crow's Nest Military Artifacts Association, Newfoundland.

Right A Red Cross vehicle with blackout blinders on the headlights, *Scenes of St. John's*. Photo by Lieut. Alice Ducile Talman, control no. 20010159-002-4, Canadian War Museum.

devastating Knights of Columbus fire that killed nearly one hundred.[11] Rumours circulated that it was sabotage, and some believe it still.[12]

As Paul Collins details in chapter 2, St John's Harbour began the war as a defended port but grew into a sizable naval base supporting the destroyers and corvettes that escorted convoys across the Atlantic. The number of Canadian warships in the harbour varied from year to year and from day to day. In 1943 there were typically fifteen warships in port, St John's served 143 escorts that year.[13] The Canadian corvettes were "mostly named after rivers," says Fraser Ellis. "I remember there was the *Skeena* and the *Esquimalt* and Indian names, the *Haida*." People called them the "Indian boats" in those days. Several interviewees remember riding in the "bumboats," the small fishing boats that ferried people from ship to shore or back again for ten cents a ride.[14] Some seamen felt "fleeced" when the price of passage jumped to fifty cents or when the boats were suddenly unavailable, stranding sailors on shore.[15]

The harbour has "always been the origin and life-blood of the town," noted Eileen Collins. It was crowded with ships of every kind.[16] Joe Prim remembers the warships, "all in grey," at anchor or tied up four or five abreast. "Merchant ships and navy ships, the whole harbour was full with them." George Ledrew accompanied his father to the waterfront as a child. During the day, he told us,

"I would walk down Water Street, go down one of the old wooden piers ... to see the congregation of merchant ships and warships in St John's Harbour. The harbour was full of ships." Occasionally an interviewee provided a panoramic view of the harbour – David Baird, for example:

> Then there were a lot of buoys in the harbour. They had three or four rows of great big steel buoys of about ten feet in diameter in the harbour and on each buoy they put merchant ships and ships generally and you sometimes [saw] three or four on each one. And I can remember with my father going up to the Lower Battery – as far as you could go – at five o'clock and looking at the ships. You probably count forty or fifty merchant ships of different sorts and navy on the South Side ... and then you come down the next morning and there wasn't a ship left in the harbour ... And lots of little boats running around, picking people up and of course a lot of these boats were run by local fishermen and everybody who had a boat would be running around, bringing people to shore.

St John's became a port of refuge for damaged ships and a safe haven for thousands of survivors. Some of these survivors had been adrift in the Atlantic for many days before being picked up by a passing ship and brought to the port. According to historians Douglas Baldwin and Gillian Poulter, "many of them were near death, or had to have their arms or legs amputated."[17] One group of fifty-three men, for example, was picked up off the coast of Iceland by a Royal Navy ship after thirteen days in open boats. Mona Wilson, the assistant Red Cross commissioner in the city, reported that after they arrived in St John's, forty-six were hospitalized and eight had to have their feet amputated.[18] Wilson estimated that 500 survivors were landed in St John's in 1941 and 5,000 more in the next eighteen months: "Sometimes there was only a handful, other times entire crews of 45 or 65 men, or crew members of several torpedoed ships – 200 or more. The biggest emergency of all was when 1,000 men were landed at one time."[19] The harbour thus represented the sober realities of the war. "The reality was there," noted James Walsh, not somewhere far away on the other side of the world.

One of the most frequently mentioned wartime stories that we heard concerned a merchant vessel that limped into the harbour, badly damaged, with a gaping hole – by all accounts – passing right through it. Several interviewees saw small boats go right through the ship. James Walsh was one of the many people who watched this spectacle with fascination. Fraser Ellis likewise remembers seeing the ship when he looked out a window of the Holloway School, where he attended the sixth grade: "Some of the Battery fishermen would literally sail through it." Two interviewees paid twenty cents each to be taken through the hole. Gilbert Oakley described what he saw: "There was one that had a lot of paper on it and there was a torpedo that went right through it. And the fishermen used to call them bumboats and they would bring sailors to the boats, tied in the middle of the harbour. He brought us and we toured the boat." Still a child

"Two of the 'O' Boats at HMC Dockyard at St. John['s] Nfld." Family photograph album of James Nicol Walkey, Halifax.

at that time, Daisy Hiscock remembers being rowed through the hole. It "felt eerie," she said.

Among the great variety of merchant vessels that called on St John's during the war were the celebrated "cattle boats" that supplied residents and the visiting forces with fresh beef. Schoolboys such as Gilbert Oakley would go down to the harbour to watch the unloading of the cattle at Neal's Wharf and see them "drive them up" Water Street. Sometimes, if the cattle were destined to go out of the city, they would be loaded onto trucks. Oakley and his enterprising friends would go down to the corner of Cochrane and Water streets and collect the coal that had fallen on the ground from passing trucks. "We would scrape it up, putting it into a bag and sell it," he recalled.

Besides the harbour, what stood out for most people about the wartime city was the blackout.[20] The city's civil defence organization called for several one-night blackouts in 1940 and 1941 before implementing a blackout for over a fortnight in early 1942. In preparation, a series of informational memoranda were published in the city's newspapers explaining the precautionary measures to be taken against attack.[21] How could a city of 50,000 people and some 8,000 buildings be concealed from sight? Civil defence officials told residents what they must do. Small shop owners were instructed to build a small interior porch with a screen to prevent light from escaping into the night.[22] Residents were taught to blacken their homes, drop sand bags on fire bombs, and designate the safest room in their home as the "Air Raid Living Room."[23] Automobile owners, in turn, were told to cover their headlights except for a small semi-circle aperture, two inches wide and an inch deep.[24] A standard headlight "mask" was later distributed. There was a constant and widespread fear of incendiary bombs igniting the densely packed wooden buildings of the city.

The first night of the extended blackout was not entirely successful. Colonel Outerbridge, head of the city's civil defences, flew over the city in an American airplane. Looking down through the bomb bay of the airplane, he discovered that automobile lights were still far too bright and that the waterfront was a blaze of light. Clearly, the list of exemptions from the blackout regulations was too long.[25] The continued lighting of the St John's waterfront and defence installations in an otherwise blacked-out city was obviously counterproductive.

A general blackout, described as the "real thing" in the *Evening Telegram*, was imposed on 6 April 1942 for the duration of the war, although it was partially lifted in August 1943.[26] The newspaper coverage of the story makes clear that this was the moment when the war truly came to St John's: "The lights are going out on the Avalon Peninsula, just as they did two and a half years ago in Europe, for the duration of the war, and we will soon be spending our nights in total blackness."[27] With this decision, residents were required to take additional precautionary measures. To avoid the use of red tail lights, automobile owners had to paint their bumpers and mudguards white and reduce their speed to just fifteen miles per hour.[28] Owners of motor vehicles protested the new rule: "Something akin to a hue and cry has been raised over the ruling that all civilian cars – whether or not they are used during blackout hours – have to be painted with a white band to make them more easily distinguishable."[29] Safety concerns and the need to cover tail lights trumped these voices of dissent. Street poles, hydrants, and fire alarm boxes were also painted with a white stripe. With no street lights and only minimal use of automobile headlights, it could be hazardous to drive at night. Dr Nigel Rusted admitted to avoiding night driving whenever possible during the blackout.

The darkness made an impression on our interviewees. "The streets were dark," recalled Louise Lambiase. So dark, in fact, it was sometimes difficult to walk on moonless nights. You "could hear footsteps and that was it," said James Walsh. Street lights were ordered turned off and every store had double doors. Often, the inside door would not open until the outside door was closed. Everyone recalled the shutters that covered house windows so that no streak of light would show. "My dad made shutters out of canvas, sail canvas, and it had wing nuts," recalled Daisy Hiscock. Hospitals had to be locked down too. Nurse A. Maude Brown recalled that this was a time-consuming and onerous job. It was also difficult on sultry summer nights for the newborn babies in the maternity ward. Dr Rusted recalled that the air could not circulate with all the blinds closed.

Guarding the gate (Harbour Grace). Control no. 19990033-012-1, Canadian War Museum.

The blackout was strictly enforced by hundreds of air-raid wardens who patrolled the nighttime streets. Some residents remember them shouting from the darkness if they saw a light; others remember a polite knock on the door. David Edwards and his father, wearing arm bands that read "ARP" for Air Raid Precaution, walked through the neighbourhood checking on the windows of their neighbours: "We had a flashlight with half the lens painted over so it wouldn't throw much of a beam ... We went around our street and two or three streets in the area, checking lights shining from windows ... And I remember the next day my father saying: 'Now, I have to go to Mrs Brown and I have to go to Mrs Whoever, tell her that last night, her lights were shining.'" These friendly reminders sometimes proved embarrassing. Patricia Winsor remembers the time when the wardens knocked on her family's door, and her father was a policeman and warden.

Newfoundland Constabulary, c. 1941. Gary Browne, Jacquey Ryan, and Stanley-Saunders Collection, Crow's Nest Military Artifacts Association.

Air-raid wardens were also responsible for dousing fires in case of an air raid. Houses were equipped with stirrup pumps and a bucket of sand. Sirens were installed in three or four places, and the city was divided up into four divisions, twelve zones, and thirty-six sections. The air-raid precaution system was tested through regular drills. Paul O'Neill described what would typically happen: "During these air-raid drills, every street had a stirrup pump put on there by the government. And there was a big sign with an 'S' put on there so that people would know it was the house with the stirrup pump." For practice, bundles of "splits" doused in kerosene were set alight in the street and the men used the stirrup pump to put it out. "It was pretty exciting for us," recalled O'Neill.

The searchlights that lit up the night sky were another feature of civil defence remembered by a number of interviewees. Stuart Fraser's father had the nerve-wracking job of testing the city's air defences:

> Father was out flying a British Hudson over the Atlantic, trying to fly in to see whether he could be detected. This was a test exercise. The defence strips were Canadian, for the most part, and they had searchlights and sound detectors to listen to the sounds of aircraft. So he would go out thirty miles from Torbay and then try to get back. And he would be flying back over the city. And my mother was terrified because the ground crew was not being notified that there was going to be an exercise. But if any plane came in over their airspace, they had to identify it. I can remember going out in the front yard – I did not know anything was going on – my mother holding my hand as if she was going to break it. And you heard this plane, they had to – I didn't find this out until many years afterwards: when they held the plane in the searchlight for so many seconds with the RCAF ... then all the searchlights of St John's would come up straight and you see them all around like that [indicates a circle of lights with his

hands]. It was a friendly aircraft. It was okay. My mother was terrified that they were going to misidentify the aircraft.

Once back on the ground, Fraser's father instructed others how to identify incendiary bombs.

Rationing came late and was limited. Tea was rationed first, and restrictions were later placed on sugar, coffee, and a handful of other products. Historian Peter Neary notes that ration books were not distributed in St John's until May and June 1943. There were also shortages of fresh fruits and other foodstuffs during the war. As a result, almost nobody interviewed had much to say when asked about rationing. Residents "had to go easy on everything," recalled Louise Lambiase. "We had a little bit of rationing," noted Ann Abraham, "but it was only sugar and tea and we had four children in the house, none of whom was able to drink tea. So mother was able to share lots with her friends." Others were more critical of the measures taken. William Pepperrell Abraham, the son of the Anglican bishop of Newfoundland, told us that food rationing in the city was nothing compared to the rationing in England.

The American consul general, George D. Hopper, would have agreed. In his dispatches to Washington, Hopper dismissed the Newfoundland government's initial attempt at rationing, which was based on the "honour system" and required no coupon books or other administration. When Commissioner John Puddester went on the radio in December 1942 and asked listeners to reduce their habitual consumption of tea by half, the result was much buying and hoarding of tea. These timid measures drew a great deal of comment from St John's newspapers as well. People wondered why Newfoundland did not implement the kind of comprehensive rationing that prevailed on the North American mainland and in Great Britain. It was "really an insult, what we called rationing," recalled William Abraham.

If people's memories did not linger on rationing, they particularly remember the many other ways that families contributed to the war effort. The Women's Patriotic Association, for example, knitted socks, sweaters, and hats for incoming survivors of torpedoed ships and for Canadian naval ratings.[30] "Everybody knitted for them," recalled June Cook. Louise Lambiase remembers that some women brought partially knitted socks to church and continued to knit during the service. Women and children also packed toiletries into duty kits, or "ditty bags" as they were known, for servicemen. Schoolchildren were asked to prepare a kit for an individual serviceman. In return, they would be told his name and perhaps receive a letter of thanks. While adults bought Victory Bonds, children bought "victory stamps" at ten cents apiece, collected scrap metal for the war effort, and gathered newspapers. Abraham recalled being told by his father that ten cents of his fifteen-cent weekly allowance should be spent this way. At Bishop Feild School, boys collected magazines and took them to the parish hall, where they would be rolled up and tied into bundles. The Church of England operated a small boat that would take these magazines out to ships anchored

The York Theatre, *Scenes of St. John's*. Photo by Lieut. Alice Ducile Talman, control no. 20010159-002-12, Canadian War Museum.

in the harbour. The bundles were then thrown on board, where they would be immediately pounced upon.[31]

HAVING CANADIANS OVER FOR DINNER

The many harbour stories told in the interviews emphasized the courage of the Canadian sailors. Thousands of residents responded to public appeals to open up their homes and their hearts to Canadian sailors and to the survivors of torpedoed ships.[32] Jean M. Murray and her father regularly brought three or four naval ratings home with them on Sundays. They were offered a hot bath and given a warm meal. Many other St John's families did the same. Jean's sympathy for these men was apparent throughout her interview: "They had such dreadful experiences at sea." Margaret Kearney spoke of the physical toll that the war took on the sailors:

> There was a young man from somewhere in Quebec ... Mother met him when she was serving over at the Knights of Columbus and told him to come to the house. When the Corvette was in town, Ted came to our house about every other evening. The last time Ted came in he must have come through the front door – it must have been evening – and he sat right down in the den and did not speak to anybody. He just sat there. And mother stayed in the den with him – there was a fire in the den, and somebody made him a cup of tea and he still did not speak. We learned later that there had been a terrible battle out in the Atlantic and that the Corvette had picked up as many survivors as it could but it couldn't [get them all].

Another naval rating invited for dinner was so exhausted that he was quickly tucked away in bed, where he slept for the next twenty-four hours. For her part, Louise Lambiase remembers that one of the young men that her family befriended this way later lost his life when his ship was torpedoed. Other memories were not so disheartening. William Pepperrell Abraham, for example, shared with us a funny story about the first time his father, the Anglican bishop of Newfoundland, invited a group of servicemen over for dinner. There was a bureau in St John's, located at the Caribou Hut, where you could ring up and arrange to have some servicemen delivered for supper. Apparently, the placement people had sent officers instead of enlisted men, as his father was an important figure in town. The evening was less than successful, as the British officers had other engagements and the evening ended early: "After that father specified what ratings."

A special effort was made at Christmastime to invite sailors over for a home-cooked meal. Patricia Winsor and her father, a member of the Newfoundland Constabulary, would go to the Caribou Hut on Christmas Day and pick up their guests: "They put out bulletins on the radio. Anybody willing to take a soldier, or sailor, one or two for Christmas, report to the Caribou Hut and they would be assigned somebody. And then, Christmas morning, my father and I and my brother would walk down to Caribou Hut. I remember it as being as high as three [guests]. And we would take these gentlemen ... home on a bus." These acts of generosity went both ways. The soldiers and sailors who were invited into private homes always brought something, maybe a box of chocolates or bubble gum for the kids.

Residents living on the South Side and in Fort Amherst felt the full weight of the Canadian occupation. Daisy Hiscock remembers how the war isolated Fort Amherst. Residents now needed a military pass to go to town, and armed guards would escort them through the military areas. "If you forgot your pass," she recalled, "we didn't get home." Canadian soldiers and sailors were constantly coming and going from the gun batteries at the end of the road, at all hours. It was as though the Hiscock family lived on the base. Helen Porter has similar memories about growing up on the South Side. She remembers the road crowded with servicemen and the ground strewn with condoms. These particular wartime narratives have a claustrophobic feel to them. Yet Daisy Hiscock's best friend married a Canadian serviceman, as did a woman "up the road." Hiscock and her neighbours never saw much of the Americans during the war, only Canadians.

The bonds of love and friendship that bound many St John's residents with Canadian sailors extended to Canadian soldiers. Several interviewees forged strong friendships with the men from the Royal Rifles of Canada, an army unit deployed early in the war. Fraser Ellis told us that his father had eight to ten soldiers from the unit over for Christmas dinner. Several other interviewees made a point of mentioning the Royal Rifles by name. This is significant because the unit was subsequently sent to reinforce the troops in Hong Kong, where it was quickly decimated by the Japanese. These headlines hit many Newfoundland families hard. They knew these men. "You don't forget these things," Ellis said.

These memories of Canadian wartime courage and sacrifice, however, contrast with recollections of an unwillingness on the part of some to engage in battle. In 1942–43 a decision was made to rotate English-speaking army units out of Newfoundland and replace them with French-Canadian regiments, whose personnel were drawn mainly from home defence conscripts who had not signed on for general service. This decision has hardly been acknowledged in the historical literature, but it was repeatedly mentioned in the interviews. While several interviewees insisted that there was no special animosity towards French Canadians, others looked down on these reluctant soldiers. Jean M. Murray spoke for many when she noted that Newfoundland was "overseas" for them, but "it wasn't the same at all." They "put in a very comfortable time here." At a minimum, the language barrier made French-Canadian soldiers appear more foreign than American GIs.[33]

It was largely because the Newfoundland government refused to allow the United States to deploy African-American units on the island that American servicemen in Newfoundland were perceived as mixing better with residents than the Canadians. Few interviewees remember seeing black servicemen during the war.[34] What they do remember, with the help of books and articles published since, is the story of the shipwrecks involving the *Truxton* and the *Pollux* on the southeast coast of the Burin Peninsula. Frank J. Kennedy, a press photographer during the war, related how the oil-covered survivors were taken to buildings in the mining town of St Lawrence and cleaned up with scrub brushes and hot water. One unconscious survivor awakened to find a woman frantically scrubbing him and reportedly said, "Lady, this is as clean as I get. I'm a black man." As the story goes, he was treated "royally" by the community and he never forgot "how good the Newfoundlanders were."[35] The moral of the story, of course, was that Newfoundlanders were free of colour prejudice.[36]

Without wishing to detract from the heroic efforts of those who saved lives or the fair-mindedness of the rescuers, the archival record suggests otherwise.

Left Inside the Knights of Columbus building/hostel on Harvey Road. Photo # 01-11-018, City of St John's Archives.

Right Able Seaman Levis Leboeuf, RCN Volunteer Reserve, 10 November 1942. No. 3525706, Library and Archives Canada.

Not only did the Newfoundland government oppose the deployment of large numbers of African Americans but black sailors stationed at Argentia were also outcasts, socially isolated and largely restricted to base. According to one May 1943 report from the U.S. Navy, the eighty black navy personnel stationed there had nowhere to spend their leisure time, as Jim Crow segregation had taken hold in neighbouring Placentia. The author of the report urged his superiors to do something to "make their existence a little more tolerable."[37]

We have some indication of how the colour issue played out in the city thanks to the editors of the *Evening Telegram*. On 10 June 1941, the newspaper ran an editorial under the defiant heading "NO COLOUR BAR HERE," condemning the proprietor of a beer saloon who had repeatedly refused to serve a black customer. Refusing to serve black servicemen in order to placate some other customers, the editor declared, defied the "principle that applies throughout the British Empire that privileges are not restricted by class, creed or colour." Such a vile practice, the editor insisted, was not going to take root in St John's, where "the British Flag still stands for certain principles, one of which is equal rights to all under the law." The editorial ended with an appeal to Newfoundlanders to "be British" and remove the colour bar.[38]

A HOME AWAY FROM HOME: WOMEN'S MEMORIES OF THE CANADIANS

The story of the Canadians' invasion of St John's is inextricably tied to the Newfoundland-run hostels that served them. The "tremendous influx" of servicemen forced the city of St John's to "devise the necessary means to provide for and care" for them in their off-hours. "It was one of the biggest jobs that St

John's ever had to face," reported the editor of the *Evening Telegram*.[39] The Canadians and the Americans generally had their "own places" to go to.[40] So too did local men and women. Newfoundland men spoke of interacting with uniformed servicemen on the streets or in their family homes. A few of them worked at the bases. One played sports with visiting servicemen. None of the local men interviewed had much to say about the dance halls or hostels that catered to the visiting forces. As these places served the visiting forces, Newfoundland men were not welcome at the Caribou Hut, the Knights of Columbus hostel, the Red Triangle, or the United Service Organization (USO) club. Yet Newfoundland women spent a great deal of time volunteering in these establishments or dancing there. These four hostels therefore loom large in the wartime stories of local women. "They [servicemen] needed looking after, so to speak," recalled Jean M. Murray.

The Caribou Hut "exemplified the gallant spirit of wartime St. John's," says historian Peter Neary.[41] Opened in December 1940, it was the first local hostel to serve visiting soldiers and sailors. Over its first year, the Caribou Hut hosted a remarkable number of activities, including fifty-nine concerts, ninety-seven movies, seventy-nine sing-songs, fifty-two dances, and twenty party nights. And the canteen served 274,909 meals. "These dances and parties provide a splendid opportunity for the men to meet the right type of young ladies in a good environment," the manager reported.[42] The hostel also had a men's club with a writing, reading, and games room.[43]

The "lady volunteers" of the Women's Patriotic Association were integral to the operation of the Caribou Hut. Jean M. Murray, a teacher, has vivid memories of her time volunteering in the canteen at the Caribou Hut, serving "bacon and eggs, bacon and eggs, bacon and eggs." In a crunch, the canteen could serve 1,400 meals in four hours. There were an estimated 350 volunteers in any given week, organized into three four-hour shifts each day. Murray volunteered three shifts per week: "You'd come home [and] sometimes you'd be so tired you wouldn't know if you'd make it." You had to do it, she insisted. She eventually did all of the scheduling for the Caribou Hut, although a YMCA man was in charge of the entire operation. Somebody else was in charge of the 250 beds on the upper floors. At this point in the interview, Murray recalled with laughter one of those stories that brings a place to life. The management had received several complaints about the cleanliness of the pillows upstairs. So she was asked to go up and investigate: "I sailed up. And I got the dear lady who was in charge of the linen and so she says, 'We are short on pillows. I got a way of getting around it ... The first night I put the pillow slip on. The next night I turn the pillow over. Third night, I turn the pillow slip inside out. And fourth night, and I turns it over. That way, I can get four nights' ... I went to the 'Y' man and told him [laughter]."

David Baird's mother also worked at the Caribou Hut. Like many other middle-class or elite women, she used to go down to the Hut once or twice a week to cook for the sailors. These women brought respectability to the hostel

Left Unidentified merchant seamen, September 1942. PA-116455, Gerald Milne Moses, Library and Archives Canada.

Right Survivors, 1942. PA-037424, Gerald Milne Moses, Library and Archives Canada.

and acted as comforting mother figures for the servicemen. The Caribou Hut must have been "semi-respectable," Ann Abraham mused, or her mother would not have gone there. She thought that these older volunteers "probably set the tone too because they [sailors] remembered their own mothers: 'Oh, here's Mum giving us a cup of tea.'"

If the older women's memories are of volunteer work in these contact zones, those of younger women likely focus on the dances. Kathleen Williams lived near the Caribou Hut, so it was only natural that she and her friends would dance with the sailors there. Occasionally, a group of American soldiers would peek in, but they never stayed long – "They would not feel invited, feel comfortable." She would go to the Caribou Hut on Thursday evenings and to the Knights of Columbus for the barn dance most Saturday nights. She liked the Canadians. Asked why, she said that they were "same as ourselves." Her parents allowed her to dance, but she had to be home at a good hour. She later married a Canadian.

"I was interested in the navy," recalled Helen Blundon. She remembers going to Saturday night dances at the YMCA and volunteering, and she showed us her official identity card for the "Canadian YMCA Volunteer Concert Party." A list of about a hundred young women was drawn up, and each had to be "checked out, to make sure." Once vetted, they were given free memberships, whereas the "boys" had to pay twenty-five cents to enter. There were concert parties and stage shows, including *Show Boat*. Everyone had a marvellous time. "We were very friendly with the boys," recalled Helen. "I was never at home." She spoke for many when she added, "It was a terrible time but I am glad I never missed it."

Women's relationships with American servicemen gave them special access to the base and to wartime luxuries. During her interview, Helen Porter advised us that "it would be nice if you could talk to somebody a bit older than me, because

Civilian workers at Fort Pepperrell. Photo #01-065-005, City of St John's Archives.

going down to the base was heaven. They wanted women there. They could not have dances without women." Louise Lambiase and her girlfriends were invited to dances on the *Edmund B. Alexander* while it still acted as floating barracks, and later they attended dances and watched movies on the base. "When *The Song of Bernadette* came out, a lot of us were invited to the movies to see it" there, recalled Margaret Kearney.

Most of the male interviewees spoke of the base as a place of employment or as a place seen at a distance. Occasionally, Newfoundland men were able to gain access to the base for leisure. As a boy, R.J. Gallagher loved the Americans "because they had lots of money." He had access to Fort Pepperrell "because of the connections with the base commander who married my sister. We had passes to go in and out the gate." Continuing, Gallagher remembered that on Thursday nights the base had a steak special for one dollar: "You could buy a steak with all the trimmings for one dollar. And all the prices were well below what they were in St John's. So that's why there were so many Newfoundland girls and Newfoundland boys – not drinking it up because we were too young to drink, but we could have the specials, all kinds of foods, for practically nothing. And to get into the movies, it was five cents at the base theatre. This is where Frank Sinatra did one of his shows."

The city's elite were frequently invited to cocktail parties and dances on the base. They were also invited just to play tennis.[44] Even so, several of the men we interviewed were keenly aware that women had special access to the base. Paul O'Neill, whose parents rented out a basement apartment to a U.S. soldier, convinced the man to take him to see the movies in the American theatre: "And, of course, all the girls got to see the movies down there."

DRUNK AND DISORDERLY?

While Newfoundland women had lingering memories of the social clubs and the U.S. base, Newfoundland working-class men did not. They had not been welcome at these places. Their leisure-time memories turned instead to the streets and to the licensed restaurants and movie houses of St John's. Joe Prim remembers when LeMarchant Road, in the "higher levels" of the city, was the main drag. "Everybody seemed to congregate on LeMarchant Road at nighttime. There was nothing else to do. There was only a few more streets in St John's – Water Street, Duckworth Street, and LeMarchant Road. There wasn't too much to do in the nighttime." Downtown streets were "filled day and night," recalled James Walsh. It was "rough and tumble" in parts of the downtown but not as bad as in Halifax.

Within days of the arrival of the *Edmund B. Alexander*, there was a sense that the city of St John's had suddenly become a "garrison town." An editorial in the *Evening Telegram* on 3 February 1941 told the paper's readers that, with local, Canadian, and American military servicemen increasingly visible, it was more important than ever to preserve "good order."[45] The newspaper reflected the moral panic felt by some residents. In June 1941 it warned readers of the growing disturbance in the streets and in licensed restaurants.[46] The docket of the Magistrate's Court was full of drunk and disorderly cases, both civilian and military. A public notice published in the newspaper indicated that the government was considering a number of proposals to restrict the sale of alcohol. All three of the propositions targeted women. It would be prohibited to sell wine or beer to women, or to men accompanied by women, after seven o'clock in the evening or altogether, and women were to be prohibited from entering a licensed restaurant.[47] Clearly, the spectres of drunken servicemen and disorderly women were fused into a single social problem threatening the social order of the city. The dearth of taverns meant that servicemen often purchased bottles of alcohol from the government store or from a bootlegger, which led to public drinking and broken glass.[48] The imposition of the blackout in 1942 fed many people's worst fears.

Newfoundland men sometimes resented the foreign servicemen who competed with them for the attention of young women. In a common refrain, James Walsh noted that "local guys didn't have money to flash around." Nor did they have access to cheap booze, silk stockings, cigarettes, and other duty-free goods. These frustrations sometimes festered until they exploded in fist fights. Frank Powers confessed that he was one of the "local toughs" who picked fights downtown with visiting servicemen. The fights began in the bars and "juke joints" soon after the Canadians arrived in the city. Powers recalled that the Canadians had big boots and weren't afraid to use them in a tussle. He described these Canadians as older and "more experienced" than "us young fellows." The Canadians were not very popular with Powers and his friends. "I could fight pretty good," he said. "I could look after myself." When the Yanks arrived in 1941, it was "more of the same." He was involved in one fight with a U.S. serviceman that turned nasty when the man almost bit off his finger. It just hung there.

Women rarely made mention of the nighttime streets of wartime St John's. The war appeared to limit women's freedom of movement in significant ways, and the streets were places of hidden danger and immoral behaviour. Margaret Kearney told us that her sense of freedom of movement in the city was curtailed in the war: "The soldiers, being soldiers, made you think twice at night. They were out drinking at night."[49] It is hard to know how class defined women's mobility in the wartime city. Certainly, women – whatever their social status – spoke of their changing attitudes to the nighttime streets in much the same way. "We didn't feel quite the same about being alone at night," recalled A. Maude Brown, a public health nurse. Eileen Collins told us this story:

> I can tell you one lovely incident with a Canadian sailor. My own little incident and I will always be grateful to him. People went around town as usual: went to the movies and walked home in the dark with a flashlight. And we weren't afraid. So we were walking home, the three of us from a late movie. We dropped off Alice and when we got to Rawlins Cross, all the troops were coming out from the airport – the party-goers, they were noisy. And we were scared and we started to run. When we stopped, there was this little sailor with his tight white and his collar and he said, "Girls, if it made you feel any better, I would walk with you." And he did. And Peg lived on Circular Road, her father was a judge. And there was a dark corner at the end of Circular Road and we walked down and walked up, and we stood on the street talking for a few moments and I thanked him ... We had a great chat. He walked me home for protection, a little Canadian sailor. He was just so nice.

Most of these women came from middle- or upper-class families. Would women of more modest backgrounds share the same understanding? It is difficult to know. June Cook always felt safe in her downtown neighbourhood. She noted that people would tell her not to go up Gower (where she lived), but she thought nothing of it.

The inclination to blame the Canadians for unruly behaviour was particularly evident in an archival file evocatively entitled "Complaints Regarding the Conduct of Canadians."[50] This file contains a large number of complaints of fights, indecent public acts, and colourful language. Despite its title (it was likely labelled years later), many of the disturbances actually involved American and Newfoundland servicemen. In March 1942 train conductors reported that they were "continually having trouble with men of the Services getting drunk on trains and causing no end of trouble for the conductors, besides delaying the trains."[51] In one instance, twenty-four artillery men were accused of being badly under the influence of liquor. Apparently, one of these men, an intoxicated sergeant, tripped while boarding the train at one of its stops, striking his head. He was knocked unconscious. The others picked him up and placed him

"British Submarine P554."
Family photograph album of
James Nicol Walkey, Halifax.

in the smoking room, thinking he was dying. A medical doctor was called, and after an examination, the sergeant was declared good to go. Later in that trip, a navy man had his face cut and an eye injured from flying glass when one of the artillerymen broke a window pane. General Page, commander of the Canadian troops, adopted a defensive attitude when Commissioner of Public Works W.W. Woods asked him to respond to the complaint, saying that he had recently seen an American NCO (non-commissioned officer) get quite drunk on the train.[52] In the meantime, the Newfoundland Constabulary dispatched a series of detectives on cross-country train journeys to ascertain how bad things really were. These reports are fascinating and merit a glance.

Sergeant M. Cahill left St John's on 30 March bound for Port-aux-Basques. He found "very few" signs of drinking. After Humbermouth, he noticed two American civilians "well under the influence" but the journey was otherwise quiet. District Inspector W.F. Case took the same trip two weeks later and painted a very different picture. Two members of the Canadian Provost Corps, or military police, did everything in their power to curb misconduct "but their numbers were inadequate." Case was incensed at the rough language used by servicemen travelling in the same compartments as women and children. It seemed to him that at times Canadian sailors "had control of the train." The immorality of these men was evident at nightfall when "most of the lights and in some cases all the lights in certain second- and first-class cars would be turned off by members of the forces and their conduct when with females can be better imagined than described." He referred specifically to the "disgusting" conduct of two soldiers seated with a woman in a first-class car: "All lights were eventually turned out,

Posted to Newfie. Watercolour by Canadian war artist Paul Goranson, 19710261-3199, Canadian War Museum.

and one of the soldiers and the girl, after being covered up with a soldier's coat, to all appearances were in the act of sexual relations." He called on the government to segregate servicemen from the travelling public.

A report filed by C. McCormack in September 1942 introduced another dimension to the disorder. A woman, already "known to police," was seen acquainting herself with a group of American soldiers, and "she became familiar with them. In one instance I noticed that she and an American soldier were about to enter the ladies toilet but when I walked in their direction she moved off and returned to her seat."[53]

Overcrowded conditions and the conduct of servicemen continued to be an issue in 1943, causing the conductor to complain about a "very rough lot of Newfoundland Navy men," about fifty in number, who got very drunk and began to fight amongst themselves in Coach 15. "It got so bad," he reported, "that the women left the car." One double window and two smaller windows were smashed. Meanwhile, in Coach 28, five military policemen had their hands full with a group of sailors who smashed two additional windows. After things quieted down a little, the conductor went into a second-class car where he encountered a Canadian soldier standing on the platform with an army rifle pointed at the front door of the coach: "I asked him what he was doing with the gun and he said he was on guard. I took the gun from him and put it in the baggage car and then reported the matter to an Officer. He had the soldier placed under arrest right away, and when searched they found 47 loaded shells with him."[54]

These few examples from the Newfoundland Railway remind us that although disorderly behaviour was not limited to Canadian servicemen, the perception that they were primarily responsible was exaggerated. Even the governor claimed that the behaviour of U.S. personnel was "exceedingly good, particularly compared to the Canadians." This viewpoint exists to this day. Joe Prim, for example, responded in the following way when asked to compare the Canadians and Americans:

> Canadians were not really accepted at all. The Americans were. They had the money. They seemed to get along better with the population than the Canadians. I don't know of any particular reason, but there used to be a lot of trouble – and mostly all the fights that started down there were Canadians. Canadians troops were involved and Canadian sailors ... Americans did not get into as much trouble. They had a different way about them. They fitted in with the people. And there were a lot of Americans living around town, with families, and they seemed to fit in and they were always open to the population. They married a lot of Newfoundlanders. They were accepted by everyone.

Several of our interviewees emphasized that Newfoundlanders cheered on the Americans in various contexts. Paul O'Neill, for example, told us about a wartime brawl that erupted in Bannerman Park between Canadian and American troops: "There were fights between Canadians and Americans. I remember one night in Bannerman Park, a fight broke out between the Americans and the Canadians. And we all rushed over – we kids – and the Americans and Canadians were punching each other and banging each other until the police arrived. It was a big melee. And we were all cheering up the Americans. 'Come on, Yanks. Come on, Yanks. Kill them. Kill them.'"

What is interesting about O'Neill's account, like so many others, is that the animus towards the Canadians is heard alongside a story of Canadian servicemen being welcomed into the family home for supper. The same pattern is evidenced in the interview with Stuart Fraser. Moments after telling us (with some relish) that the Canadian troops on parade were received in stony silence by the crowds lining the street, in contrast to the U.S. soldiers who were met earlier with wild cheers, Fraser shifts gears and tells us how his mother had Canadian servicemen over for supper most every Sunday: "She just felt these guys deserved a home-cooked meal ... Some of them spent quite a few meals in our house. Some of them kept in touch long after the war. Some of them became friends."

Did the Americans, in fact, mix with Newfoundlanders better than the Canadians? Our interviewees appear to be evenly divided in their responses. Paul O'Neill spoke for many when he told us that the Canadians were more "stand-off-ish" than the Americans: "Canada was a country we knew little or nothing about ... We had nothing to do with it. Wanted nothing to do with it." The Americans, he continued "just came in and relaxed and had a good time and took part in all the things we had going – like the regatta." Others, however, agreed with one of our interviewees when she asserted that the "Canadians were nearer to us and I think that was why we were nearer to them." The Canadians, she believed, "were more friendly" than the American servicemen. June Cook agreed: "I think the Canadians were still considered your neighbour and your friends, whereas the Americans were coming from another country."

Why has disorderly conduct been associated with the Canadians and not the Americans? One reason comes immediately to mind. With the Leased Bases Agreement, the United States enjoyed exclusive jurisdiction over all criminal cases occurring within the leased areas and concurrent jurisdiction over all other cases involving its servicemen. How concurrent jurisdiction would work was unclear, with the result that there was a great deal of conflict between the U.S. forces and the commissioner for justice and defence, L.E. Emerson. It was agreed that Newfoundland would hand over to the U.S. forces all cases of common drunkenness, disorderly conduct, and minor breaches of the Highway Traffic Act involving members of the U.S. forces.[55] There were fourteen cases of this nature pending against U.S. soldiers at the time of this agreement in August 1941, six months after their arrival.[56] No doubt hundreds of servicemen were subsequently handed over to U.S. military police. The number of serious cases involving American servicemen tried by the Newfoundland courts was thus quite small. Only forty-three U.S. soldiers or sailors served time in HM Penitentiary during the war.[57] The Canadians, without the legal standing of the U.S. bases agreement, had to live with Newfoundland custom and law. As a result, they were paraded before the Magistrate's Court and had their crimes publicized in the newspaper. Anyone reading the daily newspaper was therefore left with a distorted picture of what was actually happening.

The other factor that shaped the public's association of public drunkenness and violence with the Canadians was also related to the Anglo-American Leased Bases Agreement. Secure in their fenced-in leased base on the outskirts of St John's, the Americans could better regulate military-civilian relations. American officers were gracious hosts, and they invited the city's elite to social functions on the base. Those residents lucky enough to be invited to Fort Pepperrell

The Royal Navy anti-submarine escort carrier HMS *Smiter* (D-55) in St John's. This ship was laid down as the USS *Vermillion* but was assigned to the RN under Lend-Lease on 23 June 1943. Photo by William A. Ramsay, control no. 20030014-073-5, Canadian War Museum.

recall eating food that was otherwise unavailable to them. Dr Nigel Rusted, for example, fondly remembers eating "thick beef" at the base. He could still taste it. The generosity of the Americans is also warmly remembered. At Christmastime in 1943, for example, they brought four hundred orphaned children to the base for a party with carols and a sumptuous meal with "all the trimmings."[58] After dinner, the children were entertained with movie cartoons and a visit from Santa Claus, who gave each child a gift. Otherwise, few residents of St John's stepped foot on the base in wartime. It was a place apart. The Canadians, in contrast, did not have large blocks of land or long-term leases.

If the U.S. base at Pleasantville loomed large in the interviews, the Canadians at Lester's Field (army), Buckmaster's Field (navy), Torbay (air force), and on the South Side (army and navy) have been obscured by time. Nearly all of the Canadians' buildings were within city limits, often in highly congested areas.[59] Fraser Ellis remembers the Canadian Army facility at Lester's Field as "not very impressive." Indeed, they were "tarpaper shacks. They were just tarpaper, with strips on the top. No cement underneath; just poles." The Canadians came to

Gun play. Photo 0041 from family photograph album of John Cecil Stevens, Halifax.

be associated with shoddy construction during the war.[60] They put up buildings quickly, whereas the Americans "built for [the] long term." That Canadians did not put the extra money into equipping their troops was a constant refrain in the interviews and in the writings of historians. Bernard Ransom cited wartime observers who had said that the naval base's "curiously impermanent air" was akin to a "travelling tent show."[61]

The sharp contrast between the Canadian and American bases was described most vividly by James J. Halley. "The minute the Yanks came in, we were flush," he recalled. The Yanks had bigger trucks, cigarettes for ten cents a pack, liquor, and paid better wages. The Canadians were "poor in comparison." Throughout the interview, Haley repeatedly referred to Canadian servicemen as "lower class" and "rough." For him, Fort Pepperrell was like a "five-star hotel." The Canadians "didn't really have bases." Indeed, Haley concluded, "Yanks were prosperity. Canadians were scruff." What is left unsaid, of course, was that in 1941 Canada was at war, whereas the United States was still building peacetime bases and had won a 99-year lease to the property.

MORAL PANIC AND VD CONTROL

The dark side of the Americans' friendly invasion has been largely overlooked or at least minimized in the public memory of the war years. Most of our interviewees were children during these years, and thus they tended to be silent on the weighty issues of sex, prostitution, and venereal diseases. A few interviewees mentioned seeing signs of prostitution. James Walsh, for example, recalled teenage girls "making themselves available to the servicemen." There might have been a "scattered madam" around, but he didn't know for certain. When asked if the town had a red light district, the interviewees usually pointed to the area that had formerly been a downtown slum but had been cleared to make way for the new city hall.

In turning to wartime newspapers and archival records, we found that the friendly invasion unleashed a moral panic in St John's that resulted in the wholesale labelling of Newfoundland women of modest means – particularly women coming to St John's from coastal communities – as promiscuous.[62] A March 1943 editorial in the *Evening Telegram,* succinctly entitled "Undesirables," proved typical: "There are girls and women in the community whose behaviour makes them a disgrace to their sex. They are on the prowl for their prey at all hours of the day and night. Promiscuous in their 'loves' they brazenly accost men in the public streets, concerned with little else but fleecing those who are foolish enough to be taken in by their wiles."[63]

The climbing number of "illegitimate" births in the city and the skyrocketing birth rate overall provided a pretext for the regulation of "delinquent, disorderly and diseased females."[64] The moral panic was perhaps most evident with respect to the control of venereal disease. The *Evening Telegram* could not hide its disgust when it called sexually transmitted disease a "repulsive menace."[65]

The archival records of the U.S. Army provide an important point of entry into the subject of venereal disease control. The operating assumption in these matters was that local women were the source of infection. The army's weekly case reports asked several key questions. Who was the "source" of the infection? Had the soldier used a condom? Had he been drinking? Did he know the woman? The resulting case history identified the race and age of the soldier and the time of infection. The second part of the form asked the name or nickname of the alleged contact, her address, race, age, height, weight, eye colour, hair colour, place of employment, type of contact (friend, pickup, streetwalker, brothel, call girl), place of exposure (home, hotel, cab, auto or trailer, brothel, other), name and address of place of exposure, and the condition of the patient at the time (intoxicated, drinking moderately). To escape punishment, the U.S. serviceman had to cooperate in the identification of the woman. One report indicated that full identification of the "source" of infection was made in 100 cases, partial identification in 34 cases, and no identification in 39 cases. The final section detailed the "procurement history."[66]

Most sexual partners were identified as "pickups," young women engaged in casual sex. One of the cases involved two army privates who went into St John's in search of a good time in July 1944. They contacted a taxi driver outside the USO club and asked him for the names of some women who might "entertain" them that night. The two men were driven to a private residence where they picked up two young women. No money was exchanged. Many of the other cases involved servicemen picking up women on downtown streets. According to Lieutenant Colonel E.L. Kehoe, Medical Corps, "the cheap grade of liquor [found at 'bootleg joints'] seems to arouse them sexually. After doing considerable drinking they have no trouble contacting 'loose' women who seem to be roaming freely as 'pick-ups.' Apparently these women do not charge for their 'favours.' Many of the taxi drivers in town act as 'pimps' who know the names of available women and who are willing to drive solders to their 'hang-outs.' They also know the cheap 'dives' where soldiers can rent rooms after they pick up these girls." According to Kehoe, there were no organized houses of prostitution in St John's, only a "fairly large number" of "poorly educated girls" from the "poorer districts" who made themselves readily available to men in uniform.[67]

Historian Peter Neary has argued that because Newfoundland's administration of public health was "male dominated," it considered women the "primary carriers of infection." This is a tempting argument, since men *did* identify women as the source of their disease. Yet there may be more at work. H.M. Mosdell, Newfoundland's senior public health official, had lobbied for a "lock hospital" for years. In October 1940 he informed the commissioner of public health that the public was blissfully unaware of "how appalling is the prevalence of this disease in our midst."[68] He urged the Newfoundland Commission of Government to create a "place of detention" for the perceived sources of infection. But what is interesting here, particularly in light of what happened later, is that he recommended that diseased seamen and not local women be detained. "As in any other public health connection," he wrote, "the infection must be traced to its source." The source, in this instance, was identified as the foreign men flooding the city. With the coming of the U.S. Army to St John's, the search for the source of infection took an about-turn, and army venereal-disease-control officers began tracing the infection of servicemen back to civilian women. This U-turn reflected the bifurcated nature of VD control in St John's, with the visiting forces treating male servicemen and the Newfoundland authorities treating the women for the most part.

In the absence of organized prostitution, virtually all young Newfoundland women of modest means were suspected sources of infection. This tendency was evident when female food handlers employed at Fort Pepperrell were required to get a note from a medical doctor attesting that they were free of syphilis or gonorrhea.[69] The consul general's requirement that Newfoundland women applying for U.S. visas be likewise tested provides additional evidence of this generalized bias. The United States and Canada also strongly lobbied the Newfoundland government to create a lock hospital for women where it could enforce treatment.[70] Reflecting its punitive function, the new hospital would be operated by the Department of Defence.[71]

The sexual double standard appeared in virtually every health survey conducted by the U.S. Army during the war. These lengthy reports, several of which have been reproduced in the journal *Newfoundland Studies*, denigrate the moral standing of Newfoundland women. St John's women, we are told, were a promiscuous lot. In one exaggerated report, U.S. captain Daniel Bergsma claimed that a "large proportion" of unmarried women had "no effective inhibitions to non-marital sexual intercourse."[72] To make his point, Bergsma described a sexual free-for-all where the "least inhibited persons copulate[d] while lying on the grass beside the road" and the "more conservative" went "behind bushes, trees or houses; into alleys between the dwellings." Wartime St John's was presented as a den of immorality and social disease. The circle of blame thus extended far beyond professional prostitutes to include "pickups," roughly defined as those women who have sexual intercourse with more than one man. The sexual double standard that prevailed in the war produced a situation where women were either pure or impure, virgins or whores.[73]

How bad was the problem? The rate of infection at Fort Pepperrell in 1942 and 1943 hovered between 14 and 18 per 1,000, peaking in November 1943 with nine new cases (or 31.28 per 1,000).[74] Although the actual numbers of cases of venereal diseases were small, the U.S. Army in Newfoundland had the highest rate of infection in Eastern Defence Command, which comprised Iceland, Bermuda, and the eastern seaboard of the United States. Major General Brooks, the commanding officer, was intensely embarrassed by this fact, and he launched a full-scale assault on venereal disease within his command.[75] Yet the rate of infection among Canadian army and navy personnel stationed in St John's was considerably higher. In 1942 the Canadian Army recorded a rate of 60 per 1,000 and the navy a rate of 41 per 1,000, dropping to 32 and 26, respectively, in 1943. By 1944, the rate of venereal diseases among Canadian servicemen had plunged to 8 per 1,000.[76]

Without statistical data, it is impossible to know the full extent of VD in the civilian population of St John's. Newfoundland's VD control officer reported that the walk-in clinic in St John's treated 194 cases of syphilis and 93 cases of gonorrhea in 1944. Of these, 162 cases were new. Newfoundland's lock hospital "admitted" 90 patients that year. What thus began as a "protective fear" of female sexual vulnerability metamorphosed into the accusation that Newfoundland women were promiscuous or opportunistic. This perception would have a profound influence over the U.S. Army's wartime marriage policy.

MARRYING YANKS

The notion that Newfoundland women were dazzled by the wealth and style of American servicemen has become a commonplace in academic and popular writing about the war years. Newfoundland women supposedly preferred the Americans over the Canadians because of their money. It is still said in St John's that the American servicemen showered local women with chocolates and silk stockings. Unlike the Canadians, the Americans were more interested in sex than violence. In her published memoirs of the war years, Helen Porter wrote the following: "The Americans ... wore their hair shorter than the Canadians ... [their] faces were boyish and healthy and, if you could believe Mom and Aunt Viley, they all had good teeth ... They were loud and brash ... but they weren't especially rowdy and they seemed more interested in sex than violence ... The Canadians we weren't very fond of, at least the Canadian soldiers ... They appeared to drink a lot and fight a lot ... The Canadian sailors were all right though."[77]

Many of the interviewees had similar perceptions. "The Americans are bigger, broader, and had more money – it's as simple as that," Margaret Kearney insisted. The Americans were "all young. They were all lively," Louise Lambiase laughed. They were also "more wealthy" than the Canadians. "They bought some [gifts] for my sister Mary," recalled Margaret Kearney. "They were always polite, always. We went out with them once or twice and that was it." Picking up this theme, Eileen Collins noted that "there was fine dining for a very reasonable price [on the U.S. base]. And then, they had a PX [post exchange] where the ordinary soldier could buy anything. And the girls that went out with them had silk stockings. They were happy."

If first impressions were everything, Newfoundland women might not have given the U.S. soldiers the time of day. Upon their arrival in St John's, the soldiers on the *Edmund B. Alexander* were wearing heavy winter parkas and fur hats. It was the "first time I have seen a parka," noted Gilbert Oakley. They were "all going around with their hoods on and didn't know what to make of us and I could only see their face." Once they discarded their parkas, Newfoundlanders were much more impressed with the look of their uniforms. These guys were "beautifully dressed," recalled Margaret Kearney. "They had snazzy uniforms," agreed Eileen Collins. Almost everyone favoured the American uniform over the Canadian. For Helen Porter, the U.S. Army uniforms were "very sharp, very well fitted. Lovely caps."

By contrast, the Canadians had "more baggy pants and [the] Newfoundland militia would look even worse." Even young boys took notice. R.J. Gallagher told us that "when they [the Americans] went out on a parade, they would be all dressed to kill, the Yanks. But the Canadians were shabbily dressed." Fraser Ellis agreed: "Canadians wore mostly old heavy wool, olive drab, khaki uniforms; very uncomfortable stuff ... Not dressy. Clunky boots. When the Americans came a year later, they were dressed much [more] 'dressy.' They had more money. They looked like, how shall I say, they were paid better, dressed better." The Canadians "didn't seem to measure up."

Blacked-out headlights, c. 1942. Mary Noseworthy Hamlyn Collection and Hubert Short, Crow's Nest Military Artifacts Association.

During the war years, the United States Army in Newfoundland exhibited an extraordinary preoccupation with the marriage issue. Its policy changed constantly. Before March 1942, enlisted men wanting to marry Newfoundland women simply had to have the permission of their commanding officer.[78] This was freely given, since marriages in Newfoundland were rarely complicated by race, as was the case at the other 99-year leased bases in Bermuda and the Caribbean. This requirement was rescinded by War Department Circular Number 21, issued on 18 March 1942, only to be re-established on 22 June in the same year. On 17 November, Newfoundland Base Command (NBC) prescribed a ninety-day cooling off period once the couple had applied to be married. A soldier wanting to marry applied to the post chaplain, who then met with each party separately. The parents or guardians of the woman were required to write to the chaplain, expressing their opinion. A physical examination followed. If the soldier did not wait the prescribed ninety days, he was subject to court martial.[79] Between November 1942 and February 1943, fifteen servicemen requested that the ninety-day rule be waived owing to pregnancy.[80] This number represented 40 per cent of all applications for marriage during this period.

The rules tightened further on 11 February 1943 when the Newfoundland Base Command declared that marriages approved by "moral necessity" would no longer allow the serviceman the privilege of living off base or give his wife access to duty-free goods. A little over a week later the U.S. Army issued yet another bulletin explaining to personnel that marriage did not automatically provide a Newfoundland-born woman U.S. citizenship or the right to enter the United States. In fact, the bulletin declared that the U.S. consul general would only issue immigration visas to those wives with no criminal record and of "good moral character." The woman was required to complete a physical examination to ensure that she was not afflicted with a "dangerous contagious disease," the reference of course being to venereal diseases. The bulletin warned that Newfoundland women risked becoming stateless, as they would lose their Newfoundland citizenship upon marrying an alien. It was also noted that Newfoundland law did not permit couples to divorce. The next day, the NBC required that couples applying to marry take a Kahn or Wasserman test.[81] Finally, on 18 October 1943, permission to marry non-American women was denied altogether.[82]

The prohibition was strictly enforced, even in cases of moral necessity. Men who married without permission were subject to court martial. Despite the heavy hand of the Newfoundland Base Command, a small number of U.S. servicemen married in violation of army orders. One soldier was court-martialled in 1943; he was sentenced to one-month confinement and fined seventy-five dollars. Pri-

Avalon taxi, *Scenes of St. John's*. Photo by Lieut. Alice Ducile Talman, control no. 20010159-002-13, Canadian War Museum.

vate Carman Gill, of the coastal artillery battery, was sentenced to two and a half years hard labour for leaving the base without permission to get married on Christmas Day 1943.[83] This sentence was heralded by Hopper, who complained that most of the other sentences were for no more than four months, which was not sufficient to act as a "strong deterrent." There were two cases of desertion by U.S. servicemen who married their Newfoundland sweethearts and did not want to be sent back to the United States. Still others, after being transferred back to the States, returned to Newfoundland for a short visit to marry their girlfriends. They were therefore no longer subject to disciplinary action from NBC. Major General John B. Brooks protested that their return undermined military discipline and respect for army regulations, but to no avail.[84]

The dizzying number of directives issued by Newfoundland Base Command leading up to the prohibition, a step not mandated by the War Department in

Washington, raises the question: why? If the military's concern over the issue was not motivated by the fear of racial mixing, as was true elsewhere, what was the problem? The prohibition on marital unions was justified on military and sociological grounds. Major General John B. Brooks firmly believed that the restrictive measures were necessary in order to increase military efficiency and "overcome the handicap of divided allegiance on the part of the soldiers." The flurry of directives was thus largely a result of Brooks having taken over command of the U.S. Army in Newfoundland. Yet he received considerable support from U.S. consul general George D. Hopper, who viewed the prohibition as a "wise" and "constructive" move considering the "types" of undesirable women he thought were marrying American soldiers.[85]

The U.S. consul general believed that Newfoundland women married Yanks in order to profit from the "liberal allowances" offered U.S. citizens. He reported that there was a "noticeable increase" in the number of marriages soon after the U.S. Congress increased the allowance paid to service wives. These allowances, he continued, encouraged "local girls and their families" in their search for prospective husbands. That the Americans enjoyed a significantly higher standard of living was made clear in his reports back to Washington. While an average "outport family" earned $150 to $175 annually before the war, a soldier's wife received $660 per annum and another $264 for the first child.

Restrictions on wartime marriages between U.S. soldiers and local women served to hold down the number of marriages between American men and Newfoundland women to a fraction of what is commonly believed. In fact, George Hopper reported that there were only 350–400 of these marriages between January 1942 and April 1944. By contrast, Canada never prohibited its servicemen from marrying Newfoundland women. Canadian officers, while worried about venereal disease, generally approved servicemen's requests to be married. As a result, the number of Newfoundland women who married Canadians likely surpassed the number who married Americans during the war.[86] Historians Malcolm MacLeod and Brad Penney counted the number of marriage announcements in St John's newspapers over an eleven-month period and found this to be true.[87] They also found that 61 per cent of the Canadian servicemen named in these wedding announcements were sailors. It is significant that none of the interviewees recalled (or ever knew of) the U.S. prohibition on marriages, even with some prompting. The public memory of wartime marriages, encapsulated by the National Film Board documentary film *Yanks for Uncle Sam,* has thus served to silence this story.

BUILDING THE BASES

By contrast, the ascendancy of North American tastes, habits, and values in wartime Newfoundland was apparent to everybody.[88] Looking back, Louise Lambiase saw a wartime shift in the origin of consumer goods from England to Canada. Citing the example of children's clothing, she spoke of how her family had little choice but "to buy Canadian instead of ... European goods." This shift

South Side barracks. Photo by William A. Ramsay, control no. 20030014-074-3, Canadian War Museum.

was viewed with distaste, as Canadian goods were dismissed as "not near as good as English goods." She continued: "We [were] always British. We always bought English stuff."

The single best indication of the sea change underway, however, could be found on the country's roadways. At the outset of the war, Newfoundlanders drove on the left-hand side of the road. Harold Chancey, who was employed in the motor pool at Fort Pepperrell, remembers changing over to the other side of the road each time he entered or left the base. The U.S. buses that brought workers to and from the base likewise ran into problems when they discharged their passengers on the right-hand side, into the middle of city streets. By war's end, however, the law was changed to the (North) American standard.

The building of the U.S. base is closely associated with high wages and good times in the Newfoundland imagination. "Everybody on earth wanted to work for the Americans because they paid so well," recalled Elizabeth Scammel-Reynolds. The coming of the Americans meant a great deal to A. Doug New-

Table 4.1 Employment on Canadian and American bases in Newfoundland

Date	*Canadians*	*U.S. Army*	*U.S. Navy*	*Total*
June 1942	6,943	6,930	3,472	17,345
Sept. 1942	6,728	9,524	3,500	19,752
Dec. 1942	3,829	6,866	2,600	13,295
Aug. 1943	4,159	4,141	2,300	10,600
Dec. 1943	4,131	3,519	1,150	8,800
March 1944	3,929	2,565	982	7,476
May 1944	3,556	2,673	950	7,179
Aug. 1944	2,625	2,320	841	5,786

Source: Labour Relations Officer, Acting, to Commissioner for Justice and Defence, 29 September 1945, file 19: "U.S. Effect of Agreement on Colonies," box 365, GN 13/1/B, PANL.

bury's family. One brother, his sister, and his father worked at Fort Pepperrell. The Americans paid a "hell of a lot more money" than other employers, he recalled. Harold Chancey was one of the few interviewees who actually worked for the Americans. Shortly after the arrival of the *Edmund B. Alexander,* he was hired on as a worker in the ship's laundry room, and later, as noted above, he worked at the base in the motor pool. In comparison, Newfoundlanders had almost no memories of working for the Canadians.

Statistics compiled by the Newfoundland government, however, reveal that employment levels at the Canadian and American bases were comparable, particularly in St John's. Across Newfoundland, an estimated 20,000 people found work at any given moment at the Canadian and American bases. As the accompanying chart indicates, the United States employed nearly double the number of Newfoundlanders as the Canadians overall, but this gap would likely have been considerably smaller in St John's itself. The proportion of Newfoundlanders working on the Canadian bases also grew over time. Moreover, the archival record suggests that the Canadians employed more people indirectly than the American forces. Whereas the U.S. Army imported nearly all of its supplies by chartered vessels that off-loaded at the navy dock, the Canadian armed services obtained their supplies from local wholesalers. This method enabled the Canadians to avoid having to maintain large warehouses, stocks of goods, and shipping facilities.[89] However, it also put pressure on Newfoundland's ability to supply the necessary goods and set the Canadians up for blame in times of shortage.

The Americans paid higher wages than the Canadians in spite of the best efforts of the Newfoundland government to pressure them to hold their wages down to those already prevailing – which were far below the standard wages on the mainland. A surprising number of interviewees recalled that the Newfoundland government had worked against its own people. The "powers that be on Water Street" had kept wages down during the war, said James Walsh. They "still did," he added. What is most surprising, here, is that these efforts were supposed to be cloaked in secrecy. The government had repeatedly denied the allegation during the war, but had clearly been unconvincing. The prevailing-wage policy had dashed the hopes of many Newfoundlanders who hoped to break out of the Depression-era wages that predominated on the island. Clearly, the interviewees saw this covert policy as an act of betrayal.

If the Newfoundland government successfully held down the wage rates paid on the bases, why then are the Americans remembered for paying better wages? The answer to this question is found in the Presidential Library of Franklin D. Roosevelt in Hyde Park, New York. While Roosevelt agreed to pay prevailing wage rates in Newfoundland, he secretly directed the army and navy to pay "top scale" rather than "average scale" wages.[90] This decision resulted in wage rates that were substantially above those paid by the Canadian forces in St John's. The Canadians, to the detriment of their reputation, proved more willing than the Americans to pay the lower wage rates established by the Commission of Government as the norm. The Canadians also agreed to respect the Newfoundland government's wish that wage rates be based on those prevailing locally, which meant lower wages outside of St John's. The Americans would have none of that. Newfoundlanders working at the U.S. bases at Argentia and Stephenville received the higher wages prevailing in St John's. In so doing, the Americans earned the reputation of paying the best wages during the war. Newfoundlanders working at Fort Pepperrell also enjoyed illicit access to duty-free goods. While a pack of cigarettes retailed for thirty-five cents in St John's, the same pack cost six cents on the base.[91]

The divergent approaches taken by the Canadians and the Americans in Newfoundland was again on display in the matter of workmen's compensation. Base construction was sometimes dangerous work, and many were injured or killed on the job. In Newfoundland, injured workers had to go to court to seek compensation. There was no commission overseeing the process. Nor were there claims adjudication officers to fast-track compensation payments. Once again, the Canadians agreed to respect Newfoundland's jurisdiction in the matter, while the United States defied it, insisting that the Leased Bases Agreement gave it the right to deal with the issue.

The U.S. Congress extended its system of workmen's compensation to both U.S. nationals and local workers employed at its bases in April 1941. Henceforth, those injured were eligible to receive two-thirds of their average wages for a fixed period of time. Privately, the British and Newfoundland governments strongly opposed the measure, seeing it as breaching Newfoundland's sovereignty. Yet the U.S. system represented a significant improvement and its rates were considered far superior. It is not for nothing, then, that the United States earned the reputation of being the best employer on the island.[92] This was only possible because of the extraterritorial rights granted to the United States in the 99-year Leased Bases Agreement.

The friendly invasion has been widely credited with transforming Newfoundland "dramatically for the better."[93] The war brought prosperity and full employment to the city. The sales of war savings certificates in 1942 topped one million dollars, nearly double the amount earned in 1941.[94] For their part, insurance companies reported that the number and size of the life insurance policies being underwritten had seen a "marked increase."[95]

However, the cost of living was also on the rise and St John's was terribly overcrowded. "There were not enough places for people to live," said Joe Prim. "Anybody who had a room – it was rented." If they could, residents would rent to the families of American soldiers; they were able to pay the highest rents. The thousands of labourers who came to the city from other parts of Newfoundland to build the bases thus had great difficulty finding affordable accommodation. Fraser Ellis remembers a group of men living in squalid conditions in a neighbour's barn out on Topsail Road. They had come to work at the U.S. base and this was the best accommodation they could find. Several interviewees didn't think that there was an empty house to be found anywhere in the city.

The wartime prosperity in Newfoundland stood in sharp contrast to the meagre wages earned by the 3,419 Newfoundlanders who enlisted in the Royal Navy.[96] Their wage rates and allowances were based on the cost of living prevailing in England, not Newfoundland. A Newfoundland gunner received 50 cents a day in 1940. By contrast, a Canadian private earned $1.35 and an American enlisted man considerably more than that. No wonder Newfoundland servicemen felt ill-used. Enlistment fell off considerably in 1941 and 1942, yet the Newfoundland government refused to increase pay rates. The issue came to a head in May 1943 after a large number of Royal Navy ratings from Newfoundland were sent home on leave after eighteen months' service. In a letter to Commissioner Emerson, Captain G.B. Hope wrote:

> A serious problem has, however, arisen in dealing with them and that is the large number of them who have either become absentees or who have been in desertion. The percentage of these cases has grown to such proportions as to indicate the presence of a very serious problem ... It is apparent that the problem is social and not a disciplinary one and seems to have an economic basis. It is significant that most of these ratings who have been in desertion have been ones with dependents and have deliberately failed to return after their leave and have sought and obtained remunerative employment. Thus, in a relatively short time they have been enabled to earn a reasonable sum of money before they were apprehended or surrendered, and gave up quite willingly and accepted the risk of punishment in order to attain their financial object.[97]

Upon returning home on leave, the navy ratings found themselves at a financial disadvantage compared to civilians. They had already made it clear at an earlier meeting that the underlying issue was one of adequate pay and allowances for dependants. Ninety-four ratings had deserted since January 1942, though one rating had deserted five times in eighteen months and several others had deserted four times each. Sixteen were known to be in desertion in May 1943.[98]

CONCLUSION

The wartime impression of "friendly" Americans and "drunken" Canadians originates in Newfoundland nationalism and in the divergent actions of the Canadian and American authorities. Ironically, it was the U.S. government's willingness to defy the Newfoundland Commission of Government and impose its own laws and customs that contributed to much of its public popularity. The Americans brought jobs, higher wages, and improved workers' compensation benefits, and their bases served as models of progress and modernity. What were deemed unfriendly acts by the Newfoundland authorities were hailed by ordinary Newfoundlanders.

The Canadians, by contrast, without the legal standing afforded by the Leased Bases Agreement, had to live by Newfoundland custom and law. They therefore paid lower wages than the Americans, paid appreciably less in compensation for workplace injury, and were paraded before Newfoundland magistrates for minor violations. The fact that Canada was also a poorer country than the United States, and at war, worked against it. Canadian servicemen were themselves paid less than their U.S. counterparts, and their bases were seen as "scruff" in comparison to the Americans'. In consequence, the Canadians gained the reputation of being poor cousins to the Americans – which to some degree they were. "When all is said and done," historian Peter Neary observed, "the United States had come into Newfoundland with a first class ticket, while Canada came with a second class ticket which only the British could upgrade."[99]

5

Gate Keeping and Newfoundland Popular Culture

HMS *Burwell* gun shield art. "The Burwell gun shield represents almost everything the ship was not but no doubt wanted to be. Burwell was one of the 50 four-stackers in the US/UK deal that provided old WWI destroyers for military base leases. The destroyer was known for its poor condition and spent much of the war in port being repaired. However, here she is depicted as a heavily armoured lobster hunting down and crushing U-boats. A curious feature is that while she was a M ship, she is portrayed on a green maple leaf, the symbol used by the RCN." Gary Green, *A Guide for Some of the Gun Shield Art and Ship's Badges of the Crow's Nest Officer's Club* (St John's: Crow's Nest Military Artifacts Association, Newfoundland).

JEFF A. WEBB

As the *Edmund B. Alexander* berthed, its brass band played "Hail! Hail! The Gang's All Here" – the first of many musical performances by American servicemen that added to the cultural life of the city.[1] It was also the first of many musical performances by American servicemen to be brought to a Newfoundland audience through radio; the government-owned station, VONF, marked the occasion with a broadcast from the pier describing the ship entering the harbour.[2] Over the next few years the Canadian, British, and American servicemen were a cultural as well as a military force in Newfoundland. Contact between civilians and the servicemen of the "friendly invasion" reinforced Newfoundlanders' enthusiasm for American popular culture, but that taste had long predated the war.[3] Cultural transmission was also a two-way process; many young Americans were as influenced by their time in Newfoundland as the civilians were influenced by the servicemen. This chapter argues that the popular cultural exchanges between Newfoundlanders and Americans were mediated by institutions such as dance halls and radio stations. By "mediated," I mean both that the institutions were the medium though which culture was transmitted from one person to another and that they affected the character of culture's expressive forms. Institutions were gatekeepers in the social interactions between civilians and servicemen.

A classic study of twentieth-century Newfoundland, S.J.R. Noel's *Politics in Newfoundland*, suggests that Newfoundlanders' culture was profoundly changed by the presence of the servicemen. Noel argues that rubbing shoulders with the Americans and Canadians had made Newfoundlanders aware of the consumer culture of North America and thus encouraged the 1948 choice to join Canada.[4] Similarly, Peter Neary, author of the authoritative work on the commission government period, *Newfoundland in the North Atlantic World,* discusses the British official view that the principal social effect of the war was "the modernization of Newfoundland building, architecture, communications systems" and argues that the war aroused in Newfoundlanders "a demand for a better standard of living."[5] More recently, the historian David MacKenzie went further, suggesting that the Americans brought "exposure to new ideas and the process of modernization or 'Americanization' – [and that] had a profound impact on Newfoundland and affected the way Newfoundlanders viewed themselves and their place in the world."[6] MacKenzie does not specify what these new ideas were, and the only pieces of evidence he cites are the same official report cited by Neary and the observations of a few Americans who had not been in the country prior to the arrival of the "changes" they report observing. Those accounts must be read with caution, since we would expect American officers to imagine Newfoundlanders wanting to become more like them. The American officials had to deal with employees who worked for brief periods and then quit to return to their homes. Some authors have perceived this pattern as reflecting Newfoundlanders' pre-modern work ethic and have concluded that it improved after they rubbed shoulders with the more modern Americans. Their argument – that the example of American efficiency changed the peasant-like work habits of Newfoundlanders – has been effectively challenged by Steven High, who points to the nature of the labour market and government policy to explain high turnover rates among employees.[7]

Studies by these authors reflect the view that the country had been premodern and conservative in character until the one-two punch of the Second World War and Confederation provoked its citizens to want a twentieth-century North American lifestyle. The concept of "modernization" is out of fashion among academics, but its assumptions continue to underlie this understanding of the significance of the American presence in Newfoundland.[8] While all of the implications of this interpretation cannot be discussed in a single chapter, it is important that a focus be brought here to the institutions that brought a wartime popular culture to the people of St John's, since many scholars throughout the world, even those sceptical of modernization, hold that the mass media and popular culture play an integral role in stimulating consumer demand and in breaking down traditional ways of thinking and living.

Those who remember wartime in St John's recall the blackout, the dances, and the music. Neary comments on the effect of the Americans' presence on the popular culture of the period, suggesting that the United Service Organization (USO) and the American-owned radio station VOUS (Voice of the United States), respectively, "raised an already heady local entertainment scene to even dizzier heights" and that "opinion and popular taste were also moulded in a direction favourable to American interests."[9] These judgments seem accurate, although, as the historian Ian M. Stewart reminds us, long before 1939 people in St John's had read American magazines, listened to American radio programs, and worn the latest American fashions (Stewart believes, however, that it was the U.S. bases that extended these cultural influences to rural people, who had previously not been exposed to them).[10] The historian Carla Wheaton points out that in the early twentieth century the merchants of Water Street fully incorporated "modern" consumer culture into their department stores. In her view, the higher disposable incomes in the war years encouraged the long-standing trend among consumers, long predating the war, to want to purchase "novel" products and to prefer American-made goods over homemade.[11]

It is easy to exaggerate the novelty of American popular culture in the 1940s. Newfoundlanders had been participating in a range of North American popular culture activities for some time and had long wanted a North American consumer lifestyle. People in St John's purchased more North American goods and fewer British goods after the war than before it, but this was not because their taste had become newly Americanized through exposure to American media and contact with American servicemen. It was more the result of the disruption of British exports.

Wartime did not introduce the people of the city to new forms of popular culture; there was continuity with earlier cultural expressions. As Philip Hiscock has observed, popular culture is made of the material at hand, and long before 1940 the people of St John's made music and art out of elements both invented locally and adopted or adapted from outside.[12] Young people, in particular, listened to contemporary music, whether on phonograph records, in the movies, or at the bandstand, and they purchased sheet music of the latest hits. Swing, the popular music of the day, had its origins in African-American and European musical traditions, and despite its "American" roots was popular with diverse audiences in North America and Europe because it was an amalgam of styles. As one historian puts it, swing "was rooted in the black American experience ... [but] it became an urbane, sophisticated art, rooted in popular taste, and as a popular art form it transcended all parochialisms, creating a mass audience ... which flocked to the form because the taste was identified as a new national one: an American taste. The music's hybridity, then, was its most attractive feature."[13] Young people in St John's shared in that enthusiasm.

Before addressing the ways that Newfoundlanders engaged with popular culture in their interactions with servicemen, it is worth considering the nature of the American invasion. The American armed services expanded rapidly after the United States imposed conscription in September 1940, and thus few servicemen were career soldiers or sailors. Most of those stationed in St John's had been civilians before undertaking a brief period of basic training and perhaps some specialist training and then being posted to overseas bases. Given the nearly exclusively male character of the armed services and the pressures that suppressed individuality (common uniforms, communal dining, and communal latrines), leisure time and, especially, time with women were the only opportunities servicemen had to be individuals. Whether it was eating a meal with a family, having a surrogate mother mend a uniform and pour a cup of tea, or dancing with a pretty girl, many servicemen desired some temporary respite from the masculine, homogenizing environment. Movies and sports and dances were not just things that reminded them of civilian life and home; these leisure activities allowed off-duty men to make individual choices (and military life gave lower-ranking servicemen few opportunities to make choices). Being able to choose whether to listen to classical, Broadway musical, swing, or country, for example, allowed men to express their own taste. And given the prevailing gender expectations, men who were subordinate to those of higher ranks during on-duty hours could make decisions for the women they dated. When dancing, men led.[14]

Although foreign seamen frequently visited the port city and thus the people of St John's had more experience with people from other countries than had the residents of most North American towns, there had been no permanent presence of soldiers since the British Army garrison had left in 1870. The years of the Great Depression had not encouraged the expansion of recreational facilities and social institutions, and the city was unprepared for the influx of young men that came with the start of the war. There were two phases in the interactions between civilians and Americans in St John's. While the American base was being built, servicemen lived first on board ship and later in a tent city called "Camp Alexander." In this period, the Americans interacted with Newfoundlanders on the latter's turf and in pre-existing venues. The opening of the Caribou Hut in January 1941 provided a place for dances and other social activities, many of which had a cultural dimension. Civilians held concerts for servicemen, and servicemen entertained each other with a range of performances. Later, with the establishment of Fort Pepperrell's own facilities, the Americans entered a phase in which they were able to regulate the interactions of servicemen with civilians.

Shaping the servicemen's engagement with the host city was always a military priority, regardless of where the base was located. This was especially true when the men were not in combat; it was a challenge to maintain discipline among men who, as a result of daily interactions with civilians, might lose their preparedness and revert to civilian habits. To maintain the morale of men far from home but not fighting, the army had to offer them recreational activities. This was especially the case in St John's, for the city had little to offer the thousands of young men passing through it. Thus, not only did the Americans' ship have its own "orchestra," but the servicemen, drawn from a cross-section of America, included in their ranks some professional and many talented amateur performers. Since American policy forbade military bands from performing for money and competing with civilian establishments, the distinction between "professional" and "amateur" was fairly meaningless. The dances on board the ship and in various local venues, whatever the previous careers of the musicians, were among the most popular leisure activities for the Americans and a welcome reprieve from the mundane for young Newfoundlanders who had just lived through the Depression.

Regardless of where in the world serviceman musicians might find themselves stationed, many of them, almost upon arrival, began performing in a range

of musical styles in a range of city venues. The enlisted men loved to hear the music they had left behind in the United States, Canada, or the United Kingdom. One such concert was performed by a group of men from a Royal Navy ship, their instruments consisting of a piano, a mouth organ, a ukulele, and a guitar: "A very clever impersonation of Shirley Temple was the next number by Wm Briaris. He started his number behind the curtain and everyone in the audience was more than surprised when the curtain was drawn for it was hard to believe that the voice coming over the microphone could possibly be that of a man ... A program of this type is never complete without a black face comedian and tap dancer and the comedy skit put on by Wm Owers and Stan Mills took care of this in a very fine manner."[15]

Aerial photograph of Fort Pepperrell and Quidi Vidi Lake. Control no. 19900192-018-3, Canadian War Museum.

The music and entertainment that was favoured tended to be "popular," in the sense of mass entertainment. In the case just cited, British sailors based

Left Presentation by U.S. Army officers to civilian workers at the Fort Pepperrell base. Photo #01-065-001, City of St John's Archives.

Right Edgar Bergen and Charlie McCarthy on stage. Control no. 20030014-053, Canadian War Museum.

their show on a Depression-era Hollywood icon and an even earlier American minstrel tradition. The performance exemplified the popularity of American popular culture, although it was likely somewhat exceptional in its cross-gender and cross-race role-playing. The female impersonation in the performance was likely indicative of the character of an exclusively male shipboard life. This was not, though, the first instance of "blackface" in St John's, as local and itinerant performers had blacked up since the nineteenth century.

While men lived aboard ship and in tents awaiting the construction of barracks, servicemen performed for dances on the *Alexander* and at the many existing halls within the city.[16] The American, British and Canadian servicemen initially integrated such entertainment activities into Newfoundland's civilian venues, in which both servicemen and civilians participated as performers and audience. In this sense, the war was a vibrant period for both groups, and there were plenty of opportunities to hear live popular music: "A new dance band will make its debut at the Knights of Columbus Leave Center tonight when Bill Brokaw will present his versatile and talented Terra Novians to the patrons of the hostel. Brokaw has had many years experienced [*sic*] with nationally known 'name' bands in the United States and has gathered together a carefully selected group of musicians who can deliver old favorites, jitterbug jive, or the latest smash hits in a manner that will bring them to the forefront among local bands."[17]

For the *Daily News*, the experience the band leaders and musicians had had in the United States was evidence of their musical credentials. And during this phase, in which Newfoundland and foreign musicians mixed, there was undoubtedly informal sharing of repertoire and skills between the native-born and the recent arrivals.

With the construction of the base, the U.S. Base Command took greater control over its personnel's leisure activities. Institutions such as the USO, which opened in 1942, and the American radio station VOUS, which opened in 1943, provided venues for performance and socializing that could be policed. American commanders turned to radio broadcasting to keep in touch with the men and maintain their morale, as otherwise they had few leisure activities during their off-duty hours.[18] VOUS provided a range of American music, comedy, and sports; it explicitly sought to serve the needs of American military personnel but was also listened to by civilians.

While commanders provided entertainment to servicemen, civic leaders in St John's faced the familiar role of maintaining morale on the home front. But in this war the home front and battle front merged in unfamiliar ways. While it was thought that civilian and military social activities were ways to maintain morale among servicemen and civilians alike, the institutions that gave shape to formal interactions also served to regulate behaviour. Civilians, too, were encouraged to do their part. Many families invited servicemen into their homes for meals and companionship, forging long-lasting friendships and conducting informal exchanges of information, values, and popular culture. One of those interviewed for this project recalled servicemen playing the piano in his future wife's house.[19] In these settings, the nuclear family constrained the behaviour of the "boys" and gave them something similar to their own home.

But the size and demographics of the American presence proved challenging for a town with limited recreational facilities. The newspaper columnist Albert Perlin commented that the population of the city had with one stroke increased by 25 per cent and that this influx of men strained the infrastructure of St John's.[20] Most of the construction workers and service personnel were men, many of them young and unmarried – raising the spectre of alcohol abuse, violence, petty crime, and sexual activities outside of marriage. Not surprisingly, American officers wanted to shape these young men's leisure time in ways that maintained military preparedness, even though initially the United States was not a combatant. The officer in charge of morale for the Newfoundland Base Command, Lieutenant Colonel Henry W. Clark, reported that the troops were getting along well with local people, both because officers encouraged servicemen to be tactful and because the bases, with their bowling alleys, pool tables, and basketball courts, were self-sufficient when it came to entertaining the servicemen. Indeed, one of his objectives as morale officer was to keep the troops busy enough with "wholesome" activities that their leisure time would be used up without their having "too close contact with the natives [which] tends to reduce military efficiency."[21]

Couples dancing. Control no. 20030014-074-3, Canadian War Museum.

The boom town atmosphere in St John's, with the sudden presence of hundreds of single, young male servicemen, posed a contrast with the bleak years of the Great Depression. In her book about the Caribou Hut, writer Margaret Duley documents the new sense of sexual freedom and opportunity of those days:

> St John's became a Mecca for women. The older girls persuaded their parents it was time to leave school. The maids gave notice because they could make better money elsewhere, and stay out later at night. Every girl had a "fellah," even those who had never had a date in their lives. Some thought that the sentry box was a peaceful place for a date when the rest of the town was so crowded. Parents felt the loosening of all authority and the lowering of every moral standard. Every girl felt that her boy might

die; therefore she aimed to please. The rapidly changing dates became the same dream, only with a different face, and perhaps from another wartime service. There were many Lili Marlenes, under the lamp-posts, and by the barracks-gates.[22]

Not surprisingly, civilian and military authorities alike tried to regulate the sexual relations between the Americans and civilians, and they found that concerts, movies, and dances were a good way of doing so, since such activities could be monitored by chaperones, officers, and military police. Officials viewed with apprehension the combination of young men with cash in hand and the relative availability of alcohol. As Duley indicates, family curfews and other rules were insufficient to keep daughters and domestic servants in line in the face of an army of unmarried men and blackout regulations that ensured a degree of cover for illicit activities. Wholesome activities for servicemen, however, such as reading at the base library, bowling, boxing, listening to the radio, or going on dates to movies and dances, under careful supervision, could limit the spread of sexually transmitted diseases and unwanted pregnancies. Many of the wartime cultural activities were structured in such a way that the older generation could control the younger. The married and middle-class women who ran the Caribou Hut, for example, provided the men with playing cards, magazines, or cups of tea while they mended uniforms in need of repair.

Respectable girls were recruited as "hostesses" and dance partners for the boys, doing their part for the war effort, but not in the sense implied by Duley. The female employees of James Baird Ltd, a prominent St John's business, for example, served as hostesses at a dance at the Caribou Hut.[23] Another dance was hosted by the female employees of Bowring Brothers Ltd, one of the city's oldest

Audience at band concert. Control no. 20030014-074-4, Canadian War Museum.

and most respected firms.[24] The girls were at first unfamiliar with some of the dance steps at these parties. The wife of the owner of McMurdo's pharmacy sent its female employees, including Helen Blundon, to host a dance. Blundon later reported that the "first time I set foot on the dance floor I danced to 'In the Mood' and I didn't know how to do one thing but I wasn't long learning."[25] That song, popularized in 1939 by the Glenn Miller orchestra, achieved iconic status during the war. Not all young women were interested in dating servicemen or attending the dances. Sometimes religious conventions discouraged them from socializing with the troops. One nurse who lived in the city during the war commented that she didn't dance because of her "Methodist feet."[26] Her taste in music was primarily hymns and light classical, while her co-workers liked "cowboy" music.

After Fort Pepperrell had its movie theatre and other facilities in place, servicemen continued to participate in the social life of the city but civilians could only use the entertainment facilities at the base as the guest of a serviceman. This limited civilian attendance at American places of entertainment and controlled the kind of interactions that occurred. The base commanders' desire to allow but control the men's access to women encouraged them to act as gatekeepers. In fact, there was an actual gate that prevented Newfoundlanders from going on base without permission. Of course, the intent of the gate was not to exclude Newfoundlanders per se; this was wartime and commanders had to practise due diligence given the potential danger of spies or saboteurs. Furthermore, the base and the USO were intended to be oases of Americana for homesick Americans, and if the leisure activities were dominated by "natives," the illusion of being back home would be broken. One unintended effect of the gate, therefore, was that civilian participation in the entertainment and cultural activities of the American servicemen was limited.

Not only was the attendance of Newfoundlanders at movies shown at the base theatre limited, but the same restrictions applied to the concerts given

Civilian employees at Fort Pepperrell. Photo #01-065-006, City of St John's Archives.

Early construction of the Fort Pepperrell army base in St John's, 1941. PF-306.058, Maritime History Archive.

by visiting American entertainers (some of whom, such as Frank Sinatra and Phil Silvers, were well known to civilians).[27] Security concerns also ensured that there was no advance notice of the performers' visits to the city. An exception to such secrecy around star performers was the appearance of the American ventriloquist Edgar Bergen with his dummy Charlie McCarthy. Bergen's visit to the base was covered by the *Daily News*, and he put on a special performance for the city's children.

Newfoundland women had greater access to the entertainment on the base than Newfoundland men, since they would be invited as dates. Ann Abraham, for example, was invited to see Sinatra and remembers the other girls swooning at the concert.[28] If you add up the American serviceman's ability to invite a girl to the base, his relatively high disposable income, and his access to cheap liquor and cigarettes, it's not surprising that Americans made attractive dates and that some Newfoundland men resented the competition.[29] A few local men, though, did have access to the base entertainment. Frank Kennedy attended a show featuring Bob Hope and the band leader Les Browne (this may have been after the war) in the capacity of press photographer; years later he remembered the concert not so much because the music was new to him – he had heard the band before – but because the experience of seeing the band live was so different from hearing the music on the radio.[30]

Admission restrictions at the base might have limited civilian attendance at the Pepperrell movie theatre, but that did not prevent Newfoundlanders from seeing American movies. Several movie theatres in St John's predated the arrival of the Americans, and they showed Hollywood movies nearly exclusively. In a few cases the base showed movies before their commercial release or movies that did not play in the St John's theatres at all. But some Hollywood productions – *The Maltese Falcon* (1941), for example – were screened in the civilian theatres before they were available at Pepperrell.[31] American officials worried that the reputation of Fort Pepperrell would suffer if servicemen had to leave the base to see the most recent movies. American movies were more of a novelty at other bases, however. According to American construction worker J.E. Gilpatrick, the movie theatre at Argentia set aside a night for Newfoundlanders (who had to wear different coloured badges than American employees so that they could be distinguished). This arrangement proved very popular, "as most of the type of Newfies here have never seen pictures at all and consequently are in their glory," despite being unable to attend on all the other nights.[32]

One should not make too much of civilians' limited access to American popular culture; many Newfoundlanders listened to American radio, bought American phonograph records, and watched American movies. Some scholars have assumed that the mass media generally and Hollywood movies specifically are quintessentially "modern" and would have encouraged viewers to embrace secularization as much as a consumer lifestyle, but the evidence is ambiguous. While the audience members likely gained a skewed picture of American life, one that portrayed it as glamorous, prosperous, and white, they may also have incorporated other elements of the movies into their existing culture. Margaret Kearney commented that many of the movies she saw in this period had war-related themes, but the one that stood out in her memory was *Song of Bernadette* (1943), a film steeped in Roman Catholicism.[33] Her religion may have been reaffirmed by the movie, and the film may have had a lasting impression on her because Catholicism was important to her.[34]

Much of the social life in St John's before the war had been sponsored by particular Christian denominations, social clubs, schools, or musical organizations such as the Church Lads Brigade. Parents encouraged children to "go with your own," as David Edwards put it, to make it more likely that they would select marriage partners within their denomination.[35] In contrast, movies and dances on the base were not segregated by social class or religious denomination. A young GI would have been oblivious to the class or sectarian affiliation suggested by the school his date had attended. Similarly, the wartime dances and sports events (baseball games, for example) in the town were not segregated, which likely contributed to the long-term trend of diminishing denominational segregation in the city.

Music and dances were the mainstay of entertainment for servicemen and civilians alike, and both Newfoundland and American musicians played on

and off the base. The St John's band leader Mickey Duggan, for example, had played swing music in St John's before the war, but during the war he not only played at Pepperrell and Argentia, but also travelled to the American base at Thule, Greenland, to play for an extended period.[36] Duggan is an example of a Newfoundlander who brought the popular music of the day – music that originated in the United States – to an audience of American servicemen on a foreign base. Then there was the child singer R.J. Gallagher, who frequently sang popular music on a commercial radio show on VOCM and also performed with the Pepperrell-based big band known as the Sky Knights. Even at the age of nine, Gallagher sang at the St John's USO club, and he sometimes took a seaplane to Argentia to perform. The soldiers made a little uniform for him, complete with sergeant's stripes. The boy's repertoire included "love songs," which prompted his Roman Catholic schoolteachers and the clergy to criticize him for singing "dirty" songs. Gallagher remembers singing Broadway show tunes such as "I'll Be Seeing You" (1938), wartime popular music such as "Coming In on a Wing

U.S. soldiers going for a walk through Quidi Vidi Village, *Scenes of St. John's*. Photo by Lieut. Alice Ducile Talman, control no. 20010159-002, Canadian War Museum.

and a Prayer" (1943), and swing standards such as "Is You Is, or Is You Ain't, My Baby" (1944).[37] There were other Newfoundlanders who also performed American songs for Canadian and American servicemen. Helen Blundon and Don Jamieson (then a well-known broadcaster) were volunteers with the YMCA and organized dances and concerts for servicemen. One concert featured a unique version of *Show Boat* (the Jerome Kern and Oscar Hammerstein Broadway musical that had run in New York a number of times since 1927, had been filmed several times, and had been adapted for radio by Orson Welles in 1939). Jamieson picked out the songs and wrote the script, the Canadian navy band performed the music, and civilians in "painted faces" assumed the roles.[38]

Not all Newfoundland popular culture was "American" of course. A few Canadians and Americans discerned a particular form of local popular culture, even if their understanding of it was sometimes incomplete. One Canadian stationed in Newfoundland commented, "To the strains of a fiddle and possibly a guitar, a Newfoundlander's pleasure is at its maximum when he's whirling and stomping to the tune of the 'Squeejiggers Jug,' which starts out 'We'll rant and we'll roar like true Newfoundlanders.'"[39] That song, known as the "Ryans and the Pittmans," was a Newfoundland variant of a folk song widely known in the English-speaking world, the Newfoundland lyrics to which had been penned in 1875 by H.W. LeMessurier. It had been published in the Gerald S. Doyle songbook, the book that established the canon of Newfoundland song for a generation of Newfoundlanders and foreigners.[40] Not only was the Doyle songbook collected as a souvenir by Canadians and Americans stationed in Newfoundland, but the *Book of Newfoundland*, a compendium of essays on the culture and history of the country, was also purchased by many servicemen as a souvenir of the place where they had been based.[41]

The Canadian soldier's overall impression of Newfoundland culture was that "the Island lies off the Canadian mainland, but it is spiritually much closer to the British Isles."[42] A few Americans and Canadians embraced the local culture. Robert Macleod, a St John's musician with a repertoire that spanned many genres of popular, classical, religious, and folk music, frequently played for both civilian and military audiences, and as one scholar put it, "his house also became a focal point for many Canadian and American soldiers, particularly those who had musical abilities."[43] In addition to playing contemporary music, Macleod introduced Americans and Canadians to Newfoundland music of both ancient and recent composition. Clyde Gilmour, for example, who was stationed in St John's during the war, learned folk songs from Macleod that he later promoted as part of his collection in his role as a CBC radio host.[44] Social contacts could have important consequences. The socializing that went on between St John's businessmen, such as Gerald S. Doyle, and American officers on the "cocktail circuit" could result in the Americans participating in local charities.[45]

As inadequate as the recreational facilities in St John's were when the Canadian and American servicemen first arrived, the facilities in Argentia when the construction workers and the marines arrived offered even fewer entertainment options. One report offered this description:

American soldiers embarking on a troopship bound for home, 1945. PF-306.288, Maritime History Archive.

At the present stage in the transformation of Argentia into a United States defense base, the settlement has little to offer in the way of recreation and sport. There are no motion picture shows or hockey games to furnish entertainment, and athletic activities are restricted to walks and hikes. Making the most of what is available the Marines stationed at the base are joining enthusiastically in the old-fashioned square dances which are held regularly by the young people of the settlement. This national folk-dance of Newfoundland is new to some of the Marines, but they are learning quickly and getting a great kick out of it. The Parish hall, placed at the disposal of the young folk by the Priest, is the scene of these square dances, which up to the present time have been held once each week. There are not always enough girls to make complete sets, and sometimes men have to fill in as partners, but they all make the best of it and have a jolly good time "stepping it out." Music is supplied by a mixed orchestra comprised of musical members of the garrison, together with some local players. Sometimes waltz tunes are played and on the dance floor the visitors turn the tables on the local dancers and become impromptu dancing teachers.[46]

Another dance had the Newfoundlanders introducing the Americans to a quadrille, danced to the early nineteenth-century tune "The Banks of Newfoundland" and similar music, and this was followed later by waltzes and foxtrots, with which the Americans were more familiar.[47]

The dances and concerts, though they took place under the watchful eye of the parish priest, were sites for the exchange of dance styles and music. Not all of the American music was "popular" in the sense of being commercial music intended solely for entertainment. Soon after its opening, the Naval Air Station at Argentia had a male choir under the leadership of director and organist Donat J. Forcier, a "distinguished composer of church music."[48] Servicemen stationed in St John's performed in civilian churches as well; for example, American vocalists gave a recital at the Salvation Army Temple.[49]

The opening of the USO building on Merrymeeting Road in February 1942 provided a new focal point for American entertainment and indicated a trend towards segregating the servicemen from the Newfoundlanders. The new venue, symbolically situated in the city rather than on the base, gave the Americans greater control over which civilians would have access to American entertainment. When they did attend events at the USO club, Newfoundlanders now came as guests of the Americans, rather than the other way around. The base commanders were thus better able to shape and monitor the interactions between servicemen and civilians than they could have done in civilian-owned establishments. This didn't mean that the American officers wanted to cut off interactions between the servicemen and local women. In June 1942, thirty St John's girls received "commissions" as USO army hostesses – the nomenclature evoking the step of being admitted to the ranks of the officers.[50] The *Daily News* reported that there were more than 400 members of the "USO hostess army" and membership cards had to be produced by all visitors to the USO, although other "lady guests may be signed in for one evening."[51]

Soldiers' interaction with civilians could be controlled at officers' and service clubs. Alcohol consumption, which was sometimes a threat to military discipline, for example, could also be regulated in civilian-owned halls such as the Caribou Hut and the Knights of Columbus hostel. At one wartime dance, for example, a soft drink was at the centre of a non-sexual social activity: "The three young ladies were required to take their respective young partners on their knees and feed them Coco-Cola from a bottle to which a nipple had been affixed. The first 'baby' to finish his bottle was Geoff Stirling who was skillfully fed by Miss Jean Fox."[52] Thanks to a vigorous marketing effort, Coca-Cola was one of the products that had come to exemplify the modern consumer lifestyle and healthy leisure activities. The *Daily News* published a photograph of a female RCAF member drinking a "coke" at the USO and another of four Newfoundland girls, all members of the RCAF, at a "coke bar."[53] Parents could be reassured that daughters in uniform were having good clean fun.

The USO club not only included a range of entertainment from Newfoundland-based American servicemen musicians and performers, but brought in professional entertainers from the United States as well. One account provides something of the flavour:

> To the deafening applause of a delighted audience a series of songs comedies and dances was presented by eight celebrities of stage, radio and screen whose names are familiar to millions. They were as follows: Sid Marion, star of "Hold on to your hats" playing with Al Jolson and many other famous entertainers also in "Streets of Paris." This actor made a hit in London some time ago. Cliff ("Sharle") Hall of "Baron Munchausen" fame. Frank Conville and Sunny Dale, of Earl Carroll's Vanities. Lois Harper, musical comedy dancer. Yvette, star of National Broadcasting Company, also of the Camel Caravan program. Wini Shaw, star of the pictures "In Caliente" and "The Gold Diggers" also of Ziegfeld Follies. Irving Sacher, conductor of musical comedy shows.[54]

The USO concerts included big band dance music, comedy, and country music. One concert included a "hill billy" trio made up of infantrymen from Fort Pepperrell who dressed in costume and sang "Down That Old Texas Trail." That may have been "Ridin' Down that Old Texas Trail" or "I'll Go Ridin' Down that Old Texas Trail," the latter of which had been popularized by Gene Autry. Even before the war, Newfoundlanders were familiar with country music – live, on the radio, and through the many popular cowboy and western movies starring Autry and other singing cowboys. The same USO show included a U.S. Navy sailor, Tom Berry, "who formally played the piano in the well-known orchestra of Tommy Tucker in New York City," performing "boogie woogie selections on the piano." The program's guest vocalist was Corporal "Chick" Cumbo who sang "Miss You" and "Tangerine" (1941), a swing tune that had been popularized by Jimmy Dorsey. Cumbo was accompanied by the Pepperrell-based group the Musical Commandoes, under the direction of Technical Sergeant Harold Young. The concert included Private First Class Ira Scher performing a comedy monologue in which he imitated the voices of several movie actors.[55] In another program the Musical Commandoes performed a number of "blues" tunes, including the jazz standard "Saint Louis Blues" (1914).[56]

Morale officers approved of singing and dancing, since both encouraged the men to act in unison, much as drill did.[57] Popular morale-boosting songs such as "Coming in on a Wing and a Prayer," like many other wartime songs, were essentially singalongs. The literary historian and veteran Paul Fussell observed that even songs usually performed as solos, such as "St Louis Blues," were, in their Glenn Miller arrangement, reworked as communal marches. The singalongs and group dancing created "the sort of community awareness verging on team-spirit characteristic of wartime [that] is revealed by the all but universal knowledge of the same popular songs by all ages, classes and genders."[58]

Notwithstanding my general point about the limitations on Newfoundlanders' ability to consume American popular culture at U.S.-owned facilities, many of these concerts were broadcast on the radio for all to hear. The Newfoundland government-owned VONF broadcasted the official opening ceremonies of the USO club, including the music for the dance performed by the U.S. Army Orchestra.[59] For the duration of the war, American and Canadian concerts were frequently carried by civilian stations. Starting in October 1942, the Broadcasting Corporation of Newfoundland (BCN) carried a series of live radio variety shows from the auditorium of the USO building. High-profile entertainers from the United States, as well as servicemen stationed in St John's and Newfoundland civilians, performed for the troops.

An early radio program included the American actress and singer Joan Blondell, then visiting St John's as part of her USO tour.[60] That show exemplified the benefits implicit in cultural exchange. Not only did it include American popular music, but the tenor Irving Shectman and the Musical Commandos, as a tribute to the United States, performed "When We Sing 'America,'" a song written by Newfoundlander Charles J. White of Burin. Blondell's visit was a success, and the Fort Pepperrell Post Exchange (PX) gave her a copy of a book of Art Scammell's songs and poems as a parting gift.[61] A young man at the time, Scammell wrote poems that reflected his time as a student and teacher, and like a couple of his contemporaries, he made rural Newfoundland life a subject of literature and popular culture. Scammell had just emerged as a popular songwriter working in the Newfoundland "folksong" form, and with the support of Gerald S. Doyle, he was a leading light in Newfoundland music. Popular-music scholars Philip Hiscock and Neil Rosenberg have suggested that the up tempo rollicking comedic aspects of the songs of the Newfoundland folk repertoire were embraced by Americans stationed in Newfoundland and this tended to support stereotypes of Newfoundlanders as fun loving and unsophisticated.[62]

The Scammell songs were not all that Blondell took home with her. She had also learned a comic song, likely written by some Americans, about the slow speed of the railway. The song recounted a story of some soldiers who tied a general to the tracks to get rid of him, only to have him starve to death waiting for a train.[63] The song was the sort of compensatory narrative that Fussell identified as common in the popular culture of servicemen who sought to defend themselves against abuses at the hands of those in command.[64] Blondell sang it in a subsequent broadcast of the Armed Forces Radio Service's *Command Performance* when she returned to Hollywood, provoking an outcry in Newfoundland among those who felt their hospitality had been returned with insult.[65] The newly appointed Brigadier General John B. Brooks felt it necessary to state publicly that Blondell's remarks were in bad taste and not accurate, one of the few instances where the U.S. Command apologized.[66]

Perhaps too much was made of Blondell's misstep. After all, much of North American humour was based on the rural rube's or the unsophisticated immigrant's malapropisms or misunderstandings. Vaudeville and radio had made effective and frequent use of these gags, and in that context Blondell's song was mild. People were sensitive to insults, and Blondell's joking about the state of the railway may have hit a nerve because the railway had been an earlier era's symbol

American troopship departing for home, 1945. PF-306.233, Maritime History Archive.

of modernity and progress. The shortcomings of the slow and rickety narrow-gauge railway were therefore sore points. The *Daily News* reprinted an article from the Toronto *Globe and Mail* that had made fun of the Newfoundland Railway when discussing a USO tour. The Canadian newspaper had acknowledged that it was aware of the strains provoked by casual insults but still condescendingly portrayed Newfoundlanders as backward: "The boys there, incidentally, have annoyed the natives no end by calling them 'Newfies' and instead of referring to themselves as 'slap-happy' they say they are 'Newfie-goofie' which is a further strain on international relations. The last show the troupe gave was for the native 'Newfies' and Stroud found that they have never seen a show before, and were quite innocent as to what reaction was expected of them. He had to teach them how to applaud, and when, but gave up trying to cue them on the laughs."[67]

Readers reacted angrily to the insults of the reporters. "We were not aware that one of the objects of the 'privileged invasion' of the Americans was that of criticism," wrote Gertrude Costello in a letter to the editor. "If casting aspersions on the intelligence of our people as a form of 'gag' may be classed as criticism it is difficult to reconcile this practice with an assurance of friendship."[68] The diminutive "Newfie" was first popularized by servicemen as a short form of the place "Newfoundland," but later it was applied to the people of the country by those who were eager to distinguish themselves from the locals.[69]

These incidents are indicative of the sensitivities of many Newfoundlanders to real or imagined insults, but it would be wrong to assume that the people of St John's were rubes compared to the Americans. Undoubtedly many of the Americans, particularly the officers, had come from social positions of wealth and education, which gave them the sense that they were more sophisticated than the locals, but there were other servicemen who had never lived in a town as large as St John's.[70] A historian of the U.S. Army reported that one in three American homes in 1940 did not have running water and only 41 per cent of the Americans drafted in 1941 had graduated from high school.[71] Some of these servicemen would have thought St John's cosmopolitan. Private First Class J.W. Beardsley, for example, was still living on the *Edmund B. Alexander* when he commented to the *Daily News* that St John's nightlife was exciting.[72] The fact that the newspaper should have thought that worth reporting reveals something of an inferiority complex; the reporter looked to the outsider for validation that the town was not a backwater.

The most effective institution of cultural exchange was radio broadcasting. Newfoundland stations offered content from Britain, Canada, and the United States, and some people in the city listened to foreign stations as well. The radio station VONF provided many opportunities for American performers to entertain an audience of both servicemen and civilians. The USO radio program *Prepare for Action*, for example, was hosted by Sergeant Bud Rice, who also occasionally wrote dramatic skits for presentation.[73] Something of the flavour of the show was captured by an article in the *Daily News*:

> *Prepare for Action* the radio show of the American soldiers was broadcast again from the USO on Tuesday night over VONF and VONH. The previous two Tuesdays while the troops were quarantined transcriptions of past broadcasts were aired, but the other night once again the audience were clapping and whistling as nine o'clock came around, while Sergeant Bud Rice and Tech. Sergeant Harold Young stood ready to begin the program. In its usual variety form the show featured soldier performers and the Music Commandoes under Sergeant Young. Outstanding was pianist Gene Marshall, a recent arrival at Fort Pepperrell. Sixteen years of professional playing as an accompanist and soloist in many of the larger cities of the United States is what Private Marshall now brings with him to musical circles here and his nimble finger work and deft touch brought a ready response from the studio audience. Another instrumentalist showing fine talent was Corporal Frank Bucco who played with great finesse a six-string electric guitar. A humourous discourse on how to prepare for an attack by mosquitoes was given by "Professor Needlenose" another soldier who preferred to remain anonymous. Private Michael Pasaro sang two popular songs.[74]

Young and his Musical Commandos also performed blues.[75] As we have seen, the thousands of Americans posted to Newfoundland included some career soldiers, but most came from a variety of civilian occupations. Some had experience in radio, while many more were professional or skilled amateur musicians and performers. It is not surprising that a man such as Rice would recreate a version of an American network variety program, complete with a variety of musical styles and genres. When the run of *Prepare for Action* came to an end after five months, it was replaced by a similar program of popular and classical music performed by members of the Canadian armed services, *Comrades on Patrol.*[76] That show's debut featured "Leading Aircraftsman Pierre Rainville of the RCAF at the studio grand ... [who] selected as his contribution to the program the prelude and fugue in C minor by Bach ... Pte John Power of the Newfoundland militia ... selected one of Sigmund Romberg's songs – the title song from the operetta 'Rose Marie' followed by some more popular music."[77] The Canadian *Army Night,* on the privately owned VOCM, included rebroadcasts of Canadian programs, such as performances of Canadians stationed in St John's, and set aside a portion of each broadcast for "Newfoundland talent."[78] Captain F.R. Davies, the public relations officer with the Canadian troops, produced and directed *Stand By for Music*, a show that also drew upon many skilled musicians.

Not long after the *Prepare for Action* series ended, the American officer in charge of morale, Major G.B. Bildergack, arranged to have the BCN broadcast transcriptions from the Armed Forces Radio Service (AFRS), which was established by the American War Department in 1942. By 1 July 1943, VONF was carrying forty American War Department programs, which took up about twenty-five hours per week. With the exception of Sunday, on which the only American program the BCN carried was *Hymns from Home,* at peak the Newfoundland government-owned broadcaster provided as many as nine American programs per day in addition to the commercial American network programming it already carried.[79] The AFRS programs were popular with servicemen and civilians, and the Americans protested the Newfoundland government's decision to curtail the number of shows broadcast. Major Harford Powel, who had worked in the advertising industry in civilian life and had taken over as special service officer at Fort Pepperrell, had a low opinion of the quality of Newfoundland programming. He believed that the governors of the BCN were being unreasonable in denying Newfoundland listeners what he saw as the best programming in the world, and he reported to his superiors that the BCN's decision was based on one board member's opinion that these programs constituted "infiltration."[80] Some Newfoundland broadcasters and listeners embraced the American-style of commercial broadcasting as well as American popular culture, while others objected to them.[81]

Major General Brooks decided to establish an American broadcasting station that would be tailored to the servicemen's needs and would provide news from an American perspective, while the local radio stations would continue to provide BBC (British Broadcasting Corporation) news. Starting on 1 November 1943, station VOUS began its regular schedule from 5:30 PM to 10:00 PM. Powel recognized that Newfoundland civilians would listen to the station, but that VOUS primarily existed to maintain morale among the American servicemen.[82] The AFRS first attempted to do this by rebroadcasting American network programming and specially created entertainment programming that mimicked the radio that servicemen had listened to during their civilian lives. With this approach, the AFRS altered the repertoire of American popular culture in a several ways. First, in a process the American officials called "denaturing," advertisements and news reflecting what might be seen as petty domestic concerns were removed from the programming. For example, servicemen were kept from hearing news reports about industrial disputes when they were poorly paid and doing without basic comforts. The absence of advertising was one of the features most appreciated by civilian listeners. Second, since those in uniform were disproportionately male, the army selected shows it felt men would like – popular music (not symphonic music), sports, and comedy (no romance or serials). Survey research among a group of young recruits gave the AFRS a sense of which programs would be popular among the men. Third, just as the army and navy were racially segregated, so too was Armed Forces Radio. Musicians of African descent, for example, were restricted to one program on the schedule until 1944. Thus, Newfoundland civilian listeners, of which there were many, enthusiastically consumed American popular culture that had been tailored to the interests of young white men and that sanitized the portrayal of any conflict within the nation.

American military broadcasting was not just an avenue through which American popular culture was brought into Newfoundland. The American servicemen working at VOUS also produced their own programming. In this, their own life experiences had predisposed them to recreate the form and content of American commercial radio. Several of them had worked in civilian radio stations, either as technicians or as on-air staff. Major Powel had civilian experience in the broadcasting industry with both General Electric and WOR. In addition to this, he had worked in public relations, employing the same techniques for the manipulation of the "mass man" as those used in the advertising industry. Technician Third Grade Bud Rice had been a radio announcer for WNEW and WHN in New York in his civilian life, and several of VOUS's technicians had amateur radio experience. While Americans at both ends of the transmitter expected VOUS to be like the commercial radio they knew from before the war in tone and form, the absence of pressure to make money allowed a more relaxed tone in the local broadcasts. The amateur actors recruited among servicemen were reassured by Powel, who told them: "We're not selling time here. It doesn't matter if you run over or short a bit."[83]

Now stationed in St John's and in charge of the radio station, Powel wrote advertisements for such things as war bonds and authored about a hundred original plays and sketches devoted to interpreting Newfoundland to American servicemen to ease their adjustment to the overseas posting. Concerts of popular music, boxing matches, and quiz programs were frequently produced by volunteers among the service personnel and local civilians. A typical "orientation program" consisted of opening and closing music and a seven-minute war news bulletin (which gave the American perspective on the conflict rather than the British slant provided by the Newfoundland-owned stations). This was followed by the answer to the previous day's "thought question," which it was hoped might provoke discussion among service personnel.

In the attempt to familiarize the servicemen with Newfoundland, the orientation programs presented a portrait of the history of the country. Three out of the four extant scripts include two-minute historical sketches based on D.W. Prowse's 1895 *History of Newfoundland*. Most of the actors were local civilians who seem to have had a hand in the writing, since their social and political agendas are reflected in the scripts. These Newfoundland history radio dramas may have been prompted by an earlier recommendation that servicemen should be provided with information about Newfoundland so that they could adapt to the country more easily. In 1942 two American construction workers working at Argentia on the island's south coast were returned to the United States as "mental cases." The two civilians blamed their depression on the unending dreary weather and complained that "the community and its general facilities are, of course, not so well developed as in the United States" and that "the personnel not having been given an understanding of the reasons for conditions are not prepared for the marked change from American life." The two invalided workers suggested that if Americans were provided with information about the country before they arrived, such as a copy of the book *Newfoundland* by R.H. Tait, they might find the transition less difficult.[84]

The program used history in two ways. Depictions of Newfoundland's past could help the American servicemen better understand the contemporary social and political differences between Newfoundland and the United States and might encourage the Americans and the Newfoundlanders to get along with each other (implicit in this latter goal is the recognition that there were tensions between the servicemen and civilians). One of the odd aspects of the scripts, given that they were written by an American, is historical dialogue that seems to express anti-American sentiments. The author may have been attempting to explain to his listeners the historical reasons for the strains that sometimes appeared between the people of the two countries, or as suggested above, some locals may have contributed to the scripts. One script cited the page numbers of Prowse's book to establish its authority. The narrator claimed it was "one of the liveliest, most interesting and best illustrated histories of the world" and encouraged listeners to consult the book at a local library.

Two prominent Newfoundlanders, John Higgins and Dr Vincent Burke, acted in one of the radio plays. The narrator referred to Higgins, a lawyer and former Rhodes scholar, as "a native Newfoundlander" who reflected "the true attitude of the native of this island." The skit opened with the colonial secretary of the 1760s talking to the then Newfoundland governor Sir Hugh Palliser. Their banter served to explain to the American audience that the governor was the representative of the crown, not the government itself. It also led to a discussion of how American "invaders" take fish within Newfoundland waters. The secretary then complained that the Americans treated Newfoundlanders poorly: "The Americans are running away with our fish, Sir Hugh. The Americans are invaders ... In his own country, the American may be a diligent farmer, fisherman or mechanic. But when he comes to Newfoundland, his very nature changes. He becomes an invader. He regards us Newfoundlanders as aborigines – as savages – as were the wretched Beothucs [*sic*]."[85] Here, the actors give voice to Newfoundlanders' resentment at being treated like non-whites.[86] They were particularly antagonized by being called "natives." Presumably, it was expected that American servicemen might draw the lesson from this script that Newfoundlanders were sensitive to being treated like second-class people in their own country.

In this particular script, the Palliser character discusses the suitability of Newfoundland's climate for agriculture. The historian Prowse is cited as blaming the lack of agricultural development relative to the United States on English government policy rather than on any failure on the part of settlers. The men then segue into a discussion of salmon conservation. Passionate about the issue, the "actor" Higgins used the opportunity to promote fly fishing and condemn the practice of netting rivers. The intent of this message might have been twofold: to encourage American servicemen to take advantage of the wholesome activity of fishing and to remind civilians of conservation practices. Here, indeed, we see a cultural intervention, and perhaps significantly the character who advocates the lazy methods of harvesting salmon (netting) and demonstrates a lack of sportsmanship has an Irish name.[87] This would have been consistent with prevalent ethnic stereotypes of the day. At the end of the skit, the Palliser character anachronistically speculates that if Newfoundlanders work hard, conserve renewable resources, and "do not despise such modern inventions as greenhouses and steam heat," the country will one day not be a colony but will have the dignity of being a dominion. As was so often the case in the twentieth century, many commentators saw a supposed resistance on the part of underdeveloped colonies to "modern" methods as one of the impediments to economic performance. Americans could, and did, see themselves as exemplifying modernization while imagining that "natives" were responsible for their own backwardness. Burke, the deputy minister of education, who had trained at Columbia University and in 1921 was a founding member of the Rotary Club in St John's, worked in an anachronistic reference to that public service organization, which had originated in the United States.

A second script using the same characters allowed the narrator to criticize directly the anti-agriculture policies of Palliser for having held back Newfoundland's development. American servicemen were thus made familiar with a common nationalistic historical trope in Newfoundland, that economic development had been retarded by short-sighted English government policy – not by any inadequacies in its people.

The 28 July 1944 orientation consisted of "another proof of the long friendship, based on mutual advantage, and on inter-marriage, between Newfoundlanders, Canadians and Americans."[88] In a skit set during the war of 1812, also based on a selection from Prowse, an American privateer captures a Newfoundland trading vessel only to discover that the skippers of the two vessels are brothers who had been separated since childhood and who now find themselves on opposite sides in the conflict. The conclusion, in case anyone missed the moral, was explicitly stated: "All Newfoundlanders and all Americans are brothers." Not all of the sketches were related to Newfoundland; some dealt with themes in American history applicable to the contemporary war effort or with possible careers the servicemen might consider once they were demobilized.[89]

These orientation shows not only tried to make American servicemen more at home in Newfoundland, but provided opportunities for Newfoundlanders to communicate about matters of public concern. Powel, for one, thought that VOUS was the principal agency that represented the American armed services to civilian Newfoundlanders and thus was vital to how Newfoundlanders perceived the Americans: "This [station] has absolutely blacked out the local radio stations, except for their BBC news three times a day, and their local news. They have no talent or recordings which can compete with our transcriptions from Los Angeles. We also offer many original Army Band programs, Chapel organ recitals, and the like. VOUS has been a great maker of local good will for us, and we have been careful to ask many residents to appear on its daily orientation programs."[90]

The public relations function Powel attributed to the station presumed the existence of a civilian audience. Perhaps to boost its popularity among Newfoundlanders, the station used Newfoundland content as well as shows brought in from the United States. In a comic example that undercuts the argument that VOUS had a uniquely "American" character, Walter Bennett, who had been born in the United States to Newfoundland parents and had grown up in St John's, was drafted into the United States Army and then stationed in St John's, where he was assigned to work for VOUS. His friends quipped that his move from Forest Road to Pepperrell, on opposite sides of Quidi Vidi Lake, was a posting "overseas."[91]

VOUS gave Newfoundland civilians American music, comedy, drama, and information without listeners having to hear commercials. Likely most of the young people listened to dance music, drama and comedy shows, and latest American hits broadcast on VOUS, while mature listeners continued to avidly follow the Newfoundland news and public affairs programming on VONF. Frank Kennedy reported liking VOUS both because of the absence of advertising and because it had all the popular American radio shows, but he turned to the Newfoundland-owned stations VOCM and VONF for news.[92] Gilbert Oakley, similarly, remembers hearing the news on VONF (Barrelman and O.L. Vardy's international news) and listening to comedy programs (such as *It Pays to Be Ignorant*) on VOUS and dramas (such as *The Shadow* and *The Lone Ranger*) on the commercial stations.[93] David Edwards remembers listening to the latest swing music on the American station.[94]

Although it makes intuitive sense to assume that American music had a great effect on Newfoundland popular culture, that seems not to have been the case. The authors of a study of the "roots and sources of Newfoundland popular music" began with the assumption that the American bases had a "major influence in introducing popular music, especially Country-Western music," but they found little evidence to support that. While their informants agreed that the American presence was an outlet for popular music, the authors suggested that "Newfoundlanders influenced American taste in music rather than vice-versa."[95] Newfoundland musicians and listeners had gathered music from published sources, continental radio stations, phonographs, and travel, never from a single medium. Informants on the west coast of the island, for example, reported learning songs from stations in the Canadian Maritime provinces as well as from the eastern seaboard of the United States. It would be an exaggeration to claim that Newfoundland music was overwhelmed by the American popular culture conveyed through VOUS broadcasts.

Various intellectual and artistic contacts between Newfoundlanders and outsiders were promoted by the war. Some of these were ephemeral, but for those who had post-war careers in Newfoundland, the effects were long-lasting. The cultural interactions involving the print medium were less public than performance-related interactions, and it is difficult to be precise about the extent of their influence, but some examples serve to illustrate my point. Fort Pepperrell not only had performers, of course, but being a cross-section of American society, it also included a number of intellectuals. Given the interest in the commercial potential of civilian aviation, it is not surprising that the *Daily News* took note of the "most scholarly officer at Fort Pepperrell," an officer who held a doctoral degree and whose thesis was on the international law of aviation.[96] Similarly, the censor at the base had in his pre-war life been assistant curator of herpetology for the American Museum of Natural History in New York.[97] And Surgeon Lieutenant Commander Wellman of the Royal Canadian Navy spoke at the Rotary Club on psychiatry, bringing recent developments in the discipline to a Newfoundland audience.[98]

Personal interactions with Americans and Canadians may have encouraged artistic experimentation among Newfoundlanders. St John's-born aspiring poet Michael Harrington worked for the Americans between 1941 and 1943. His first book of poetry, *Newfoundland Tapestry*, was published in Texas after his boss at Pepperrell, a Texan, brought the young man's poetry to the publisher's attention.[99] These poems exemplify my larger theme: they work within the modernist poetic forms then emerging in Britain and the United States, and they take as their subject the Newfoundland experience. Harrington was a nationalist intellectual who explicitly attempted to forge a Newfoundland modernist literature, rather than reject modernism as a foreign style. There were others among his peers who shared a similar agenda. In 1943 the Art Students' Club of Memorial University College organized a public exhibition of the artwork of servicemen, in this way encouraging a creative leisure activity for the soldiers and bringing such amateur efforts to public viewing and critical appreciation. Over 600 people saw the exhibition within the first few days. The paintings included watercolours of naval vessels by S.A. Clarke, RCNR.[100] After working for the Americans at Argentia, the aspiring Newfoundland painter Reginald Sheppard travelled to Canada to enlist in the Royal Canadian Air Force, only to be posted to Gander, where he was tutored by a Britain-trained painter.[101] Sheppard and his wife went on to train a new generation of Newfoundland artists after the war. Certain items of Newfoundland material culture took on new meanings for foreign servicemen searching for something of the place to send home to their families. The Newfoundland-born librarian at Argentia, Louise Lambiase, reported that when she visited St John's, many of the American servicemen asked her to bring them NONIA (Newfoundland Outport Nursing and Industrial Association) sweaters to send to their wives back home.[102] These sweaters, handknitted in a Newfoundland style, made good souvenirs. The effect of these exchanges of material culture defies measurement.

CONCLUSION

Looking back on St John's in wartime, Helen Blundon reflected: "It was a terrible time, but I'm glad I never missed it."[103] Compared to life during the bleak years of the Depression, the Second World War was a time when young people embraced American dance music, movies, and Coca-Cola with a degree of frenetic enthusiasm. None of these cultural forms or commodities were new to people in the city, but the contrast between the boomtown atmosphere of wartime St John's and the pre-war life in the same small town could hardly have been greater. Added to that excitement was the very real sense among many that each experience could be the last – that one's friend or boyfriend might soon die in the fight against Hitler. The Canadian and American servicemen and civilians filled many of their leisure hours with music. Wartime swing sessions, barn dances, and other performances had a lasting impression on the city.

A few American musicians made St John's their home after the war, which encouraged the misconception that the friendly invasion had introduced American popular music to a land of folk music. The idea that Newfoundland was transformed from a tradition-bound, backward area of the world into a secular, capitalist, and innovative place through the actions of American business and military might is a common trope. That impression is not accurate. Long before the *Edmund B. Alexander* docked, phonographs, movies, live concerts, travellers, and radio had introduced Newfoundlanders to jazz, early variants of country music, and many other musical forms. While there is no doubt that the AFRS programming and the American servicemen themselves provided more American popular music during wartime than had been available before, each of these musical styles had been popular with younger listeners before the war. Swing and country music were twentieth-century American musical art forms, and they emerged in St John's not long after their inception and shaping in the barn dances and night clubs of the United States. Not everyone liked the modern American popular culture of wartime, but whether one embraced it or not had more to do with one's generation than with one's place of birth. Older people, as well as military and civilian authorities, were less likely to like popular music and movies and more likely to worry about the sexual behaviour of youth than young people in the city.[104] As one correspondent to the *Daily News* pointed out, the generation that liked swing were "fighting the greatest battle the world has already seen" and insisted that they were "entitled to our fun."[105]

Even the interest taken by Newfoundlanders in "folk" music (such as Scammell's songs, the Doyle songbook, and the work of musicians like Macleod) can be seen as a modern people's attempt to forge a new Newfoundland national culture that exemplified humane values, continuity, and community in the face of Nazism and disruption. We need not assume that their interest in traditional music was a reflection of cultural conservatism or anti-modernism just because it drew upon continuity with a Newfoundland past.

Part of the reason that the modernization theory passed out of fashion among academics was that scholars realized that there was more than one path to modernity. Despite the problems with the modernization concept, however, a few scholars have described Newfoundland as having remained "traditional" until events such as the arrival of the Americans or political union with Canada provoked its people to embrace modern ways of life. No compelling case has been made for this interpretation. Long before the war, Newfoundlanders had embraced the modern and the industrial.

Newfoundlanders have taken more than one road to modernity. Reeves has pointed out that at the beginning of the twentieth century some Newfoundlanders were "aping the American type."[106] Korneski has suggested that the enthusiasm for modern railway building in the late nineteenth century was tied to a popular desire for a "British society," and this would entail recreating Newfoundlanders as individuals with the proper gender roles. The Newfoundland Railway was as much an imperial project as a desire to embrace North American–style wage labour.[107] The choice was not between traditionalism and a modern American lifestyle; Newfoundlanders could embrace a modern culture of Britishness or American values. Perhaps the Confederate Association slogan, "Confederation – British Union," represented an attempt to find common ground between Newfoundlanders' seeing themselves as Britain's oldest colony and their accepting that the country was part of North America.

Military authorities tried to confine interactions between servicemen and civilians to the movie theatre, the dance hall, and the family parlour and to limit the sex in the sentry box. American popular culture could channel people into working together, but a few people of the older generation disapproved of the popular music anyway. The St John's social and commercial elite were as likely to look to Britain as to North America in matters of taste and culture, and they may have, as did conservatives in the United Kingdom, looked upon American popular culture as degenerate.[108] Opposition to American popular culture is not reflected in the interviews for this project. Most of the respondents had been children during the war, and their views of popular music varied from enthusiasm to indifference. But evidence suggests that many older people during and after the war continued to favour British popular culture.

Just as the U.S. Army was not the homogenous entity that it might have appeared to be from outside, civilians experienced different engagements with Americans. People's interactions with the servicemen and their popular culture varied with their generation, sex, and class. Women and men experienced the war differently. While it is a bit of an exaggeration to say that the local men worked alongside the foreigners and the women dated them, gender roles did affect how individuals gained access to and were influenced by cultural interchange. Moreover, middle- and upper-class civilians interacted with foreigners differently than did the poorly educated and economically marginal.

Radio was a significant factor on the home front. There were literally dozens of regular and occasional broadcasts devoted to war purposes. This was a war in which the home front and the battle front overlapped; civilians in Europe bore the brunt of the casualties and civil societies became militarized. North America was spared the most horrific aspects of the war, but radio brought the conflict into people's homes. This made war an experience that was mediated by radio broadcasts for many people. Hollywood movies and popular songs adopted patriotic and martial themes. In the case of Newfoundland, implicit within the wartime culture was the tension between British and American popular culture. Wartime promotion of American popular culture may have raised Newfoundlanders' expectations of a North American consumer lifestyle after the war and thus helped prepare the ground for political union with Canada, but it only marked an acceleration of an existing trend, in Newfoundland and elsewhere, towards higher levels of consumption of North American goods and media. On the other hand, the BBC and the Newfoundland radio stations also tried to reforge the ties of King and Country and remind Newfoundlanders that they were fighting a British war.

American bases in many parts of the world, especially during the Cold War when the bases accommodated the spouses and children of service personnel, may have served as modernizing models for local populations to emulate. The bases, with their schools, sidewalks, bowling alleys, women in pants, and so on, differed greatly from the Japanese or the Saudi host society.[109] Local populations may have copied the technology, architecture, and social styles that they came into contact with at the bases, but they may also have developed reactionary attitudes towards the Americans. But Fort Pepperrell during the Second World War was not a self-contained bubble that recreated America in a radically different country. The base on the shore of Quidi Vidi Lake had gates, but the gates allowed passage in both directions. Newfoundland in 1940 was culturally similar to the United States, and American popular culture had long been available in the city. Wartime was a culturally vibrant time, and the civilian and military institutions mediated the cultural interchange.

6

Mona Wilson and the Canadian Red Cross

GILLIAN POULTER AND
DOUGLAS O. BALDWIN

HMCS *Transcona* gun shield art. "Transcona, now a part of Winnipeg, was founded as a service centre for the railway and hence, the mighty 2-8-4 locomotive breaking up the Nazi swastika." Gary Green, *A Guide for Some of the Gun Shield Art and Ship's Badges of the Crow's Nest Officer's Club* (St John's: Crow's Nest Military Artifacts Association, Newfoundland).

> She is known all over St. John's, from the sailor on the street to the Governor of Newfoundland ... Miss Wilson has not only served our men with unselfish devotion, but she has made a permanent contribution towards a better understanding between Newfoundland and Canada.
>
> Clara F. McEachren, "Canadian Red Cross in Newfoundland"

The influx of Canadian service personnel into Newfoundland at the beginning of the Second World War quickly taxed St John's medical, recreational, and temporary housing facilities. The city was also home to the Royal Canadian Navy (RCN), which helped escort convoys of ships on the North Atlantic Run, and thus additional care was required for the thousands of shipwrecked sailors left stranded by German submarine attacks. Lionel Chevrier, Canada's minister of transport, later recalled, "It was quickly apparent that extraordinary measures were necessary to provide facilities ashore for rest, relaxation, recreation and welfare of officers and men and to receive and care for survivors landed after ship wreck, etc."[1] The Canadian Red Cross stepped in to take on a large share of this responsibility.

Soon after the first Canadian soldiers landed in St John's, the Canadian Red Cross Society convened an emergency executive meeting to appoint a representative in Newfoundland. Although the terse notes of that meeting mentioned that Miss Mona Wilson was "thoroughly conversant with conditions there" and recommended that she be asked to serve as assistant commissioner,[2] she had never been to Newfoundland and knew very little about it. However, her work

as provincial director of public health nursing on Prince Edward Island was well known to the Red Cross executive, and Wilson had two close friends on the society's National Women's War Work Committee who recommended her for the position.[3] After receiving a leave of absence from the Prince Edward Island government, Wilson became assistant Red Cross commissioner of Newfoundland.

With no existing organization in the country, Wilson faced an imposing task. Her mandate was to care for the physical and social needs of Canadian men stationed in Newfoundland, but "no programme directive had been given to me by the Can. Red Cross, other than to do what I could to help," Wilson later recalled.[4] Although she was given no specific instructions, Wilson had vast experience in taking on such a challenge. Her background in the Balkans with the American

Surrendered German U-boat U-190 in St John's Harbour, June 1945. Department of National Defence Fonds, PA 145584, Library and Archives Canada.

Mona Wilson, assistant Red Cross commissioner, Newfoundland. Authors' collection.

Red Cross after the First World War and her work in rural Prince Edward Island had prepared her for what was needed. Her letters, diaries, and official reports outline the work of the Red Cross in Newfoundland and provide glimpses of the wartime city and its people.

Whereas other chapters in this anthology detail the reaction of Newfoundland children, women, and the general population to the invading Canadians, this chapter examines the reactions of one Canadian towards wartime St John's and its people. Given Mona Wilson's experiences, it appears that the claims of such nationalist historians as John FitzGerald that Newfoundlanders despised the invading Canadians are clear exaggerations.[5] Although Wilson's experiences confirm most of the interpretations made by the other authors in this collection, she had her own unique observations. What, for example, are we to make of her lamentations about the lack of shopping facilities and restaurants in St John's when other chapters note their large numbers? Noteworthy for its absence is the lack of any mention of disorderliness in the streets or even a hint that Newfoundlanders treated her differently because of her nationality.

Mona Gordon Wilson was born in 1894 in the prestigious Rosedale area of Toronto, Ontario, where the family rubbed shoulders with the city's elite.[6] Nursing was one of the few avenues available to women who desired a professional career and a measure of independence, and this led Wilson to enrol in the prestigious Johns Hopkins Hospital nursing program. Following graduation in 1918, she enlisted in the United States Army Nursing Corps to assist in the closing of American base hospitals in France. The next year, she joined the American Red Cross Society and departed for Siberia, which was in the throes of a Communist revolution and the Allied intervention. Quartered in Vladivostok, Wilson spent eight tension-filled months working in a women's medical ward and training Russian nurses' aides in the principles of practical nursing. In May 1920 the American Red Cross sent Wilson to Tirana, Albania, to conduct home visitations in that war-ravaged country. Late in June, amidst a barrage of shells, Wilson hurried to the Adriatic coast to assist the Red Cross medical unit located only ten kilometres from the warring Albanian and Italian armies. In August, Wilson was dispatched to Dubrovnik on the Dalmatian coast to care for 30,000 White Russian refugees. April 1921 found her in Vir Pazar, Montenegro, where she organized mothers' clubs to teach the benefits of fresh air, infant care, and personal hygiene, and accompanied mobile public health clinics into the mountains.

Like other nurses who have served in war zones abroad, Wilson was not content with the prospect of civilian nursing when she returned to Toronto in 1922.[7] Instead, she earned a Public Health Nursing Diploma at the University of Toronto and became chief Red Cross public health nurse in Prince Edward Island the following year. In the absence of a provincial health department, Wilson and her small staff ministered to the island's health needs. When the provincial government established a Department of Health in 1931, Wilson became provincial director of public health nursing. Except for the period of the Second World War, she held this position until her retirement in 1961. By the time she passed away twenty years later, Wilson had been awarded the highest honour in international nursing (in 1963 she was the ninth Canadian to receive the Florence Nightingale Award), in Girl Guides (the Beaver Award in 1957), and in Prince Edward Island (Island Woman of the Century in 1967).

Harbour viewed from gun emplacement at Cabot Tower. Z-1605, Department of National Defence, Library and Archives Canada.

With this extensive background in nursing and pubic health administration, Wilson was well prepared to face the task of organizing the activities of the Canadian Red Cross in wartime St John's. Fortunately for historians, Wilson maintained an extensive correspondence with friends and family, sporadically maintained a diary, and kept the numerous drafts of her many speeches to women's and public health organizations.[8] Mona Wilson's extensive overseas experiences, her familiarity with rural people and Maritime culture, her insightful nature, and her penchant for writing down her thoughts make her an excellent observer of wartime St John's.

Wilson's wartime narrative must, however, be interpreted within the context of her experiences, personality, class, and gender. Wilson was steeped in nursing traditions premised on respect for hierarchical authority. Rather than forming close associations with her workers, Wilson relied upon a large network of like-minded women of similar class for emotional support.[9] These companions were usually service-minded, independent, middle- to upper-class single women. Wilson was not sympathetic to any attempt to challenge traditional gender roles or to contravene the dictates of "ladylike" behaviour.[10] When the Canadian Red Cross Society supplied Wilson with several young female volunteers to assist her in Newfoundland near the end of the war, she attempted to limit the women's social activities and insisted that they behave like officers and ladies and maintain a friendly but non-familiar attitude towards the rank and file. Although they occasionally had a good laugh together, Mona Wilson and her staff existed in two separate worlds after working hours, and when the Red Cross recommended that Mona share a house with these women, she objected to living in such "close proximity to my workers."[11] Despite Wilson's sense of privilege, she got along exceedingly well with all classes of people in her work. Eleanor Wheler, who had worked with the Victoria Order of Nurses in New Brunswick and had been a nursing supervisor in Ontario before moving to Prince Edward Island, was particularly impressed with her. "She loved directing, she had a tremendous enthusiasm for it, it was her whole life." One day, Wheler, recalled, Wilson "went with me out to this dirty, neglected home, where the kids were full of head lice, I wondered how she would tackle it, and she was wonderful ... she could get down to their level."[12]

Wilson arrived in St John's to take up her post as assistant Red Cross commissioner on 4 October 1940. During her first few days in the city, she walked around town, climbed Signal Hill, and addressed several volunteer organizations. Operating from her room on the fifth floor of the Newfoundland Hotel, Wilson explored the town's resources and arranged with customs and railway officials to admit and transport Red Cross supplies free of charge. Although the vast bulk of goods were to be provided by the Red Cross National Women's War Work Committee in Toronto, shipping would take time and Wilson foresaw that she would need things quickly when emergency situations arose.[13] On these occasions she would have to buy what she could in St John's, so she also surveyed the city for suitable shops and met with their managers to enlist their support. "From then on," Wilson noted in her diary, "they proved to be friends indeed and later helped me out of many a supply difficulty."

Knowing how vital volunteers would be to the success of her Red Cross programs, Wilson quickly established friendly relations with existing service organizations. During the next few weeks, she contacted church groups, the Girl Guides, and several volunteer women's organizations, and called upon the health department, the St Johns Ambulance,[14] and military officials. Her best connection was with the Women's Patriotic Association.[15] Before the war was two weeks old, the governor's wife, Lady Walwyn, had organized a public meeting in St John's to revive the Women's Patriotic Association of Newfoundland (WPA). The WPA had provided material comforts for Newfoundland's soldiers and sailors in the First World War, and Lady Walwyn envisioned it playing a similar role in this war. Following this 21 September meeting, about 300 St John's women, including the wives of many of the "best" families in the city, registered to start work immediately. The number of branches grew steadily until it reached 409 at the war's conclusion.[16] The WPA provided woollen sweaters, scarves, socks, mitts, and other comforts to each departing member of Newfoundland's armed forces.[17] On Wilson's second day in St John's, Lady Walwyn invited her to a meeting of the WPA, and she immediately became good friends with WPA secretary Caroline Hutchinson, whose brother Wilson had known in Charlottetown.

The YMCA, the Salvation Army, the Canadian Legion, the Ladies' Auxiliary of the Benevolent Irish Society, the Omrac Sewing Club, and the Knights of Columbus, among other groups, also provided volunteer services for the Canadian, American, and Newfoundland armed forces.[18] Two days prior to Wilson's arrival in Newfoundland, the St John's War Services Committee was established to coordinate the activities of these service organizations, and it convinced the Newfoundland government to loan it the old King George V Seamen's Institute at 93 Water Street as a hostel for members of the armed forces. In addition, the government agreed to contribute $5,000 and pay the salaries of the custodial staff.[19] The hostel was renamed the Caribou Hut in honour of the Newfoundland Regiment in the First World War, whose emblem was the caribou, the symbol of plenty. With Wilson's urging, the Canadian Red Cross contributed $1,000 for the hostel's furnishings and Torontonians donated books and magazines for the library.[20]

THE CARIBOU HUT

The Caribou Hut was officially opened on 23 December 1940, and it was there that Wilson established the first Canadian Red Cross office. It was a five- to ten-minute walk from her room in the Newfoundland Hotel, and each morning she passed a monument outside the hotel dedicated to Ethel Dickinson, who, the inscription read, "gave her life while tending patients at the King George V Institute" during the 1918 influenza epidemic. Farther down the hill, between Duckworth and Water streets, was a First World War memorial, and across the street was the place where Sir Humphrey Gilbert first landed in Newfoundland in 1583. To the rear of the Caribou Hut was the harbour where Wilson spent many nights waiting for ships returning with survivors.

The Caribou Hut was a place where military personnel, merchant seamen, and civilians could meet and relax. Although the YMCA had offered to provide a professional manager for the hostel, he had not arrived, and the War Services Committee accepted Wilson's offer to take charge of the hostel in the interim.[21] It was a "very hectic & exciting" month, Wilson noted in her diary. As manager, she was responsible for selecting paint colours, interviewing painters and carpenters, recruiting people to do odd jobs, delousing mattresses, washing blankets, and spraying sleeping quarters against "creepy crawlies." With the help of several work parties of Canadian soldiers, Wilson put the hostel into working order in just under two months.[22] In addition to these responsibilities, she was always "chatting with the troops, answering the phone a million times a day, and dashing to four hospitals in different parts of the city to visit my sick sol-

A party at the Caribou Hut. Authors' collection.

diers, sailors and men of the merchant marine." Then there were the numerous trips to customs and the freight sheds each time a shipment of supplies arrived from Canada, followed by the difficulty of borrowing a truck and getting the supplies stored in the warehouse. During this two-month period, Wilson lost twelve pounds, seldom returned home before 7:30 at night and often worked until 10:30. Wilson relinquished her managerial role to Mr Herbert A. Messacar when he arrived in April 1941, but remained a permanent member of the Caribou Hut Committee's executive.[23] Even after the Canadian Red Cross moved its office to another building, Wilson continued to support the Caribou Hut, and as the historian of the Hut wrote, "whenever there was giving to be done the Canadian Red Cross seemed to always be at the top of the list with service and goods."[24]

The Caribou Hut was bigger than its name implies. When completed, it boasted more than 200 beds, along with bowling alleys, a canteen that remained open from 6 AM to 1 AM, the city's only indoor swimming pool, card games, five- and ten-pin bowling lanes, a reading room, darts, table tennis, a large fireplace, dances and musical entertainment, bingo nights, a lending library, and even counselling services.[25] These activities were reported regularly in the St John's newspaper. When Wilson, ever the watchful observer, noticed that the men only participated in square dances, she arranged for a local teacher and a group of young women to offer dance classes. The first class attracted twelve men, and by early 1941 Wilson was organizing dances for upwards of 500 people. The Caribou Hut also offered activities for the mothers and wives of servicemen. In April 1941, for instance, the women were invited to attend a "Talkie Pictures and Musical Programme." The Caribou Hut provided a much needed and appreciated service, one that was praised as being a vital part of the war effort.[26]

The idea of providing sailors and servicemen with a "home away from home" was far from new.[27] Like other such establishments in the past, the Caribou Hut was designed to provide servicemen with a wholesome, respectable, family-like environment. St John's mayor Carnell, for example, declared, "It is very desirable that there should be sufficient places of amusement, clean, brightly lit and attractive, supplying wholesome entertainment for our own young people and for the young men and young women of the various services who for the time being are making their home with us."[28]

RED CROSS SERVICES

When Wilson arrived in St John's, there was limited entertainment available for the Canadian troops (even restaurants were closed on Sundays), so she quickly telephoned the city's permanent Canadian and British residents and asked them to invite Canadian servicemen for Christmas dinner.[29] When this effort proved successful, she recruited the wives of Canadian bankers and businessmen to make clothes and supplies for the servicemen. As more servicemen's wives sailed to Newfoundland to be with their husbands, Wilson's group of volunteers swelled to about seventy strong, and she established separate committees to visit the men in the hospitals, collect reading materials and create hospital libraries, look after the supplies in the warehouse, arrange entertainment, and make hospital supplies.[30] Other services included finding apartments and nurse maids for the newly arrived Canadian families.

The Red Cross office, conveniently situated in the Caribou Hut a block away from the WPA headquarters, soon became a centre of information for Canadians living in St John's. The volunteers responded to a variety of requests, advising the servicemen where to eat and how to find relatives, mending and sewing their clothing, finding them a date or a nursemaid, and even buying clothes for a bride

A spot of tea or coffee for all callers at the Canadian Red Cross office. Authors' collection.

Mona Wilson in front of the Red Cross office. Authors' collection.

in England whose only measurements were "tall and slim." The office also provided comfort and companionship for the service wives who were thousands of miles away from home and faced the ever-present fear that their husbands might never return. Civilians and servicemen dropped in for coffee in the morning and cookies and tea in the afternoon. "She set up a small office," the secretary of the WPA later wrote in praise, "and one of her first modest requests was for a tea-set, kettle, tea, cocoa, canned milk to make a home-like spot."[31]

In May 1941 Wilson moved the Red Cross office and workroom to the ground floor of the Knights of Columbus building on Water Street, opposite the Caribou Hut, providing more room and a view of the harbour. Two years later, the noisy presence of the new Merchant Seamen's Club on the second floor, and water damage caused by a serious fire, convinced Wilson to move the office a block farther south on Water Street.[32] By now Wilson was renting five storage warehouses, including one at Botwood. To guard against potential bombing raids, she equipped each warehouse with a complete range of supplies. "We worked continually under the strain of limited time," Wilson wrote, "sorting, counting, packing the piles and piles of comforts when two or three groups of ships were in port at one time, and for merchant ships too, so the deliveries would be made before the ships sailed. The sailing hours were shrouded in secrecy and frequently were changed."[33]

By the end of 1941 there were three Canadian hospitals in St John's and one each in Botwood and Gander. The Red Cross provided these hospitals with sheets, beds, triangular bandages, and operating-room supplies, many of them made by Wilson's volunteer sewing committees. That year the Red Cross shared its two new mobile hospital units with the St John's Ambulance and several Newfoundland hospitals whose doctors were not acquainted with the technology.[34] Later, similar supplies were distributed to outport hospitals, and the Red Cross assisted the Department of Health with its blood donor clinics. Working under the direction of the Nursing Sisters of the Naval Hospital, Red Cross volunteers provided sterilized supplies and surgical linens for ship sick bays. The Nursing Sisters' quarters received radios, chairs, bedside lights, and curtains, as did the patients' recreation rooms. Since the military hospitals also treated civilians, the Red Cross supplied them with layettes and children's clothing.

Wilson's most challenging task was caring for the survivors of stricken vessels in the North Atlantic. The WPA had been providing shipwrecked sailors with a new kit of clothes, but shortly after Wilson arrived, ninety-five survivors from a

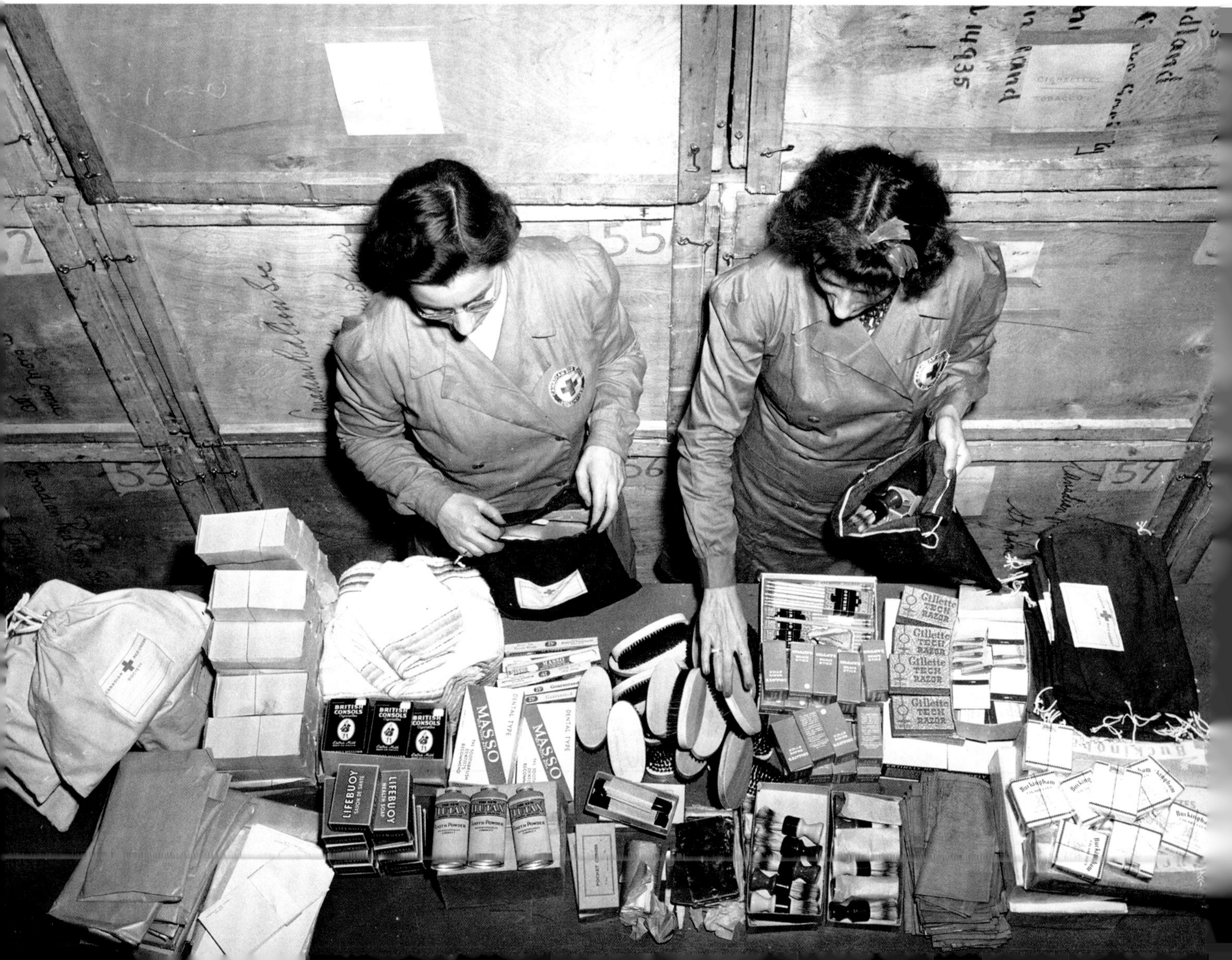

Naval officers' wives filling comfort bags for survivors. P0003127, Public Archives and Records Office of Prince Edward Island.

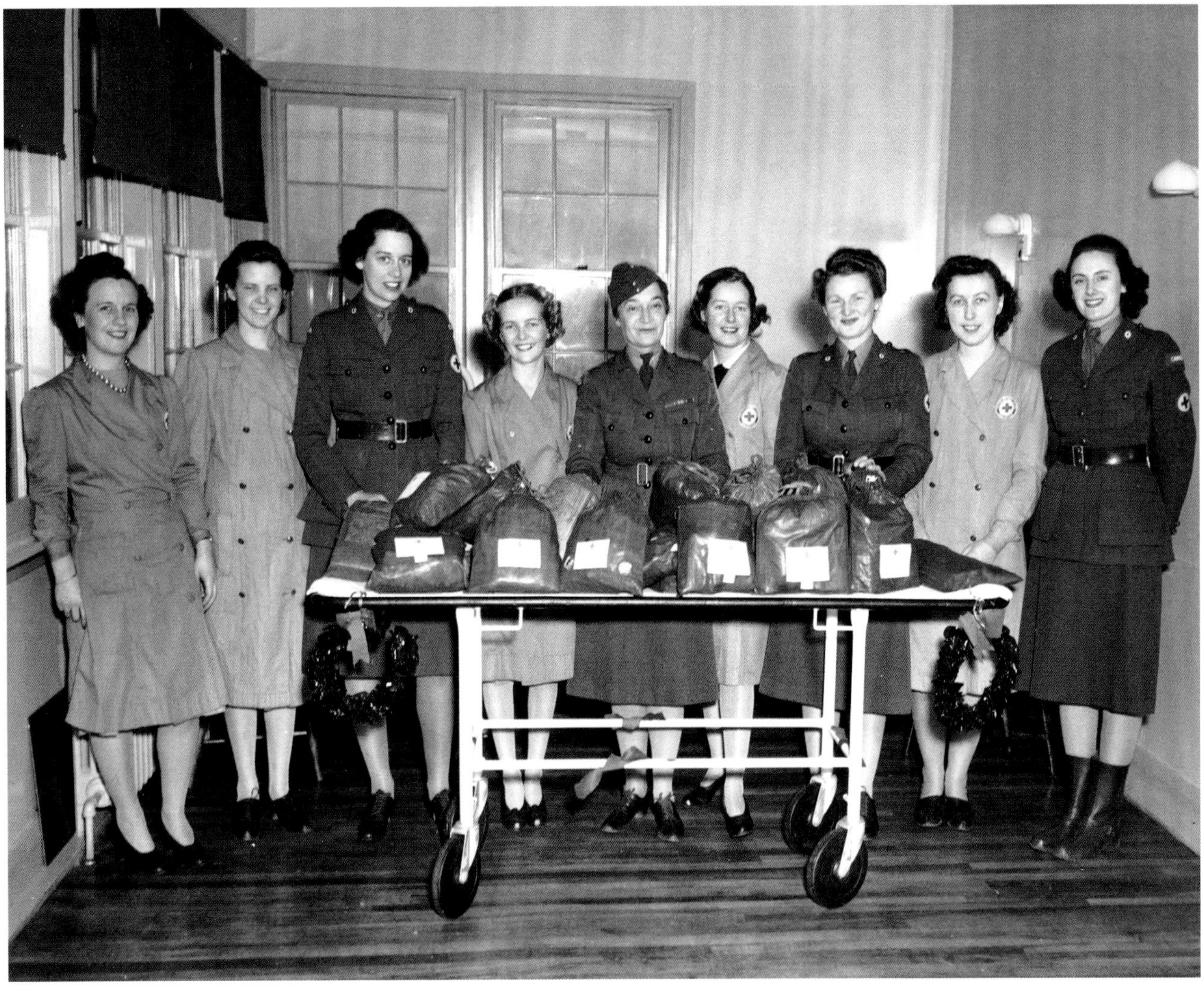

convoy attacked by the *Admiral Scheer* were brought in to St John's by the merchant cruiser *Jervis Bay*. Although she had insufficient supplies on hand for so many people, Wilson promised the WPA that the Red Cross would provide both emergency clothing and ablutionary supplies for each survivor, and then she asked her volunteers if they could do it. The volunteers rose to the challenge. As Wilson described it, "One lady accompanied me hurriedly down town where we bought material and had it sent back to the office by special messenger, where the ladies immediately started cutting out and sewing the bags, while we went from wholesale to wholesale store purchasing razors, shaving soap and brushes and all the other toilet articles and stationery which make these little bags just the very first thing a survivor wants to receive. The next day the ladies helped distribute the bags. That sent their enthusiasm sky rocketing and from then on they met every emergency with the same quick dispatch and undaunted spirit."[35]

Mona Wilson and volunteers with ditty bags. NF 3740.8, Department of National Defence,

Wilson established sewing committees of fifteen to twenty wives to make these "comfort" or "ditty" bags. The bags were filled with shaving equipment, toothbrushes and paste, cigarettes, combs, soap, towels, writing paper and pencils, and then put into large dunnage bags containing an overcoat, underwear, sweater, socks, sneakers, a cap, mitts, and a suit of clothes. Every day there was "a mad dashing to the wholesale department and searching for clothing and more clothing. This meant going to all the shops along Water St. before a sufficient quantity of any one thing could be accumulated."[36] That year the volunteers made over 1,200 articles. By 1943, Wilson was coordinating over 300 women, and the sewing groups' production soared from 5,300 articles in 1942 to over 7,000.[37] Navy, air force, and army wives met separately and often had different tasks related to the special needs of their menfolk. Navy wives, for example, made leather vests, toques, and minesweeper mitts.

The Red Cross office had to be ready for action at any hour of the day or night, especially between the summer of 1941 and June 1943, when the Battle of the Atlantic was at its height. Wilson reported that 500 survivors landed in St John's in 1941, followed by more than 5,000 in the next eighteen months.[38] The workdays were fifteen hours long, with many all-night sessions. One emergency followed another. No sooner had one group of survivors been outfitted, than a message came that twenty shipwrecked sailors had landed at a small village on the coast 150 kilometres away, and Wilson had to organize a convoy of trucks with food and clothing for the trip over narrow, icy roads. Survivors were brought in by naval escorts, small rescue trawlers, or individual fishing crafts. Some men had been adrift in lifeboats for many days and were near death or had to have their arms or legs amputated after spending too many hours in the bitterly cold ocean. Sometimes only a handful of men needed care; other times an entire crew was rescued. Once, a thousand survivors arrived in St John's on the same day, but all were greeted by Wilson and her volunteers and given the supplies they needed. The following selection from Wilson's diary for the first week of October 1941 indicates the frantic level of activity:

> Two groups of survivors arrived, 30 Dutchmen & 36 Englishmen ... Given comfort bags (greatly appreciated), trousers, braces or belts, shirts, running shoes, underwear. Dutchmen left by destroyer following morning. Great scurry getting them off and new group clothed which arrived just before departure of Dutch. Sewing committee working feverishly to make comfort bags. Also made 24 prs lap stockings and 6 operating suits for RCAF Hosp, Gander – all most beautifully done – raised moral amazingly. Woolen comforts asked for by several ships, supply exhausted and wire sent for more to be rushed.[39]

Wilson took great pride in being at the pier to greet every survivor, regardless of the weather. "At any hour of the day or night," she recalled, "the telephone might ring, there would be a message from the port officer, – 'friends outside,' or 'at the usual place at 2 am.' In wartime, telephone messages were guarded. I

would ask 'Many?' also 'Large?' also 'Color?'" If the survivors arrived at night, Wilson hurriedly phoned her volunteers, dressed, dashed to her station wagon parked a couple of blocks down the street from the hotel and drove around the city to collect her helpers. Returning to the office, the women laid out clothing for the survivors, and then walked a hundred metres to the pier to wait for the rescue ship to loom out of the darkness, lit only by the port and starboard lights. As Wilson explained, "The decks would be lined with the men who had been rescued from the sea looking down and wondering what fate lay ahead for them." Wilson and her volunteers were a welcome sight: "[O]ften the captain would call down from the bridge to me. Those who had brought survivors in before said they always felt so relieved to know I would be there. Many times I would have to rush back to the office for an armful of shoes so the men could come ashore, their own shoes lost when the ship was torpedoed, or would find a man wrapped

Mona Wilson welcoming survivors at Canadian Red Cross headquarters. NF 201-2, Department of National Defence.

in a blanket borrowed from the ship because his clothes had been blown off."[40] Those who did not need hospital treatment were taken across the street to the Red Cross office, where they were given clean clothing and a bed was arranged for them at the Caribou Hut, the YMCA, or the Knights of Columbus hostel.[41]

In addition to helping these survivors, Wilson was an inexhaustible worker. She helped at the Caribou Hut; spoke at functions for graduating nurses, Girl Guides, Army Nursing Sisters, Rotary Clubs, and Girls' Bible Classes; participated in radio broadcasts to raise money for various volunteer organizations; wrote articles for the *Canadian Red Cross Despatch*; made regular trips to Botwood and Gander and later to Lewisporte, where a third hospital was built; drove military men out into the country for picnics; and just kept "the whole show running smoothly." In preparation for Christmas she arranged for the St John's Cadets and the Girl Guides to come to the Red Cross office every Saturday morning from October onwards to wrap gifts for the servicemen and for the

Lascars from India – merchant seamen survivors landed in St John's. C-053589, Department of National Defence Fonds, Library and Archives Canada.

women in the Merchant Marine Hospital. Despite the constant work, Wilson confided that she would not exchange her job for any other.[42]

Delivering mail to ships. Z-1323, Department of National Defence Fonds, Library and Archives Canada.

Under Wilson's leadership, the Red Cross was ready to deal with any island disaster. The Knights of Columbus fire showed Wilson at her best. In December 1942, the Knights of Columbus hostel burned to the ground, killing a hundred people who had been trapped in the inferno.[43] Because the telephone company had suspended all communications, Wilson had to drive all over town to collect volunteers to help feed the patients and make dressings. When she learned that the hospital needed twenty additional arm baths for burn immersion, she jumped into action. "They weren't to be found anyplace," she later wrote. "All windows had been boarded up. It was a Sunday, but we got various managers of wholesale departments to allow us to poke through their shelves for anything which would do for a substitute, but without success. Then we found a tinsmith who gathered all his men together and made the arm baths in record time."[44] The Canadian Red Cross donated dressings, sheets, and blood plasma to the hospitals treating the victims. The greatest demand, however, was for sulfadi-

Country drive and picnic for hospital patients. Authors' collection.

azine, a new anti-burn drug not yet available in Canada. Wilson wired these needs to the Canadian Red Cross commissioner, who phoned Trans-Canada Airways requesting that a plane be held in readiness and then contacted a hospital in New York to fly a shipment of sulfadiazine to Toronto. Sixteen hours after Wilson learned about the emergency, 2,000 tins of dry blood serum and twenty pounds of sulfadiazine arrived in St John's.[45] Later, the national commissioner of the Canadian Red Cross wrote: "Another feature of disaster preparedness which really grew out of the tragic fire at St. John's Newfoundland, is that dry blood serum is now available in every part of Canada in case of civilian disaster."[46]

Wilson assisted in several other emergencies, including when supplies had to be sent to an isolated base by dog team or dropped by parachute to a troop train caught in the snow. When the main street in Harbour Grace burned to the ground, Wilson immediately rushed her volunteers to the scene. The finance commissioner, who had flown to the site of the disaster, remarked, "Ah, here the Red Cross is again. Always on hand when there is a job to be done." This was not an isolated remark, as Wilson always sought to ensure that the Red Cross symbol was visible for all to see on crisis occasions.[47]

Coming from Prince Edward Island, Mona was accustomed to short summers; however, she found St John's "so dirty, cold & foggy that to get any summer weather at all it is necessary to get even a few miles away from it."[48] So, during the few holidays Mona allowed herself, she liked to explore the countryside, which she admired for its "harsh and dramatic beauty." In a talk to the Prince Edward Island Women's Institute following the war, Mona described "the great high, menacing rocks rising a sheer 100–200 ft. out of the sea & in a storm the serf breaking in great geisers & with wind & snow adding to the savagery of the picture." She later noted: "There are great long bodies of water stretching as far as 30–40 miles into the interior from the sea & when one flies over Nfld one is impressed by the mass of water – an amazing mass of streams, rivers, ponds and lakes also vast forests, rock and bog. Only the coast is settled with small villages – called outports & a few settlements along the RR."[49]

Wilson was particularly fascinated with the outports. One holiday she toured the coastline aboard the *Northern Ranger*, which was making its last delivery of the season before ice closed the harbours. The *Northern Ranger* cruised between such narrow passageways that she had the impression she could touch both sides if she stretched out her arms. Wilson was intrigued with the variety of supplies the ship carried: "100 lb bags of flour, of sugar, bags of coal, an outboard motor, cartons from Eaton's (maybe from their catalogue – always so useful and

Mona Wilson with Major Moore and Major Klock: "Taken for a drive into the country." Authors' collection.

well-thumbed) by people not conveniently near shops, even a wood stove was deposited into one dory."[50] On another holiday, Wilson vividly recalled the fishermen's return after a season of fishing:

> Searchlights showed the wharf packed with humanity and freight ... what a melee. Luggage right to end of dock piled high. Gangplank unsteadily balanced on 2 oil drums, but before it was raised men clamoured over sides like pirates boarding a ship. Such confusion, shouting, and heaving around of luggage. Streamed aboard carrying kettles (must always have their tea), cartons, carpet bags, flour sacks, pillow cases, potato bags, mattress ticking, paper bags, suit cases, sea boxes of all sizes, shapes and colours, tied with rope and trunks wives. Children – pets and animals crated, guns, rods, harpoons.[51]

Several times a Canadian naval boat took Wilson to see icebergs outside St John's Harbour, which she found a thrilling sight. At least once, Wilson escorted naval officers on a drive "to see a bit of the country," and they climbed up the cliffs outside St John's to see the icebergs. "To our amazement from that eire [*sic*] position we counted no less than twenty small icebergs in the vicinity ... it was a very exciting scene to watch for half an hour or so."[52]

THE WARTIME CITY

Mona Wilson was fascinated by the city and recorded her impressions in her diary and in letters to friends and family. She loved watching the fishing fleets unloading their fish at the docks and the bumboats ferrying passengers across the harbour. "The waterfront is a veritable forest of masts when the schooners bring in their catch," she noted. "Everywhere there seems to be a reek of fish which one soon gets used to – most unique to see the rows of fishing flakes and the stages cleverly built."

Except for a short stay at Mrs Hattie Cowan's boarding house, "the nicest one in the city," on Topsail Road, Wilson rented a room in the Newfoundland Hotel.[53] This seven-storey, yellow-brick building was the finest hotel in the country. It had been furnished from England, and included telephones and baths in each room, tennis courts, and a skating rink. The Newfoundland Escort Force was initially headquartered here and the flag officer Newfoundland Force and his staff occupied the top floors. Wilson photographed the view from her fifth-floor room, revealing a bustling but not prosperous city.

The high unemployment rate during the Depression had brought a steady decline in the standard of living. Few people could afford to make repairs on their homes. St John's "is interesting," Wilson informed her sister,

> very old of course and very dingy. The houses are built right on the streets up against another in endless rows. Very foreign looking, or possible like the old part of Quebec City. The most ordinary looking house on the out-

Sorting fish, 1945. Wilson noted on the back of the photo that this was "probably dried cod or haddock." P0003128, Public Archives and Records Office of Prince Edward Island.

> side however, may be most charmingly arranged inside – they really are most surprising. Many of the old houses have no central heating, only fireplaces in the rooms. I went to look for rooms in one of these the other day. Most antiquated bathroom and kitchen with no end of pipes visible, funny little fireplaces, and the unevenness of the floors and stairs could be felt at each step.[54]

This impression was not just Wilson's Canadian prejudice. Less than five months later, the archbishop's pastoral letter stated that some sections of St John's were so poorly lighted and ventilated that they were a "disgrace to the city." Later, the Commission of Enquiry into Housing and Town Planning reported that St John's was "dirty, congested, ill-built, and planless," and that approximately 70 per cent of the city's 6,500 houses were "substandard."[55]

Even though she was familiar with rural poverty from her years in Prince Edward Island, Wilson was shocked by the poverty-stricken conditions in Newfoundland. The island's tuberculosis mortality rate was triple Canada's, and its infant mortality was double.[56] "Never in any place on this side of the Atlantic have I seen such undernourished and miserable looking children apparently so poorly fed and clothed," Wilson remarked to a friend. Since 14 per cent of the city's homes did not have sewage connections, two-wheeled horse-drawn carts, with burning torches on the back to ward off the flies, regularly collected sewage

Wilson wrote on the back of the photo: "taken from my window in the Newfoundland Hotel, 1945." Authors' collection.

buckets from the front of each house.[57] The Canadian troops nicknamed these vehicles "chariots," or "honey wagons."[58] American authorities also complained of unhygienic restaurants, salons, and other public places.[59] In many areas of town there were still horse troughs. "Everyone says the poverty is terrific," Wilson noted, "but I don't see how this could be avoided with the high cost of living. Practically all food is imported and the tariffs are terrific. It is almost impossible to get a tin of vegetables or fruit under 30c, butter is 50c, lb, tea 85c, coal $25 a ton. A bar of Ivory soap for washing is 30c etc, and cornflakes 30c. I've forgotten how many thousands are on the dole, and there are many organizations for sewing for the poor of the outports."[60]

Wilson could shop for herself in the Canadian forces canteen, where prices were lower, but inflation was more of a problem for civilian residents. In August 1941, she noted that most commodities were "twice as dear here as in Canada."[61] Although the food controller pegged food prices in May of the following year, Wilson wrote two months later that prices had increased by 35 per cent in the previous month, particularly for gas, cabbage, butter, and soft coal. She also complained about the rationing of canned milk, coffee, tea, and sugar. Canned goods were especially hard to come by.[62] In the summer of 1943 she noted that tires and spare parts were so scarce that cars were disappearing from circulation.[63] Wilson's correspondence to her sisters indicates that ladies' items were also difficult to find. Although Bowring Brothers, Ayre and Sons, James Baird, and the Royal Stores department stores were all located along Water Street, Wilson's letters are replete with requests for cotton dresses, frocks, slips, girdles, fleece-lined boots, stockings, cotton gloves, "posh" shoes, and a sports hat. Even when Wilson did find something she liked, the storekeepers might reply, "Sorry, but it is out of stock at present, meaning 6 months to a year."[64] After one unsuccessful shopping trip she lamented that there was no "decent place to go to revive one's drooping spirits with a spot of tea. Not a good restaurant in the city that is not dear or serves good food – and after 8 pm it is impossible to get a bite in the hotel. What a country! Oh for a Honey Dew or a Murray's."[65]

Since the Canadian hospitals were located at opposite ends of the city, Wilson initially relied upon bus service to get around. Unfortunately, the busses broke down regularly, "but how was one to know about that after standing on a street corner freezing in the icy wind for an hour or more waiting hopefully! The simplest way to get to the base at Lester's Field from where I lived was a good half hours pull up a steep hill, usually with a haversack filled with heavy magazines on my back, and then another three quarters hour walk to the General Hospital, stopping in at two other civilian hospitals on the way. No, those days were not easy," Wilson recalled, "but the men were sick and alone in a strange country and it was my job to make them feel that the Red Cross was their real friend."[66] The arrival of a green Red Cross station wagon in late April 1941 brought an end to Wilson's long, "wearisome trudging by foot, tram, and bus" around St John's.

"Walking on the streets is quite a hazardous adventure," she observed in her diary:

> The hills are terrific and both the sidewalks (such as they are) and the roads are horribly slippery. There are only a few streets in the city that are paved and so far I have only found pavement on sidewalks of two streets. There are narrow footpaths built up with a curb for future paving I suppose, but at present they are of rolled dirt and gravel, are most uneven and very treacherous for walking. One continually must keep one eyes glued to the path ahead. Most of the people walk on the road in a most nonchalant manner and must be a most frightful nuisance for motorists ... We used to worry in Charlottetown about the children sliding [sledding] on the grades, but heavens! that wasn't a patch on what they do here – simply swarms of them on almost every street slipping down the hills onto cross roads with street cars, trucks and what have you. They tell me usually several are killed each winter.[67]

Discarded bottles added to the hazardous condition of the streets. Wilson found the evidence of constant drunkenness "appalling" and attributed the littered bottles to the lack of drinking facilities. The men, she wrote, "have to buy a bottle and as after awhile a bottle becomes a nuisance to carry around its contents are consumed straight then the bottle heaved off into space."[68]

Mona Wilson in the Red Cross station wagon. Authors' collection.

Evidence of the war became more tangible in St John's when weekly air raid practices began. The city's civil defence organization called for several one-night blackouts in 1940 and 1941, beginning at 6:30 PM, before implementing a blackout for a fortnight in early 1942.[69] Movies began at 5:30 in the summer so the audience could return home in daylight. "The first night of the black-out," Wilson reminisced,

> I had been so desperately busy all day that I had quite forgotten to have the headlights of the car blackened. These were required to be completely painted black except for a 2 x 1 inch patch of light! There were no street lights on or any in the houses or buildings. I was in a great rush, but, of course, hadn't gone any distance when I was stopped by one of the constabulary. These tall men wore dark grey ankle-length great coats and high black fur caps and really were quite awesome. However, they were familiar with our Red Cross service so, after explaining my mission, I turned off the headlights and was allowed to proceed through the dark streets without any light whatsoever. Fortunately the streets were deserted. When I finally arrived on the pier without mishap, one of the Naval officers came to my assistance with a roll of black electric tape with which he covered the headlights except for the small patch of light allowed.[70]

PUBLISHED BY AUTHORITY

Under the provisions of the Defence Regulations 1939, the Governor-in-Commission has been pleased to make the following orders.

The 25th day of May, 1940.

L. E. EMERSON,
Commissioner for Justice.

1. All public street lights in the City of St. John's shall be reduced to 50 per cent of their present lighting value.

2. No lights of any description (other than street lights) on the outside of any buildings within the City of St. John's or within one mile thereof, shall be lit after the coming into force of this order, provided however that door lights in front of a building may be lit for necessary temporary use.

3. No lights shall be lit in any building in the City of St. John's unless the direct reflection towards the sky is eliminated by the bulbs or lights being above the permanent structure of the window or unless the windows or lights of such buildings are covered by blinds or shades which confine the glare within the building.

4. No lights shall be allowed to remain lit in any unoccupied building in the City of St. John's ,whether such building shall be unoccupied temporarily or permanently.

5. Head lights used on any motor vehicle in or near the City of St. John's, or on any road approaching St. John's from which lights may be visible at sea, shall be obscured by blackening or covering with a non-light penetrating shield or material the upper portion of the lens down to a line one inch above the centre of the bulb, and by blackening or covering with dark non-reflecting material the lower portion of the reflector up to a line one inch above the centre of the bulb.

6. On the sounding of an Air Raid Alarm, all street lights and all lights showing any light that may be observed from the street shall be immediately extinguished and shall so remain until the 'all clear' signal has been sounded, and all motor vehicles shall immediately haul close to the side of the road or sidewalk and park and shall extinguish all lights and remain so parked with lights out until the 'all clear' signal has been sounded.

7. It shall be the duty of the members of the Constabulary and all A. R. P. wardens to see that these regulations are strictly obeyed and all orders issued by them for the better observance of these Rules and Regulations shall be forthwith carried out.

8. Any person contravening the provisions of this order shall on summary conviction thereof be subject to a fine of not more than one hundred dollars and in default of payment thereof imprisonment for a term not exceeding one month.

9. This order shall come into effect on the first day of June, 1940.

CIVIL DEFENCE

INFORMATOIN MEMORANDUM No. 13

MOTOR VEHICLE LIGHTS DURING BLACKOUT

For the sake of clarity, the requirements regarding lights on motor vehicles are set out below. WHAT IS NEW IN THE REGULATIONS IS PRINTED IN CAPITAL LETTERS.

The requirements, in so far as they affect headlights, are in force until a special mask is officially approved and made available.

DIGEST OF REGULATIONS

1. The entire headlight lens must be blacked out with the exception of a semi-circular aperture of this size and shape.

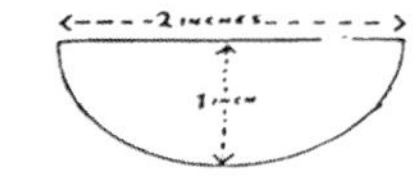

2. This clear space is so located on the lens that the centre of the top line is in front of the centre of the lens and the top line is horizontal across the centre of the lens.

3. EXCEPT IN CARS WITH SEALED BEAM HEADLIGHTS, THE BULB IN EACH HEADLIGHT MUST NOT EXCEED 32 CANDLE POWER.

4. (a). THE SEMI-CIRCULAR APERTURE MUST BE COVERED WITH A MIST COAT OF WHITE PAINT OR OTHER SUBSTANCE WHICH WILL PRODUCE THE EFFECT OF A LIGHT FROSTING.

(b) THIS MIST COAT OF PAINT MUST BE APPLIED MORE HEAVILY IN THE CASE OF VEHICLES HAVING SEALED BEAM HEADLIGHTS, SO AS TO REDUCE THE AMOUNT OF LIGHT DISPLAYED TO THAT PERMITTED FOR VEHICLES NOT SO EQUIPPED.

(The purpose of the mist coat of paint is to diffuse and reduce the beam of light shining through the semi-circular aperture).

5. All the rest of your headlights must be blacked out.

6. The front of your car will look like this:—

You may have:

(a). One red light at the rear, if possible on the right hand side, which must show to the rear and not upwards. THIS LIGHT MUST BE SO BLACKED OUT OR SHADED THAT LIGHT IS PASSED THROUGH A CIRCULAR APERTURE NOT EXCEEDING ONE INCH IN DIAMETER.

(b). One small white light to illuminate your number plate. BUT IT MUST BE SHADED SO THAT NO LIGHT IS VISIBLE FROM ABOVE.

You may have:

The red light which is temporarily shown by the application of the foot brake. BUT IF YOU DO SO THIS LIGHT MUST BE SO BLACKED OUT OR SHADED THAT LIGHT IS PASSED THROUGH A CIRCULAR APERTURE NOT EXCEEDING ONE INCH IN DIAMETER, WHICH SHOWS TO THE REAR AND NOT UPWARDS.

8. This memorandum is issued solely for the guidance of motorists and is not a legal interpretation of the Regulations.

COMMON FAULTS

The principal irregularities which have been noted, and which will in future be corrected by Police and Civil Defence Officers, are:

(a) The semi-circular aperture is either not frosted at all, or the frosting has been removed opposite the bulb.

(b) No tail lights showing at all.

(c) Bulbs of over 32 candle power being used.

(d) Sealed beam headlights not reduced by increased density of the mist coat of paint to the equivalent of the light permitted on vehicles not so equipped.

(e) The semi-circular aperture reversed, or placed above the centre line of the lens.

L. C. OUTERBRIDGE, Lt.Col.
Director of Civil Defence.

11th April 1942

CUT THIS OUT AND KEEP IT.

DON'T SAY LATER YOU NEVER KNEW

Left Blackout announcement, *Evening Telegram*, 22 May 1940. Used with permission of the *Telegram*.

Right Civil Defence Information Memorandum No. 13, *Evening Telegram*, 11 April 1942. Used with permission of the *Telegram*.

Despite these occasional frustrations, Wilson found the islanders "overpoweringly hospitable" and was impressed by their friendliness, ingenuity, enjoyment of "the simple things of life," and their "zest for living."[71] Shortly after arriving in Newfoundland, Mona took the train to Corner Brook. "This provided me with an insight into the enthusiasm and attitude of Newfoundlanders towards their way of life," she later noted.[72] At this time she also met the Rendells. "How lucky for me, as that delightful family with their wonderfully warm hospitality so typical of the Newfoundlanders took me to their hearts and made me feel welcome and very much at home throughout my five years in Newfoundland," she recalled. The islanders' sense of humour could "keep one in convulsions of laughter for hours on end with their tall stories."[73] However, when Wilson was intent on her job, some of these characteristics were not always appreciated. She wrote a friend that although it was often difficult to get people moving in Prince Edward Island, "believe me it isn't a patch on what one has to contend with here. 'Time' as we value it is just non-existent."[74] Another time, when Wilson was having difficulty obtaining supplies, she wrote: "Life is certainly hard – nothing is easy here – there is a struggle every day over something or other. It wears me down."

As a staunch Canadian, Wilson often made a point of noting that her volunteers were Canadians – army and navy wives and the wives of Canadian bankers and businessmen stationed in St John's. In editing the drafts of her many talks, Wilson frequently inserted the qualifier "Canadian" where appropriate. For example, she wrote: "The house was not equipped for overnight guests, but Mrs. McClenahan, in charge, (a Canadian), rose to the occasion." Or, the survivors stayed at "the newly opened [handwritten "Canadian" later inserted] YWCA Hostel." These entries were typical of the careful distinction Wilson made between Canadians and Newfoundlanders. She recognized that St John's was a city occupied by foreign forces whose presence caused some resentment. Early in her stay on the island, she escorted a dozen Canadian officers to a local party. The men were dressed in their finest and Wilson later commented, "[E]ven if they are not exactly welcome here in their present capacity, at least they are bound to make an impression and let's hope create a good feeling of friendliness between two countries of the Empire. After all, I suppose no country really enjoys the invasion of another country."[75]

Wilson's gender also shaped her wartime experiences in the city. Her rank as assistant commissioner was equivalent to the rank of captain, which meant that the servicemen often saluted her.[76] "I was the first woman in a service uniform to be seen on the streets of St. John's," she later wrote, "and apparently was quite a curiosity. I was amused to find that occasionally I would be followed by a few children marching in line. I presume they were playing at imagining themselves as part of the Army."[77] In a similar comment that shows her awareness of the uniqueness of her situation, Wilson wrote that when the Red Cross two-ton truck arrived, "it practically held up the traffic on Water St. while the drivers of other vehicles slowed down or stopped to watch. The tram conductors also stopped their trams so the passengers could have a good look! Apparently they

Miss Maud Krumm and the Red Cross truck. P0003128, Public Archives and Records Office of Prince Edward Island.

had never seen a woman drive a truck of any kind and this was a large one."[78] To speed the admittance of supplies from Canada through Customs and Immigration, Wilson did without a broker, and although "[i]t just 'wasn't done' to have a woman messing around the piers," she was soon "passed through Customs and Immigration without any difficulty."[79] Thus, Wilson broke many gender barriers in her work, but her writings convey the sense that she did so on the strength of her social background, professional training, and administrative competence rather than because of any feminist leanings.

The work of the Red Cross straddled the military-civilian divide. Although it "wasn't done" to have women on piers, the services provided by the Canadian Red Cross were considered as being within the realm of women's sphere. Thus the appointment of an eminently capable woman like Mona Wilson to a position in which she outranked many men was deemed appropriate, especially since it freed another man for war work on the front lines.[80] Providing clothing, toiletries, and medical supplies to enlisted and merchant seamen helped return them to sea quickly and fully recovered. The Caribou Hut ensured that servicemen on the loose in St John's were provided with opportunities for wholesome entertainment in the company of respectable women.[81] The Red Cross workers and volunteers visiting the hospitals acted as surrogate female family members, caring for wounded men who were away from home. They soothed brows, sewed, cooked, entertained and generally acted as substitutes for mothers, sisters, and wives, reinforcing the family bonds seen as so vital to social stability. In the gendered ideology of the time, it was only women who could provide care like this; men would not do.[82] Wilson may have been a figure of some curiosity and awe on the streets of St John's, but no questions were raised about the suitability of her presence there.

Wilson's social background added to her acceptability. She was quickly invited to join the active social life enjoyed by St John's social elite, and was soon swept up in a social whirl of dinners, teas, and parties. After her first few weeks in Newfoundland, she wrote remorsefully to a friend in Charlottetown: "Now I regret having kept my nose so steadily to the grind in PEI and so lost all the social graces. My inability to play bridge, mix easily with strangers, and chat incessantly is indeed a handicap."[83] The next year she complained to her sister: "Heavens the parties! The pace is too strenuous for me. I have been aboard corvettes for luncheons and dinners, and cocktail parties on British sloops."[84] When Wilson moved the Red Cross office to the Knights of Columbus building, she invited Governor and Lady Walwyn, members of the government, the mayor of St John's, the Canadian commissioner, and the commanding officers of the Newfoundland, American, and Canadian armed forces to the official opening. The Walwyns took an active interest in the Red Cross "and were frequent callers at our office ... and Lady Walwyn occasionally helped with the distribution of clothing to shipwrecked survivors." Although Wilson made no mention of bowling, watching any of the many hockey games, or going to a movie at the Capitol, Nickol, York, Star, or Crescent theatres, when her workload lightened in 1943 she began to play badminton, an activity she later expanded to Wednesday and Sunday nights. As she claimed later, "there was never a dull moment in this port."[85]

POST-WAR BENEFITS

More-efficient radar detection systems, new tactics, and air protection brought a virtual end to the Battle of the Atlantic late in 1943. By then, Wilson calculated, the Red Cross had helped approximately 6,000 survivors and supplied more than two million items. As the action shifted away from the North Atlantic, American and Canadian servicemen, who at one time numbered over 16,000, left Newfoundland for other theatres. The decline in the number of survivors needing care provided a welcome relief. Ironically, it was only at this time that the Canadian Red Cross Society, astonished by the burden that Wilson shouldered alone, recommended that she be given full-time help.[86] In mid-July 1943, three members of the Canadian Red Cross Uniformed Corps (Transport Sec-

tion) arrived to assist Wilson; they were followed in April by two women from the Nursing Auxiliary section.

Since the hard work of attending to survivors was virtually over, Wilson took this opportunity to expand the society's activities and augment civilian services. Some of the corps women provided occupational therapy at the Canadian hospitals in St John's, Botwood, and Gander. Others taught home nursing and first aid classes, helped at blood donor clinics, and instructed expectant mothers in the Canadian Naval Well Baby clinics. When the war concluded, Wilson arranged for the corps women to meet each incoming transport vessel and provide the returning veterans with chocolates, cigarettes, "and smiles." They also assisted the WPA in helping the wives and children of the Newfoundland Foresters.

Wilson spent the last months of her stay off-loading the Red Cross's supplies and equipment, ensuring that Newfoundland would benefit once the war was over. Some surplus stock was transferred to Europe and the Far East, but most of the medical supplies, including the station wagon and the truck, went to New-

Part of the Canadian Red Cross staff: Betty Smith, Maud Krumm, Mona Wilson, May Boyle, and Dorothy Martin (Christmas 1944?). Authors' collection.

foundland's Department of Public Health and to local hospitals. At the end of October 1945, Wilson transferred the remaining clothing and packing cases to the WPA, which, on her suggestion, moved into the Red Cross office and later transformed itself into the Newfoundland Red Cross Society.[87] Other supplies were donated to the hostels of the Knights of Columbus and the YMCA. Following a sad farewell, Wilson sailed for Halifax on 31 October 1945.

Several years after Wilson had left St John's, the president of the WPA claimed, "No report that has, or may be written, can ever pay sufficient tribute or do justice to Miss Wilson. Those of us who witnessed the efficiency with which she organized her volunteers, cared for the needs of servicemen, together with her readiness to rush assistance to local communities which suffered disaster, felt that the Canadian Red Cross was really something."[88] Likewise, the 1944 Annual Report of the Canadian Red Cross Society stated, "No one in the services of the Canadian Red Cross Society ... has done a more outstanding piece of work than Miss Wilson." As the *Canadian Red Cross Despatch* explained, "Miss Wilson has not only served our men with unselfish devotion, but she has made a permanent contribution towards a better understanding between Newfoundland and Canada."[89] In the occupied city of St John's, the maternal nature of the services provided by the Red Cross had blurred the divisions between military and civilian and set the groundwork for future relations between Canada and Newfoundland.

Part 3 | Conclusion

7

The Occupation of St John's in Global Perspective

HMS *Dianthus* gun shield art. "The gun shield shows a ram butting a U-boat. This commemorates Dianthus sinking U-379 not by depth charges but by ramming her several times. The badge shows the flower for which the corvette was named with the motto, 'Small but Hardy,' underneath. The crew taking delivery of the new Flower Class corvette knew nothing about the flower and consulted a seed catalogue. It described the plant as small but hardy! The crew thought it an apt description of the vessel and adopted it as the corvette's motto." Gary Green, *A Guide for Some of the Gun Shield Art and Ship's Badges of the Crow's Nest Officer's Club* (St John's: Crow's Nest Military Artifacts Association, Newfoundland).

KEN COATES AND WILLIAM R. MORRISON

On 29 January 1941, a large number of American forces arrived in St John's, Newfoundland, on the troopship *Edmund B. Alexander*. The start of this friendly invasion overwhelmed the capital of the Dominion of Newfoundland, bringing both economic opportunity and social disruption to the community. St John's was transformed by the experience and emerged from World War II in dramatically different shape than it had entered it. The effort to understand the impact of the American occupation on St John's requires, however, a view of the episode that goes beyond simply local events, for the presence of the Americans, their effect on local customs, the development of new wartime infrastructure, and the inevitable conflict of values and experiences that resulted from large-scale cultural mingling were part of a global phenomenon that has been called the "American Rampant."[1] It was the first worldwide expansion of the United States and the first stage in the establishment of the American Empire, a geopolitical force that would dominate the globe for more than a half a century after the end of World War II.

While one could certainly examine the American occupation of St John's as a local phenomenon, the analysis of the Newfoundland and Labrador experience benefits more from an understanding of the broader patterns and significance of the wartime expansion of the United States of America. Though no German troops had invaded the dominion, Newfoundland's troops, like those of the rest of the Commonwealth, were participants in the war, and the battle for the North Atlantic provided real and tragic evidence of the violence and devastation associated with the expanding conflict. In this environment, the arrival of the American soldiers was both a welcome and an intensely local event, with the impact and consequences felt very close to home. It is important to remember, however, that the American deployment of troops and associated workers in Allied countries represented one of the fastest and largest distributions of military personnel in history, that this deployment transformed the American outlook on and experience of much of the globe, that America's international presence and profile changed both dramatically and permanently in a matter of a few months, and that the St John's experience was replicated around the globe. The St John's situation was complicated by the arrival of Canadian forces alongside the American military and civilian personnel. In this regard, Newfoundland experienced a double invasion, one in which historical memory has treated the Americans more positively than the Canadian interlopers.

THE HISTORIOGRAPHY OF THE FRIENDLY INVASIONS

The vast literature on the American engagement in World War II has focused on its military and political aspects and has provided insights into the social and economic impact of the war in the United States and other countries.[2] Over the past twenty years, consideration of the effect of the war has broadened considerably, to include such crucial themes as World War II as an element in the liberation of African Americans[3] and Native Americans, the ecological implications of widespread military activity, and the influence of cultural imagery on the conduct of war. Historians in a number of different countries have begun to examine the impact of America's many "friendly invasions," their studies covering regions as diverse as Iceland and the Caribbean, Great Britain and Australia, the Canadian North and New Zealand.[4] The American interventions are viewed as an interesting and in some instances crucial element in national history; with surprisingly few exceptions, the American military expansion is not viewed as a global or international phenomenon.

It is odd that the global impact of the war has attracted so little attention, beyond general analyses of the war as the starting point for the expansion of the American Empire. A review of the various local, regional, and national histories of the American invasions – many repeating the old British cliché of the Yankees as "over-paid, over-sexed and over here"[5] – reveals surprising commonalities in the Allied experience of American occupations. In community after community, the arrival of the American soldiers sharply altered the local economy, brought Americans and locals into direct and extended contact for the first time, introduced foreign nationals to the reality of American racism and segregation, created tensions and opportunities in gender relations, tested the tolerance and patience of local officials, created new infrastructure, and introduced American popular culture, wealth, and values to populations that previously had formed most of their ideas of the new North American superpower from watching Hollywood movies.

It is only natural that historians should emphasize local and national circumstances and highlight the regional impact of the American occupations rather

Surrendered German submarine U-190, May 1945. 2007-8 Album, James Hawke Collection, Crow's Nest Military Artifacts Association.

than search for commonalities across the globe. There is no automatic reason, for example, for historians of Newfoundland to look to Bermuda for lessons about local conditions or to believe that developments in Brisbane are germane to efforts to understand developments close at home.[6] Despite promising beginnings, the sub-discipline of world history has been slow to attract practitioners – beyond the world history courses that have been substituted for the old standard Western Civilization overview. There are a number of reasons for this, starting with the difficulty inherent in understanding developments in dozens of different regions, the challenge of searching archives and libraries around the world, and the inevitable linguistic, cultural, and historiographical barriers involved in looking at comparative developments in many different locations. This said, there are many phenomena, from the spread of ideas to environmental change, from political movements to technological transformations, including the impact of Americans overseas during World War II, that would very much benefit from a global perspective.

The collection in this volume, rather uniquely among the global literature on the subject of the American invasions, combines broad, conceptual, and community-level descriptions of the friendly occupation with highly personalized descriptions, drawn from extensive oral history collections, of the impact of the arrival of the U.S. troops. The accounts of those who experienced the occupation offer a nuanced picture of the American presence, just as the political and military assessments place the local and personal developments in broader context. Other areas likewise experienced dual (or more) friendly invasions. In Great Britain, after all, there were hundreds of thousands of Canadian and other troops in addition to the massive American contingent. The analysis here of the combined impact of the Canadian and American occupation looks beyond the lingering animosity towards Canada and Canadians – a vestigial legacy of the post-war Confederation debates – to explain how legal and political arrangements helped create different realities for the two friendly military groups. The St John's experience was among the most intense, long lasting, and transformative of the American peaceful invasions. In many parts of the Americas, the U.S. forces came and went quickly, or removed themselves almost entirely from the scene after the war. In Newfoundland's case, World War II built upon earlier relations, dramatically reoriented the community, and shaped St John's' long-term view of itself, Canada, and the United States. As the recollections of St John's residents reveal, the events of war remain deeply imbedded in the personal and collective consciousness of Newfoundlanders.

THE ST JOHN'S OCCUPATION IN GLOBAL CONTEXT

By the 1930s it looked as though the United States, in the aftermath of the carnage and disillusionment of World War I, had retreated permanently into a protectionist shell. Congress rejected President Woodrow Wilson's entreaties to assume a position of international leadership, dooming the League of Nations in the process. With bitter memories of the loss of 50,000 men in a European war that had not made the world safe for democracy, Americans showed no interest in extending hegemony after 1920, except to some degree in a commercial sense to Latin America. The roller-coaster economic expansion and collapse of the 1920s and 1930s both celebrated and tested the resilience of the American economy, but both eras saw the country shunning any global responsibilities. The Great Depression, made worse by the retreat into protectionism, raised even greater fears about the dangers of international engagement.

Even as militarism triumphed in Japan and Germany and as Nazi occupations of German territories in Europe and Japanese aggression against China foreshadowed war, most Americans preferred to hunker down and focus on the challenges created by an ecological catastrophe on the Great Plains, the turmoil that followed the stock market crash of 1929, and the growing unemployment lines that plagued the entire nation. The neutrality acts passed by Congress in the late 1930s, among them laws forbidding the sale of armaments to belligerents and the arming of American merchant ships, showed the pacifist temper of the country. As late as early December 1941, a week before the attack on Pearl Harbor, the America First Committee, an organization vehemently opposed to American participation in the war, boasted a membership of over 800,000.[7] When the rest of the world plunged into war in 1939, the United States stayed on the sidelines, capitalizing on new markets for American-made military hardware, shoring up friendly nations through various Lend-Lease programs, and permitting a few adventurous souls to join the British or Canadian armed forces in their battles with the Germans. While President Roosevelt may have desired more rapid intervention, memories of World War I and the political power of the America First movement made it necessary for him to move very cautiously towards war. But despite this, the United States did take steps to ready itself for international military engagement. The Lend-Lease program of 1941 that shored up Britain by providing war material on credit was a brilliant move in this direction, as was the 1940 deal by which the United States gave Britain some old naval vessels in return for bases in the Caribbean and Newfoundland and Labrador.[8]

The history of Newfoundland's early engagement in World War II is well known. The Dominion of Newfoundland entered the war on 3 September 1939, automatically following Great Britain's declaration of war on Germany (Canada waited a week and voted separately to declare war). The following year, Canada secured permission to station troops at several Newfoundland and Labrador sites and took steps to integrate Newfoundlanders into the Canadian armed forces. The destroyers-for-bases deal, signed in September 1940, included the right to build military facilities in Newfoundland, which sat on critical naval routes and flight paths between North America and Europe. American bases were subsequently constructed at Argentia, Stephenville, and Fort Pepperrell and other military stations in St John's. Major air bases at Gander, Goose Bay, and Torbay played a crucial role in the air strategy in the North Pacific. Over the winter of 1940–41, the American presence in the war expanded dramatically, initially through the shipments of American-built bombers to Great Britain and then, in January 1941, through the arrival of the first American troops in Newfoundland. For the duration of the war, as discussed in the other chapters in this book, the Americans transformed St John's and much of Newfoundland, boosting the economy, marrying local women, constructing new facilities, and even altering the political culture of the region to the point where many local people were prepared to consider annexation to the United States.[9]

On the global scale, the Japanese attack on Pearl Harbor shocked the United States out of its illusion that it could avoid participation in the global war. The American army had had several years to prepare for what the prescient had realized was their inevitable entry into the war on the Allied side. Even so, daunting logistical challenges lay ahead as the United States mobilized for a multi-front war, rushed to the defence of the battered United Kingdom, and took steps to stop the aggressive advance of the Japanese in the Pacific. In the early months of 1942, the United States had few military personnel overseas, lacked the infrastructure to deliver men and supplies to the fronts in Europe and Asia, and did not have a detailed strategy for moving swiftly to a wartime footing. What the United States did have, in abundance, was money, manpower, a huge industrial machine, and the American can-do spirit, the last liberated by the government's willingness to spend lavishly, though often wastefully. They also had a profound sense of urgency. German submarines were attacking shipping in the North Atlantic, carrying the campaigns into the waters off Newfoundland. Japanese aggression in the North Pacific, which eventually resulted in enemy troops occupying part the Aleutian Island chain, showed that the continent was vulnerable to enemy attack.

Not surprisingly, therefore, much of the early effort focused on solidifying the defence of North America. Newfoundland had been so strategically crucial that the Americans moved quickly to develop naval and aviation facilities in the dominion. Similarly, the United States started in 1939 to build the Northwest Staging Route, a series of airfields linking Edmonton, Alberta, and the highly vulnerable Territory of Alaska. In one of the greatest wartime construction projects in history, the Americans built a 1,500-mile highway linking Dawson Creek, British Columbia, and Fairbanks, Alaska, between April and November of 1942. In short order, the Northwest defence projects expanded to include oil production in Norman Wells, Northwest Territories; pipelines linking Norman Wells, Whitehorse, and various highway locations; additional roads along the pipeline supply and construction routes; and a communications network tying the far northwest to the rest of the continent. On a smaller scale, the Americans also undertook Project Crimson, building a network of air bases that provided an alternative route between the Midwest and Europe, using Frobisher Bay on Baffin Island as the key facility in the network.

The Newfoundland and Canadian activities solidified the defence of North America. In the case of the Newfoundland bases, the facilities were urgently required and played a vital role throughout the war. Thousands of planes, hundreds of ships, and tens of thousands of military personnel passed through Newfoundland during this period, repeatedly demonstrating the value of the strategic investments. The Northwest projects, on the other hand, were arguably a waste of money from a military perspective. The American armed forces had argued against the construction of the highway and supporting facilities, and the Canadian government disputed the location of the route connecting Edmonton to Whitehorse and Fairbanks. The U.S. government persisted, more for reasons of morale and publicity than for military necessity. The highly pub-

licized construction of the Alaska Highway received much more attention in the American press than did the more militarily important Newfoundland bases, reassuring the North American public that the government would stop at nothing to defend the continent. By 1943, with the Japanese pushed out of Kiska and Attu in the Aleutian Islands and with the Battle of Midway in June 1942 tipping the balance in the North Pacific in the Allies' favour, the Northwest defence projects were downgraded in importance, leaving the Alaska Highway only partially rebuilt and the massive Canol (Canadian Oil) pipeline and refinery project underutilized and largely unneeded. (The Whitehorse refinery closed shortly after the end of the war and was relocated to Alberta; the pipeline was dismantled and taken to Texas.) The Newfoundland bases, in contrast, remained active and of critical importance throughout the war and beyond, highlighting the dominion's crucial strategic location and long-term contribution to the war effort.

"Newfy V.E. Day," 8 May 1945. Control no. 19840030-100, Canadian War Museum.

Simultaneously, the United States prepared itself for the fastest and largest overseas mobilization of military and support personnel in world history. Even the activities of the British Empire at its height paled in comparison to the size, scale, and rapidity of the American overseas expansion between 1941 and 1945.

The tasks varied little from country to country. Where military facilities already existed, the Americans shipped in supplies, soldiers, aviators, and naval personnel. They stationed ships, planes, and fighting units on both the Pacific and the Atlantic fronts. In most places, however, existing facilities were inadequate for the size and nature of the planned friendly invasion. As a consequence, the Americans dispatched construction crews to build roads, airfields, ports, dormitories, warehouses, and the other facilities needed to house, supply, and support hundreds of thousands of U.S. soldiers. There was not a great deal of careful planning behind these activities, and as a result, the bases built in Surinam, Tonga, and the Canadian Northwest proved to be of little long-term value. It is important to recall, however, that the outcome of the war was unknown and unknowable in the period between December 1941 and the summer of 1943; indeed, and scholars remind us of this, save for tactical and strategic errors on the part of the German and Japanese military leadership, the war might well have gone in different directions. As a result, and fuelled by American wealth and personnel, the safest option was clearly to blanket the Allied world, defend it against further Axis encroachment, and prepare for the planned assaults on the enemy.

In later years, as criticism of the American Empire mounted, countries that had welcomed these friendly invasions would come in retrospect to resent them, at least to some degree. They would see in them the manifestation of Yankee imperialism, would note the rapid expansion of American corporate influence around the globe – what critics referred to as "Coca-colonization" – would decry the impact of American popular culture, and would point to the distortions of local social and economic conditions that resulted from the wartime invasions.[10] Commentators would emphasize that the experience also revealed the shortcomings of the American value system and mindset, from crass commercialism, abundant wealth, and racism, to cultural insensitivity. Many would find reasons to denounce the American presence and to wish, ahistorically, that the friendly invasions had never occurred, or at least that they had been more carefully managed by regional and national governments.

The benefits of hindsight were obviously not available in 1941–42, when the Axis powers seemed destined for global supremacy and Hitler's 1,000-Year Reich seemed a distinct possibility. Within a few months of the United States entering the war, Japanese and German power reached its peak, with the battles on the Eastern Front ravaging Russia and pulverizing southeast Europe and with the Japanese seemingly unstoppable as they island-hopped across the Pacific, overrunning the British bases in Hong Kong and Singapore and entrenching themselves in Southeast Asia. Australia went so far as to prepare plans to abandon vast areas of the north and west of the country, believing that a retreat into the southeast corner was the only possible survival strategy. On the Western Front, the Germans had ended the Battle of Britain – the massive bombardment of England – in May 1941 and diverted most of their resources to the east. But the seemingly impenetrable fortifications along the northern coast made the reconquest of France and the Low Countries a daunting prospect.

In country after country the arrival of scores of thousands of American soldiers and support personnel was widely and justly celebrated. In Australia and New Zealand, for example, which had thousands of their soldiers deployed on the European front, there was much rejoicing when American reinforcements arrived. The prospect of Japanese invasion dimmed considerably when military fortifications were expanded on New Zealand's North Island and when the Americans assumed responsibility for the defence of Australia and solidified military facilities along the Queensland coast. Canadians and Newfoundlanders likewise celebrated the Americans' arrival, for it signalled a turning point in the war. And in the United Kingdom, having hundreds of thousands of American soldiers on hand provided both protection against the long-threatened invasion and the resources needed to contemplate the retaking of the continent. It would be worth a good deal to have been able to see the expression that crossed Winston Churchill's face when he was told of the bombing of Pearl Harbor.

Early in World War II, it became clear that modern warfare rested as much on supply-chain management – delivering food, material, armaments, and equipment when and as needed – as it did on military prowess. Many more military and civilian personnel were engaged in supply and support functions than in actual combat roles, for the scale of armaments required, the number of military personnel involved, and the vast distances to be covered produced formidable logistical challenges. As a consequence, the Allied forces had to protect all crucial sources of supply, all manufacturing sites, and all shipping routes, this necessity alone justifying much of the investment in Newfoundland. In addition, preparations had to be made for the planned offensive operations on both fronts. In Europe, this required supply and equipment units in the United Kingdom and North Africa. In the Pacific, the Allied/American strategy focused on retaking the Philippines – a requirement set by Douglas MacArthur, who was humiliated at having been forced to retreat from the American colony – and then island-hopping to the Japanese mainland. To accomplish both tasks, the Americans worked very quickly to build up Allied bases in Australia, which served as the centre of the Allied effort in the Pacific, and to strenthen facilities on islands still held by the Allies in the South Pacific. Major bases were hastily constructed on Tonga, Fiji, and dozens of other small and isolated islands in the region, providing support facilities for airborne and naval engagement with the Japanese.

The American expansion was not limited to countries facing imminent invasion. Unable to predict the future directions of the war, the Americans also recognized that naval, submarine, and air war stretched the boundaries of combat considerably. Furthermore, the ideological and political aspects of the war, particularly those involving alleged and potential subversive and fifth column activities, meant that the Allied forces had to reinforce the pro-democracy presence in areas not yet affected directly by war. For two major reasons, therefore, the United States established military and supply bases in far-flung corners of the world. Some made great strategic sense, such as the major air force base in Reykjavik, Iceland, which subsequently became a cornerstone of Iceland's economy.

HMCS *Burlington* victory party, 1945. 2007-8 Album, Herbert Roberts Collection, Crow's Nest Military Artifacts Association.

The U.S. base in Bermuda provided long-distance supply support for American ships and planes operating in the central Atlantic. Within a few months, American personnel had been dispatched to India, Panama, Brazil, and dozens of other locations around the globe. In little more than a year, the American military presence had expanded from a North American–centric strategy to global engagement. The world would never be the same again.

While their priorities focused on the war effort, the Americans were not above contemplating long-term possibilities. American businesses followed the troops and support personnel overseas, most famously with the Coca-Cola Company carrying its now-ubiquitous beverage to the corners of the earth and building more than sixty new bottling plants overseas to supply Americans. In the Canadian Northwest, American personnel cast hungry eyes on uranium deposits near Great Bear Lake, leading the British government to intervene and convince Canadian authorities to watch American developments in the region more closely. American soldiers, most of whom had never before been outside the United States, discovered new opportunities for investment and business development; substantial post-war economic activity was rooted in the experiences of American personnel overseas during the war. The U.S. government, particularly President Roosevelt, believed that the United States needed to take a more active international role, arguing that the intentional isolationism of the post–World War I era had made a second global conflagration possible. From the outset, key American political and military leaders hoped to prevent a post-war retreat into isolationism. In their minds – and this was confirmed through their immediate post-war actions – the United States had to use its wartime activities as a footprint for global influence.

The scale and breadth of American expansionism during World War II was breathtaking. Within little more than a year, by January 1943, the United States had over a million troops overseas. Two years later, the number had increased to over five million, with three million located in the European theatre. At that time, the American armed forces had 15,000 in the Canadian Northwest (plus an even greater number of civilian workers), more than four times as many (65,000) in Panama, 37,000 in Iceland, 23,000 in Fiji, more than 30,000 in New Caledonia (the French colony in the South Pacific), 33,000 in the Solomon Islands, and over 115,000 in Australia and New Guinea. The changing fortunes and requirements of war dictated significant shifts in personnel in the coming two years, with the Americans moving troops and supply personnel within and between theatres. Newfoundland, with slightly more than 6,000 American military personnel in place in April 1945, attracted a much smaller number than many other places, although the transient population passing through St John's was extremely high.

By 1945, the American presence overseas was impressive. With millions of men (and thousands of women, particularly in the nursing corps and in secretarial roles) distributed around the globe, the United States had established a truly international footprint. While armies of liberation and military occupation comprised most of the American forces, the friendly invasions accounted for substantial numbers of support troops and civilian workers. The numbers told only part of the story, for each occupation involved the construction of major facilities and the improvement of local infrastructure through the development of roads, radio and telephone connections, ports, barracks, movie theatres, canteens, and the like. In countries around the world, the Americans had arrived to provide protection, reassurance, and freedom. And with the war winding down in 1945, it was increasingly clear that a long-term change had occurred. In some places, it was evident that the Americans had no intention of leaving quickly and were solidifying their wartime military facilities, while in others, they left as soon as the fighting stopped. In all these locations, save for the homelands of the Axis powers (and even there to some extent), the Americans were viewed as saviours, allies, and protectors. These were friendly invasions, even while they were disruptive, transformative, and largely determined by forces outside local control.

The arrival, activities, and subsequent departure of the American military had profound implications for the communities and regions involved. In most Allied cities, the Americans' arrival was heralded by parades and celebrations of relief and optimism – Australia was an example. By the time they left – where they did – their departure was also often greeted with relief, in the manner of relatives who have overstayed their welcome. In between, there were times of great cooperation, romance and friendship, conflict and bitterness. In Australia, the defining event of the darker aspect of the occupation was the Brisbane riot of November 1942, a drink-induced conflict that unleashed pent-up frustrations, particularly those of Australian servicemen. The Americans brought

Table 7.1 U.S. armed forces, global distribution, April 1945

Country	*American Forces*	*Country*	*American Forces*
Iceland	8,152	New Hebrides	7,706
United Kingdom	486,726	Fiji	429
Europe	2,435,597	Tongawera	11
Mediterranean	499,179	Aitutaki	12
Africa and Middle East	35,156	New Caledonia	63,938
Ascension	1,192	Australia	24,740
Persian Gulf	20,793	New Zealand	155
India	161,036	Brazil	4,860
Ceylon	1,350	Caribbean	35,993
Burma	2,594	Panama Canal	37,017
China	40,456	Bermuda	2,594
Philippines	527,433	*Newfoundland*	*6,123*
Okinawa	67,495	Greenland	2,705
Palau	12,400	Canada	2,094
Iwo Jima	13,687	Alaska	60,196
New Guinea	233,717		
Marianas	116,885		
Bismarck Island	3,130		
Marshalls	2,627		
Gilbert Islands	225		
Nukufetau	13		
Solomon Islands	28,382		
Hawaii	175,228		
Line Island	980		

Note: Does not include forces in transit or based in the continental United States of America.

Source: K.S. Coates and W.R. Morrison, *The Alaska Highway in World War II: The U.S. Army of Occupation in Canada's Northwest* (Norman: University of Oklahoma Press, 1992), 5.

money, often well out of proportion to local wages and standards, and their activities often sparked short-lived economic booms. But their presence forced up prices, created labour shortages, and distorted local supplies, a particularly noticeable phenomenon in the South Pacific islands, where the arrival of the Yankees echoed the earlier discoveries of the islands by Europeans, as recounted in local lore. The American military men mingled freely with local women, and this led to marriages, divorces, and many broken hearts when the Yankees left, as well as not a few children of uncertain parentage. Social relations were particularly complicated in the United Kingdom, where English women, less racist than American women, engaged in interracial relationships that caused conflict among American troops. Within a brief, intense period, with emotions heightened by the uncertain terrors of war, the friendly invaders had a significant impact on the people and communities with whom they came into contact. St John's, Newfoundland, was in most respects little different.

CHARACTERISTICS OF THE FRIENDLY INVASIONS

While circumstances varied among countries, cities, and regions, the various friendly invasions shared consistent patterns. Among the defining characteristics of this important global phenomenon were the following, each of which can be seen to have operated, at least in part, in St John's:

Redefining Urban Spaces

Most of the military establishments were in or near existing towns, which in turn were often located around port facilities or at key transshipment points. As a consequence, these towns, some of them quite small when the Americans arrived, found themselves facing major development pressures. St John's, as described so effectively in this volume by C.A. Sharpe and A.J. Shawyer, was as profoundly affected as any community in the world, with major investments in its infrastructure, the rapid broadening of the city's footprint, and the general improvement of the urban environment. St John's was a markedly different community at war's end, and its subsequent development continues to reflect this wartime activity. Whitehorse in the Yukon grew overnight from about 400 residents to more than 10,000. The Americans built freely, adding buildings, facilities, and infrastructure where needed and without much consideration of cost or the capacity of local ratepayers to maintain the newly constructed elements. Through the friendly invasions, therefore, the urban footprint was often redefined, typically by way of the major expansion of transportation facilities and the general growth of the town. In the post-war period, the former military encampments and facilities were either converted to residential or commercial purposes or torn down and replaced by more appropriate buildings for the sites. Very few of these towns escaped the war without major modifications to their urban shape and function, and subsequently townspeople spent several generations adapting to decisions made in haste and with little thought of the future. Few towns, however, had been recast as profoundly as St John's, Newfoundland, by the combined military expenditures of two visiting friendly allies.

Economic Prosperity and New Foundations

By the end of the 1930s, much of the world was in the grip of a painful and prolonged economic depression. The start of the war exacerbated existing problems while solving others. Rationing quickly became commonplace. Shortages of key goods were accepted as an inevitable cost of war. Unemployment disappeared, partly because so many men were in uniform and partly because of the enormous growth of defence industries, but wages were held in check by war-strapped governments. And then the Americans arrived, spending freely both officially and personally, with money to burn on all measure of items. They also brought with them surplus supplies of food, personal goods, equipment, and other hard-to-find items. Within days of the Americans' arrival, the effects could be felt working their way through the local economies. Local labour was in high demand, wages spiked, and local stores, bars, and restaurants celebrated the cash-rich newcomers. Local companies complained about the unfair competition, but generally to little avail, as wartime needs took priority. The boom proved short-lived, but the Depression-era realities did not return at war's end. No community touched by the friendly invasion was as poor in 1945 as it had been in 1939. The American period was widely seen as the catalyst that destroyed the Great Depression and brought about renewed prosperity. The arrival in St John's of more than 15,000 people had obvious implications for the prosperity of the community. So, too, did the major overhaul of the port facilities. St John's entered the war, as Paul Collins describes in chapter 2 of this volume, as a "defended port" and ended the war as a major military establishment. The community remembers the war as a time of prosperity – ensured by the free-spending Americans and the smaller Canadian investments – but also as a turning point in the city's rise to prominence.

Social Relations and War Brides

The arrival in town of swarms of young men at a time when many of the local men were off on military service caused an inevitable stir. The situation in St John's differed from that in other areas in that there was also a significant Canadian presence in the city. The Canadians did not come off well in the comparison, a perspective skewed a little by post–World War II debate about Newfoundland's controversial decision to join Confederation. Within the community, U.S.-Newfoundland marriages and more temporary unions were commonplace – perhaps 25,000 strong in total – despite regular efforts by the U.S. authorities to curtail such pairings. More globally, the Yankees were viewed as being different, friendly, chivalrous towards women (a particularly important fact in Australia), wealthy, and fun-loving – all of which made them particularly desirable to women on the home front. Physically, they were often seen as being more attractive. In Britain, for instance, compared to the local males, they tended to be taller and stronger and usually had better teeth. Dances, parties, and other events drew the men and women together; human nature took many to the next step. In the months following, romances became love affairs and often turned into hastily arranged marriages. Local men, including those overseas in the service, resented the Yankees' intrusion on their women. Anger and conflict was not unusual. At war's end, tens of thousands of war brides and wartime mothers awaited news from their American husbands or boyfriends that they would be reunited in the United States.[11] Some of the military personnel were killed in action and the planned reunions never took place. In other instances, the men reneged on their wartime promises. But others returned home and arranged for their wives to join them in the United States. The path was not always easy, for the euphoria of wartime romance was often poor preparation for post-war marriage and parenthood in a foreign land. Around the world, however, the "over-sexed and over-here" Americans left a romantic legacy of considerable proportions, as well as many unclaimed offspring. In St John's the prevailing memory of the social aspects of the American experience was more positive than the norm (the view of Canadians proved to be more negative at a macro level but equally positive in personal terms).

Race Relations and Attitudes towards American Racism

At the beginning of World War II, it was the official policy of United States not to permit African Americans to engage in combat. They were trained in segregated groups and then served for the most part in supply and construction units, supporting the war effort behind the scenes. Many other countries found the racial policies of the American military difficult to take. In Australia, the clear discrimination towards black soldiers sparked many Australians to rethink their own shameful treatment of Aborigines. In New Zealand, where the Maori figured more prominently in national life, the Kiwis were furious about American racism. British women and men were much more accepting of interracial relationships than most Americans; such relationships in Great Britain, however, often sparked a reaction from white American troops, thus reinforcing the notion that America was unjust in its treatment of African Americans. Racism was the greatest scar on the American character in this era, and people in other countries thought less of them as a result. Assumptions about the pervasiveness of racism in the United States would linger well after the end of the war, and with good reason.

African-American military personnel did not figure prominently in St John's experience of the war, largely owing to the Newfoundland government's insistence that black troops be kept off the island (however, a small number of African Americans did come through St John's on a transient basis). As a consequence, this issue did not resonate with Newfoundlanders, although the government's ban demonstrates the degree to which race relations influenced the management of the friendly invasions. To the degree that Newfoundlanders came in direct contact with African Americans, their approach was generally more positive and closer to the British experience than that of other countries.

Overlapping Government Jurisdictions

The arrival of the Yankees raised serious questions about matters of governance and social control. The host nations had no choice but to welcome the Americans and consider the details later. But the Americans, for their part, did not want their soldiers and other workers coming under foreign control. Essentially, the host countries had to agree to American legal extraterritoriality, allowing the United States to retain both military and civil jurisdiction over its nationals for the duration of the war. For most countries, this was their first direct experience of the political and administrative realities of dealing with the United States on a regular basis. Most of the arrangements worked out smoothly, however, and given the large number of military personnel, the heated circumstances, and the potential for cultural misunderstanding, it is surprising that the problems were not worse than they were. In all these countries, Americans were often accused of bellicosity and their Military Police were blamed for using aggressive tactics. Americans accused of crimes against civilians were on occasion slipped out of the country before legal proceedings could begin. Host countries sometimes withdrew complaints when they discovered that American military justice was faster and more severe than their own civilian courts. In subsequent decades, many of these countries would find their legal and administrative affairs entangled with American practice. The wartime experience with extraterritoriality proved a sound foundation for many of these later relationships. The situation in St John's proved to be somewhat at odds with the prevailing pattern. Canadian troops came under British and therefore local law, and thus found themselves dealt with in the same manner as local residents. Ironically, this legal equality appears to have made the prevailing view of Canadians harsher than that of the Americans, who came under the jurisdiction of American military courts. The public record indicates that there were systematic problems with Canadians but very few with Americans, largely because the U.S. authorities dealt with such affairs separately.

Impact of American Popular Culture and Materialism

Armies carry national cultures with them, and the Americans brought a particularly aggressive and wide-ranging form of their popular culture. They came with baseball bats and the latest movies, chewing tobacco, Coca-Cola, and condoms. The soldiers could buy cigarettes at discounted rates (they became a parallel currency in some places), and American chocolate soon developed a wide following. They brought nylons, magazines, and newspapers – all the accoutrements of a society where mass advertising was finding its feet and where commercialized culture was overwhelming traditional forms of entertainment. The Americans shared their culture with gusto and as a rule showed little interest in local traditions or activities, although of course there were exceptions – some Americans in Britain were anglophiles, while others were completely ignorant of anything beyond their own borders. For their part, the host countries were finally able to reconcile their ill-formed views of the United States – created in large part through Hollywood movies – with the real thing. In this instance, they encountered a perhaps unrepresentative segment of the American reality – the troops, who were young, overwhelmingly male, military-minded, regionally and culturally mixed, and on the verge of engaging in combat. Nevertheless, to many locals, the Yankees seemed to match the cinematic ideal that had started to define the country for the world – there were the polite young men wooing the women, the free-spending Yanks who offered a glimpse of American wealth, and the dashing and aggressive soldiers about to go off to war. People in many parts of the world were experiencing their first prolonged encounter with American popular culture, and they generally liked what they saw. The troops had, unintentionally, created a global market for what Americans had to say, perform, sing, play, and, later, sell. Newfoundlanders, of course, had greater and longer-term access to American popular culture than Allied countries not in North America. Still, the memories of St John's residents are filled with recollections of American wealth, access to luxury goods thanks to the Yankees, and other pieces of Americana. The wartime experience brought Newfoundland closer to the North American consumer culture and accelerated the process of distancing St John's from its British past. In this, Newfoundland was part of the global process of Americanization through popular and material culture.[12]

Re-militarization of Regional Cultures

World War II re-militarized vast expanses of the world. In few places was this as dramatic as in St John's and Newfoundland, with their strong military traditions and deeply painful memories of the dominion's engagement in World War I. Before the war and after the retreat of the European empires, military conflict was generally localized, fought in long and protracted battles over site-specific areas. The new warfare, with bombers, radar, submarines, transoceanic supply lines, and the like, brought the war into many distant areas of the globe. Communities protected by distance and isolation from military conflict, from Whitehorse in the Yukon to Cairns on the northern Queensland coast to Goose Bay in remote Labrador, found themselves in the middle of an international conflict. The American presence – the hundreds and thousands of soldiers, airplanes, warships, barracks, and the various accoutrements of war – provided a stark reminder of the new reality: war was inescapable, and so, it seemed, were the Americans. Communities came to realize that distance was no longer a protector, that war could and did strike quickly, and that military protection had become increasingly important. The globalization of military awareness continued after the war, reinforced by the Cold War between the United States and the Soviet Union. The refurbishing and expansion of the port facilities, the construction of military bases around the city, and the wartime and post-war presence of American troops brought home to St John's a new reality, one marked by direct engagement with global militarization. The uncertainties that obtained throughout the war would linger long into the post-war period.

Post-War Implications and American Influence

Not only war was inescapable, so too, it proved, was Coca-colonization. World War II was America's coming-out party. And like a debutante freed from parental constraints, the United States had no intention of retreating into its pre-war shell. In those places of ongoing strategic significance, such as Newfoundland and Labrador, the Americans did not soon leave, maintaining a military presence and building on the collaborations and security partnerships established during World War II. In other instances, like Australia and the Canadian Northwest, the Americans began to pull out before the end of the war and retreated in full as soon as conditions permitted. But in all cases, the American influence never fully retreated. American investments tended to follow U.S. wartime activities, both through servicemen who had made contacts in the region during the war and had returned afterwards, and through companies that had developed ties with new countries as a result of the friendly occupations. The United States emerged from the war as the world's most important military and political power, but much of its sustained strength rested on the expansion and entrenchment of American popular culture and commerce. Those countries that hosted the Americans during the war benefited from the wartime economic engagement, and most of them retained strong ties with the United States thereafter.

Wartime expansion established a footprint for the American Empire, allowing the United States, with its former enemies Germany and Japan, to become the strongest economic force in world history. Newfoundland had long been part of the British Empire and a military extension of the home country. In World War II, St John's became the epicentre of a tripartite militarization: it experienced a declining British connection, a strengthening tie to the Canadian armed forces, and a dramatic and impressive American military presence. The Americans did not leave – practically or metaphorically – at the end of the war, and Newfoundlanders came to understand that they were now an integral part of the post-World War II American Empire.

CONCLUSION

The social, economic, cultural, and political changes described in the other chapters in this collection were very real and had profound implications for St John's and for Newfoundland and Labrador. The American occupation is appropriately understood, therefore, as a transformative event in the history of the city and dominion, one with lasting implications for the urban landscape, the community's sense of America, and its understanding of its place in the geopolitics of the globe. At the same time, it is vital to realize that the St John's situation shares a great deal in common with what happened in Brisbane, Australia; Auckland, New Zealand; Edmonton, Alberta; Reykjavik, Iceland; Prince Rupert, British Columbia; Cairns, Australia; and dozens of other communities around the world. The arrival of the American Rampant was one of the most vigorous and significant developments of the World War II era, with implications that reflected both the military activities of the period and the broader impacts associated with the arrival of thousands of intense, largely friendly, and always interesting Americans in the far and distant corners of the Allied world.

The American occupation of St John's was therefore a far from solitary or unique event in world history. In fact, the opposite is the case. St John's was an active participant in one of the most pivotal events of the twentieth century: the emergence of the United States on the world stage. In ways large and small, from encouraging a worldwide interest in American movies to reinforcing the fact that the United States was emerging as the wealthiest and most dynamic country on earth, the wartime occupations of Allied countries changed America's role in the world. And just as the U.S. Army of Occupation left mixed memories in St John's – the relief of protection and support offset by concern about the Yankees' gaucheries, racism, and occasional arrogance – the Americans made complicated impressions of themselves around the world. Their allies – saved from attack and possible enemy invasion by the timely arrival of the American war machine – came to understand the benefits and consequences of bedding down with the United States. In St John's and elsewhere, the legacy of the Americans' invasion in World War II conflated all these sentiments and more, creating the ambivalence towards the United States that dominated the non-Communist world after World War II and remains one of the most prevalent and important sentiments in international affairs.

While St John's fits within the global context, the community's response to the Americans has its unique characteristics. St John's responded more positively – both during the war and subsequently – to the American presence than did other countries experiencing friendly invasions. Newfoundland's profound sense of vulnerability, its fear of imminent attack, and its strong concern about the potential loss of Great Britain to the Nazis conditioned the dominion to appreciate and support the arrival of the Yankees. The generally positive response of St John's to the presence of U.S. troops, reinforced by extensive and collaborative post-war relations, has meant that its citizens have retained fond memories of the World War II experience. The large number of war brides, the pervasive impact of American popular culture, and the formidable physical legacy left by wartime construction are evidence that St John's' experience of the U.S. forces was more substantial, deeper, and longer-lasting than was the case in other parts of the world. The war was, after all, a shared experience with the United States, and Newfoundlanders could see the immediate importance of a sizable American military presence in their midst. While cities and regions around the world demonstrated ambivalence towards their American allies, St John's offered the Americans a welcoming and supportive environment. The stereotype of the "ugly American" – rich and aggressive, self-important and aloof – did not work for the citizens of St John's, Newfoundland.

Notes

Abbreviations

AP	author's possession
CRCS	Canadian Red Cross Society
DHH	Directorate of History and Heritage
DND	Department of National Defence
LAC	Library and Archives Canada
MUNFLA	Memorial University of Newfoundland Folklore and Language Archive
NARA	National Archives and Records Administration
NOIC	naval officer in charge
NSHQ	Naval Service Headquarters
PANL	Public Archives of Newfoundland and Labrador
PAPEI	Public Archives of Prince Edward Island
PJBD	Permanent Joint Board on Defence
TNA [PRO]	The National Archives, Public Record Office
WPA	Women's Patriotic Association of Newfoundland

Introduction

1 Cecil Hutchens, 1 March 1941. A copy of the letter is in the possession of the editor.

2 While some readers will insist that the U.S. bases in Newfoundland were never part of the Anglo-American "destroyers-for-bases" deal, as they were gifts, freely given, the archival record suggests otherwise. All the bases were leased for ninety-nine years, and no distinction was made in the March 1941 Leased Bases Agreement that governed them. The rhetorical distinction between "gifted" and "exchanged" bases in the original announcement, like the insistence on this distinction today, had everything to do with race and national pride. See, for example, High, *Base Colonies in the Western Hemisphere,* esp. chap. 1.

3 "Mr. Roosevelt's Message to Congress on Bases," *Royal Gazette and Colonist Daily* (Bermuda), 5 September 1940, 3. See also, "The Big Deal," *Time Magazine,* 16 September 1940; and Francis Brown, "For America the Horizons Widen," *New York Times,* 15 September 1940, 109.

4 The Newfoundland Airport at Gander was heralded as one of the biggest aerodromes in the British Empire. Conn, Engelman, and Fairchild, *Guarding the United States*, 358.

5 Neary, "Newfoundland and the Anglo-American Leased Bases Agreement," 517.

6 Hutchens, letter to parents, 1 March 1944.

7 Bob Benson, "The Call to Arms," *Evening Telegram* (St John's), 9 November 1996, A1. A second newspaper article on Cecil Hutchens appeared a decade later; see Tara Bradbury Mullowney, "U.S. trooper came 'overseas,'" *Evening Telegram*, 8 February 2006.

8 Bob Benson, "The Call to Arms," *Evening Telegram*, 9 November 1996, A1.

9 Cecil Hutchens, interviewed by Stephen MacPherson, 27 August 2007. All of the interviews have been donated to the Centre for Newfoundland Studies at Memorial

University and the Centre for Oral History and Digital Storytelling at Concordia University. The Johnson Family Foundation also has a copy of all the interviews.

10 This situation is beginning to change with the publication of several recent books by local historians, including Gary Browne, *To Serve and Protect: The Newfoundland Constabulary on the Home Front in World War Two*; Gene Quigley, *Voices of World War II: A Collection of Oral Histories*; and William Rompkey, *St. John's and the Battle of the Atlantic*. This wave of popular history is also evidenced in Halifax with the publication of Stephen Kimber, *Sailors, Slackers, and Blind Pigs: Halifax at War*; and William Naftel, *Halifax at War: Searchlights, Squadrons and Submarines, 1939–1945*.

11 For the impact of the bases, see Neary "'A Mortgaged Property'"; and Neary's important book *Newfoundland in the North Atlantic World*. A similar emphasis on the U.S. bases can be seen in MacLeod, *Peace of the Continent*; Mackenzie, "A North Atlantic Outpost"; and my own *Base Colonies in the Western Hemisphere*, which focuses on the impact of the ninety-nine-year-leased bases in Newfoundland, Bermuda, Trinidad, St Lucia, Antigua, British Guiana (Guyana), Jamaica, and the Bahamas.

12 Ransom, "Canada's Newfyjohn Tenancy."

13 As always, there are exceptions. See, for example, Browne, *To Serve and Protect*.

14 Paul O'Neill, interviewed by Kenny Hammond (13 September 2007).

15 Editorial, "Occupation of St. John's," *Evening Telegram*, 3 February 1941.

16 Ling, "'Share of the Sacrifice,'" 49.

17 Newfoundland Railway Office of the General Manager, *Monthly Bulletin* (St John's), 15, no. 1 (1 November 1939), MG 273, 2.01.001, Provincial Archives of Newfoundland and Labrador (hereafter PANL), St John's, NL.

18 "US is negotiating for British bases, plan with Canada," *New York Times*, 17 August 1940.

19 Alfred B. Morine, "Fortify Newfoundland to defend Canada," *Globe and Mail*, 27 July 1940. The Nova Scotia–born letter writer had a personal connection to Newfoundland, having sat in the Newfoundland House of Assembly for many years.

20 "Canada to spend a million in Newfoundland," *Toronto Daily Star*, 16 August 1940. Canada's associate minister of national defence, C.G. Power, visited St John's in August 1940 to confer with Newfoundland's governor. According to the *Hamilton Spectator*, "History was made when the minister stepped ashore from a rowboat at Bay Bull's Big Pond, eight miles from here, last night. The plane that had dropped down on the lake a few minutes beforehand carried the first Canadian cabinet minister ever to visit on a mission of such import." The *Edmund B. Alexander* it wasn't, but the visit sealed what the Canadian journalist provocatively called a "confederation of defence." "Defence Minister Completes his Survey of Newfoundland," *Hamilton Spectator*, 21 August 1940.

21 Greenslade Commission: Reports on Social and Economic Conditions, file 2, box 5, John W. Greenslade Papers, Library of Congress, Washington, DC.

22 Dziuban, *Military Relations between the United States and Canada*.

23 Charles Hurd, "Roosevelt puts Canada pact first," *New York Times*, 21 August 1940.

24 "Barter with Britain," *New York Times*, 8 September 1940, 121.

25 Readers of the *New York Times* could follow the friendly invasion step-by-step. In September 1940 the cruiser USS *St Louis*, carrying Rear Admiral Greenslade and the Board of Naval Experts, visited the city in order to finalize the location of the ninety-nine-year-leased bases. "Scan Newfoundland base sites," *New York Times*, 17 September 1940. Readers also learned of St John's essential role as a port of refuge. In the "epic battle" between the British merchant cruiser *Jervis Bay* and a German warship, the outgunned ship went down "with her guns blazing," which enabled thirty of thirty-eight ships in the convoy to escape. The story was accompanied by a photograph of the surviving crew members taken in St John's. "Crew of the Jervis Bay, heroes of an epic battle of the sea, reach a Canadian port," *New York Times*, 14 November 1940, 3. Other news stories told of the daring rescue of survivors in the North Atlantic. In June 1941, the U.S. Coast Guard cutter *General Greene*, which was taking on supplies in St John's, made a five-day dash to pick up thirty-nine survivors after eight of nine boats in a convoy were sunk south of Cape Farewell, Greenland. The survivors were crowded into two boats: "None of the rescued men was able to talk after five days of cold and exposure. They were from the refrigerator ship Marconi. They were brought to St. John's." See "8 ships in convoy sunk," *New York Times*, 9 June 1941, 8.

26 "First defenders off for new base," *New York Times*, 16 January 1941.

27 "Harold Denny, "We begin to man our new bases," *New York Times*, 19 January 1941.

28 Stanley Truman Brooks, "Newfoundland as defense outpost would provide US with strategic air-sea bases,"

St Louis Post-Dispatch, 29 August 1940. Before the war, Brooks had been paid by the Newfoundland Tourist Board to write articles promoting Newfoundland in the United States. It was therefore only natural that American newspaper editors asked him to comment on the bases agreement.

29 Stanley Truman Brooks, "Newfoundland – Gibraltar of the North," *Christian Science Monitor,* 14 September 1940.

30 Governor Humphrey Walwyn, governor of Newfoundland, in his end-of-war assessment to the Dominions Office, 15 October 1945, CO 971/21/7, 81868, Public Record Office, London, England.

31 Rose, "Sex, Citizenship, and the Nation," 1148. The social consequences of friendly invasion during the Second World War can be seen in Australia: Kay Saunders and Helen Taylor, "The Reception of American Servicemen in Australia during World War II: The Resilience of White Australia," *Journal of Black Studies,* June 1988, 331–48; Daniel E. Potts and Annette Potts, *Yanks Down Under, 1941–1945: The American Impact on Australia* (Oxford: Oxford University Press, 1985).

32 With the prevalence of moral discourses in wartime, gender naturally becomes central to the war stories being told. The wholesale labelling of young women from outport communities living in the city as promiscuous is not dissimilar to the moral panic that prevailed on the North American mainland and in Great Britain. Pierson, "*'They're still women after all,'*" 15; Rose, "Sex, Citizenship, and the Nation," 1148.

33 As part of this project, I examined dozens of interview transcripts and listened to many oral history recordings held at the Folklore and Language Archives at Memorial University. These interviews, conducted mainly by students in the 1970s and 1980s, record the war stories of an older generation. Unfortunately, these interviews cannot be easily quoted owing to the absence of consent forms. Moreover, we would have had to track down the interviewers to get their permission to share these stories. While this book would have benefited from their inclusion, the stories resemble those told by the fifty people we interviewed in 2007.

34 Fifty men and women responded to our public appeal for interviewees. Our appeal was carried on local radio stations and newspapers, and the Royal Canadian Legion and several seniors' homes provided contacts, as did the family connections of some of our contributors and interviewers. Even our posters elicited some response.

35 FitzGerald, "'The difficult little island,'" 23.

36 Major, *As Near to Heaven by Sea,* 369.

37 Labour Relations Officer to Commissioner for Justice and Defence, 29 September 1945, file 19: US Effect of Agreements on Colonies, box 365, GN 13/1/B, PANL.

38 George D. Hopper, "Political Developments during the Month of April, 1942," box 48, RG 84, St John's Consulate, General Records, 1936–49 (1942), National Archives and Records Administration (hereafter NARA), College Park, Maryland.

39 Jane Lewis and Mark Shrimpton, "Policymaking in Newfoundland during the 1940s: The Case of the St. John's Housing Corporation," *Canadian Historical Review* 75, no. 2 (1984): 210.

40 William E. Cole Junior, "Annual Economic and Financial Review Newfoundland, 1942," 5 April 1943, file 1943, box 53, RG 84, St John's Consulate General's Records, 1936–49, NARA.

41 George D. Hopper. "Political Developments during the Month of April, 1942," box 48, RG 84, St John's Consulate, General Records, 1936–49 (1942), NARA.

42 These statistics can be found on a case by case basis. "Classification of American Persons Committed to H.M. Penitentiary since January 1st, 1941 to Date," 5 October 1945, file 19: US Effect of Agreement on Colonies, box 365, GN 13/1/B, PANL.

43 Governor Walwyn to the Right Honourable the Viscount Addison, Secretary of State for Dominion Affairs, 15 December 1945, file 19: US Effect of Agreement on Colonies, box 365, GN 13/1/B, PANL.

44 Governor Humphrey Walwyn to the Right Honourable the Viscount Addison, Secretary of State for Dominion Affairs, 15 October 1945, file 19: US Effect of Agreement on Colonies, box 365, GN 13/1/B, PANL.

45 Ibid.

46 George D. Hopper, "Political Developments during the Month of December, 1942," box 48, RG 84, St John's Consulate, General Records, 1936–49 (1942), NARA.

47 Writing in July 1945, H.A. Winter admitted that the "great consensus of opinion seems to regard [this change] as inevitable sooner or later." H.A. Winter, Commissioner for Public Utilities and Supply, Memorandum for Commissioners of Government, "Proposed Change of the Rule of the Road," 13 July 1945, file 8: PU-General-1945, box S5-1-3, GN 38, PANL.

48 Major, *As Near to Heaven by Sea,* 371.

49 Coates and Morrison, *The Alaska Highway in World War II*, 238. For more on the economic impact, see Coates and Morrison's *Working the North: Labor and the Northwest Defense Projects, 1942–46*.
50 Reynolds, *Rich Relations*, xvii. For Newfoundland, see Webb, "VOUS – Voice of the United States," 87–99.
51 These were power-laden encounters. Gilbert M. Joseph defines *encounter* as the "range of networks, exchanges, borrowings, behaviours, discourses, and meanings whereby the external became internalized." Joseph, "Close Encounters," 5.

Chapter One

1 Jamieson, *No Place for Fools*, 30.
2 "Will aid defence of Newfoundland," *St John's Evening Telegram*, 7 September 1939, 4.
3 Fraser, "Newfoundland's Contribution to Canada," 252.
4 The British Admiralty was an important landowner, but with the exception of some RN ships, few British servicemen were based in St John's. Most British personnel were based at the airports in Gander and, eventually, Goose Bay.
5 It has been impossible to find a definitive total for the number of military personnel based in St John's. Local archival sources were unable to provide the number we sought, and the academic literature is more confusing than helpful. Hiller ("Newfoundland Confronts Canada 1867–1949," 374) says that in 1943 the peak military presence consisted of 10,000 American and 6,000 Canadian personnel. The same number for Canadians is also found in MacKay, *Newfoundland in North Atlantic Strategy in the Second World War*, with the caveat that this was for garrison personnel only. The maximum number of Canadian Army personnel assigned to "W" Force is 5,700 but not all were based in St John's (Nicholson, *More Fighting Newfoundlanders*, 520). The number of RCN personnel posted to HMCS Avalon was 3,365 in January 1944 and 4,096 in July according to Tucker (*Naval Service of Canada*, 531). Base complement, including both RCN and WRCNs (Women's Royal Canadian Naval Service) personnel peaked at 5,500 in early 1945. MacLeod and Penney, "Sailors Ashore." The Newfoundland Heritage website suggests that there were about 2,000 RCAF personnel in St John's and about 16,000 Canadian troops in Newfoundland at any given time. The highest estimate, given without attribution, is 13,200 American and 19,200 Canadian servicemen in Newfoundland, but certainly not in St John's, at the end of 1942. FitzGerald, "'The difficult little island,'" 24.
6 Cardoulis, *Friendly Invasion*, 52.
7 Noel, *Politics in Newfoundland*, 507.
8 Sharpe, "'The Race of Honour'"; and *Encyclopedia of Newfoundland*, 5:625.
9 The Newfoundland Ranger Force, created in 1935 and modelled on the Royal Canadian Mounted Police (RCMP), was intended to serve remote areas of Newfoundland. It was wound up in 1950. Because of their obsolete weapons the Rangers were "practically unarmed for the purpose of modern warfare." "Remarks on Newfoundland Defence Scheme by a Sub-committee of the Imperial Defence Committee," June [ ], 1937, in Bridle, *Documents on Relations*, 14.
10 Act 37, 3 September 1939. Between 1934 and 1949 Newfoundland was governed by an appointed Commission of Government. For an introduction to this critical aspect of Newfoundland's history, see Hiller, *Confederation*; and Neary, *Newfoundland in the North Atlantic World*, chaps 2–4.
11 Governor to Commander-in-Chief, America and West Indies, 3 September 1939. GN 4/1/D, box 20, file G/302.3, Public Archives of Newfoundland and Labrador.
12 "Enlistment in British Army, Navy, Air Force is open here," *Evening Telegram*, 5 September 1939, 3.
13 Act 47, 18 November 1939.
14 Initially these were the crewmen of ships seized in Newfoundland ports and from enemy ships captured at sea. "Internment Camp," *Evening Telegram*, 16 October 1939, 4.
15 Wells, *The Newfoundland Regiment*, 6; and Browne, *To Serve and Protect*, 33–7.
16 Act 45, 31 October 1939.
17 Telegram 236, Governor of Newfoundland to Dominions Secretary, 27 September 1938, in Bridle, *Documents on Relations*, 26.
18 Telegram 276, Dominions Secretary to Governor of Newfoundland, 30 August 1939, in Bridle, *Documents on Relations*, 39.
19 Nicholson, *More Fighting Newfoundlanders*, 523; and J57-'39, Emerson to Commission, 13 September 1939, GN 38, S4-1-4, file 1, PANL.
20 Browne, *To Serve and Protect*, 41.
21 Wells, *The Newfoundland Regiment*, 6; Kavanagh, "W Force," 80; and Nicholson, *More Fighting Newfoundlanders*, 525.
22 Ted Pritchard, personal communication.

23 Memorandum by Joint Staff Committee, Ottawa, 22 March 1937, in Bridle, *Documents on Relations*, 12.
24 German U-boats returned on two occasions in the fall of 1942, sinking a pair of ore carriers each time. Neary, *The Enemy on Our Doorstep*; and Hadley, *U-Boats against Canada*.
25 Telegram 59, Dominions Secretary to Secretary of State for External Affairs, 6 September 1939, in Stacey, *Arms, Men and Governments*, 537.
26 Prime Minister to High Commissioner of Great Britain, 16 March 1940, in Bridle, *Documents on Relations*, 64.
27 516 K/21 High Commissioner of Great Britain to Prime Minister, 26 March 1940, in Bridle, *Documents on Relations*, 69.
28 Unfortunately, the battery was sited to protect only the loading piers, with the regrettable consequence that when ore carriers moored to the southeast of the island were torpedoed in the fall of 1942, the guns could not be brought to bear on the attacking U-boats. Gordon Wells, personal communication.
29 Wells, *The Newfoundland Regiment*, 5.
30 Telegram 408, Secretary of State for Dominion Affairs to Governor, 6 November 1939, GN 38, S5-5-2, file 2, PANL.
31 J.W. Herbertson made this remark in October 1939. Quoted in MacKenzie, *Inside the Atlantic Triangle*, 31.
32 Telegram 374, Secretary of State for Dominion Affairs to Governor, 5 June 1941, in Bridle, *Documents on Relations*, 79.
33 J24-'40, 7 June 1940, GN 38 S4-1-2, file 2, PANL.
34 Telegram G.S. 0371, "Most Immediate. Rush. Secret," Chief of the General Staff to District Officer Commanding Quebec, for Officer Commanding Black Watch, 16 June 1940, in Bridle, *Documents on Relations*, 117.
35 J72-'39, Memorandum for Commission from L.E. Emerson, 23 November 1939, GN 38, S4-1-4, PANL. See also "Transferred," *Evening Telegram*, 6 December 1939, 5.
36 J24-'40, Memorandum for Commission from L.E. Emerson, 10 July 1940, GN 38 S4-1-2, file 7, PANL. The field was not returned to St Bonaventure's College until the summer of 1945. J and D 22-'45, Emerson to Commission, 10 May 1945, GN 38, S4-1-2, file 7, PANL.
37 Assistant Secretary, Department of Public Works, to City Clerk, 26 June, 1940, Jackman Collection, City of St John's Archives, file J1; "New quarters for local militia force," *Evening Telegram*, 19 July 1940, 4.
38 Plan 1242, 10 November 1942, RG 4.3, 41/83, PANL; and "Good progress made on militia barracks," *Evening Telegram,* 20 September 1940, 4.
39 Nicholson, *More Fighting Newfoundlanders*, 524.
40 Wells, *Newfoundland Regiment*, 5.
41 MacKay, "Newfoundland in North Atlantic Strategy," xxii. In stark contrast to the relationship between Newfoundland and the United States, Canada and Newfoundland never worked out a general defence agreement. They contented themselves with arrangements to cover specific defence requirements as they arose. The system worked well. In Telegram 138 of 31 May 1943 from the governor to the dominions secretary, the governor argued against any further extension of American jurisdiction, noting that "[t]he Canadians have all three forces here in large numbers and no questions of jurisdiction arise." GN 38 S3-5-3, file 20, PANL.
42 The Newfoundland Visiting Forces (British Commonwealth) Act (Act 29, 15 October 1940), based, *mutalis mutandis*, on the Canadian legislation, permitted Canada to station its armed forces in Newfoundland and put the militia under Canadian operational control. This led to an immediate improvement in equipment and morale (Wells, personal communication). The Newfoundland Militia was granted full regimental status on 2 March 1943 by the Newfoundland Militia Act, Act 6, 16 March 1943.
43 Minutes of a meeting at St John's to discuss bilateral defence questions, 20 August 1940, in Bridle, *Documents on Relations*, 159.
44 Minutes of a meeting at St John's to discuss bilateral defence questions, 20 August 1940, in Bridle, *Documents on Relations*, 159. The arrangements made by Power were confirmed by the second recommendation of the Permanent Joint Board of Defence. It required "strengthening the defences of Newfoundland ... the measures to include increasing Canadian garrisons" (Stacey, *Arms, Men and Governments,* 344). All the recommendations of the PJBD are reproduced in Dziuban, *Military Relations*, 347.
45 They were not the first Canadian troops to arrive in St John's – this honour belongs to the Queen's Own Rifles, who disembarked here on their way to relieve the Black Watch at Gander and Botwood. They "attracted much attention as they marched up Water Street this forenoon." "Here, there and everywhere," *Evening Telegram*, 26 October 1940, 4.
46 Telegram 48, Governor to Secretary of State for External Affairs, 1 October 1940; and Secretary of State for External Affairs to Governor, 3 October 1940, in Bridle, *Documents on Relations*, 134, 135.

47 The documentary record gives no indication of the reason this location was chosen, nor do we know why it was decided that the Canadian authorities would have to deal individually, and on their own, with private owners. The land could have been expropriated by the commission under the Emergency Powers (Defence) Act, no. 25, 20 September 1940.

48 Kavanagh, "W Force," 86.

49 Cyril Lynch (Royal Canadian Corps of Signals, retired), personal communication.

50 Murray, *Cows Don't Know It's Sunday,* 11, 51–2, 118–20, 303; and "Early driving for cattle," *Evening Telegram*, 7 December 1945.

51 Department of National Defence Plan 91826, Map Division, Queen Elizabeth II Library, Memorial University of Newfoundland.

52 Fitzgerald "'The difficult little island,'" 23. See also High, chapter 4, this volume.

53 What is as surprising as the lingering criticism of the quality of the buildings is the faint footprint that the massive Canadian presence in the city left behind. The Newfoundland and Labrador Heritage website, which has entries for all the American facilities, as well as for those of the RCN and the RCAF, makes not a single mention of Lester's Field Camp or any of the other Canadian Army sites.

54 Governor to Secretary of State for External Affairs, Ottawa, 7 January 1941, GN 38, S4-2-2, file 16, PANL.

55 The artillerymen, typical Canadians, had already commenced hockey practice by the end of October, using borrowed skates and sticks, while waiting for their baggage to arrive. "Canadian artillery hockey practice begins at Arena," *Evening Telegram*, 28 October 1940, 9. The season started in earnest early the next year with six teams, in two divisions, the players wearing either Toronto Maple Leafs or Montreal Maroons jerseys. The "hard fought" games generated considerable local interest, in part because of two equipment innovations – the Canadians wore felt shoulder-arm-elbow pads and footless hockey stockings! "Military hockey starts," *Evening Telegram*, 16 January 1941, 10.

56 The lack of appropriate manufacturing capacity in Newfoundland meant that all military equipment had to be imported from overseas. The searchlights were manufactured by the Canadian General Electric Company in Peterborough, Ontario.

57 Gard, *Hiking the East Coast Trail*, 12; and Plan "Nfld. 174," Department of National Defence, Directorate of Works and Accommodations, 12 September 1949 (Plan H215), City of St John's Archives.

58 Schwerdt to Emerson, 2 February, 1942, GN 4/1/D, numbered series, box 12, file 11/02/37, PANL.

59 Gard, *Hiking the East Coast Trail*, 17.

60 The three forts were manned by the 103rd Coast Battery, Royal Canadian Artillery: "A" Troop at Cape Spear, "B" Troop at Fort Amherst, and "C" Troop at Fort Chain Rock. The Newfoundland Regiment took over the Cape Spear battery in June 1943 and manned it until its decommissioning on 30 June 1945. Wells, *The Newfoundland Regiment*, 84. The Americans built an "aircraft warning station" just south of the lighthouse in the spring of 1942, and the RCN maintained the Port War Signal Station here as well.

61 This battery was of symbolic value only until February 1942, when the ammunition finally arrived. The 1890s vintage guns came from Fort Mott, New Jersey. They could throw a 250-kg shell up to 13 km. The guns were not returned, and the barrels remain at the Cape Spear National Historic Site.

62 The need for harbour defence was not illusory. On 3 March 1942, a U-587, presumably trying to sink the sealing vessel *Terra Nova* to block the harbour entrance, fired two torpedoes, one exploding in front of No. 1 Gun at Fort Amherst and the second against the North Head (Ozorak, *Abandoned Military Installations of Canada,* 269; and Hebbard, "The day the Germans torpedoed St. John's," *Evening Telegram*, 3 March 1996, 5). Two ships were sunk less than 125 miles from the harbour: the British *King Malcolm* on 30 September 1941 and the Greek *Mount Kitheron* on 25 January 1942. The Greek ship was sunk by U-574, which was itself sunk with all hands off Cape Sable on 31 July 1942 by a Hudson aircraft of 113 Squadron, based at Yarmouth – the first kill for Eastern Air Command. Mines were laid in the approaches to St John's Harbour by U-220 in the winter of 1942–43 (Lawrence, *Victory at Sea*, 76), and on 10 October 1943 two ships came to grief on them: the British ore carrier *Pensolver* and the American *Delisle*. On 1 February 1944, U-845, trying to steal into the harbour, ran aground on a rock less than 900 yards from Cape Spear. Refloated after a desperate struggle, the boat lay surfaced for some hours before limping away, undetected either by radar or human observation. U-845 was sunk on 10 March 1944, and the interrogation reports of the surviving crew made Canadian military authorities aware of this debacle. Hadley, *U-Boats against Canada*, 200.

63 Constable Coveyduck to Chief of Police, 26 May 1943, GN 13/1/B, box 390, file 46, PANL.

64 W.J. Robinson, Chief Engineer, Department of Public Works, to Secretary of Public Works, 8 June 1943, GN 4/1/D, box 38, file G/480/7, PANL.

65 The first such batteries appeared in the fall of 1941. Three sites, each accommodating about twenty men, were established on the Cape Spear Road by the 16th A/A Battery, S/L Troop, Royal Canadian Artillery. Earnshaw to Emerson, 14 August 1941, GN 4/1/D, box 38, file G/480/3, PANL.

66 The 40-mm (1.57-inch) Swedish-designed Bofors guns deployed in St John's were manufactured by the Otis Fensom Elevator Company in Hamilton, Ontario.

67 The 25th and 26th Anti-Aircraft Regiments, Royal Canadian Artillery, were mobilized in St John's on 1 June 1942, consisting of six and eight batteries respectively. Light Batteries were located at Fort Amherst; on the South Side Hills; on Campbell Avenue; at St George's Field on Merrymeeting Road; on the roof of a building on George Street; on the Hill O'Chips; and at the Bell Island piers. Efforts were made to integrate these installations into the fabric of the city to the greatest extent possible, although this was often difficult. An officer of the Royal Canadian Engineers wrote to the city clerk in July 1942 with regard to the A/A crew hut to be built at the corner of Buchanan and George Streets. He had originally intended to clad the hut with asbestos, cedar-grained shingles on the walls "to preserve the appearance of the building in the downtown section, and to provide a measure of fire protection." But, he said, he had now learned that none were available locally, and it would be necessary to have the shingles shipped from Canada. This would take three months, assuming they were available at all. So he asked for permission to use "a standard 95 pound building paper" instead. Major C.B. Bate to J.J. Mahoney, 10 July 1942, Jackman Collection, City of St John's Archives, file J1. Heavy Batteries were located at Torbay Airport, on Blackhead Road and Pennywell Road, and beside Kenny's Pond. Some sources suggest there was also a Light Battery in Calver's Field on Newtown Road, but we believe that this was probably the headquarters of the 25th A/A Regiment and No. 5 Gun Operations Room. Searchlights were sited on the Cape Spear Road in 1941, and a searchlight troop was posted to Bell Island in the summer of 1943, manning two lights, one on a pier and the other on a beach. There were other searchlight installations but we have not been able to identify them. Ozorak, *Abandoned Military Installations*, 265; Michael Harrington, "The coastal guns that guarded St John's," *Evening Telegram*, 17 April 1988, 5.

68 Minute 851-42 of the Commission of Government, re: PU133-'42, 30 October 1942, GN 4/1/D, box 38, file 1, PANL.

69 R.R. Sheldrick, Staff Captain (Q), Force "W," to John F. Calver, 1 May 1941. Calver Family Papers, Archives and Special Collections Division, QEII Library, Memorial University; Sheldrick to W.P. Ryan, City Engineer, 29 May 1941, Jackman Collection, City of St John's Archives, file J2.

70 R.S. Furlong to L.E. Emerson, Commissioner for Justice and Defence, 15 March 1943, GN 13/1/B, box 23, file 24, PANL.

71 L.F. Page, Officer Commanding Canadian Troops in Newfoundland, to J.J. Mahoney, City Clerk, 24 February 1943, GN 13/1/B, box 23, file 24, PANL.

72 "Buildings near Belvedere," *Evening Telegram,* 2 April 1943, 3; and "Canadian buildings ordered removed: Chief of Police unable satisfy Council fire proofing proposed would remove hazard," *Evening Telegram,* 16 April 1943, 3. There were at least a half-dozen buildings within the 300-foot radius, including three barrack blocks. Unfortunately, the written record goes silent now, and it has not been possible to determine whether the demolition was ever carried out, although on 16 April 1943 the mayor instructed the city solicitor to prepare a demolition order. Andrew Carnell to C. O'N Conroy, 16 April 1943, Jackman Collection, City of St John's Archives, file J2.

73 "Unsafe buildings to be placarded: Building permit for canteen on Circular Road refused," *Evening Telegram,* 27 March 1942, 3; and "Council refuses permit for Canadian Army building," *Evening Telegram*, 26 February 1943, 3.

74 City Clerk to Commanding Officer, Canadian Defence Headquarters, 13 March 1942; G.O.C. Commanding Canadian Troops in Newfoundland to City Clerk, 20 March 1942, Jackman Collection, City of St John's Archives, file J2.

75 Philip Field, personal communication.

76 Murray, *Cows Don't Know It's Sunday*, 256.

77 See, for example, GN 4/1/D, box 38, file G/480/5, "Canadian Army Rifle Range near Windsor Lake, 1943–44"; file G/480/6, "Canadian Army Battle Range, Cape Spear Road, 1943," PANL.

78 Churchill, *The Second World War: Their Finest Hour,* 398. The destroyers he sought were of the so-called

Town Class, built prior to 1920 and laid up since 1922 at Philadelphia.

79 The Anglo-American Leased Bases Agreement of 27 March 1941 was based on an exchange of notes on 2 September 1940 between the Marquis of Lothian, British ambassador to the United States, and Cordell Hull, the American secretary of state. The negotiation of this agreement was more complex than usually reported. The best evaluation of its difficult birth is in Reynolds, *The Creation of the Anglo-American Alliance.*

80 Telegram 1812, Dominions Secretary to High Commissioner of Great Britain, 14 August 1940, in Bridle, Documents on Relations, 241.

81 Ambassador of Great Britain in the United States (Lord Lothian) to Secretary of State of United States (Cordell Hull), 2 September 1940, "Most Secret and Personal," in Bridle, *Documents on Relations*, 252. The base sites in Newfoundland were covered by the same stipulations as those in the West Indies, but the fact that they were not offered as a *quid pro quo* for the destroyers was crucial to Churchill's reluctant acceptance of the agreement. In this chapter we discuss only the main army base in St John's. There was also a large naval base at Argentia, protected by the adjacent army base of Fort McAndrew, and Harmon Air Force Base at Stephenville.

82 Dziuban, *Military Relations*, 162. Furthermore, article 2 ("Non-User") of the Leased Bases Agreement 1941 said that the United States "shall be under no obligation ... to provide for the defence [of the leased areas]."

83 In August the commander-in-chief of the America and West Indies Station offered this opinion:"At the risk of infringing on political and possibly financial questions consider Naval and Air Bases in Newfoundland should be Canadian, United States of America having right to use only. Case is different in West Indies where U.S.A. object is direct defence of Canal Zone and Caribbean, and leased bases are reasonable. In Newfoundland case, while object is defence of U.S.A., Canada, a first class power, lies between and should be responsible for defence of north-east gateway on behalf of both parties. A third party assuming rights in Newfoundland will in my opinion, lead to endless trouble in years to come. Strongly urge leases of bases in Newfoundland to U.S.A. be not granted if this can possibly be avoided and provided Canada can undertake to provide efficient bases herself." Commander-in-Chief, America and West Indies Station, to Admiralty, Telegram 464, 25 August 1940, GN 4/1/D (numbered series), box 11, file 11/02/28, PANL.

84 "Letter from the Prime Minister to the Commissioner for Defence," *Evening Telegram*, 27 March 1941.

85 81 Telegram 211, Dominions Secretary (from Emerson and Penson) to Governor, 19 March 1941, GN 38 S4-2-3.1, file 14a, PANL.

86 J64-'40, Emerson to Commission, 1 November 1940, GN 38, S4-2-1.1, file 8, PANL.

87 J74-'40, Emerson to Commission, 28 November 1940, GN 38, S4-2-1.1, file 8, PANL.

88 American Bases Act, "An Act to give effect in Newfoundland to an agreement made between the government of the United Kingdom and the United States of America relating to the establishment of naval and air bases in Newfoundland, and to authorize the execution of a lease under the said Agreement and for other purposes," Act No. 12, 11 June 1941.

89 The title of the Act is misleading. President Roosevelt agreed to Canadian and British requests that no existing military facilities be included within the areas to be leased, so the Americans could not lease pre-existing bases. And the cost of building bases on the chosen sites was sometimes enormous. The naval and air base at Argentia cost $44,912,927, making it the most expensive wartime base outside the United States. Goodheart, *Fifty Ships That Saved the World*, 228.

90 "Members of Board United States Naval Experts Visiting," *Evening Telegram*, 16 September 1940, 4.

91 This account of the events of 16–21 September 1941 is based on the minutes of meetings between the government and Greenslade's board. Greenslade Papers, box 6, file 6 NF, Library of Congress, Washington, DC. This material was kindly made available by Steven High.

92 Telegram 87, Governor to Dominions Office, 12 February 1941, GN 4/1/D, box 32, file G/441, PANL.

93 According to Lothian's note, the sites would be "free from all rent and other charges other than such compensation to be mutually agreed on to be paid by the United States in order to compensate the owners of private property for loss, expropriation or damage arising out of the establishment of the bases and facilities in question."

94 D26/21/2, Governor to Dominions Secretary, 30 December 1940, GN 31/3A, PANL.

95 Telegram 82, Governor to Dominions Secretary, 8 February 1942, GN 38, S4-2-3, file 3a, PANL.

96 Despatch 96, Governor to HM Ambassador, Washington, 18 February 1941, GN 38, S3-5-2, file 7, PANL.

97 Governor to Secretary of State for External Affairs, 2 October 1940, in Bridle, *Documents on Relations*, 748.

98 See the discussion in High, "From Outport to Outport Base," 87–93.

99 This discussion of the requisitioning of property in Pleasantville is based on documents in GN 4/3, boxes 12 and 13, PANL.

100 "St. John's extends warm welcome to American troops; U.S. transport reaches St. John's, entered port early this morning under own power without difficulty. largest ship ever to enter port," *Evening Telegram*, 29 January 1941, 3.

101 GN 38, S4-2-3, U.S. Joint Defence Board, 1941, PANL.

102 44 Rennies Mill Road. "New Headquarters for U.S. Base Command," *Evening Telegram*, 21 May 1941, 4.

103 Cardoulis, *Friendly Invasion*, 48. William Pepperrell, born in the Thirteen Colonies, is best known for his role in capturing the French fortress of Louisburg for the British in 1745.

104 Steven High, personal communication.

105 Dziuban, *Military Relations*, 167.

106 Peter Neary, "Newfoundland and the Anglo-American Leased Bases Agreement," 517. It has proved impossible to find an accurate count of the number of Newfoundlanders employed on base construction. The general consensus is that the peak number, reached at the end of 1942, was approximately 20,000, of which two-thirds were employed on American army or navy projects. High, *Base Colonies*, 69.

107 High, "Working for Uncle Sam," 87.

108 "Workmen's quarters," *Evening Telegram,* 24 December 1941, 3.

109 G.O.C. Atlantic Command to Secretary, Department of National Defence, 6 March 1941, in Bridle, *Documents on Relations*, 289.

110 Dziuban, *Military Relations*, 168.

111 Candow, *A Structural and Narrative History*, 127.

112 Dziuban, *Military Relations*, 174.

113 During 1942 there was extensive U-boat activity in the Gulf of St Lawrence, at Bell Island, and in the Cabot Strait. More than two dozen ships were sunk between May and September 1942.

114 Candow, "The Tactical Role of American Armed Forces at Signal Hill," 26.

115 Cardoulis, *Friendly Invasion*, 54.

116 Searchlight sites were set up at Blackhead Road, Freshwater Bay Ridge, Cape Spear Road, Maddox Cove, Long Pond Road, Thorburn Road, Upper Battery Road, Torbay Road, Outer Cove, and the White Hills. Gun sites were established at Flatrock, Torbay, Middle Cove, Outer Cove, Logy Bay, Blackhead, Robin Hood Bay, Red Cliff, and Topsail Head. Parrot, "On the Perimeter," 185; and Dziuban *Military Relations*, 175.

117 Major General G.C. Brant to Commissioner for Defence, 10 December 1941, GN 31/3B, file WU47, PANL.

118 Governor to Dominions Office, telegram 87, 11 February 1941, and telegram 99, 19 February 1941, GN 4/1/D, box 32, file G/441, PANL.

119 J6-'41, Emerson to Commission, 14 February 1941, GN 38, S4-1-6, file 1, PANL. The Commission of Government granted permission to U.S. forces to develop more than twenty sites outside the leased areas, both on the island and in Labrador. Browne, *To Serve and Protect*, 221.

120 Acts of the Honourable Commission of Government of Newfoundland 1942, Act No. 19, 27 June 1942. Both local newspapers published editorials on 22 June 1942 roundly criticizing this further erosion of Newfoundland sovereignty. The Canadian high commissioner apprised the secretary of state for external affairs of local sentiment in Despatch 382 of 26 June. Bridle, *Documents on Relations*, 310.

121 Plans 745, "Ammunition Storage Area, Property Ownership," 2 June 1941; and 4558, "Property Ownership, Vicinity of the Ammunition Storage Site," 8 April 1941, RG 4.3, 41/83, PANL.

122 Map 4568, RG 4/3, 41/83, 3 December 1942, PANL; and "Fort Pepperrell Property Lines and Property Ownership," "St. John's Army Post, Boundary Lines and Property Ownership, April 7, 1941," War Department Corps of Engineers, U.S. Army, City of St John's Archives.

123 Since the Americans imported most of their materials and supplies, they were worried about their supply chain. The harbour at Argentia was operating at full capacity, as the main American base was constructed there, and the development of Harmon Air Base near Stephenville overtaxed the port capacity of Port aux Basques and that of the Newfoundland Railway. The army supply dock in St John's was very close to Fort Pepperrell. Cardoulis, *Friendly Invasion*, 50.

124 This discussion of the requisitioning of property in the battery is based on files in GN 4/3, boxes 11 and 12, PANL.

125 Air Officer Commanding, Eastern Air Command, to Secretary, Department of National Defence, 29 May 1940, in Bridle, *Documents on Relations*, 77.

126 Woods to Minister of National Revenue, 17 April 1941, in Bridle, *Documents on Relations*, 462.

127 A property commissioner/land surveyor from the Canadian Department of Transport (whose signature is illegible) met with the farmers in the schoolhouse on Portugal Cove Road to negotiate the amount of compensation. His report is dated 10 June 1941. GN 4/1/D, box 34, G/449, PANL.
128 Minutes of a meeting at Ottawa to discuss bilateral defence questions, 19 April 1941, in Bridle, *Documents on Relations*, 185.
129 Enclosure to Memorandum from Department of External Affairs to Cabinet Committee on Reconstruction, 5 September 1945, in Bridle, *Documents on Relations*, 1417.
130 One of the larger radar sites was at Flatrock, to which the men were bussed daily from their barracks at Torbay Airport. Parrott, "On the Perimeter," 183.
131 This was necessary because the first two had not been oriented correctly with respect to the prevailing winds and the flying conditions were made more difficult as a result. Burchell to Keenleyside, 30 August 1943. In Bridle, *Documents on Relations*, 474.
132 Douglas, *Creation of a National Air Force*, 473, 385–6.
133 The term "scarecrows" is used in Douglas, *Creation of a National Air Force*, 469, referring to the fact that even the sighting of an aircraft usually caused a U-boat to submerge immediately in the hope of escaping attack. This caused the boat to lose contact with potential targets, and its slow speed underwater made it difficult to regain contact. Thus, even as scarecrows, aircraft played a vital role. For at least the first three years of the war, the corvettes of the RCN performed a similar role, since their primary mission was to ensure the "safe and timely arrival of the convoy" rather than destruction of U-boats. Bercuson and Herwig, *Deadly Seas*, 62.
134 A detachment of four Hudson bombers from No. 11 (BR) Squadron began operating from Torbay on 26 November 1941. They were joined on 9 June 1942 by the Hurricanes of No. 125 (F) Squadron. Over the course of the war a variety of aircraft operated out of Torbay (Hurricane, Hudson, Ventura, Liberator, and Canso), flown by Nos 5, 11, 113, and 145 (BR), and 125 and 128 (F) Squadrons. Kostenuk and Griffin, RCAF.
135 Parrott, "On the Perimeter," 101.
136 Rompkey, *St. John's and the Battle of the Atlantic*, 44.
137 Plan 11.01.680, City of St John's Archives; Government of Newfoundland Registry of Deeds, vol. 165, folio 271, 14 November 1941; vol. 166, folios 275–7, 23 December 1941; and Memo to Asst. Deputy Minister of Justice, Canada, 7 November 1942, GN 13/1/B, box 390, file 19, PANL.
138 C.M. McEwen, Air Officer Commanding, No. 1 Group Headquarters, to W.P. Ryan, City Clerk, 14 August 1942, Jackman Collection, City of St John's Archives, file J2; Ozorak, *Abandoned Military Establishments*, 258; and *1963 Fire Insurance Atlas*, City of St John's Archives.
139 Bashow, *All the Fine Young Eagles*, 245.
140 Douglas, *Creation of a National Air Force*, 465.
141 The etymology of the term "Newfyjohn" is discussed in Kirwin, "Miscellany," 33–4. It is suggested that in the beginning the name was used to distinguish the city from Saint John, New Brunswick.
142 Newfoundland Defence Scheme, 4 May 1936, in Bridle, *Documents on Relations*, 2.
143 Collins, "First Line of Defence."
144 In 1939 the RCN had 13 ships and 2,891 personnel. In 1945, with 434 warships and 92,441 men and women in uniform, it was the third-largest navy in the world, after the U.S. Navy (USN) and the RN. Milner, *North Atlantic Run*, 141. The number of personnel expanded by a ratio of 32 to 1, and the number of major ships by 44 to 1. Graves, *In Peril on the Sea*, 231.
145 Bercuson, *Maple Leaf against the Axis*, 36.
146 Telegram 171B/20, Admiralty to NOIC, 20 May 1941, GN 38, S4-2-3.3, file 4, PANL.
147 Telegram 2232Z/20, NOIC to Admiralty, 20 May 1941, GN 38, S4-2-3.3, file 4, PANL.
148 Telegram 2108Z/21, NSHQ to Admiralty, 21 May 1941, in Bridle, *Documents on Relations*, 560.
149 HMCS *Agassiz, Alberni, Chambly, Cobalt, Collingwood, Orillia,* and *Wetaskiwin.*
150 Schull, *Far Distant Ships*, 68.
151 Hadley, "The Popular Image of the Canadian Navy," 36.
152 Telegram 287, Governor to Dominions Office, 6 June 1941, GN 38, S4-2-4, file 2, PANL.
153 That is, mooring buoys in the middle of the harbour.
154 One depot ship, 7 destroyers, 12 corvettes (5 for local defence), 4 sloops, 6 mine sweepers, 1 store ship, 1 large oiler, 1 small oiler, 2 tugs, 1 water boat, 3 harbour patrol craft, 4 Fairmiles, 4 lighters, 6 harbour duty boats, and 2 examination vessels.
155 Repair facilities were already strained. Between July and December 1940, a total of 126 vessels were repaired in the Newfoundland Dockyard: 102 merchantmen and 24 HM destroyers. On one day in December there were 46 steamers in port, 35 needing repairs. Many of these vessels were more than twenty years old and their plating had deteriorated, making repairs more extensive and time-consuming than would be the case for newer ships. Superintendent of the Newfoundland Dockyard

to the Manager, 27 February 1941, GN 38 S5-1-2, file 9, PANL.

156 Tucker, *Naval Service of Canada*, 190; Telegram 1140, Dominions Secretary to High Commissioner of Great Britain, 28 June 1941; Telegram 666, Dominions Secretary to Governor, 19 July 1941; Telegram 377, Governor to Dominions Secretary, 21 July 1941; and Telegram 682, Dominions Secretary to Governor, 25 July 1941, in Bridle, *Documents on Relations*, 577–88.

157 Lamb, *Corvette Navy*, 92. As late as 1943 naval ratings were still accommodated in a Great Lakes steamer designated *Avalon II.* Miller, *St. John's Naval Guide Book*.

158 Lamb, *Corvette Navy*, 92.

159 The major owners were Bowring Brothers, Job Brothers, Baine Johnston's, and Imperial Oil.

160 Ransom, "Canada's 'Newfyjohn' Tenancy," 57.

161 This discussion of the requisitioning of Water Street property is based on files in GN 4/3, box 15, PANL.

162 The field took its name from Patrick Buckmaster, a butcher who had used it for grazing, but it had also been used as a golf course (O'Neill, *Oldest City*, 641) and as the site for a visiting circus (Advertisement, *Evening Telegram*, 3 January 1936).

163 Government of Newfoundland, Registry of Deeds, vol. 221, folio 539, 7 October 1950.

164 Pugsley, *Saints, Devils and Ordinary Seamen*, 106.

165 "His Excellency officiates at Flag Raising Ceremony: Dedication Exercise at Naval Barracks at Buckmaster's Field," *Evening Telegram*, 7 December 1942, 3.

166 A field of command-detonated mines was laid on the seabed outside the eastern end of the Narrows. They were controlled by an officer and ratings housed at Fort Amherst.

167 Flag Officer, Newfoundland Force to Commissioner for Public Utilities, 25 August, 1941, in Bridle, *Documents on Relations*, 589.

168 Milner, *Canada's Navy*, 102.

169 Tucker, *Naval Service of Canada,* 203.

170 Ibid., 198.

171 Lockwood to Burchell, 9 May 1942, GN 4/1/D, numbered series, box 24, file 19/01/53, PANL.

172 British Admiralty Delegation in Washington to Commissioner of Public Works and Utilities, 14 April 1943, GN 38, S5-1-3, file 12, PANL.

173 E.G.M. Cape of Montreal was the major contractor for this expansion. Tucker, *Naval Service of Canada,* 199.

174 This discussion of the requisitioning of property on the South Side is based on files in GN 4/3, box 17, PANL.

175 Porter, *Below the Bridge.*

176 Telegram 38, High Commission in Newfoundland to Secretary of State for External Affairs, 11 April, 1943, in Bridle, *Documents on Relations*, 613.

177 Telegram 68, Burchell to Woods, 18 August 1942, GN 4/1/D, numbered series, file 19/01/56, PANL.

178 PJBD Journal of Discussions and Decisions, Report of Service Representatives, 24–25 August 1943, in Bridle, *Documents on Relations*, 622.

179 Ten properties were expropriated in Bay Bulls, one of them the home of a seventy-five-year-old widow who had lived in the house since the day of her marriage, fifty years earlier. PU96(b)-'42, 21 October 1942, GN 38, S5-1-2, file 2, PANL.

180 Tucker, *Naval Service of Canada,* 199.

181 James Kirby and Aubrey Halfyard, personal communications.

182 Wright, *October*, 43.

183 Editorial: "Windsor Lake Supply'," *Evening Telegram*, 4 March 1941.

184 Minutes of a meeting at St John's to discuss bilateral defence questions, 14 April 1941, in Bridle, *Documents on Relations*, 175; and Hopper to Woods, 22 June 1943, GN 4/1/D, box 19, file G/208, PANL. Portugal Cove Road, leading to Torbay Airport, was a particularly contentious issue. It was, apparently, not the policy of the Canadian government to pay for a hard surface on roads leading to airports, but the high commissioner suggested that in this case an exception might be made, and proposed to share the cost with the commission. PU109-'42, 23 September 1942, GN 38, S5-1-2, file 2, PANL.

185 "City council to appoint building and electrical inspector next month: Resolution on taxation of military buildings in the city," *Evening Telegram*, 17 December 1943, 3.

186 High Commissioner to Under-Secretary of State for External Affairs, 30 June 1944, in Bridle, *Documents on Relations*, 880.

187 High Commissioner to Under-Secretary of State for External Affairs, 10 February 1945, in Bridle, *Documents on Relations*, 966.

188 Order-in-Council P.C. 4849, 16 July 1945, in Bridle, *Documents on Relations*, 884.

189 Plan Books 1940–1942, City of St John's Archives.

190 "War buildings to go," *Evening Telegram*, 7 December 1945.

191 "Editorial: Responsibilities to be faced," *Evening Telegram*, 21 March 1942, 6.

192 The fire at the Imperial Oil Company on 24 June 1944 reminded everyone of the ever-present danger of fire. See Rompkey, *St. John's and the Battle of the Atlantic,* 45. There was also the possibility that a deliberate destruction of military facilities might be undertaken under a "scorched earth" policy. See Collins, chapter 2, this volume.

193 Woods to Emerson, 3 April 1943, GN 4/1/D, box 38, file G/480/11, PANL.

194 NOIC to Woods, 23 May 1945. GN 4/1/D, box 38, file G/480/9, PANL.

195 Rent Restriction Regulations, *Newfoundland Gazette* 17, no. 52 (30 December 1941); "Order restricting increase in rents," *Evening Telegram,* 2 January 1942, 3; and "Overcrowding," *Evening Telegram*, 10 June 1943, 6.

196 Neary, *Newfoundland in the North Atlantic World*, 484; "600 men now employed at U.S. Army Base at Quidi Vidi," *Evening Telegram,* 26 February 1941.

197 *Commission of Enquiry into Housing and Town Planning in St. John's Third Interim Report*, 1943.

198 Commissioner for Public Health and Welfare (Puddester) to High Commissioner for Canada (C.J. Burchell), 6 December 1943, GN 38, box 6-1-7, file 4A, PANL.

199 Phyllis Meschino, personal communication.

200 Cardoulis, *Friendly Invasion*, 52.

201 The Air Officer Commanding No. 1 Group wanted all dependants sent home. The Flag Officer Newfoundland was surprised to learn of this because, in his opinion, the presence of wives in port was critical to maintenance of morale among sea-going personnel, and thought the same would be true of aircrew. The three service heads resolved the issue by agreeing on a quota of dependants permitted to live in St John's: 400 for the RCN, 280 for the Army and 60 for the RCAF. See Bridle, *Documents on Relations*, 859, 862.

202 "Families living in one room owing to lack of houses," *Evening Telegram*, 21 October 1943, 3.

203 See, in this volume, Collins, chapter 2; Poulter and Douglas, chapter 6; and Lorenzkowsi, chapter 3. The clubs included the Salvation Army Red Shield Centre at Lester's Field Camp; the Terra Nova Club, operated by the United and Presbyterian churches at the corner of LeMarchant Road and Barter's Hill; the Knights of Columbus hostel on Harvey Road; the Caribou Hut, run by the Canadian Club of St John's in the King George V Seaman's Institute on Water Street; the Crow's Nest Officers' Club at Queen's Beach; the American United Service Organization (USO) club on Merrymeeting Road; the YMCA's Red Triangle Hut on Water Street West; the Allied Merchant Seaman's Hostel at King's Beach; and the Allied Merchant Seaman's Officers' Club on Cochrane Street; and the YWCA's Leave Centre for Women on Cochrane Street.

204 Stacey, *Arms, Men and Governments*, 180.

205 PJBD Journal of Discussions and Decisions, Report of Service Members, 7–8 November 1945, in Bridle, *Documents on Relations*, 972.

206 Despatch 261, High Commissioner in Newfoundland to Secretary of State for External Affairs, 3 July 1946, in Bridle, *Documents on Relations*, 972; and "Canadian Forces withdraw," *Evening Telegram*, 29 June 1946, 6.

207 Memorandum from Director of External Operations, Wartime Information Board (G.W. McCracken), to General Executive Manager, Wartime Information Board (A.D. Dunton), 17 April 1944, in Bridle, *Documents on Relations*, 872.

208 Lamb, *Corvette Navy*, 92.

209 Display advertisement, *Daily News,* 21 March 1946, 2.

210 "Hut must come down," *Evening Telegram,* 12 April 1946.

211 "Purities allowed to take over Canadian Army buildings," *Evening Telegram*, 29 March 1946.

212 "Condition of Lester's Field strongly condemned," *Daily News*, 2 May 1947.

213 Despatch 116, Dominions Secretary to Governor, May 16, 1946, in Bridle, *Documents on Relations*, 987.

214 Deputy Minister of National Defence for Naval Services to Under-Secretary of State for External Affairs, 20 May 1946, in Bridle, *Documents on Relations*, 990. See also Ozorak, *Abandoned Military Installations*, 27.

215 About 1,000 Newfoundlanders continued to be employed on the site after 1945. High Commissioner in Newfoundland to Secretary of State for External Affairs, 3 July 1945, in Bridle, *Documents on Relations,* 1050.

216 In Mount Pleasant Cemetery.

217 H.A. Winter to Secretary of State for Dominion Affairs, 5 October 1945, quoted in Strauss, "The Americans Come to Newfoundland," 560.

218 The St John's Housing Corporation Act, 1944, and the St John's Housing Corporation (Lands) Act, 1944. See Sharpe, "Mr. Dunfield's Folly."

219 Mellin, "Modernism in Newfoundland," 18–21.

220 "Address by Hon. Justice Dunfield at Conference," *Daily News*, 18 September 1943, 8. See Shawyer and Sharpe, "Addressing the Legacy of the Modern on Newfoundland."

221 Roberts, *Canada and the War at Sea,* 22.

Chapter Two

1 British historian Andrew Williams sums up Canada's participation in the Atlantic campaign in just two sentences. Oddly enough, in those two sentences he recognizes Canada's "extraordinary contribution" to the Allied victory in the Atlantic. See Williams, *The Battle of the Atlantic,* 287. American historians tend to lump all Commonwealth forces under the catch-all phrase "British forces."

2 Milner, *North Atlantic Run* (Toronto: University of Toronto Press, 1985). In his memoir, *U-Boat Killer,* Donald Macintyre is very critical of the RCN. Commander Macintyre felt that Canada should have swallowed its national pride and simply turned over its ships and men to the Royal Navy. Macintyre's attitude towards the RCN is indicative of the relationship between officers of the RN and RCN. Numerous RCN officers complained to higher authority of the RN's condescending attitude towards all "colonial" personnel, not just Canadian. Capt. (D), Newfoundland, to Commodore (L), Western Approaches, 9 July 1943, RG 24, vol. 11, 943, Library and Archives Canada (hereafter LAC). See also O'Mayne, *Betrayed.*

3 Hadley, *U-Boats against Canada* (Montreal and Kingston: McGill-Queen's University Press, 1985). Previously, Canada's naval historiography basically consisted of Joseph Schull's official operational history of the RCN during the Second World War, *The Far Distant Ships,* first published in 1952, and Gilbert Tucker's two-volume *The Naval Service of Canada,* also published in 1952. The two parts of the second volume of the official history, *No Higher Purpose* and *Blue Water Navy,* were published in 2002 and 2006, respectively.

4 Halifax had been an established naval base since before the First World War, but during the Second World War it never provided convoy escort further than the Newfoundland Grand Banks. It was, and remains, Canada's most important Atlantic naval base and, from April 1943, the headquarters of the Canadian Northwest Atlantic Command. All of the RCN's wartime bases were sub-commands of Halifax. However, HMCS Avalon was the only RCN base developed during the war in which the commanding officer held the title of Flag Officer Commanding and up until 1943 answered to Halifax only on manning issues.

5 The Canadians arrived in 1940 and were encamped in Lester's Field. The Americans arrived in January 1941 and constructed Fort Pepperrell on the shores of Quidi Vidi Lake.

6 Milner, *Canada's Navy,* 89–90.

7 Hadley, *U-Boats against Canada,* 29.

8 Tucker, *Naval Service of Canada,* 203; Schull, *Far Distant Ships,* 68.

9 German, *The Sea Is at Our Gates,* 93.

10 Ibid.

11 Lamb, *Corvette Navy,* 52.

12 A Canadian exception is Sydney, Cape Breton. However, Sydney was more a convoy assembly base and home to local escort forces, and remained active long after the Second World War. See Tennyson and Sarty, *Guardian of the Gulf.* See also Shirlaw, *Point Edward.*

13 Cadigan, *Newfoundland and Labrador*; Neary, *Newfoundland in the North Atlantic World*; O'Neill, *The Oldest City.*

14 See Ransom, "Canada's 'Newfyjohn' Tenancy"; and Collins, "'First Line of Defence.'" Unfortunately, Kerry Badgley's short article in the *Archivist* on the proposed Scorched Earth Policy in place for St John's was subsequently the centrepiece of a minor controversy. See Badgley, "'Rigorously Applied in Practice,'" 38. Also see Daniel Leblanc, "Canada's plan to torch St John's," *Ottawa Citizen,* 30 May 1998, A1; Daniel LeBlanc, "Upper-Canadian arrogance," *Ottawa Citizen,* 31 May 1998, 1; and Collins, "'Canada's Plan to Torch St John's.'"

15 See Christopher A. Sharpe and A.J. Shawyer, chapter 1, this volume.

16 See Steven High, chapter 4, this volume.

17 See Gillian Poulter and Douglas O. Baldwin, chapter 6, this volume.

18 See Barbara Lorenzkowski, chapter 3, this volume.

19 Steven High argues that this distinction was a purely political one, to make the deal more palatable to the colonies' white population. See High, *Base Colonies in the Western Hemisphere,* 213–14.

20 Cardoulis, *A Friendly Invasion,* 19. For further discussion on the American presence in Newfoundland, see Neary, *Newfoundland in the North Atlantic World 1929–1949,* 135; MacKenzie, *Inside the Atlantic Triangle,* 46–52; Reynolds, *The Creation of the Anglo-American Alliance,* 121–32, 169–75; and Whitham, "On Dealing with Gangsters."

21 Secretary of State for External Affairs to Governor of Newfoundland, 2 September 1939, in Bridle, *Documents on Relations,* 1:41. See also Extract from a Speech by Prime Minister, 8 September 1939, in Bridle, *Documents on Relations,* 1:43.

22 *The Mackenzie King Record,* vol. 1: *1939–1944* (Toronto: University of Toronto Press, 1960), 202; and Minutes of a Meeting of War Cabinet Committee, 17 September 1940, in Bridle, *Documents on Relations,* 1:99. See also Minutes of a Meeting of War Cabinet Committee, 10 June 1941, in Bridle, *Documents on Relations,* 571; High Commissioner in Newfoundland to Secretary of State for External Affairs, 3 December 1941, in Bridle, *Documents on Relations,* 115; Secretary of State for External Affairs to Dominions Secretary, 2 March 1941, in Bridle, *Documents on Relations,* 103. For a further examination of Newfoundland's strategic importance, see Lower, "Transition to Atlantic Bastion."

23 Public Archives of Newfoundland and Labrador (hereafter PANL), GN 38, S4-1-2, file J12(a)-40, Governor to Secretary of State For Dominion Affairs, 17 September 1940.

24 PANL, GN 38, S4-1-2, file 2: J12-49, Memorandum for Commission, 23 March 1940.

25 Tarrant, *The U-Boat Offensive,* 101.

26 "The Pit," "The Black Pit," and "The Gap" were all names for the area in the mid-Atlantic where the convoys travelled unescorted, or lightly escorted, from the point at which the RCN escorts left them and their rendezvous with RN warships east of the United Kingdom. It was also referred to as the "Air Gap" as ASW aircraft from Newfoundland, Iceland, and the U.K. did not have the range to patrol it. The Allies finally "closed the Gap" in 1943 with the introduction of VLR (Very Long Range) aircraft of American manufacture and escort carriers that accompanied convoys to supply air cover.

27 Department of National Defence (hereafter DND), Directorate of History and Heritage (hereafter DHH), NHS 8000, 1, Lt Stuart Keats, The Royal Canadian Navy in Newfoundland, 1940–1944, 25 October 1944.

28 LAC, Record Group (RG) 24, vol. 3892, NSS 1033-6-1, pt 1, "Nfld. Convoy Escort Forces. Gen. Data and Correspondence," NSHQ to Admiralty, 21 May 1941; LAC, RG 24, vol. 3892, NSS 1033-6-1, pt 1, "Nfld. Convoy Escort Forces. Gen. Data and Correspondence," NSHQ to Admiralty, 29 May 1941. See also Douglas, Sarty, and Whitby, *No Higher Purpose,* 183.

29 During the first four months of the war (September–December 1939), U-boats sank over a half million tonnes of British shipping, including the aircraft carrier HMS *Courageous* and the battleship *Royal Oak,* the latter at anchor at Scapa Flow. See Tarrant, *The U-Boat Offensive,* 84.

30 Johnson, *Corvettes Canada,* 3.

31 Ibid.

32 Ibid.

33 Dr Roger Sarty of Wilfrid Laurier University suggests that it was possibly the fine job that the naval officer in charge at St John's, Capt. C.M.R. Schwerdt RN, and his staff did in preparing the U.K.-bound ex-USN destroyers for their transatlantic voyage that introduced the Admiralty to the idea of establishing a forward escort base there.

34 MacKenzie, *Inside the Atlantic Triangle,* 71.

35 Douglas, *Creation of a National Air Force,* 383. The Canadians were not the only ones who were concerned about an American presence in Newfoundland. In a telegram to the secretary of state for dominion affairs, the commander-in-chief, America and West Indies Station, recommended that Canada shoulder sole responsibility for the defence of Newfoundland. He felt that giving the United States leases in Newfoundland would lead to "endless trouble in the years to come." PANL, GN 38, S4-2-1.1, file 13, Admiralty 464, CinC, A&WE to Secretary of State, DA, 25 August 1940.

36 Douglas, *Creation of a National Air Force,* 386.

37 Minutes of a Meeting of Cabinet War Committee, 29 October 1941, in Bridle, *Documents on Relations,* 110.

38 LAC, RG 24, vol. 3892, NSS 1033-6-1, pt 1, "Nfld. Convoy Escort Force. Gen. Data and Correspondence.," Lt-Col. K.S. Maclachlan, Assistant Deputy Minister of Naval Service, and Admiral P. Nelles, Chief of Naval Staff, "Notes for Minister of National Defence," 1 July 1941. See also Stacey, *Arms, Men and Government,* 311.

39 Minutes of Meeting of Cabinet War Committee, 20 June 1941, in Bridle, *Documents on Relations,* 572.

40 Milner, *Canada's Navy,* 93.

41 Douglas, *The Creation of a National Air Force,* 383.

42 Minute, 17 June,1941, Admiralty Minute Series M.09406/41, The National Archives, Public Record Office (hereafter TNA [PRO]), Kew, UK, ADM 116/4387, copies at DND, DHH. See also Governor to Secretary of State for Dominion Affairs, 17 September 1940, PANL, GN 38, S4-2-1, file 13, 602-40. Ottawa assured the Newfoundland government that no formal plans had been made. See Secretary of State for External Affairs, Ottawa to Governor, 1 October 1940, PANL, GN 38, S4-2-1.1, file 13, 51–40.

43 The Lend-Lease Bill permitted the United States to provide war supplies to Great Britain without the latter having to pay for them. Up to this point, Britain had to

pay for any supplies "cash and carry" and its foreign cash reserves were exhausted.

44 In response to the slow pace of negotiations, Roosevelt suggested to the British ambassador to Washington, Lord Halifax, that the pending Lend-Lease Bill could be in jeopardy if agreement were not soon achieved. See Conn, Engelman, and Fairchild, *Guarding the United States,* 373.

45 Neary, "Newfoundland and the Anglo-American Leased Bases Agreement," 510.

46 MacKenzie, *Inside the Atlantic Triangle,* 51.

47 LAC, RG 24, vol. 11, 956, NFM 2-8, Emerson and Pension to Governor, 19 March 1941.

48 LAC, RG 24, vol. 11, 956, NFM 2-8, Governor to Emerson and Pension, 17 March 1941; "Letter from Prime Minister to Commissioner of Defence," *Evening Telegram* (St John's), 27 March 1941.

49 Neary, "Newfoundland and the Anglo-American Leased Bases Agreement," 514.

50 Dominions Secretary to Governor of Newfoundland, 23 May 1941, in Bridle, *Documents on Relations,* 560.

51 Ibid., 561.

52 NSHQ to Admiralty, 29 May 1941, in Bridle, *Documents on Relations,* 565.

53 Minutes of a Meeting of Cabinet War Committee, 20 June 1941, in Bridle, *Documents on Relations,* 571–4.

54 TNA (PRO), Kew, UK, ADM 116/ 4387, copies at DND, DHH, Admiralty Minute Series M.09812/41, Minute, H.N. Morrison, Head of Military Branch, 27 July 1941.

55 Minutes of a Meeting of Cabinet War Committee, 15 July 1941, in Bridle, *Documents on Relations,* 584.

56 TNA (PRO), Kew, UK, ADM 1/4387, Government of Newfoundland to Dominions Secretary, 6 June 1941.

57 TNA (PRO), Kew, UK, ADM 116/4387, copies at DND, DHH, Admiralty Minute Series M.01127/41, Memo, Military Branch, 20 July 1941.

58 TNA (PRO), Kew, UK, ADM 116/4387, copies at DND, DHH, Admiralty Minute Series M.09406/41, Minute, 17 June 1941.

59 Tucker, *Naval Service of Canada,* 192.

60 DND, DHH, FOMR, NSS-1000-5-20, vol. 1, CCNF to NSHQ, 30 June 1941.

61 Capt. Schwerdt had been serving as the governor's private secretary and took over as naval officer in charge at the start of hostilities. He was later seconded to the RCN and eventually became senior naval officer (SNO) at Sydney, N.S.

62 HF/DF stood for "High Frequency Direction Finding," a method of locating U-boats by triangulating their radio signals to U-Boat Command. DND, DHH, FOMR, NSS-1000-5-20, vol. 1, CCNF to NSHQ, 30 June 1941.

63 DND, DHH, Monthly Report on Proceedings, NSS-1000-5-13.5, Lt-Cdr R.U. Langston RCNR (for NOIC) to NSHQ, 31 March 1941.

64 For an extensive examination of Canada's defensive presence in Newfoundland, including airport and coastal protection, see Kavanagh, "W Force." See also Sarty, *Maritime Defence of Canada,* 155.

65 German, *The Sea Is at Our Gates,* 90–1.

66 DND, DHH 81/520/1440-166/25 II (1), Report, Engineer-in-Chief to CNS, Ottawa, 9 June 1941.

67 As Newfoundland's main port, St John's supplied all the communities spread along the island's considerable coastline, as well as in Labrador.

68 See also Ransom, "Canada's 'Newfyjohn' Tenancy," 53–5; and DND, DHH 81/520/1440-166/25 (1), Reports, R-Adm. Sheridan and Adm. Bonham-Carter to NOIC, St John's, dated 5 June 1941 and 4 June 1941.

69 LAC, RG 24, vol. 3892, NSS 1033-6-1, pt 1, "Nfld. Convoy Escort Forces. Gen. Data and Correspondence," Admiralty to CincWA, CinC Home Fleet, CNS, 4 June 1941.

70 Ransom, "Canada's 'Newfyjohn' Tenancy," 55. See also MacKenzie, *Inside the Atlantic Triangle,* 71.

71 DND, DHH, FOMR, NSS-1000-5-20, vol. 1, Murray to NSHQ and CincWA, July 1941.

72 DND, DHH, FOMR, NSS-1000-5-20, vol. 1, Murray to NSHQ and CincWA, August 1941.

73 There are a few interpretations for what "SC" stood for. Gilbert Tucker says it stood for "Sydney-Clyde," while Marc Milner suggests that it originally meant "Sydney Convoy" but was changed to "Slow Convoy" after these convoys were transferred to New York in 1941. The confusion could result from the sources referenced. For example, the RCN called HX convoys "Halifax Convoys," while the RN referred to them as H(omeward) from (Halifa)X convoys.

74 LAC, FONF, RG 24, vol. 11,953, file 1-1-1, vol. 1, Monthly Reports, FONF, September 1941.

75 As quoted in Milner, *North Atlantic Run,* 64.

76 Only two U.S. Coast Guard cutters remained for transatlantic escort duty.

77 Murray's promotion to rear admiral in December 1941, making him equal in rank to the commanding officer, Atlantic Coast (COAC), situated in Halifax, gives some indication of the importance NSHQ placed on the Newfoundland station. However, while Murray reported directly to NSHQ for administrative and disci-

plinary matters, he was dependent upon the COAC for manning, a situation that caused some friction between the two commands.

78 By May 1942, the RCN was also escorting Canadian-flagged tankers to and from the Caribbean as a result of the carnage being wrought there and along the American eastern seaboard by U-boats. See Douglas, Sarty, and Whitby, *No Higher Purpose,* 412; and Fisher, "'We'll Get Our Own,'' 33–9.

79 LAC, FONF, RG 24, vol. 11,951, Brant to Admiral Commanding Newfoundland, 24 December 1941.

80 LAC, RG 24, vol. 11,956, Secretary of State for Dominion Affairs to Governor, 8 April 1941.

81 "Says Newfoundland was included in Hitler's plans," *Evening Telegram,* 13 July 1944.

82 LAC, RG 24, vol. 11,953, file 1-1-1, vol. 1, "Report of Proceedings for Month of March, 1942, by Maintenance Captain, Captain of the Port," 10 April 1942. U-boats also attacked shipping at the Wabana anchorage twice in the fall of 1942, sinking four ships, and set up an automated weather station in northern Labrador in 1943. See Hadley, *U-Boats against Canada.*

83 LAC, RG 24, vol. 11,927, MS 1400-4, vol. 1, "Denial Plans – Naval Installations, Equipment and Supplies," 23 September 1942. For an in-depth examination of the RCN's denial plan for St John's, see Collins, "Canada's Plan to Torch St John's."

84 Ransom, "Canada's 'Newfyjohn' Tenancy," 60.

85 LAC, RG 24, vol. 3892, NSS-1033-6-1, pt. 1, CCNF to NSHQ, 22 November 1941.

86 DND, DHH, FOMR, NSS-1000-5-20, vol. 1, FONF to NSHQ, January–May 1942.

87 DND, DHH, NHS 8000, 23, Lt Stuart Keats, "The Royal Canadian Navy in Newfoundland, 1940–1944," October 1944.

88 LAC, RG 25, series 62, vol. 3198, file 5206-40, Burchell to Scott MacDonald, 16 April 1943.

89 The earliest report of the landing of Battle of the Atlantic survivors at St John's was dated June 1941. See "Sixty-Four survivors of torpedoed ships reach Newfoundland port," *Evening Telegram,* 16 June 1941.

90 DND, DHH, NHS 8000, 25, Lt Stuart Keats, "The Royal Canadian Navy in Newfoundland, 1940–1944," October 1944.

91 LAC, RG 28, vol. 129, file C-3-21, 3, Minutes of Combined Canadian, United Kingdom and United States Committee to Examine Repair Problem for Warships and Merchant Vessels on the East Coast of Canada and Newfoundland, 12 August 1943. Orders issued by the RN Maintenance Office in February 1943, as cited in Milner, *North Atlantic Run,* 219.

92 Of the forty-eight days worked by the dock in September and October, thirty-six were taken up with naval usage.

93 Tucker, *Naval Service of Canada,* 203. See also Ransom, "Canada's 'Newfyjohn' Tenancy," 58–61.

94 PANL, GN 38, S4-2-1.1, file 9, 578-42, Secretary of State for Dominion Affairs to Governor, 16 October 1942.

95 Ransom, "Canada's 'Newfyjohn' Tenancy," 59–60.

96 LAC, RG 25, series 62, vol. 3198, file 5206-40, C.J. Burchell, High Commissioner for Canada, St John's, to Scott MacDonald, Department of External Affairs, Ottawa, 16 April 1943.

97 "Mechanics to train at local dockyards," *Evening Telegram,* 22 August 1941, 4.

98 DND, DHH, FOMR, NSS-1000-5-20, vol. 1, CCNF to NSHQ, 30 June 1941.

99 High Commissioner in Newfoundland to Commissioner for Public Utilities, 18 August 1942, in Bridle, *Documents on Relations,* 603–4.

100 Ibid., 606.

101 The RCN escorted mainly SC convoys, which because of their slow speed of advance were easier to find and stay in contact with than fast convoys. Indeed, after the Canadian, or "C", groups were pulled out of the Atlantic in the winter of 1943, the British (B) and American (A) escort groups that replaced them did not fare any better.

102 Milner, "Squaring Some of the Corners," 132. See also Milner, "Royal Canadian Navy Participation," 65–81.

103 DND, DHH, ADM 116/4540, Minute M.012347/42 and Notes by Admiralty M. Branch, 23 September 1942.

104 DND, DHH 81/520/1440-166/25 II (1), Reports on St John's Repair Facilities, DSR to CNEC, Ottawa, 19 April 1943.

105 ASDIC equipment, now called SONAR, sent out a sound pulse underwater much like radar, and a return echo would indicate the presence of a submerged submarine. See Ransom, "Canada's 'Newfyjohn' Tenancy," 64.

106 LAC, RG 25, series 62, vol. 3198, file 5206-40, D.B. Carswell, Controller of Ship Repairs and Salvage, to A.J. Martin, Department of Munitions and Supply, 27 April 1943.

107 DND, DHH 81/520/1440-166/25 II (1), Seal to Admiralty, Report on Repair Facilities, 7 April 1943. See also TNA, Kew, UK, DO35/1368, FONF to Admiralty, 14 April 1943.

108 Working-up practices were discontinued in late 1942 when Pictou and St Margaret's Bay, Nova Scotia, came

into use. Refresher training continued to the end of the war. See DND, DHH, NHS 8000, 1–6, "Harbour Training in St John's - Summary of General Development," 28 June 1945.

109 LAC, RG 24, vol. 11, 505, 335.4.1, vol. 1, "Commanding Officer H.M. M.A.S.T.U. No. 11 to FONF, September 1, 1942.

110 DND, DHH 81/520/1440-166/25 II (1), Seal to Admiralty, Report on Repair Facilities, 7 April 1943.

111 LOng-RAnge Navigation. The Loran system utilized radio signals to aid in navigation.

112 DND, DHH, NHS 8000, 1–6, "Harbour Training in St John's - Summary of General Development," 28 June 1945.

113 DND, DHH, NHS 8000, 1–6, "Harbour Training in St John's - Summary of General Development," 28 June 1945.

114 Minutes of a Meeting of Cabinet War Committee, 16 April 1943, in Bridle, *Documents on Relations*, 616–17.

115 LAC, RG 25, series 62, vol. 3198, file 5206-40, Malcolm MacDonald, High Commissioner for the United Kingdom, to A. Robertson, Under-Secretary for External Affairs, Ottawa, 12 April 1943.

116 LAC, RG 28, vol. 129, file C-3-21, Minutes of Combined Canadian, United Kingdom, and United States Committee to Examine Repair Problem for Warships and Merchant Vessels on the East Coast of Canada and Newfoundland, 12 August 1943, 3–7.

117 Tucker, *Naval Service of Canada*, 531.

118 Zimmerman, "The Social Background of the Wartime Navy," 275. RCNR officers were mostly older, recommissioned former RN and RCN officers. Most held senior administrative positions in Ottawa, Halifax, and overseas.

119 Evidence suggests that this reliance on public facilities and the lack thereof were root causes of the VE (Victory in Europe) Day riots at Halifax in 1945. See Caldwell, "The VE Day Riots in Halifax," 3–20. Indeed, some argue that the lack of established naval recreational facilities was at the heart of the RCN's morale problem, not outdated equipment. See O'Mayne, *Betrayed*, 82.

120 Unless otherwise noted, all information concerning facilities available to naval personnel comes from Miller, *St John's Naval Guide Book*.

121 "Police ask order against beer parlours," *Evening Telegram*, 30 January 1941.

122 "Two motor boats collide in harbour," *Evening Telegram*, 10 January 1941. Also see "Harbour Regulations," *Evening Telegram*, 27 June 1941.

123 Duley, *The Caribou Hut*, 28.

124 "Official opening of St John's 'Y' Hostel," *Evening Telegram*, 10 January 1942.

125 "Criminal cases show increase over 1940," *Evening Telegram*, 31 December 1941.

126 "Very busy year in Magistrate's Court," *Evening Telegram*, 31 December 1943.

127 "Chinese café gutted by naval ratings," *Evening Telegram*, 27 December 1941.

128 See Steven High, chapter 4, this volume.

129 PANL, GN 38, S4-2-4, file 3, Welty to Emerson, 4 October 1941; PANL, GN 38, S4-2-7, file 16, Emerson to Welty, 7 October 1941; "Are any exempt?" *Evening Telegram*, 5 December 1941.

130 Banister, *Equal to the Challenge*, xvi; "Wren establishment here second largest in the R.C.N.," *Evening Telegram*, 8 August 1944.

131 Banister, *Equal to the Challenge*, 177.

132 Ibid., 454.

133 Ibid., 458.

134 Ibid., xvii.

135 Tucker, *Naval Service of Canada*, 322.

Chapter Three

1 See, in particular, Tuttle, *"Daddy's Gone to War,"* x.

2 Meyers and Poutanen, "Cadets, Curfews, and Compulsory Schooling"; Keshen, *Saints, Sinners, Soldiers*, 194–227; Sethna, "Wait till your father gets home"; and Johnston, "The Children's War."

3 Christine Hamelin, "A Sense of Purpose"; and Lewis, "'Isn't this a terrible war?'"

4 I have borrowed the metaphor of the "winds of childhood" from Neil Sutherland, who in turn encountered it in Gabrielle Roy's *The Fragile Lights of Earth*. See Sutherland, *Growing Up*, 3–23. Although Sutherland does not devote a separate chapter to children's wartime experiences, his account is rich with childhood memories of the war.

5 Lunn, "This isn't really a story," 46.

6 As Neil Sutherland has suggested, "a series of unconnected but vivid vignettes suggests a childhood as yet not reflected upon or put in a final perspective and comes closer to the events of childhood, with all of their sensual and emotional freight." See Sutherland, *Growing Up*, 7.

7 Interview with Paul O'Neill, 13 September 2007.

8 These twenty-five interviews have been chosen from the project's total of fifty life-course interviews for their

vivid memories of growing up – or coming of age – in wartime St John's.

9 Lowenthal, *The Past Is a Foreign Country.*

10 Barman, "'Oh, No!,'" 54, 56.

11 Ibid., 203. Memorable wartime memoirs of children growing up in these seaports include Porter, *Below the Bridge;* Alan Wilson, "A Young Maritimer in the 1930s and '40s"; and Budge Wilson, "To live in Halifax, Nova Scotia." See also the oral history recollections in Montgomery, "'The war was a very vivid part of my life.'"

12 Interview with Joe Prim, 27 September 2007.

13 Interviews with Helen Porter, 28 August 2007; Margaret Kearney, 1 October 2007; and George Ledrew, 29 August 2007. The memory of the second submarine raid on Bell Island in November 1942 is one of the few personal notes historian Peter Neary shares in his *Newfoundland in the North Atlantic World, 1929–1949*, 163.

14 For recent explorations of the history of childhood in a Canadian context, see, for example, Parr, introduction to Janavocek and Parr, eds, *Histories of Canadian Childhood and Youth*; and McIntosh, "Constructing the Child."

15 Valentine, "Children should be seen and not heard," 210.

16 Interview with Ann Abraham, 11 August 2007.

17 Porter, *Below the Bridge,* 67–8.

18 Ibid., 5; and Collins, "'First Line of Defence,'" 24.

19 Quoted in Baldwin and Poulter, "Mona Wilson and the Canadian Red Cross," 284.

20 Interview with Stuart Fraser, 20 August 2007.

21 Interview with Ann Abraham, 11 August 2007.

22 Interview with Eileen Collins, 27 August 2007.

23 Interviews with Norman Crane, 7 September 2007; Patricia Winsor, 29 August 2007; Eileen Collins, 27 August 2007; and Paul O'Neill, 13 September 2007.

24 Porter, *Below the Bridge*, 39–40.

25 Interviews with Margaret Kearney, 1 October 2007; Ann Abraham, 11 August 2007; Eileen Collins, 27 August 2007; and Patricia Winsor, 29 August 2007. See also the religious divisions described by British war brides who arrived in Newfoundland in the mid-1940s as described in Casey and Hanrahan, "Roses and Thistles."

26 Interviews with Patricia Winsor, 29 August 2007; and Eileen Collins, 27 August 2007.

27 Interview with Tom Goodyear, 27 August 2007.

28 Interviews with Joe Prim, 27 September 2007; and David Edwards, 28 August 2007.

29 Nasaw, *Children of the City* (1985), 31.

30 MacKenzie, "A North Atlantic Outpost," 53.

31 Porter, *Below the Bridge,* 27–8.

32 Interviews with Margaret Kearney, 1 October 2007; David Baird, 12 September 2007; and Frankie O'Neil, 28 August 2007.

33 Porter, *Below the Bridge*, 60.

34 Interview with Paul O'Neill, 13 September 2007.

35 Interview with Joe Prim, 27 September 2007.

36 For a point of comparison, see Keshen, "The Children's War: 'Youth Run Wild,'" in his *Saints, Sinners, Soldiers*; and Tuttle, "Working Mothers and Latchkey Children," in his *"Daddy's Gone to War."*

37 Forestell, "Times Were Hard," 161 (quoted in Cullum and Baird, "A Woman's Lot," in Kealey, *Pursuing Equality,* 100).

38 Forestell, "Women's Paid Labour in St. John's," 64.

39 Canadian navy officer Don McClure, who was stationed in St John's between 1941 and 1945, was struck by the "class distinctions in St John's that we didn't have in Victoria ... The business people, they nearly all had outport girls working for them as servants. They'd live in-house and do the chores." See interview with Don McClure, 23 September 2007.

40 Interviews with Eileen Collins, 27 August 2007; Joe Prim, 27 September 2007; and James Walsh, 21 September 2007.

41 Interview with Norman Crane, 7 September 2007.

42 Wheaton, "'... as modern as some of the fine new department stores,'" 203–4.

43 Interview with Patricia Winsor, 29 August 2007.

44 Interview with R.J. Gallagher, 29 September 2007.

45 Interview with Gilbert Oakley, 22 September 2007.

46 Interview with Joe Prim, 27 September 2007.

47 Sutherland, *Growing Up*, 24, 47.

48 "My father rarely talked ... He never talked to me once ... He never talked much about anything."

49 Porter, *Below the Bridge*, 5. Interviews with Helen Porter, 28 August 2007; and Patricia Winsor, 29 August 2007.

50 Interviews with James Walsh, 21 September 2007; and Eileen Collins, 27 August 2007.

51 Interviews with Eileen Collins, 27 August 2007; and James Walsh, 21 September 2007.

52 Sutherland, *Growing Up*, 80.

53 Interview with Joe Prim, 27 September 2007.

54 Interviews with Norman Crane, 7 September 2007; and David Edwards, 28 August 2007.

55 Wilson, "To live in Halifax, Nova Scotia," 173–4. For the chasms of communication that separated men on the battlefield from friends and relatives at the home front, see Keshen, *Propaganda and Censorship.*

56 Interview with James Walsh, 21 September 2007.
57 In order to protect would-be volunteers from the taunts and ostracism that "slackers" faced, the government "began distributing rejection badges to those Newfoundlanders who had volunteered for active service." See Neary, *Newfoundland in the North Atlantic World*, 117. For the public censure meted out to "slackers," see the interview with Paul Neill, 13 September 2007; and Porter, *Below the Bridge*, 65–6.
58 Porter, *Below the Bridge*, 68.
59 Interviews with David Baird, 12 September 2007; and James Walsh, 21 September 2007.
60 Christopher Chapman, "In 1939, thousands of miles from the outbreak of war, the lives and fortunes of many Canadian families changes," and Patricia Galloway, "'My mother is not a lady,' I said with conviction," in Galloway, *Too Young to Fight*, 111, 12.
61 Interviews with Eileen Collins, 27 August 2007; Helen Porter, 28 August 2007; Margaret Kearney, 1 October 2007; and Paul O'Neill, 13 September 2007.
62 As James Walsh recalls, "Occasionally, there would be other people in the house because not everybody at the time had a radio. We were one of the few people in our area who had a radio." Interview with James Walsh, 21 September 2007.
63 Interview with Vicki Cheeseman, 30 August 2007.
64 Interview with Gilbert Oakley, 22 September 2007. In a similar vein, Stuart Fraser recalls that "as a kid, you had to be quiet at twelve o'clock every day because the news was on." Interview with Stuart Fraser, 20 August 2007.
65 Interview with Patricia Winsor, 29 August 2007.
66 Interviews with Paul O'Neill, 13 September 2007; and Stuart Fraser, 20 August 2007.
67 Interviews with George Ledrew, 29 August 2007; James Walsh, 21 September 2007; Paul O'Neill, 13 September 2007; and R.J. Gallagher, 29 September 2007.
68 Interviews with Margaret Kearney, 1 October 2007; and Ann Abraham, 11 August 2007.
69 Interview with Helen Blundon, 28 August 2007; and Porter, *Below the Bridge*, 65.
70 Interview with Vicki Cheeseman, 30 August 2007.
71 Interviews with Patricia Winsor, 29 August 2007; Ann Abraham, 11 August 2007; and Helen Porter, 28 August 2007. See also Porter, *Below the Bridge*, 65.
72 Porter, *Below the Bridge*, 68.
73 *Evening Telegram* (St John's), "U.S. troopship now in Newfoundland waters," 25 January 1941; and "St. John's extends warm welcome to American troops," 29 January 1941.
74 Interviews with Margaret Kearney, 1 October 2007; and Thomas Doyal, 21 August 2007.
75 Interviews with Helen Porter, 28 August 2007; George Ledrew, 29 August 2007; and Paul O'Neill, 13 September 2007.
76 Interview with Joe Prim, 27 September 2007.
77 Interviews with George Ledrew, 29 August 2007; and David Baird, 12 September 2007.
78 The piers fell victim to the national harbour reconstruction of the early 1960s. The reconstruction destroyed Helen Porter's South Side neighbourhood and culminated in the bulldozing of a local landmark, St Mary's Church, in the name of progress and development. See Porter, *Below the Bridge*, 124–5.
79 Interview with Eileen Collins, 27 August 2007.
80 Porter, *Below the Bridge*, 19.
81 Ibid., 4, 65, 1–2; and interview with Helen Porter, 28 August 2007.
82 Interviews with Eileen Collins, 27 August 2007; and Gilbert Oakley, 22 September 2007.
83 Interviews with R.J. Gallaghar, 29 September 2007; Helen Porter, 28 August 2007; Eileen Collins, 27 August 2007; and Stuart Fraser, 20 August 2007.
84 Interview with Margaret Kearney, 1 October 2007; Porter, *Below the Bridge*, 71.
85 Porter, *Below the Bridge*, 71; and interview with R.J. Gallagher, 29 September 2007.
86 Quoted in Baldwin and Poulter, "Mona Wilson and the Canadian Red Cross," 203.
87 Interviews with Stuart Fraser, 20 August 2007; and Joe Prim, 27 September 2007.
88 See, for example, the recollections of Margaret Kearney ("The Americans fitted into the social life of the city"), Joe Prim ("They fitted in well with the people"), and Thomas Doyal ("They fit in fine").
89 Interview with Paul O'Neill, 13 September 2007.
90 Porter, *Below the Bridge*, 71.
91 Interviews with Ann Abrahams, 11 August 2007 and Patricia Wilson, 29 August 2007.
92 Interview with Don McClure, 23 September 2007.
93 "NBC Flashes," *Evening Telegram*, 26 July 1941 and 2 August 1941.
94 Interview with David Baird, 12 September 2007.
95 Interviews with Ann Abraham, 11 August 2007; David Edwards, 28 August 2007; Vicki Cheeseman, 30 August 2007; Stuart Fraser, 20 August 2007; and Paul O'Neill, 13 September 2007. See also Paul O'Neill's recollection: "Every Sunday, we had sailors and soldiers at the table, Canadian soldiers and English." For friendships forged

between Newfoundland hosts and Canadian guests and boarders, see the interviews with Frankie O'Neil, 28 August 2007; and James Walsh, 21 September 2007.

96 *Evening Telegram*, 20 December 1941.

97 Interview with Patricia Winsor, 29 August 2007. It is no coincidence that the Christmas guests were mostly Canadian, as the American servicemen enjoyed many amenities, including excellent food, on the military base Fort Pepperrell.

98 Interviews with Ann Abraham, 11 August 2007; and Vicki Cheeseman, 30 August 2007.

99 Interview with Ann Abraham, 11 August 2007. See also David Edwards, 28 August 2007.

100 Interview with Margaret Kearney, 1 October 2007.

101 Tuttle, *"Daddy's Gone to War,"* 3.

102 *Evening Telegram*, 15 October 1942. See also the interviews with Helen Porter, 28 August 2007; Ann Abraham, 11 August 2007; David Edwards, 28 August 2007; and James Walsh, 21 September 2007.

103 As recalled in Frank J. Kennedy, *A Corner Boy Remembers*, 170.

104 Neary, *Newfoundland in the North Atlantic World*, 163; and interviews with Helen Porter, 28 August 2007; and Ann Abraham, 11 August 2007.

105 Interviews with James Walsh, 21 September 2007; Gilbert Oakley, 22 September 2007; Kathleen Williams, 28 August 2007; Helen Porter, 28 August 2007; Margaret Kearney, 1 October 2007; Ann Abraham, 11 August 2007; Eileen Collins, 27 August 2007; David Edwards, 28 August 2007; and Paul O'Neill, 13 September 2007.

106 See, for example, the interviews with Ann Abrahams, 11 August 2007; James Walsh, 21 September 2007; Joe Prim, 27 September 2007; Gilbert Oakley, 22 September 2007; Margaret Kearney, 1 October 2007; Stuart Fraser, 20 August 2007; and Eileen Collins, 27 August 2007. For the experiences of children elsewhere in North America, see the literature cited in notes 1 to 5 above.

107 Porter, *Below the Bridge*, 72.

108 Tuttle, *"Daddy's Gone to War,"* x.

109 In her study of children's play in turn-of-the-century Los Angeles, the historian Victoria B. Brown has similarly noted "boys' freedom to roam at will, to have contact with nature, to deal with foreigners, to get into trouble." By contrast, she observes that girls "retired" from the world of "physical play and adventurous outings" at the onset of adolescence. See Brown, "Golden Girls," 252.

110 Rotundo, "Boy Culture," 339.

111 Interviews with Ann Abrahams, 11 August 2007; and Patricia Winsor, 29 August 2007. Vicki Cheeseman, as well, who attended an amalgamated school in a company town in the interior, fondly remembers her school days: "I always loved school. There was lots of sports – winter skiing, snowshoeing, groups were together more ... We had a wonderful lab which was unheard of in these days. There was outdoor recreation." Interview with Vicki Cheeseman, 30 August 2007.

112 Interview with James Walsh, 21 September 2007.

113 For a point of comparison, see Rotundo, "Boy Culture," 339.

114 Interview with Joe Prim, 27 September 2007.

115 Interview with George Ledrew, 29 August 2007.

116 Interview with Ann Abraham, 11 August 2007.

117 Interview with James Walsh, 21 September 2007.

118 Interview with Ann Abraham, 11 August 2007.

119 Interviews with James Walsh, 21 September 2007; and Gilbert Oakley, 22 September 2007. In addition, two of our male interviewees joined the Church Lads Brigade. See interviews with David Edwards, 28 August 2007; and Gilbert Oakley, 22 September 2007.

120 Interview with Paul O'Neill, 13 September 2007.

121 Interviews with Stuart Fraser, 20 August 2007; and Patricia Winsor, 29 August 2007.

122 Interviews with David Edwards, 28 August 2007; and Gilbert Oakley, 22 September 2007.

123 Interview with Paul O'Neill, 13 September 2007.

124 Interview with Gilbert Oakley, 22 September 2007. On boys' fascination with fire, see also Rotundo, "Boy Culture," 341; and Brown, "'Golden Girls,'" 250.

125 Interviews with Paul O'Neill, 13 September 2007 and Stuart Fraser, 20 August 2007.

126 Interview with Helen Porter, 28 August 2007.

127 As the historian Ruth Roach Pierson has argued in an influential work, there existed considerable continuity between women's pre- and post-war roles in Canada. At war's end, Pierson holds, public opinion once again relegated women to the private sphere of home and hearth. In Newfoundland, where paid employment for married women remained the exception even during the war years, the boundary between the private and the public spheres was not subject to similar intense questioning. It remains to be seen whether or not the war years inspired subtle processes of change in gender roles in St John's, much as they did elsewhere across the continent. See Pierson, *"They're still women after all,"* 216. For studies that emphasize change over continuity

in women's wartime roles, see Strong-Boag, "Canada's Wage Earning Wives," 9; Sangster, *Earning Respect,* 229; and Davis and Lorenzkowski, "A Platform for Gender Tensions," 431–65.

128 Interview with Patricia Wilson, 29 August 2007.

129 Interviews with Ann Abraham, 11 August 2007; and Eileen Collins, 27 August 2007.

130 Interviews with Vicki Cheeseman, 30 August 2007; Stuart Fraser, 20 August 2007; and James Walsh, 21 September 2007.

131 Interviews with James Walsh, 21 September 2007; and Norman Crane, 7 September 2007.

132 Interview with David Edwards, 28 August 2007.

133 Interview with Joe Prim, 27 September 2007.

134 Interview with Margaret Kearney, 1 October 2007.

135 Interviews with Gilbert Oakley, 22 September 2007; and James Walsh, 21 September 2007. See Davis and Lorenzkowski, "A Platform for Gender Tensions," 435; and, for an earlier time period, Rudy, *The Freedom to Smoke.*

136 Interviews with David Baird, 12 September 2007; Paul O'Neill, 13 September 2007; and Thomas Doyal, 21 August 2007.

137 *Evening Telegram*, 16 July 1941.

138 "NBC Flashes," *Evening Telegram*, 11 July 1941.

139 Interview with Kathleen Williams, 28 August 2007.

140 Interviews with Margaret Kearney, 1 October 2007; Eileen Collins, 27 August 2007; and Vicki Cheeseman, 30 August 2007.

141 Kennedy, *A Corner Boy Remembers*, 161. As two of our women interviewees emphasized, although they frequently went to social dances, they never had an American or Canadian serviceman boyfriend. Here, a line was drawn – albeit implicitly – between socializing in public and the exchange of physical intimacies of any kind.

142 See, for example, interviews with Eileen Collins, 27 August 2007; Ann Abraham, 11 August 2007; and Paul O'Neill, 13 September 2007. As Thomas Doyal recalls, "We had maids in those days who came to town from the outports. To walk from where we lived to downtown St John's was a pretty awkward walk for a young girl, with a tent city of several thousand soldiers behind us. So we had to provide cash for taxis. My mother would drive them to town and give them extra money to come home by cab." Interview with Thomas Doyal, 21 August 2007.

143 Interview with Margaret Kearney, 1 October 2007.

144 Interview with Eileen Collins, 27 August 2007.

145 For making this connection, I am indebted to Brown, "Golden Girls," 249.

146 See, for example, the interview with Patricia Winsor, 29 August 2007.

147 This transformation is charmingly captured in Wik, *Henry Ford and Grass-Roots America.*

148 Interviews with Ann Abraham, 11 August 2007; David Edwards, 28 August 2007; and Don McClure, 23 September 2007; and "NBC Flashes," *Evening Telegram*, 26 July 1941 and 2 August 1941.

149 Interviews with Patricia Winsor, 29 August 2007; Ann Abraham, 11 August 2007; and Norman Crane, 7 September 2007.

150 Interviews with Patricia Winsor, 29 August 2007; and Joe Prim, 27 September 2007.

151 Interview with David Baird, 12 September 2007.

152 "NBC Flashes," *Evening Telegram*, 31 May 1941.

153 Ibid., 20 June 1941.

154 Ibid., 6 December 1941.

155 "Eleven-year-old child victim of fatal accident," *Evening Telegram,* 2 June 1941.

156 "One child instantly killed, brother critically injured," *Evening Telegram,* 7 July 1941. Gilbert Oakley also describes this tragic incident in his interview on 22 September 2007.

157 "Three persons killed and four others injured when struck down by motor car," *Evening Telegram,* 2 November 1942.

158 Valentine, "Children should be seen and not heard," 210.

159 "NBC Flashes," *Evening Telegraph*, 11 October 1941. These tentative beginnings were later formalized in "traffic control plans" for elementary schoolchildren, who were shepherded across busy thoroughfares by senior college girls acting as traffic guards. See "Traffic Control for Children," *Evening Telegraph*, 23 March 1944.

160 *Evening Telegraph*, 11 July 1941.

161 Ibid., 11 October 1941.

162 As Spike wrote in his column "NBC Flashes," "Pedestrians too, we think, should be a little more careful. Jaywalking always has been dangerous – always will be! And walking in the streets at any time – even though the sidewalks are wet – is bad business. Now that the snow is gone – is there any good reason why the sidewalks shouldn't be used. Seems to us that the streets are crowded enough – without cars and trucks having to dodge people on foot too!" *Evening Telegram,* 31 May 1941.

163 "Traffic Matters," *Evening Telegram,* 7 November 1941.
164 "Save the Children," *Evening Telegram,* 3 January 1942.
165 "Children's Playground Association," *Evening Telegram,* 28 May 1942.
166 Ibid.
167 Tuttle, *"Daddy's Gone to War,"* 94.
168 Interview with James Walsh, 21 September 2007.
169 Interview with Stuart Fraser, 20 August 2007.
170 Porter, *Below the Bridge,* 67.
171 Nasaw, *Children of the City,* 24.
172 Valentine, "Angels and Devils," 585–6.
173 Interview with Margaret Kearney, 1 October 2007.

Chapter Four

1 War Diary, General Staff, "W" Force, Newfoundland, 29 January 1941, vol. 13807, C-3, RG 24, LAC.
2 Cardoulis, *Friendly Invasion*. Other estimates range as high as 35,000. See Major, *As Near to Heaven by Sea,* 374. Unless otherwise indicated, quoted material in this chapter originates in the fifty oral history interviews conducted with wartime residents for this project. These interviews will be publicly accessible at the Centre for Newfoundland Studies Archives at Memorial University.
3 For the Canadian presence, see Ransom, "Canada's Newfyjohn Tenancy"; Kavanagh, "W Force"; and Paul Collins, "'First Line of Defense.'" The American invasion is examined in Neary, *Newfoundland in the North Atlantic World, 1929–1949*; MacLeod, *Peace of the Continent*; and a series of articles published by Steven High, "The Racial Politics of Criminal Jurisdiction in the Aftermath of the 'Destroyers-for-Bases' Deal, 1940–50" and "Working for Uncle Sam."
4 John Edward FitzGerald, "'The difficult little island,'" 23.
5 See ibid. For more on the academic debate over nationalist historiography, see Jerry Bannister, *Politics of Cultural Memory.*
6 Jerry Bannister credits the cultural revival beginning in the 1960s for the later resurgence of nationalist sentiment in Newfoundland. Integral to Newfoundland nationalism, he says, is the turn to an idyllic past. Bannister, "Making History."
7 Sociologist James Overton has presented a compelling case that the controversy surrounding union with Canada has led some nationalists to deny the existence of widespread poverty before the war. Anyone who has sifted through the reports filed by the Newfoundland Rangers stationed in coastal communities knows this to be untrue.
8 For a comparative study of the social and economic impact of the leased-bases deal on these territories, see High, *Base Colonies.*
9 Jean Murray, interviewed by Kenneth Hammond. See also Harding, "Glorious Tragedy."
10 For more on radio in wartime St John's, see Webb, "VOUS—Voice of the United States."
11 Neary, *Newfoundland in the North Atlantic,* 155.
12 One of the most confident assertions that the fire was the result of Nazi sabotage can be found in Major, *As Near to Heaven by Sea,* 378.
13 Ransom, "Canada's 'Newfyjohn' Tenancy," 57.
14 Cecil Hutchins, interviewed by Steven MacPherson, 27 August 2007.
15 Fleeced, "Pirates in the Narrows," letter to the editor, *Evening Telegram* (St John's), 20 January 1942; "Fleecing seamen," editorial, *Evening Telegram,* 20 January 1942.
16 Collins, "'First Line of Defence,'" 24.
17 Baldwin and Poulter, "Mona Wilson and the Canadian Red Cross," 287.
18 Mona Wilson quoted in ibid., 296.
19 Mona Wilson quoted in ibid., 301.
20 The blackout was helpfully defined for readers as a "constant condition of preparedness" but where "normal life and business goes on." Civil Defence, Information Memorandum No. 2, "Blackout," *Evening Telegram,* 14 January 1942.
21 Civil Defence, Information Memorandum No. 1, "General organization," *Evening Telegram,* 10 January 1942.
22 Civil Defence, Information Memorandum No. 3, "Blackout," *Evening Telegram,* 17 January 1943.
23 Civil Defence, Information Memorandum No. 8, "Fire bombs," *Evening Telegram,* 7 February 1942.
24 Civil Defence, Information Memorandum No. 4, "Blackout," *Evening Telegram,* 20 January 1942.
25 "Civil defence director's air survey of blackout," *Evening Telegram,* 27 January 1942, 3.
26 "Blackout effective from April 6th," *Evening Telegram,* 24 March 1942.
27 "Blackout for duration," *Evening Telegram,* 24 March 1942.
28 "Blackout rule," *Evening Telegram,* 1 April 1942.
29 "To paint or not," *Evening Telegram,* 14 April 1942.
30 Editorial, "Their care and comfort," *Evening Telegram,* 8 January 1942, 6.

31 William Pepperrell Abraham, interviewed by Kenneth Hammond.

32 The Wanderers Club, which maintained the Hospitality Registration Bureau at the Caribou Hut, coordinated these efforts.

33 The archival record supports the oral interviews in every respect. The U.S. consul general, for example, reported in July 1943 that Newfoundlanders were keenly aware when Canada deployed a French-language unit to the island. Canada's high commissioner in St John's likewise observed that the deployment of French Canadians to Newfoundland, estimated to be "at least the majority of the Canadian Armed Forces," had a negative effect on public opinion: "For while there is no marked feeling against French-speaking Canadians as such, Newfoundlanders have come to realize more than they had before that Canada is not an Anglo-Saxon country." More important, perhaps, was the sense that these were reluctant soldiers. High Commissioner for Canada to Secretary of State for External Affairs, 25 September 1944, file 2828-40, pt 5.1, vol. 8480, RG 25, LAC.

34 The oral history interviews do not reveal much beyond the occasional sighting. A. Doug Newbury, while still a teenager, met these men while playing basketball against ship teams and the Americans. He would sometimes hear comments about the black Americans from some of the other Yanks. Gilbert Oakley told us the story of a riot – "over girls, I guess" – when "a black man and a white man [were] fighting ... and then the white man struck the black man in his face, and then he said, 'Look, red blood.' He didn't know the difference." In the context of the interview, it appears that the white man Oakley referred to came from the city.

35 Compare this version with that of R.J. Gallagher, who was only a young boy when the ships were wrecked: "A lot of the sailors swam ashore and jumped right off the ship and of course, all the oil of the ship was in the water. They were all covered in oil. And the residents, the women and the men, went down there with ropes and over a big cliff, they hauled the Americans up on top of the cliff, and the women took them back to the houses and stripped them naked and washed all the oil off. And this guy, they were scrubbing him down and he kept yelling and yelling. And was a black man. He wrote a book about it and donated the money to the [town] council and they built a park and named it after him. And he comes here, every year, on the anniversary of the sinking of the two ships. And they were scrubbing him and scrubbing and it wasn't oil. It was a black man."

36 That the memory of the *Truxton* lives on is evidenced in the honorary doctorate awarded to Lanier Philips, the only African-American crew member to survive the sinking of the USS *Truxton*, by Memorial University in 2008. The biographical note on Philips distributed to the public for the occasion suggests that during his rescue he was "treated with dignity and full respect for the first time in his young life." It goes on to say that this experience motivated him to become active in the civil rights movement of the 1950s and 1960s.

37 "Notes on Argentia," n.d. (approximately May 1943, based on its placement in the file), file: "Argentia, Newfoundland, 1941–1948," box 33, Naval Historical Centre (NHC), Washington Navy Yard. See also file: "Jean Byers: A Study of the Negro in Military Service" (June 1947), box 783, RG 341, HQ, USAF; and Deputy Chief of Staff, Director of Personnel Procurement and Training, Executive Office Records of Racial Policies, 1944–50, National Archives and Records Administration (hereafter NARA).

38 Editorial, "No colour bar here," 10 June 1941.

39 Editorial, "Another hostel opened," *Evening Telegram,* 10 January 1942.

40 Helen Blundon, interviewed by Nancy Rebelo.

41 Neary, *Newfoundland in the North Atlantic World,* 121.

42 "Caribou Hut manager's report for first year," *Evening Telegram,* 20 January 1942, 7. See also Duley, *The Caribou Hut.* Duley calculates the hostel's wartime activities as follows: 1,518 movies, 459 dances, 205 Sunday night singsongs, etc.

43 The three other major hostels or clubs were opened in 1941 and 1942. The USO club was a "two-storey frame building with cedar clapboard siding. It is finished with wallboard and hardwood floors and trim. The building is spacious, well lighted, conveniently laid out, and is equipped with the most modern fixtures. The basement has four bowling alleys. On the ground flat there is a large club room and shower baths." "USO Centre nears completion," *Evening Telegram* (7 January 1942), 3; the Red Triangle Club was erected on Water Street by the Canadian YMCA. "Red Triangle Club officially opens today," *Evening Telegram,* 9 January 1942, 3.

44 James J. Halley, an influential lawyer, remembers using the base's tennis courts, while Dr Nigel Rusted remembers attending cocktail parties and dances on the base.

45 Editorial, "Occupation of St. John's," *Evening Telegram,* 3 February 1941.

46 "Time for Action," *Evening Telegram,* 19 June 1941, 6.

47 Public Notice, *Evening Telegram,* 19 June 1941, 5.

48 Editorial, "This intemperance," *Evening Telegram,* 9 April 1942.
49 Margaret Kearney, interviewed by Kenneth Hammond.
50 File: "Complaints Regarding Conduct of Canadians 11/02.42," GN 4/D1, Public Archives of Newfoundland and Labrador (hereafter PANL).
51 General Manager of Newfoundland Railway to W.W. Woods, 16 March 1942, enclosed "Report of Conductor in Charge of Express Train That Left St John's March 9, 1942 to Gander," file: "Complaints Regarding Conduct of Canadians 11/02.42," GN 4/D1, PANL.
52 General Page to W.W. Woods, 20 March 1942, file: "Complaints Regarding Conduct of Canadians 11/02.42," GN 4/D1, PANL.
53 C. McCormack, 9 November 1942, "Observations on Conduct of Passengers on Newfoundland Railway Government Express between St. John's and Port-aux-Basques on September 8 and 9 and Return Journey on September 11 and 12," file: "Complaints Regarding Conduct of Canadians 11/02.42," GN 4/D1, PANL.
54 Harry Shortall, Conductor, to W. Fitzpatrick, Superintendant, 14 March 1943, file: "Complaints Regarding Conduct of Canadians 11/02.42," GN 4/D1, PANL.
55 Chief of Police to Assistant Chief of Police, 19 November 1941, file: U.S. Army, box 401, GN 13/2/A, PANL.
56 Joseph Seaward, Sergeant to Chief of Police, 8 April 1941, file: U.S. Army, box 401, GN 13/2/A, PANL.
57 While these offences varied in kind, they include only single cases of manslaughter, rape, and attempted rape as well as four indecent assaults, three malicious woundings, and three cases of assaulting a police officer. "Classification of American Persons Committed to H.M. Penitentiary since January 1st, 1941 to Date," 5 October 1945, file: U.S. Effect of Agreement on Colonies, box 365, GN 13/1/B, PANL.
58 George D. Hopper, "Political Developments during the Month of December, 1943," box 61, RG 84: St John's Consulate General Records, 1936–49 (1944), NARA.
59 George D. Hopper, "Political Developments during the Month of December, 1942," box 48, RG 84, St John's Consulate General Records, 1936–49 (1942), NARA.
60 The city council complained that the city's fire regulations were being ignored by the Canadian construction companies, but the U.S. consul general doubted that the charge could be sustained, "as no one could claim that construction methods used by Canadian authorities could be less efficient than those employed locally, since the great majority of the buildings of St. John's are regarded as fire-traps." George D. Hopper, "Political Developments during the Month of December, 1942," box 48, RG 84, St John's Consulate General Records, 1936–49 (1942), NARA.
61 Ransom, "Canada's 'Newfyjohn' Tenancy," 57.
62 Historian Ruth Roach Pierson has shown that in 1940s Canada a similar moral panic resulted in the labelling of Canadian servicewomen as promiscuous. Pierson, *"They're still women after all,"* 15.
63 Editorial, "Undesirables," *Evening Telegram,* 25 March 1943.
64 Historian Ruth Haywood found that the number of illegitimate births climbed from 80 in 1939 to 233 in 1943. The Waterford Hall Home for Infants in St John's, which cared for illegitimate children ages three months to two years, was opened that year. Overall, 1943 saw 70 per cent more births than 1939. Haywood, "'Delinquent, Disorderly and Diseased Females," 67–9.
65 Editorial, "Venereal diseases," *Evening Telegram,* 11 February 1943.
66 For more, see High, "'From Outport to Outport Base.'"
67 E.L. Kehoe, Captain, Medical Corps, VD Control Officer, NBC to VD Control Officers at Newfoundland bases, 27 April 1944, file: "Venereal Disease," box 46, RG 338, NARA.
68 H.M. Mosdell, Secretary of Public Health, to Commissioner, 30 October 1940, file 3: VD, 1938-42, box S6-1-2, PANL.
69 Herbert T. Berwald to Commanding Officer, 1 October 1942, file: "Sanitary Reports," box 19, RG 338 NBC, NARA.
70 Captain Daniel Bergsma, Medical Corps, "Venereal Disease and Other Health Problems in Newfoundland," 1 December 1942, file: "Venereal Disease," box 19, RG 338: NBC, NARA.
71 The spread of venereal disease was an age-old problem for the armed services. British military records for the nineteenth century, for example, reveal that VD was responsible for one in three sick cases involving military personnel. Admissions in 1864 were a staggering 290.7 per 1,000, according to historian Judith Walkowitz. To limit the spread of infection, Great Britain passed three contagious disease acts that established eighteen "subjected districts" around key garrisons. In these special areas, plainclothes policemen were given broad powers to have women examined by an army or navy physician. If found to be effected, the woman would be detained

in a lock hospital until cured. Poor women bore the brunt of state power, and during their confinement they were subjected to "lessons in deference, respectability, and personal cleanliness." Walkowitz, *Prostitution and Victorian Society*, 1–2, 60.

72 Captain Daniel Bergsma, quoted in Neary, "Venereal Disease and Public Health Administration," 144.

73 Pierson, *"They're still women after all,"* 179.

74 Statistical Compilation of Venereal Disease Rates and Numbers of Cases, file: "Venereal Disease Reports," box 46, RG 338, NARA.

75 All officers would henceforth "exhaust every means" to prevent and control "this serious reflection on the intelligence, discipline and reputation of this command." To track the problem, NBC compiled its cases for individual units. Units found to have high rates of infection would be collectively punished: their leave would be curtailed or other privileges taken away. "For sometime this command has maintained the highest rate of venereal diseases of any area in Eastern Defense Command. This situation can and must be corrected." John B. Brooks, Major General, U.S. Army, Commanding Newfoundland Base Command, "Record of Venereal Diseases," 6 May 1944, file: "Venereal Disease Reports," box 46, RG 338, NARA.

76 Annual Report, 1944, Division of Venereal Disease Control, file 6: "VD," box S-6-5-2, RG 38, PANL.

77 Porter, *Below the Bridge*, 69–71.

78 Headquarters, Newfoundland Base Command, Memorandum No. 23, "Marriages," 4 March 1943, file: "Marriages," box 20, NBC, RG 338, NARA.

79 Newfoundland Base Command, HQ, "Marriages," 22 July 1943, file: "Marriages," box 20, NBC, RG 338, NARA.

80 Jerome S. Arnold, Major, Adjutant General (by Command of Brigadier General Brooks), "Policy of Newfoundland Base Command on Marriages of Enlisted Personnel Locally," 19 February 1943, file: "Marriages," box 20, NBC, RG 338, NARA.

81 Kahn's and Wassermann's tests were simple quantitative tests for syphilis. Kathryn E. Kennedy, "Tests for Syphilis," 713–14.

82 Various bulletins, file: "Marriages," box 20, NBC, RG 338, NARA.

83 G.D. Hopper, U.S. Consul General, "Marriage Policy of Newfoundland Base Command," 21 April 1944, file: "Genealogy and Race," box 25, RG 338, NARA.

84 Major General John B. Brooks to Major General Guy V. Henry, Senior U.S. Army Member, Permanent Joint Board of Defense, 15 April 1944, file: "Genealogy and Race," box 25, RG 338, NARA.

85 George D. Hopper, U.S. Consul General, "Marriage Policy of Newfoundland Base Command," 21 April 1944, file: "Genealogy and Race," box 25, RG 338, NARA.

86 The Registrar of Births, Marriages and Deaths maintained by the Department of Health and Welfare had been notified of thirty-eight Newfoundland women marrying Americans, forty marrying Canadian soldiers, and seven marrying Canadian naval ratings by 18 November 1941. Editorial, "Marriages to soldiers," *Evening Telegram*, 18 November 1941.

87 MacLeod and Penney, "Sailors Ashore."

88 Neary, *Newfoundland in the North Atlantic World*, 236.

89 William E. Cole, Jr, "Annual Economic and Financial Review, Newfoundland, 1942," 5 April 1943, file 1943, box 53, RG 84: "St John's Consulate General Records, 1936–1949," NARA.

90 A letter from Navy Secretary Knox to Lawrence Cramer is cited in "How the Caribbean Met Its Caribbean problems," no date, file A8-1 (d), "Caribbean Islands and the War," box 23, RG 43, Anglo-American Caribbean Commission, 1940–46, NARA.

91 Commissioner for Finance to Commissioner for Justice and Defence, 11 September 1945, file 19: "U.S. Effect of Agreement on Colonies," box 365, GN 13/1/B, PANL.

92 Mrs Jewell W. Swofford, Chair, U.S. Employees Compensation Commission, 9 July 1942, box 3797, 811.34544, RG 59, NARA.

93 Major, *As Near to Heaven by Sea*, 369.

94 Ibid.

95 William E. Cole, Jr, "Annual Economic and Financial Review, Newfoundland, 1942," 5 April 1943, file: 1943, box 53, RG 84, NARA.

96 Ling, "'Share of the Sacrifice." See also Benoit, "Urbanizing Women Military Fashion."

97 G.B. Hope, Captain, RCN, Naval Officer in Charge, St John's, to L.E. Emerson, 24 May 1943, box 390, GN 13/2/A, PANL.

98 Lieutenant Commander Balfour, Executive Officer of HMCS *Avalon*, felt "'that in the majority of instances the rating, on return to his home, found great changes in social conditions since the outbreak of war.'" Memorandum of Meeting Held to Discuss Newfoundland Ratings, 11 May 1943, box 390, GN 13/2/A, PANL.

99 Neary, *Newfoundland in the North Atlantic World*.

Chapter Five

1 *Daily News* (St John's), 30 January 1941.
2 Memorial University of Newfoundland Folklore and Language Archive (hereafter MUNFLA), F27111/79-007 (CD657).
3 Webb, "Repertoire and Reception."
4 Noel, *Politics in Newfoundland,* 263–4.
5 Neary, *Newfoundland in the North Atlantic World,* 213.
6 MacKenzie, "A North Atlantic Outpost," 52.
7 High, "Working for Uncle Sam."
8 There is a perceptive critique of the traditional/modern view of Newfoundland culture in Pocius, *A Place to Belong.*
9 Neary, *Newfoundland in the North Atlantic World,* 210.
10 Stewart, "The 'Revolution of 1940' in Newfoundland," 79–80.
11 Wheaton, "'... as modern as some of the fine new department stores."
12 I thank the folklorist and mass media scholar Philip Hiscock for pointing this out to me.
13 Jacques, "Listening to Jazz," 69.
14 I thank Alison Jacques for pointing out the implications of who leads on the dance floor.
15 *Daily News,* 10 August 1942.
16 For example, the Men's Service Club of Cochrane Street Church held a concert featuring Newfoundland, Canadian, and American musicians. *Daily News,* 27 February 1941.
17 *Daily News,* 9 October 1942.
18 Webb, "VOUS – Voice of the United States."
19 David Edwards interview.
20 "Wayfarer," *Daily News,* 28 October 1941.
21 National Archives and Records Administration (hereafter NARA), RG 338, Newfoundland Base Command, Decimal File, box 20, file 353.8, Henry W. Clark, Morale Report for Newfoundland Base Command, 3 June 1943.
22 Duley, *The Caribou Hut,* 17.
23 *Daily News,* 12 February 1941.
24 Ibid., 31 May 1941.
25 Helen Blundon interview.
26 A. Maude Brown interview.
27 Paul O'Neill interview.
28 Ann Abraham interview.
29 James Walsh interview.
30 Frank Kennedy interview.
31 NARA, RG 160, Records of HQ Army Service Forces, Office of Director of Personnel, Special Services Division, General Records 1941–44, box 44, "Information Telephoned to Major Newman by Mr Murray, Army Motion Picture Service, 31 July 1942."
32 Letter to wife, 12 July 1941, J.E. Gilpatrick Collection, Newfoundland Historical Society Collection.
33 Margaret Kearney interview.
34 For the interplay between church concerns about morality in movies and the mass market for entertainment in the city earlier in the century, see Moore, "Early Picture Shows."
35 David Edwards interview.
36 Frankie O'Neil interview.
37 R.J. Gallagher interview.
38 Helen Blundon interview.
39 *Daily News,* 27 October 1941.
40 Rosenberg, "The Gerald S. Doyle Songsters."
41 Gwyn, *Smallwood,* 53; and Smallwood, *The Book of Newfoundland.*
42 *Daily News,* 27 October 1941.
43 Guigné, *Folksongs and Folk Revival,* 99.
44 Ibid., 255n14.
45 Thomas Doyle interview.
46 *Daily News,* 27 February 1941.
47 Ibid., 19 April 1941.
48 Ibid., 13 May 1942.
49 Ibid., 19 May 1942.
50 Ibid., 4 June 1942.
51 Ibid., 25 July 1942.
52 Ibid., 27 January 1943.
53 Ibid., 27 July 1942, 3 August 1943
54 Ibid., 2 February 1942.
55 Ibid., 22 October 1942.
56 Ibid., 8 and 14 January 1943.
57 Smith, *God Bless America,* 70, 132.
58 Fussell, *Wartime,* 188.
59 *Daily News,* 7 February 1942.
60 Ibid., 13 October 1942.
61 Ibid., 13 and 16 October 1942. The gift was likely Arthur Scammell's *Songs of a Newfoundlander* (St Jérôme, QC: J.H.A. Labelle, 1940).
62 Hiscock, "Folk Programming versus Elite Information"; and Rosenberg "The Canadianization of Newfoundland Folk Songs."
63 R.J. Gallagher interview.
64 Fussell, *Wartime,* 90.
65 Barrelman Papers, 2.02.071, Letter from Miss Ruth Way, Grand Falls, 24 January 1943, Archives and Manuscript Division, Queen Elizabeth II Library, Memorial University of Newfoundland (hereafter QEII Library). Ruth Way reports listening to *Command*

Performance and being angered by Joan Blondell's performance.

66 *Daily News,* 29 January 1943.

67 Ibid., 27 April 1942, article reprinted from *Globe and Mail.*

68 Ibid., 12 May 1942.

69 Story, Kirwin, and Widdowson, *Dictionary of Newfoundland English,* 343.

70 Louise Lambiase interview.

71 Reynolds, *Rich Relations,* 76–7.

72 *Daily News,* 6 February 1941.

73 Ibid., 22 October 1942, 12 November 1942.

74 Ibid., 4 February 1943.

75 Ibid., 8 and 14 January 1943.

76 NARA, RG 338, Newfoundland Base Command, Decimal File, box 20, file 353.8, Henry W. Clark, Morale Report for Newfoundland Base Command, 3 June 1943; and *Daily News,* 27 February 1943.

77 *Daily News,* 3 March 1943.

78 Ibid., 7 October 1942.

79 NARA, RG 84, Foreign Service Posts, Consul General St John's, Newfoundland, box 57, file 000.77, Major Harford W.H. Powell, Special Service Officer, to Commanding General, Newfoundland Base Command, 1 October 1943.

80 NARA, RG 84, box 57, file 000.77, Powel to Commanding General, Newfoundland Base Command, 1 October 1943.

81 Webb, *Voice of Newfoundland,* 172–7, 198.

82 NARA, RG 84, box 57 file 000.77, Major Harford W.H. Powel, Special Service Officer, to Commanding General, Newfoundland Base Command, 1 October 1943.

83 NARA, RG 338, box 23, file "Radio Broadcasts," "VOUS The United States Army Station in Newfoundland," Newfoundland Base Command.

84 Tait, *Newfoundland: A Summary of the History and Development of Britain's Oldest Colony from 1497 to 1939* (Harrington, NJ: Harrington Press, 1939).

85 Archives and Manuscript Division, QEII Library, coll. 087, 4.14.002, "Shall we give Newfoundland back to the Beothuks."

86 High, *Base Colonies in the Western Hemisphere,* 14.

87 Archives and Manuscript Division, QEII Library, coll. 087, 4.14.002, "Shall we give Newfoundland back to the Beothuks."

88 Archives and Manuscript Division, QEII Library, coll. 087, 4.14.002, "Orientation: Friday, 28 July 1944."

89 For example, see Archives and Manuscript Division, QEII Library, coll. 087, 4.14.002, Orientation Program, 3 February 1944.

90 NARA, RG 338, Newfoundland Base Command, Decimal File 1945, box 47, file 676.3, Harford W.H. Powel to Colonel John R. Reitemeyer, 14 February 1945.

91 David Edwards interview.

92 Frank Kennedy interview.

93 Gilbert Oakley interview.

94 David Edwards interview.

95 Posen and Taft, "The Newfoundland Popular Music."

96 *Daily News,* 19 April 1943.

97 Ibid., 3 March 1943.

98 Ibid., 25 September 1943.

99 Michael Francis Harrington, *Newfoundland Tapestry* (Dallas: Kaleidograph Press, 1943).

100 *Daily News,* 9 August 1943, 23 October 1943.

101 Gard, "Pioneering Art," 20.

102 Louise Lambiase interview.

103 Helen Blundon interview.

104 See, for example, the newspaper columnist Albert Perlin's (the Wayfarer) condemnation of swing music in the *Daily News,* 29 November 1941.

105 "Another One," letter to editor, *Daily News,* 1 December 1941.

106 Reeves, "Aping the 'American Type.'"

107 Korneski, "Race, Gender, Class, and Colonial Nationalism."

108 Reynolds, *Rich Relations,* 38–40.

109 The base may have served as an example to Newfoundlanders in some cases. Commissioner H.A. Winter met with commanders at Fort Pepperrell to plan for the inspection tour of the base to be taken by 200 Newfoundland teachers, who would then be able to tell their students about the Americans and their base. *Daily News,* 21 July 1942.

Chapter Six

1 Chevrier, *Canada's Merchant Seamen,* 5.

2 Minutes of the Sub-Committee of the Canadian Red Cross Society, 16 August 1940, Canadian Red Cross Society Archives, Ottawa (hereafter CRCS Archives).

3 Interview with Mona Wilson's sisters, Margaret Keenleyside and Jane Hamilton, Toronto, 1986.

4 After returning to Prince Edward Island, Wilson typed a seventeen-page, single-spaced foolscap history of her years in Newfoundland, entitled "Five Years of War Service for the Canadian Red Cross in Newfoundland, 1940–1945," Acc. 3652, Public Archives and Records Office of Prince Edward Island (hereafter PAPEI). This

manuscript has been reprinted in Baldwin and Poulter, "Mona Wilson and the Canadian Red Cross."

5 FitzGerald, "'The difficult little island,'" 23. For more on this debate, see chapter 5 by Steven High, this volume.

6 Details about Wilson's life and career are drawn from Baldwin, *She Answered Every Call.*

7 This was true for both world wars. See Mann, *The War Diary of Clare Gass,* xxxiv; and Toman, *An Officer and a Lady,* 156.

8 This material is in the Prince Edward Island Public Archives and Record Office.

9 See Baldwin, "Interconnecting the Personal and Public."

10 Women's entry into the military raised public fears about their potential loss of femininity and sexual promiscuity. In the Canadian context, this is discussed in Pierson, *"They're still women after all"*; and Keshen, *Saints, Sinner, and Soldiers.* For Great Britain, see Rose, "Sex, Citizenship, and the Nation."

11 Interview with corps woman J. Kirby MacNeill Small, Ottawa, 11 June 1992; and follow-up correspondence, 8 August 1992.

12 Interview with Eleanor Wheler, 21 August 1987; and Eleanor Wheler, "Some Memories of Public Health Nursing in P.E.I." (January 1973), Acc. 3150, PAPEI.

13 The Canadian Red Cross National Women's War Work Committee shipped over two million items to Newfoundland. The most numerous items were woollen caps and mitts, socks, sweaters, and items for the ditty bags. A label on every article of clothing read "Gift of the Canadian Red Cross Society." Other supplies came from people who read accounts about and by Wilson in the *Canadian Red Cross Despatch* or in the local press, or heard one of Wilson's several radio broadcasts. Annual Report of the National Women's War Work Committee, 1944; and Porter, *To All Men,* 73–4.

14 The International Red Cross recognized the Newfoundland District of the St Johns Ambulance Brigade Overseas as the de facto British Red Cross Association of Newfoundland. Dr Cluny MacPherson was its representative in St John's.

15 Unless otherwise noted, the information on the WPA was derived from its quarterly meeting reports and its annual reports from 1939 to 1945, P8/B/13, Public Archives of Newfoundland (hereafter PANL).

16 The WPA transferred its clubrooms on Queen Street to the Caribou Hut in January 1941. Women's Patriotic Association of Newfoundland, Annual Report for 1940; and Nicholson, *More Fighting Newfoundlanders,* 539.

17 The wool was provided by the Canadian government, which released 20,000 pounds of raw wool from the Riverside Woollen Mills at cost. *Telegram* (St John's), 1 February 1940.

18 In 1941 the Salvation Army opened a recreation hut at Lester's Field. The United and Presbyterian churches operated the Terra Nova Club as a recreational centre. The Red Triangle, the YMCA hostel on Water Street West, officially opened in January 1942. The Knights of Columbus hostel on Harvey Road opened a month earlier.

19 Initially, the WPA clubhouse on Queen Street provided food and entertainment for the troops. St John's War Services Association, Minutes, 2 October and 4 November 1940, P8/B/15, PANL; Canadian Club, Minute Book, 4 September 1940, P8/B/1, PANL; 3 January 1941, War Diary, Force W, RG 24, vol. 13807, Library and Archives Canada (hereafter LAC).

20 Two years later, Wilson convinced the national association to contribute an additional $1,000.

21 The information on the YMCA was derived from documents at the St John's YMCA offices and from Hurst, *The Canadian Y.M.C.A. in World War II,* 138–42.

22 Wilson even served as a waitress for the Hut's first New Year's Eve gathering. St John's War Services Association Executive Minutes, 18 February 1941, P8/B/15, PANL.

23 *Evening Telegram* (St John's), 10 April 1941, 11. Ralph Smith took over in June 1942.

24 Duley, *The Caribou Hut,* 23.

25 By 1943, the Caribou Hut had thirty-seven permanent staff members. WPA Annual Reports; *Avalon News,* January 1944; *Evening Telegram,* 14 October 1941, 13.

26 For example, *Evening Telegram,* 14 November 1942, 6; and 15 June 1942, 2.

27 In the nineteenth century, sailors in port were viewed as potential victims of unscrupulous "crimpers" who supplied them with alcohol, enticed them with prostitutes, and took their hard-earned wages. Philanthropic reformers sought to establish seamen's homes where, as Darcy Ingram notes, the presence of respectable middle-class female volunteers "would provide a surrogate home where clients would be appropriately acculturated." The same notion was the basis for the Maple Leaf Clubs run in England by the Canadian Red Cross during both world wars. Darcy Ingram, "Saving the Union's Jack: The Montreal Sailors' Institute and the Homeless Sailor, 1862–98," *Negotiating Identities in 19th- and 20th-Century Montreal,* eds. Bettina Bradbury and

Tamara Myers (Vancouver: UBC Press, 2005: 49–76. See also, Judith Fingard, *Jack in Port: Sailortowns of Eastern Canada* (Toronto: UTP, 1982) and Roald Kverndal, *Seamen's Mission: Their Origin and Early Growth* (Pasadena: William Carey Library, 1986).

28 Quoted in *Evening Telegram*, 17 June 1943.

29 The Wanderers Club operated a Hospitality Registration Bureau in the Caribou Hut for citizens willing to entertain members of the Newfoundland armed forces and merchant marine. Many residents, especially at Christmas, responded to public appeals to open up their homes to Canadian sailors and the survivors of torpedoed ships. For more on Newfoundland citizens' response to Canadian servicemen, see chapter 3 by Barbara Lorenzkowski and chapter 4 by Steven High, this volume.

30 The hospitalized men called these women the "ladies in blue," after their blue Red Cross smocks.

31 McEachren, Clara F. "Canadian Red Cross in Newfoundland." *Canadian Red Cross Despatch*, September/October 1944.

32 In May 1943 Wilson had made a radio appeal for contributions on behalf of the Merchant Seaman's Club. Shortly after the club opened in June, a serious fire broke out and cascades of water from the firemen's hoses poured into the Red Cross office below.

33 Baldwin and Poulter, "Mona Wilson and the Canadian Red Cross," 300.

34 "Report of the Activities of the Canadian Red Cross Society in Newfoundland," August 1941, Acc. 3652, PAPEI.

35 "Report of the Activities of the Canadian Red Cross Society in Newfoundland," 1940–41, Acc. 3652, PAPEI. By 1942 the Red Cross had taken over this responsibility, with occasional help from the WPA.

36 Wilson's handwritten notes entitled "Nfl'd Story," written for her proposed biography, series 6, file 3, Acc. 3652, PAPEI.

37 Annual Reports of the Activities of the Canadian Red Cross Society in Newfoundland, Acc. 3652, PAPEI.

38 Wilson's Newfoundland Diary, file 81, acc 3652, PAPEI (hereafter Wilson Diary).

39 Wilson Diary.

40 Baldwin and Poulter, "Mona Wilson and the Canadian Red Cross," 16.

41 Wilson, "Nfl'd Story." The Salvation Army and the Sailors and Soldiers club provided similar services.

42 Wilson to Ruth Barton, 20 June 1943, Acc. 3652, PAPEI.

43 *Evening Telegram*, 15 December 1942. For more on this fire, see chapter 2 by Paul Collins, this volume.

44 Baldwin and Poulter, "Mona Wilson and the Canadian Red Cross," 22. For the Knights of Columbus fire, see Fitzgerald, *Newfoundland Disasters*; and *The Canadian Medical Association Journal*, 47, no. 3, March, 1943.

45 Canadian Red Cross, Sub-Committee Minutes of the Central Council, 21–22 January 1943, CRCS Archives.

46 Report of the National Commissioner, Dr F.W. Routley, to the Central Council on the activities of the Red Cross nationally, 1942. The Red Cross was instrumental in the dissemination of blood products and other medical advances. See Porter, *To All Men.*

47 "Report of the Canadian Red Cross Corps Newfoundland, August 1944," Acc. 3028, PAPEI; and correspondence with Jean K. Small (Nursing Auxiliary), 8 August 1992.

48 Mona to Ruth Barton, 14 August 1945, Acc. 3652, PAPEI.

49 Mona's notes for her speech to the P.E.I. Women's Institute Chapter, file 16, series 6, Acc. 3652, PAPEI.

50 Mona Wilson, "Nfl'd Story," notes on changes, file 20, Acc. 3652, PAPEI.

51 Mona's notes for her speech to the P.E.I. Women's Institute Chapter, file 16, series 6, Acc. 3652, PAPEI.

52 Mona Wilson, "Nfl'd Story," notes, file 20, Acc. 3652, PAPEI.

53 Since the boarding house was on the other end of the city from the Red Cross office and was expensive, Wilson returned to the Newfoundland Hotel. The chapters in this volume by Steven High (chapter 5) and C.A. Sharpe and A.J. Shawyer (chapter 1) discuss the "housing crisis" in St John's.

54 Wilson to Jane, 1 September 1940. Letter in author's possession (hereafter AP).

55 *Evening Telegram,* 25 February 1941, 12 June 1943.

56 The *Evening Telegram* reported in 1942 that approximately 4 to 5 per cent of the population had tuberculosis and that enteritis had killed more than fifty children in the previous two months as a result of uncovered garbage cans (30 January and 25 February 1942). Some scholars, including sociologist James Overton, deny the existence of widespread poverty in St John's before the war. See chapter 5 by Steven High, this volume, for more on this topic.

57 *Evening Telegram*, 25 February 1941

58 Sergeant Thomas Miller's opinion of Newfoundland, 27 October 1941, LAC, vol. 2793, file 7410-17.

59 *Telegram*, 27 November 1942.

60 Rough drafts of reports, file 6, series 3, Acc. 2652, PAPEI.

61 Wilson to her sister Jane in Toronto, 26 August 1941, AP.

62 Wilson to Amy Palmer, 21 July 1942, Acc. 3652, PAPEI. See chapter 5 by Steven High for a discussion on the limited impact of rationing.

63 Wilson to Ruth Barton, 20 June 1943, Acc. 3652, PAPEI.

64 Wilson to Jane, 24 August 1941, AP.

65 Ibid. Paul Collins, however, in chapter 2, this volume, notes that there was a wide variety of restaurants from which to choose, ranging from the Newfoundland Hotel to lunch counters on Water and Duckworth streets to tearooms on Henry Street and Rawlins Cross.

66 Baldwin and Poulter, "Mona Wilson and the Canadian Red Cross," 11. The city bus routes were extended to include all of Water Street in May 1940.

67 Wilson, "Nfl'd Story." A 30 May 1941 editorial in the *Evening Telegram* commented on the number of children hit by cars: "They dart into the street from the cover of parked cars; they rush from intersecting streets into the main thoroughfare ... it is only a matter of time before one is killed or seriously hurt." For more on city streets and the impact of military vehicles on them, see the chapters in this volume by A.J. Shawyer and C.A. Sharpe (chapter 1) and Barbara Lorenzkowski (chapter 3).

68 Wilson to Ruth Barton, 1 April 1943, Acc. 3652, PAPEI. For more on public drunkenness, see chapter 4 by Steven High, this volume.

69 For more on blackouts, see chapter 4 by Steven High.

70 Wilson, "Nfl'd Story."

71 Ibid.

72 Ibid.

73 Wilson's notes for her speech at the annual dinner of the P.E.I. nurses association in 1947 and her notes for a speech to the P.E.I. Women's Institute Chapter, file 16, series 6, Acc. 3652, PAPEI.

74 For instance, when one small window of the Red Cross office was smashed during the war, Wilson was exasperated that it took from June to October to get it replaced. Wilson to Amy Palmer, April 1941, Acc. 3652, PAPEI.

75 Rough drafts of reports, dated 25 November 1940, series 6, file 3, Acc. 3652, PAPEI.

76 Wilson wrote: "The lads wear me out snapping to attention and saluting. I draw the line at saluting in return and that sort of rot. But my face is always stiff at the end of a day after smiling sweetly all day at all and sundry!!" Wilson to Jane, 24 August 1941, AP.

77 Wilson, "Nfld Story." According to Barbara Lorenzkowski (chapter 3, this volume), many children considered the Canadian uniforms to be unflattering, so perhaps Wilson's interpretation of the children's actions was inaccurate.

78 Ibid.

79 Ibid.

80 Pierson, in *"They're still women after all,"* argues that this type of opportunity for women was merely temporary and that after the war gender roles were firmly reinstated. Keshen, in *Saints, Sinners,* takes a more optimistic view, seeing the wartime experience as providing a basis for the women's movement in the next generation. Wilson certainly saw her time in St John's as a highlight of her career. After the war she tried hard to secure a position with several overseas relief organizations, hoping for similar challenges and autonomy, but her age was against her and she rather reluctantly returned to her work on Prince Edward Island.

81 Nurses were often expected to attend dances at the Caribou Hut as part of their job, and their presence conferred an aura of respectability on the events. This was not unique to St John's; see Toman, *An Officer and a Lady,* 102–18. The long-standing effort to eliminate any hint of sexuality from nursing is traced in McPherson, "The Case of the Kissing Nurse." This type of control began to break down in the aftermath of the Second World War.

82 Sarah Glassford characterizes the work of the Canadian Red Cross in the First World War in a similar fashion in "'The Greatest Mother in the World': Carework and the Discourse of Mothering in the Canadian Red Cross Society during the First World War," *Journal of the Association for Research on Mothering* 10, no. 1 (2008): 219–32.

83 The first year, Wilson spent most evenings at the Caribou Hut, either working, teaching dance classes, watching a movie, or participating in singalongs. Wilson to (?) on P.E.I., 29 October 1940, Acc. 3652, PAPEI.

84 Wilson to Jane, 12 July 1941, AP.

85 Title of an article Mona Wilson wrote for *Canadian Red Cross Despatch*, March 1944, 3.

86 The National Women's War Work Committee had made a similar request in March 1941, to which the Canadian Red Cross executive had agreed but upon which it had not acted. Minutes of the Sub-Executive Committee of the Canadian Red Cross Society, 3 March 1941, CRCS Archives.

87 Lady Walwyn noted in November 1945, "It is unthinkable that such a grand organization, with such an outstanding war record, should disband," and sug-

gested that the WPA reconstitute itself as the National Newfoundland Red Cross Association. "6th Annual Meeting of the W.P.A. – Association may continue as Nfld. Red Cross Organization," *Daily News* (St John's), 21 November 1945.

88 Caroline Hutchinson to McKenzie Porter regarding his history of the Canadian Red Cross Society, 29 September 1958, CRCS Archives.

89 McEachren, "Canadian Red Cross in Newfoundland"; also see Canadian Red Cross, National Executive Minutes, 21 June 1944, CRCS Archives.

Chapter Seven

1 Coates and Morrison, "The American Rampant." This article provides an extensive review of the historiography of American "friendly invasions" to 1991.

2 Paul Fussell's *Wartime: Understanding and Behavior in the Second World War* (1989) is a helpful introduction to the social themes of the war.

3 B. Nalty, *Strength for the Fight: A History of Black Americans in the Military* (New York: Free Press, 1988).

4 One of the best works in the field is Reynolds, *Rich Relations.*

5 Moore, *Over-Sexed, Over-Paid, and Over Here.*

6 Moore, *The American Alliance*; and Potts and Potts, *Yanks Down Under, 1941–45.*

7 See Sarles, *A Story of America First.*

8 See Kimball, *Most Unsordid Act.*

9 In addition to the excellent articles in this collection, see High, *Base Colonies in the Western Hemisphere.*

10 See Wagnleitner, *Coca-Colonization and the Cold War.*

11 See Shukert and Scibetta, *The War Brides of World War II.*

12 There is a huge literature on American culture both at home and overseas during and after the war. Representative examples are M.K. Winchell, *Good Girls, Good Food, Good Fun: The Story of USO Hostesses during World War II* (Chapel Hill: University of North Carolina Press, 2008); Robert Heide and John Gilman, *Home Front America: Popular Culture of the World War II Era* (San Francisco: Chronicle Books, 1995); P.D. Bielder, *Good War's Greatest Hits: World War II and American Remembering* (Athens: University of Georgia, 1998); and N. Polmar and T.B. Allen, *World War II: America at War 1941–1945* (New York: Random House, 1995).

Bibliography

Badgley, Kerry. "'Rigorously Applied in Practice': A Scorched Earth Policy for Canada and Newfoundland during the Second World War." *Archivist,* no. 116 (1998): 38–43.

Baker, Melvin, and Robert D.W. Pitt, eds. *Dictionary of Newfoundland and Labrador Biography.* St John's: Harry Cuff Publications, 1999.

Baldwin, Douglas. "Interconnecting the Personal and Public: The Support Networks of Public Health Nurse Mona Wilson." *Canadian Journal of Nursing Research* 27, no. 3 (Fall 1995): 19–38.

– *She Answered Every Call: The Life of Public Health Nurse, Mona Gordon Wilson, 1894–1981.* Charlottetown: Indigo Press, 1997.

Baldwin, Douglas, and Gillian Poulter. "Mona Wilson and the Canadian Red Cross in Newfoundland, 1940–1945." *Newfoundland and Labrador Studies* 20, no. 2 (2005): 281–311.

Banister, Lisa, ed. *Equal to the Challenge.* Ottawa: Queen's Printer, 2001.

Bannister, Jerry. "Making History: Cultural Memory in Twentieth-Century Newfoundland." *Newfoundland Studies* 18, no. 2 (2002): 175–94.

– *The Politics of Cultural Memory: Themes in the History of Newfoundland and Labrador, 1972–2003.* St John's: Royal Commission on Renewing and Strengthening Our Place in Canada, 2003.

Barman, Jean. "'Oh, no! It would not be proper to discuss that with you': Reflections on Gender and the Experience of Childhood." *Curriculum Inquiry* 24, no. 1 (1994): 53–67.

Bashow, David L. *All the Fine Young Eagles: In the Cockpit with Canada's Second World War Fighter Pilots.* Toronto: Stoddart, 1996.

Benoit, Cecilia. "Urbanizing Women Military Fashion: The Case of Newfoundland Women." In *Their Lives and Times, Women in Newfoundland and Labrador: A Collage,* edited by Barbara Neis, Carmelita McGrath, and Marilyn Porter, 113–27. St John's: Killick Press, 1995.

Bercuson, David. *Maple Leaf against the Axis: Canada's Second World War.* Toronto: Stoddart, 1995.

Bercuson, David, and Holger H. Herwig. *Deadly Seas: The Story of the St Croix, the U305 and the Battle of the Atlantic.* Toronto: Random House, 1997.

Bridle, Paul, ed. *Documents on Relations between Canada and Newfoundland.* Vol. 1. Ottawa: Queen's Printer, 1974.

Brown, Victoria B. "Golden Girls: Female Socialization among the Middle Class of Los Angeles, 1880–1910." In *Small Worlds: Children and Adolescents in America, 1850–1950,* edited by Elliott West and Paula Petrik, 232–54. Lawrence, KS: University Press of Kansas, 1992.

Browne, Gary. *To Serve and Protect: The Newfoundland Constabulary on the Home Front, World War Two.* St John's: DRC Publishing, 2008.

Cadigan, Sean. *Newfoundland and Labrador: A History.* Toronto: University of Toronto Press, 2009.

Caldwell, R H. "The VE Day Riots in Halifax, 7–8 May 1945." *Northern Mariner* 10, no. 1 (2000): 3–20.

Candow, James E. *A Structural and Narrative History of Signal Hill National Park and Area to 1945.* Ottawa: Parks Canada, 1979.

– "The Tactical Role of American Armed Forces at Signal Hill, Newfoundland, during World War II." *Newfoundland Quarterly* 88 (1993): 25–9.

Cardoulis, John. *A Friendly Invasion: The American Military in Newfoundland, 1940–1990.* St John's: Breakwater Books, 1990.

Casey, G.J., and Maura C. Hanrahan. "Roses and Thistles: Second World War Brides in Newfoundland." *Newfoundland Studies* 10, no. 2 (1994): 240–9.

Chevrier, Lionel. *Canada's Merchant Seamen.* Ottawa: King's Printer, 1945.

Churchill, Winston Spencer. *The Second World War: Their Finest Hour.* Boston: Houghton Mifflin, 1949.

Coates, Kenneth, and William R. Morrison. *The Alaska Highway in World War II: The US Army of Occupation in Canada's Northwest.* Toronto: University of Toronto Press, 1992.

– "The American Rampant: Reflections on the Impact of the U.S. Armed Forces Overseas during World War II." *Journal of World History* 2, no. 2 (Fall 1991).

– *Working the North: Labor and the Northwest Defense Projects, 1942–46.* Anchorage: University of Alaska, 1994.

Collins, Paul. "'Canada's Plan to Torch St John's': Upper Canadian Arrogance or Tabloid Journalism." *Newfoundland Studies* 24, no. 2 (Fall 2009).

– "'First Line of Defence': The Establishment and Development of St. John's, Newfoundland as the Royal Canadian Navy's Premier Escort Base in the Second World War." *Northern Mariner/Le Marin du nord* 16, no. 3 (2006): 15–32.

– "War At Sea: Newfoundland's Role." Newfoundland and Labrador Heritage Website. http://www.heritage.nf.ca/law/war_at_sea.html (accessed February 2009).

Commission of Enquiry on Housing and Town Planning in St John's (1943), *Third Interim Report.*

Commission of Government of Newfoundland. *Acts of the Honourable Commission of Government of Newfoundland 1939–1945.* St John's: King's Printer.

Conn, Stetson, Rose C. Engelman, and Byron Fairchild. *Guarding the United States and Its Outposts.* Washington, DC: Center of Military History, 1964.

Cullum, Linda, and Maeve Baird, with Cynthia Penny. "A Woman's Lot: Women and Law in Newfoundland from Early Settlement to the Twentieth Century." In *Pursuing Equality: Historical Perspectives on Women in Newfoundland and Labrador,* edited by Linda Kealey, 66–162. St John's: Institute of Social and Economic Research, 1993.

Curry, Frank. *War at Sea: A Canadian Seaman on the North Atlantic.* Toronto: Lugus Publications, 1990.

Davis, Donald F., and Barbara Lorenzkowski, "A Platform for Gender Tensions: Women Working and Riding on Canadian Urban Public Transit in the 1940s." *Canadian Historical Review* 79, no. 3 (1998): 431–65.

Douglas, W.A.B. *The Creation of a National Air Force: The Official History of the Royal Canadian Air Force.* Vol. 2. Toronto: University of Toronto Press, 1986.

Douglas, W.A.B., Roger Sarty, and Michael Whitby, et al. *No Higher Purpose: The Official Operational History of the Royal Canadian Navy in the Second World War, 1939–1943.* Vol. 2, pt 1. St Catharines, ON: Vanwell Publishing, 2002.

– "No Higher Purpose: The Official Operational History of the Royal Canadian Navy in the Second World War, 1939–1943." *Canadian Historical Review* 85, no. 3 (2004).

Duley, Margaret. *The Caribou Hut: The Story of a Newfoundland Hostel.* Toronto: Ryerson Press, 1949.

Dziuban, Stanley. *Military Relations between the United States and Canada, 1939–1945.* Washington: Office of the Chief of Military History, Department of the Army, 1959.

Easton, Alan. *50 North: An Atlantic Battleground.* Toronto: Ryerson Press, 1963.

Fingard, Judith. *Jack in Port: Sailortowns of Eastern Canada.* Toronto: University of Toronto Press, 1982.

Fisher, Robert C. "'We'll get our own': Canada and the Oil Shipping Crisis of 1942." *Northern Mariner/Le Marin du nord* 3, no. 2 (1993): 33–9.

Fitzgerald, Jack. *Newfoundland Disasters.* St John's: Creative Book Publishing, 1984.

FitzGerald, John Edward "'The difficult little island' that 'must be taken in': Canadian Interests in Newfoundland during World War Two." *Newfoundland Quarterly* 35 (Spring 2001): 21–8.

Forestell, Nancy F. "Times Were Hard: The Pattern of Women's Paid Labour in St. John's between the Two World Wars." *Labour/Le Travail* 24 (Fall 1994).
– "Women's Paid Labour in St. John's between the Two World Wars." MA thesis, Memorial University of Newfoundland, 1987.
Fraser, A.M. "Newfoundland's Contribution to Canada." *International Affairs* 4, no. 5 (1949): 250–60.
Fussell, Paul. *Wartime: Understanding and Behavior in the Second World War.* New York: Oxford University Press, 1989.
Galloway, Priscilla. *Too Young to Fight: Memories from Our Youth during World War II.* Toronto: Stoddart, 1999.
Gard, Peter. *Hiking the East Coast Trail: Book #1, Fort Amherst to Petty Harbour–Maddox Cove.* St John's: East Coast Trail Association, 2001.
– "Pioneering Art." In *Sheppard: A Life Composed,* edited by Ronald Rompkey, Reginald Sheppard, and Helen Parsons, 17–84. St John's: Breakwater Books, 2005.
German, Tony. *The Sea Is at Our Gates: A History of the Canadian Navy.* Canada: McClelland & Stewart, 1990.
Glassford, Sarah. "'The Greatest Mother in the World': Carework and the Discourse of Mothering in the Canadian Red Cross Society during the First World War," *Journal of the Association for Research on Mothering* 10, no. 1 (2008): 219–32.
Goodheart, Philip. *Fifty Ships That Saved the World: The Foundation of the Anglo-American Alliance.* New York: Doubleday, 1965.
Government of Newfoundland. *Ledger of the Commission of Enquiry on Housing and Town Planning in St John's* (1942–43).
Graves, Donald. *In Peril on the Sea: The Royal Canadian Navy and the Battle of the Atlantic.* Toronto: Robin Brass Studio for the Canadian Naval Memorial Trust, 2003.
Guigné, Anna Kearney. *Folksongs and Folk Revival: The Cultural Politics of Songs of the Newfoundland Outports.* St John's: Institute for Social and Economic Policy, Books, 2008.
Gwyn, Richard. *Smallwood: The Unlikely Revolutionary.* Toronto: McClelland & Stewart, 1968.
Hadley, Michael. "The Popular Image of the Canadian Navy." In *A Nation's Navy: In Quest of Canadian Naval Identity,* edited by Michael Hadley, Rob Huebert, and Fred Crickard, 35–56. Montreal and Kingston: McGill-Queen's University Press, 1996.
– *U-Boats against Canada: German Submarines in Canadian Waters.* Montreal and Kingston: McGill-Queen's University Press, 1985.
Hamelin, Christine. "A Sense of Purpose: Ottawa Students and the Second World War." *Canadian Military History* 6, no. 1 (1997): 34–41.
Harding, Robert J. "Glorious Tragedy: Newfoundland's Cultural Memory of the Attack at Beaumont Hamel, 1916–1925." *Newfoundland and Labrador Studies* 21, no. 1 (2006).
Harrington, Michael Francis. *Newfoundland Tapestry.* Dallas: Kaleidograph Press, 1943.
Haywood, Ruth. "'Delinquent, Disorderly and Diseased Females: Regulating Sexuality in Second World War St. John's, Newfoundland." MA thesis, Memorial University of Newfoundland, 2002.
High, Steven. *Base Colonies in the Western Hemisphere, 1940–1967.* Toronto: Palgrave-Macmillan, 2009.
– "From Outport to Outport Base: The American Occupation of Stephenville, 1940–1945." *Newfoundland Studies* 18, no. 1 (2002): 84–113.
– "The Racial Politics of Criminal Jurisdiction in the Aftermath of the 'Destroyers-for-Bases' Deal, 1940–50." *Journal of Imperial and Commonwealth History* 32, no. 3 (September 2004): 77–105.
– "Working for Uncle Sam: The 'Comings' and 'Goings' of Newfoundland Base Labour, 1940–1945." *Acadiensis* 32, no. 2 (2003): 84–107.
Hiller, James K. *Confederation: Deciding Newfoundland's Future, 1934 to 1949.* St John's: Newfoundland Historical Society, 1998.
– "Newfoundland Confronts Canada, 1867–1949." In *The Atlantic Provinces in Confederation,* edited by E.R. Forbes and D.A. Muise, 349–81. Toronto: University of Toronto Press, 1993.
Hiscock, Phillip. "Folk Programming versus Elite Information: The Doyle Bulletin and the Public Despatch." *Culture and Tradition* 12 (1988): 41–59.
Hurst, Alan M. *The Canadian Y.M.C.A. in World War II.* N.p.: National War Services Committee of the National Council of Young Men's Christian Associations of Canada, n.d.
Ingram, Darcy. "Saving the Union's Jack: The Montreal Sailors' Institute and the Homeless Sailor, 1862–98." In *Negotiating Identities in 19th- and 20th-Century Montreal,* edited by Bettina Bradbury and Tamara Myers, 49–76. Vancouver: University of British Columbia Press, 2005.

Jackson, F.L. "The Rise and Fall of the Newfoundland State." In F.L. Jackson, *Surviving Confederation.* St John's: Harry Cuff Publications, 1968.

Jacques, Geoffrey "Listening to Jazz." In *New Approaches to the Twentieth Century: American Popular Music,* edited by Rachel Rubin and Jeffrey Melnick, 65–92. Amherst: University of Massachusetts Press, 2001.

Jamieson, Don. *No Place for Fools: The Political Memoirs of Don Jamieson.* St John's: Breakwater Books, 1989.

Johnson, Mac. *Corvettes Canada.* Toronto: McGraw-Hill Ryerson, 1994.

Johnston, M. "The Children's War: The Mobilization of Ontario Youth during the Second World War." In *Patterns of the Past: Interpreting Ontario's History,* edited by Roger Hall, William Westfall, and Laurel Sefton MacDowell, 356–80. Toronto: Dundurn Press, 1988.

Joseph, Gilbert M. "Close Encounters." In *Encounters of Empire: Writing the Cultural History of US–Latin American Relations,* edited by Gilbert M. Joseph, Catherine C. LeGrand, and Ricardo D. Salvatore. Durham, NC: Duke University Press, 1998.

Kavanagh, Robert. "W Force: The Canadian Army and the Defence of Newfoundland in the Second World War." MA thesis, Memorial University of Newfoundland, 1995.

Kennedy, Frank J. *A Corner Boy Remembers: Growing Up in St. John's.* St John's: Breakwater Books, 2006.

Kennedy, Kathryn E. "Tests for Syphilis: The Kahn Test." *American Journal of Nursing* 30, no. 6 (1930): 713–14.

Keshen, Jeffrey. *Propaganda and Censorship during Canada's Great War.* Edmonton: University of Alberta Press, 1996.

– "Revisiting Canada's Civilian Women during World War II." *Histoire sociale/Social History,* November 1997, 239–66.

– *Saints, Sinners, Soldiers: Canada's Second World War.* Vancouver: University of British Columbia Press, 2004.

Kimball, Warren F. *Most Unsordid Act: Lend-Lease, 1939–1941.* Baltimore: Johns Hopkins, 1969.

Kimber, Stephen. *Sailors, Slackers, and Blind Pigs: Halifax at War.* Halifax: Anchor Canada, 2003.

Kirwin, William J. "Miscellany." *Regional Language Studies* 20 (2007): 33–4.

Korneski, Kurt. "Race, Gender, Class, and Colonial Nationalism: Railway Development in Newfoundland, 1881–1898." *Labour/Le Travail* 62 (2008): 79–108.

Kostenuk, Samuel, and John Griffin. *RCAF: Squadron Histories and Aircraft, 1924–1968.* Toronto: Samuel Stevens, 1977.

Kverndal, Roald. *Seamen's Mission: Their Origin and Early Growth.* Pasadena, CA: William Carey Library, 1986.

Lamb, James B. *The Corvette Navy: True Stories from Canada's Atlantic War.* Toronto: Macmillan, 1977.

Lawrence, Hal. *Victory at Sea: Tales of His Majesty's Coastal Forces.* Toronto: McClelland & Stewart, 1989.

Lewis, Jane, and Mark Shrimpton. "Policymaking in Newfoundland during the 1940s: The Case of the St. John's Housing Corporation." *Canadian Historical Review* 75, no. 2 (1984).

Lewis, Norah. "'Isn't this a terrible war?' The Attitudes of Children to Two World Wars." *Historical Studies in Education/Revue d'histoire de l'éducation* 7, no. 2 (1995): 193–215.

Ling, Katherine Anne. "'Share of the Sacrifice': Newfoundland Servicewives in the Second World War." PhD thesis, Memorial University of Newfoundland, 2001.

Lowenthal, David. *The Past Is a Foreign Country.* New York: Cambridge University Press, 1985.

Lower, A.R.M. "Transition to Atlantic Bastion." In *Newfoundland: Economic, Diplomatic, Strategic Studies,* edited by R.A. MacKay, 484–508. Toronto: Oxford University Press, 1946.

Lunn, Janet. "This isn't really a story. It's a collection of memories about a few years in my life." In *Too Young to Fight: Memories from Our Youth during World War II,* edited by Priscilla Galloway. Toronto: Stoddart, 1999.

McEachren, Clara F. "Canadian Red Cross in Newfoundland." *Red Cross Despatch,* September/October 1944.

McIntosh, Robert. "Constructing the Child: New Approaches to the History of Childhood in Canada," *Acadiensis* 28, no. 2 (Spring 1999): 126–40.

Macintyre, Donald. *U-Boat Killer: Fighting the U-boats in the Battle of the Atlantic.* London: Weidenfeld and Nicolson, 1956.

MacKay, R.A. "Newfoundland in North Atlantic Strategy in the Second World War." In *Documents on Relations between Canada and Newfoundland.* Vol. 1: *1935–1949,* edited by Paul Bridle, xix–lxiii. Ottawa: Queen's Printer, 1974.

– *Newfoundland in North Atlantic Strategy in the Second World War.* Ottawa: Information Canada, 1974.

–, ed. *Newfoundland: Economic, Diplomatic, and Strategic Studies.* Toronto: Oxford University Press, 1946.

MacKenzie, David. *Inside the Atlantic Triangle: Canada and the Entrance of Newfoundland into Confederation, 1939–1949.* Toronto: University of Toronto Press, 1986.

– "A North Atlantic Outpost: The American Military in Newfoundland, 1941–1945." *War and Society* 22, no. 2 (2004): 51–74.
MacLeod, Malcolm. *Peace of the Continent: The Impact of Second World War American Bases in Newfoundland.* St John's: Harry Cuff Publishers, 1986.
MacLeod, Malcolm, and Brad Penney. "Sailors Ashore: RCN Interactions with Civilian Society at St. John's, 1941–1945." Paper presented to the Newfoundland Historical Society's 2002 Colloquium on Newfoundland and World War Two.
Macpherson, A.G., ed. *Four Centuries and the City: Perspectives on the Historical Geography of St. John's.* St John's: Memorial University of Newfoundland, 2005.
McPherson, Kathryn. "The Case of the Kissing Nurse: Femininity, Sexuality, and Canadian Nursing, 1900–1970." In *Gendered Pasts: Historical Essays in Femininity and Masculinity in Canada*, edited by Kathryn McPherson, Cecilia Morgan, and Nancy M. Forestell, 3–22. Don Mills, ON: Oxford University Press, 1999.
Major, Kevin. *As Near to Heaven by Sea: A History of Newfoundland and Labrador.* Toronto: Viking, 2001.
Mann, Susan, ed. *The War Diary of Clare Gass, 1915–1918.* Montreal and Kingston: McGill-Queen's University Press, 2000.
Mellin, Robert. "Modernism in Newfoundland." *Canadian Architect* 45 (2000): 18–21.
Meyers, Tamara, and Mary Anne Poutanen. "Cadets, Curfews, and Compulsory Schooling: Mobilizing Anglophone Children in WW II Montreal." *Histoire sociale/Social History* 38, no. 76 (2005): 367–98.
Miller, D.C., ed. *St. John's Naval Guide Book.* St John's: Blackmore, 1943.
Milner, Marc. *Battle of the Atlantic.* St Catharines, ON: Vanwell Publishing, 2003.
– *Canada's Navy: The First Century.* Toronto: University of Toronto Press, 1999.
– *North Atlantic Run: The Royal Canadian Navy and the Battle for the Convoys.* Toronto: University of Toronto Press, 1985.
– "Royal Canadian Navy Participation in the Battle of the Atlantic Crisis of 1943." In *The Good Fight,* edited by J.L. Granatstein and Peter Neary, 158–74. Toronto: Copp Clarke, 1995.
– "Squaring Some of the Corners." In *To Die Gallantly,* edited by Timothy J. Runyan and Jan M. Copes, 121–36. Boulder, CO: Westview Press, 1994.
Montgomery, Emilie L. "'The war was a very vivid part of my life': British Columbia School Children and the Second World War." MA thesis, University of British Columbia, 1991.
Moore, J.H. *The American Alliance: Australia, New Zealand and the United States, 1940–1970.* Melbourne: Cassell Australia, 1970.
– *Over-Sexed, Over-Paid, and Over Here.* St Lucia: University of Queensland Press, 1981.
Moore, Paul S. "Early Picture Shows at the Fulcrum of Modern and Parochial St John's, Newfoundland." *Newfoundland and Labrador Studies* 22, no. 2 (2007): 447–71.
Murray, Hilda Chaulk. *Cows Don't Know It's Sunday: Agricultural Life in St John's.* St John's: Institute for Social and Economic Policy, 2002.
Naftel, William. *Halifax at War: Searchlights, Squadrons and Submarines, 1939–1945.* Halifax: Formac, 2008.
Nasaw, David. *Children of the City: At Work and at Play.* Garden City, NY: Anchor Press/Doubleday, 1985.
Neary, Peter. "Canada and the Newfoundland Labour Market, 1939–49." *Canadian Historical Review* 62 (1981): 470–95.
– "A Mortgaged Property: The Impact of the United States on Newfoundland, 1940–49." In *Twentieth Century Newfoundland: Explorations,* edited by J.K. Hiller and Peter Neary, 179–93. St John's: Breakwater Books, 1994.
– "Newfoundland and the Anglo-American Leased Bases Agreement of 27 March 1941." *Canadian Historical Review* 67, no. 4 (1986).
– *Newfoundland in the North Atlantic World, 1929–1949.* Montreal and Kingston: McGill-Queen's University Press, 1988.
– "Venereal Disease and Public Health Administration in Newfoundland in the 1930s and 1940s." *Canadian Bulletin of Medical History* 15 (1988).
– *White Tie and Decorations: Sir John and Lady Hope Simpson in Newfoundland, 1934–36.* Toronto: University of Toronto Press, 1996.
Neary, Peter, and Patrick O'Flaherty. *Part of the Main: An Illustrated History of Newfoundland and Labrador.* St John's: Breakwater Books, 1983.
Neary, Steve. *The Enemy on Our Doorstep: The German Attacks at Bell Island, Newfoundland, 1942.* St John's: Jesperson Press, 1994.
Nicholson, G.W.L. *More Fighting Newfoundlanders: A History of Newfoundland's Fighting Forces in the Second World War.* St John's: Government of Newfoundland, 1969.

Noel, S.J.R. *Politics in Newfoundland.* Toronto: University of Toronto Press, 1971.
O'Mayne, Richard. *Betrayed: Scandal, Politics and Canadian Naval Leadership.* Vancouver: University of British Columbia Press, 2006.
O'Neill, Paul. *The Oldest City.* Erin, ON: Press Porcepic, 1975.
Ozorak, Paul. *Abandoned Military Installations of Canada.* Vol. 3: *Atlantic.* Published by author, 2001.
Parr, Joy. Introduction to *Histories of Canadian Childhood and Youth,* edited by Nancy Janavocek and Joy Parr, 1–7. Don Mills: Oxford University Press, 2003.
Parrott, William C. "On the Perimeter: A Reconstruction of the Military Geography of Newfoundland and Labrador during the Second World War, 1939–1945." MA thesis, Memorial University of Newfoundland, 1993.
Pierson, Ruth Roach. *"They're still women after all": The Second World War and Canadian Womanhood.* Toronto: McClelland & Stewart, 1986.
Pocius, Gerald L. *A Place to Belong: Community and Everyday Space in Calvert, Newfoundland.* Athens and London: University of Georgia Press, 1991.
Porter, Helen. *Below the Bridge: Memories of the South Side of St. John's.* St John's: Breakwater Books, 1979.
Porter, McKenzie. *To All Men: The Story of the Canadian Red Cross.* Toronto: McClelland & Stewart, 1960.
Posen, Sheldon, and Michael Taft. "The Newfoundland Popular Music Project." *Canadian Journal for Traditional Music,* 1973. http://cjtm.icaap.org/content/1/v1art4.html.
Potts, E.D., and A. Potts. *Yanks Down Under, 1941–45.* Melbourne: Oxford University Press, 1985.
Pugsley, William. *Saints, Devils and Ordinary Seamen: Life on the Royal Canadian Navy's Lower Deck.* Toronto: Collins, 1946.
Quigley, Gene. *Voices of World War II: A Collection of Oral Histories.* St John's: Jesperson Publishing, 2006.
Ransom, Bernard. "Canada's 'Newfyjohn,' Tenancy: The Royal Canadian Navy in St. John's, 1941–1945." *Acadiensis* 23, no. 2 (Spring 1994): 45–71.
Reeves, William. "Aping the 'American Type': The Politics of Development in Newfoundland, 1900–1908." *Newfoundland Studies* 10, no. 1 (1994): 44–72.
Reynolds, David. *The Creation of the Anglo-American Alliance, 1937–1941: A Study in Competitive Co-operation.* Chapel Hill: University of North Carolina Press, 1981.
– *Rich Relations: The American Occupation of Britain, 1942–1945.* New York: Random House, 1995.
Roberts, Leslie. "Canada and the War at Sea." In *Canada's War at Sea.* Vol. 2, edited by Stephen Leacock and Leslie Roberts. Montreal: Alvah M. Beatty, 1944.
Rompkey, Bill, ed. *St. John's and the Battle of the Atlantic.* St John's: Flanker Press, 2009.
Rose, Sonya O. "Sex, Citizenship, and the Nation in World War II Britain." *American Historical Review* 103, no. 4 (1998): 1147–76.
Rosenberg, Neil. "The Canadianization of Newfoundland Folk Songs; or the Newfoundlanization of Canadian Folksongs." *Journal of Canadian Studies* 29, no. 1: 55–73.
– "The Gerald S. Doyle Songsters and the Politics of Newfoundland Folksongs." *Canadian Folklore canadien* 13, no. 1: 45–57.
Rotundo, E. Anthony. "Boy Culture." In *The Children's Culture Reader,* edited by Henry Jenkins, 337–62. New York: New York University Press, 1998.
Rudy, Jarrett R. *The Freedom to Smoke.* Montreal and Kingston: McGill-Queen's University Press, 2005.
Sangster, Joan. *Earning Respect: The Lives of Working Women in Small-Town Ontario, 1920–1960.* Toronto: University of Toronto Press, 1995.
Sarles, Ruth. *A Story of America First: The Men and Women Who Opposed U.S. Intervention in World War II.* Westport, CT: Praeger, 2003.
Sarty, Roger. *The Maritime Defence of Canada.* Toronto: Canadian Institute of Strategic Studies, 1996.
Schull, Joseph. *The Far Distant Ships: An Official Account of Canadian Naval Operations in the Second World War.* Ottawa: King's Printer, 1950.
Sethna, Christabelle. "Wait Till Your Father Gets Home: Absent Fathers, Working Mothers and Delinquent Daughters in Ontario during World War II." In *Family Matters: Papers in Post-Confederation Canadian Family History,* edited by Lori Chambers and Edgar-André Montigny, 19–37. Toronto: Canadian Scholars' Press, 1998.
Sharpe, C.A. "Mr. Dunfield's Folly: The Development of Churchill Park Garden Suburb in St. John's." In *Four Centuries and the City: Perspectives on the Historical Geography of St. John's,* edited by Alan G. Macpherson, 83–122. St John's: Memorial University of Newfoundland, 2005.
– "'The Race of Honour': An Analysis of Enlistments and Casualties in the Armed Forces of Newfoundland, 1914–1918." *Newfoundland Studies* 4 (1988): 27–55.
– "'... to arouse our city from its deathlike apathy, from its reproachable lethargy, from its slumber of indus-

trial and social death.' The 1939 St. John's Municipal Housing Scheme." *Newfoundland Studies* 16 (2000): 47–66.

Shawyer, C.A., and A.J. Sharpe. "Addressing the Legacy of the Modern in Newfoundland: Churchill Park Garden Suburb in St. John's." In *Conserving the Modern in Canada: Buildings, Ensembles and Sites: 1945–2005*, edited by Susan Algie and James Ashby, 125–33. Winnipeg: Winnipeg Architecture Foundation, 2007.

Shirlaw, David J. *Point Edward: Canada's Forgotten Naval Base.* Lexington, MA: Lexington Press, 1999.

Shukert, E.B., and B.S. Scibetta. *The War Brides of World War II.* Novato, CA: Presidio Press, 1988.

Smallwood, J.R. *The Book of Newfoundland.* St John's: Newfoundland Book Publishers, 1937.

Smith, Kathleen E.R. *God Bless America: Tin Pan Alley Goes to War.* Lexington: University of Kentucky Press, 2003.

Stacey, C.P. *Arms, Men and Governments: The War Policies of Canada 1939–1945.* Ottawa: Queen's Printer, 1970.

Stewart, Ian M. "The 'Revolution of 1940' in Newfoundland." MA thesis, Memorial University of Newfoundland, 1974.

Story, G.M., W.J. Kirwin, and J.D.A. Widdowson. *Dictionary of Newfoundland English,* 2nd ed. Toronto: University of Toronto Press, 1990.

Strauss, Richard. "The Americans Come to Newfoundland." In *The Book of Newfoundland.* Vol. 6, edited by Joseph R. Smallwood. St John's: Newfoundland Book Publishers, 1967.

Strong-Boag, Victoria. "Canada's Wage-Earning Wives and the Construction of the Middle Class, 1945–60." *Journal of Canadian Studies* 29 (1994): 5–25.

Sutherland, Neil. *Growing Up: Childhood in English Canada from the Great War to the Age of Television.* Toronto: University of Toronto Press, 1997.

Tait, Robert Holland. *Newfoundland: A Summary of the History and Development of Britain's Oldest Colony from 1497 to 1939.* Harrington, NJ: Harrington Press, 1939.

Tarrant, V.E. *The U-Boat Offensive, 1914–1945.* Annapolis, MD: Naval Institute Press, 1989.

Tennyson, Brian, and Roger Sarty. *Guardian of the Gulf: Sydney, Cape Breton, and the Atlantic Wars.* Toronto: University of Toronto Press, 2000.

Toman, Cynthia. *An Officer and a Lady: Canadian Military Nursing and the Second World War.* Vancouver: University of British Columbia Press, 2007.

Tucker, Gilbert. *The Naval Service of Canada: Its Official History.* Vol. 2: *Activities on Shore during the Second World War.* Ottawa: King's Printer, 1952.

Tunbridge, John E. "The Churchill-Roosevelt Bases of 1940: The Question of Heritage in Their Adaptive Re-use." *International Journal of Heritage Research* 10 (2004): 229–51.

Tuttle, William M. *"Daddy's Gone to War": The Second World War in the Lives of America's Children.* New York: Oxford University Press, 1993.

Valentine, Gill. "Angels and Devils: Moral Landscapes of Childhood." *Environment and Planning D: Society and Space* 14 (1996): 581–99.

– "Children should be seen and not heard: The Production and Transgression of Adults' Public Space." *Urban Geography* 17, no. 3 (1996): 205–20.

Wagnleitner, Reinhold. *Coca-Colonization and the Cold War.* Chapel Hill: University of North Carolina Press, 1994.

Walkowitz, Judith. *Prostitution and Victorian Society: Women, Class and the State.* Cambridge, UK: Cambridge University Press, 1980.

Webb, Jeff A. "Repertoire and Reception: Musical Culture in St John's Newfoundland, 1930–1945." *Journal of Canadian Studies* 42, no. 2 (2008): 117–39.

– *The Voice of Newfoundland: A Social History of the Broadcasting Corporation of Newfoundland, 1939–1949.* Toronto: University of Toronto Press, 2008.

– "VOUS – Voice of the United States: The Armed Forces Radio Service in Newfoundland." *Journal of Radio Studies* 11, no. 1 (2004): 87–99.

Wells, Gordon C. *The Newfoundland Regiment (1939–1946): War on the Home Front.* Trinity, NL: Oceanside Press, 1997.

Wheaton, Carla Jane. "'… as modern as some of the fine new department stores … can make it': A Social History of the Large Water Street Stores, St. John's, Newfoundland, 1892–1949." PhD thesis, Memorial University of Newfoundland, 2003.

Whitham, Charlie. "On Dealing with Gangsters: The Limits of British 'Generosity' in the Leasing of Bases to the United States, 1940–41." *Diplomacy and Statecraft* 7, no. 3 (1996): 589–630.

Wik, Reynold M. *Henry Ford and Grass-Roots America.* Ann Arbor: University of Michigan Press, 1973.

Williams, Andrew. *The Battle of the Atlantic.* London: BBC Worldwide, 2002.

Wilson, Alan. "A Young Maritimer in the 1930s and '40s: A Memoir." In *Children's Voices in Atlantic Literature and Culture: Essays on Childhood,* edited by Hilary Thompson, 114–23. Guelph, ON: Canadian Children's Press, 1995.

Wilson, Budge. “To live in Halifax, Nova Scotia, is to be aware of the shadow of war – even in peacetime.” In *Too Young to Fight: Memories from Our Youth during World War II,* edited by Priscilla Galloway, 172–87. Toronto: Stoddart, 1999.

Wright, Richard B. *October.* New York: HarperCollins, 2007.

Zimmerman, David. “The Social Background of the Wartime Navy: Some Statistical Data.” In *A Nation's Navy: In Quest of Canadian Naval Identity,* edited by Michael L. Hadley, Rob Hubert, and Fred W. Crickard, 256–79. Montreal and Kingston: McGill-Queen's University Press, 1996.

Contributors

DOUGLAS BALDWIN, retired Acadia University history professor and freelance writer, has lectured in Japan, Great Britain, and the United States. Among his thirty books is the biography *She Answered Every Call: The Life of the Public Health Nurse, Mona Gordon Wilson, 1894–1981* (Charlottetown: Indigo Press, 1997).

KEN COATES is professor of history and dean of arts, University of Waterloo. He has written extensively on the history of northern Canada and on the regional impact of wartime military projects. With W.R. Morrison, he has written on the global experience of American soldiers and civilian personnel overseas during the Second World War.

PAUL COLLINS is finishing his PhD in history at Memorial University of Newfoundland, concentrating on the development of HMCS Avalon, the Royal Canadian Navy's escort base at St John's during the Second World War. He is the author of *Dangerous Waters* and has written a number of articles on the RCN's presence in Newfoundland during those turbulent years.

STEVEN HIGH is Canada research chair in public history at Concordia University and co-director of the Centre for Oral History and Digital Storytelling. He is the author of *Base Colonies in the Western Hemisphere* (2009) as well as of several other articles exploring the social and economic impact of the Anglo-American destroyers-for-bases deal in Newfoundland, Bermuda, and the British Caribbean.

BARBARA LORENZKOWSKI teaches at Concordia University in Montreal. She is the author of *Sounds of Ethnicity: Listening to German North America, 1850–1914*

(Winnipeg: University of Manitoba Press, 2010) and is currently working on a book manuscript on "The Children's War: Growing Up in the Seaport Cities of St. John's, Halifax and Saint John, 1939–1945."

WILLIAM R. MORRISON is professor of history at the University of Northern British Columbia. *Arctic Front*, his most recent book (co-authored), won the 2009 Donner Prize for best book on Canadian public policy.

GILLIAN POULTER is associate professor in the Department of History and Classics at Acadia University. She is the author of *Becoming Native in a Foreign Land: Sport, Visual Culture and Identity in Montreal, 1840–1885* (Vancouver: University of British Columbia Press, 2009) and of several articles exploring the cultural construction of identity. Her current research examines the ways in which people, particularly women, commemorate their lives and those of their families.

CHRISTOPHER A. SHARPE is professor of geography at Memorial University of Newfoundland. He has a long-standing interest in the home-front geography of the Newfoundland and Canadian war effort, especially its impact on the urban landscape. He is the author of the three war plates in volume 3 of the *Historical Atlas of Canada*.

A.J. SHAWYER, PhD, is a retired associate professor of geography, Memorial University of Newfoundland. She has researched cultural landscapes – contemporary and historical, urban and rural, and institutional – as expressions of policy. She also has experience in the museum profession.

JEFF A. WEBB is an associate professor of history at Memorial University and editor of the journal *Newfoundland and Labrador Studies*. He has published many essays in political and cultural history and is the author of *The Voice of Newfoundland: A Social History of the Broadcasting Corporation of Newfoundland.*

Index

ABCI (American British Conversations) agreement, 87–8, 96
Aborigines, treatment of in Australia, 265
Abraham, Ann, 117, 129, 133, 134, 135, 138, 140, 143, 155, 156, 163, 169, 201
Abraham, William Pepperrell, 163, 165
Act for the Defence of Newfoundland, 24
Admiral Scheer, 231
African-Americans: liberation of, 252; servicemen, 166–7, 265
age: as category of historical analysis, 113; children and, 124; oral history and, 115
"Air Gap." *See* "Pit, The"
air-raid drills, 141–2, 161, 162, 242
Alaska, 256
Alaska Highway, 256–7
alcohol use, 171, 197, 199, 206
Aleutian Islands, 256, 257
America First movement, 255
American Bases Act (1941), 43
American Bases (Supplementary Bases) Act (1942), 51
American Empire, 251, 252, 268; criticism of, 258
Americanization, 18, 192, 193
"American Rampant," 251, 268
American Red Cross Society, 223
Americas and West Indies Command, 91
Anglo-American Cable Company, 105
Anglo-American Leased Bases Agreement (1940), 41–2, 47, 70, 84, 90, 176, 188, 271n2. *See also* destroyers-for-bases deal
anti-aircraft batteries, 37–41, 49, 93
anti-modernism, 218
Anti-Submarine Warfare, 100–2
Argentia, U.S. base in, 17, 43, 98, 151, 167, 188, 202–3, 204–6, 255, 278n81, 278n89, 279n123
Armed Forces Radio Service (AFRS), 211–12, 217; absence of advertising on, 212; *Command Performance*, 208
ASDIC (Allied Submarine Detection Investigation Committee), 86, 100
Atlantic Charter, 95
Auckland (New Zealand), 268
Australia: African-American servicemen in, 265; U.S. servicemen in, 252, 259, 261, 264, 267, 273n31
Autry, Gene, 207
Avalon Telephone Company, 105
Avalon II, 281n157
Axis powers, 258
Ayre and Sons, 241

Badgley, Kerry, 283n14
Baine Johnston's, 281n159
Baird, David, 125–6, 130, 133, 147, 158, 168
Baldwin, Douglas, 158
Bally Haly Golf and Country Club, 44, 103
"Banks of Newfoundland, The," 206
Bannister, Jerry, 292n6
Barman, Jean, 114–15
Barn Dance, The, 136
bases, U.S.-leased, 3, 6, 17, 32, 41–4, 47, 155, 185–9. *See also under individual base locations*
"Battery," the, 22, 26, 44, 51, 52, 66, *90*
Battle of Britain, 258
Battle of Midway, 257
Battle of the Atlantic, 9, 58, 81–3, 116, 135, 232, 246
Bay Bulls, 69, 75, 98, 99
Beardsley, J.W., 210
Beaumont Hamel, battle of, 13, 23, 155
Bella Vista Country Club, 103
Bell Island, 24, 27, 76, 84, 116, 156; defence of, 25–6
Bennett, Walter, 215
Benson, Bob, 5
Bergen, Edgar, *196*, 201
Bergsma, Daniel, 181
Bermuda, 181, 253; U.S. base in, 3, 41, 84, 91, 155, 183, 260
Berry, Tom, 207
Bildergack, G.B., 211
Bishop Feild School, 129, 138–9, 163
blackouts, 141–2, 159–61, 171, 192, 199, 242, *243*
"Black Pit, The." *See* "Pit, The"
"Black" plan, 90
black servicemen, 166–7, 265

Black Watch, 85; Royal Highland Regiment, 27
Blondell, Joan, 208, 297n65
Blundon, Helen, 128, 169, 200, 204, 217
Board of Arbitration, 44, 46, 52, 61, 68
Board of Experts, 42–3, 45, 272n25
Bonaparte, Napoleon, 3
Book of Newfoundland, 204
Botwood: Canadian hospital in, 230, 247; defences for, 54; harbour and seaplane base at, 24, 26, 84
Bowring Brothers Ltd, 199, 281n159
Boyle, May, *247*
boys, wartime experiences of, 138–41
Brant, G.C., 97
Brazil, 260
Brisbane (Australia), 253, 268; riot in, 261
Bristol, Admiral, 96
British Admiralty, 55, 86, 87, 96, 100, 101, 274n4; docking facilities and, 98; property requisitions by, 59–60, 62; St John's base and, 58, 71, 74, 91–4
British Admiralty Delegation (BAD), 94, 98, 100
British Broadcasting Corporation (BBC), 156, 211, 219
British Caribbean, U.S. bases in, 3, 41, 155, 183, 252
British Columbia, 122
British Empire, 257, 268
British Red Cross Association of Newfoundland, 298n14
Broadcasting Corporation of Newfoundland (BCN), 208, 211; *Hymns from Home*, 211
Brokaw, Bill, 196
Brooks, John B., 184–5, 208, 211, 272n28
Brooks, Stanley Truman, 12
Brown, A. Maude, 156, 160, 172
Brown, Victoria B., 290n109
Browne, Les, 201
Buckmaster, Patrick, 281n162
Buckmaster's Field, 62–3, 66, 75, 177
"bumboats," 157
Burchell, Charles, 99, 105
Burke, Vincent, 213

Cabot Tower, 93, 97, *224*
Cadigan, Sean, 83
Cahill, M., 173
Cairns (Australia), 267, 268
Calver's Field, *40*, 74
Camp Alexander, 46, 47, *48*, 194
Canada: agreement with Newfoundland, 29; agreement with United States, 27; air force of, 8, 22, 54–7, 70, 73, 76, 85, 94, *144*, *154*, 177, 206; annexation of Newfoundland by, 153; army of, 8, 22, 30, 33–41, 56, 70, 73, 177; arrival of military in St John's, 30–46, 152; attitudes towards of Newfoundland, 70–1; *Comrades on Patrol* radio program, 211; defence of continent by, 12, 24; defence of Newfoundland by, 84; financial assistance to St John's by, 71, 91, 101; financing of St John's airport by, 54; fortification of Newfoundland by, 11; marriage between servicemen and Newfoundland women, 185; naval heritage of, 81–2; navy of, 8, 9, 22, 56, 57–70, 73, 76, 81–108, 177, 220, 280n144; radio content from, 210; rate of VD infection among servicemen, 181; relationship with Newfoundland, 26; role of in Battle of the Atlantic, 9; securing of Newfoundland by, 4; servicemen of, 13–16, 22, 131–2, 152, 155, 164–7; title to land in Newfoundland, 54; unruly behaviour by servicemen, 172; vs United States, views on, 152–5, 166, 175–6, 178–9; view of Newfoundland by, 21; U.S. servicemen in North of, 252, 258, 261, 267; War Cabinet, 71, 99; women's memories of servicemen, 167
Canadian General Electric, 276n56
Canadian Legion, 105, 226
Canadian Manufacturers Association, 86
Canadian Naval Service Headquarters (NSHQ), 57, 85–6, 99–100
Canadian Naval Well Baby clinics, 247
Canadian Northwest Atlantic Command, 283n4
Canadian Provost Corps, 173
Canadian Red Cross, 18, 84, 220–48; Annual Report (1944), 248; and military-civilian divide, 245; National Women's War Work Committee, 221, 225; Nursing Auxiliary, 247; post-war benefits of, 246–8; services of, 228–36; Uniformed Corps (Transport Section), 246–7; volunteers, 225, 228, 230–2
Canadian Red Cross Despatch, 234, 248
Canol (Canadian Oil) pipeline, 257
Cape Farewell (Greenland), 272n25
Cape Spear, 276n60; counter-bombardment battery, 35, *37*, *74*, 76; DEMS training, 101; Port War Signal Station, 63, 93, 94, 101
Caribou, 135, 137, 156
Caribou Hut, 105, 133, 134, 165, 168–9, 194, 198, 199, 206, 229, 234; as centre of information for Canadians, 228; Newfoundland men not welcome at, 168; volunteer work at, 155, 168; Wilson and, 226–8, 234, 246
Carnell, Andrew, 228
Case, W.F., 173
"cattle boats," 159
Chamberlain, Neville, 125
Chancey, Harold, 186, 187
Chapman, Christopher, 126
Cheeseman, Vicki, 126, 128, 133, 134, 143, 146
Chevrier, Lionel, 220
childhood, gendered worlds of, 116
children: effect of occupation on, 113–50; geographies of, 116, 117–25; historians of, 115; mobilization of, 113, 139–40; traffic and, 116
Children's Playground Association, 149
China, 255
Christian Brothers' Monastery, 27
Christian Science Monitor, 12
Churchill, Winston, 41–2, 85, 86, 89, 91, 94, 97, 126, 259, 278n81
Churchill Park, 78
Church Lads Brigade, 143, 202, 290n119
City Club, 103
City of Dieppe, 96
Civil Air Administration War Group, 26
civilians: interaction between military personnel and, 73, 176, 191, 194, 196, 197, 199, 206, 219, 226; limitations on access to bases, 194, 200–2, 206–7, 218
Clam, 96
Clark, Henry W., 197
Clarke, S.A., 216
class, 13; childhood and, 116, 118–20, 124; oral history and, 115; Wilson and, 224–5
Coca-Cola, 206, 260
"Coca-colonization," 258, 267
Cold War, 219, 267
Collins, Eileen, 117, 118, 124, 126, 130, 143, 146, 157, 172, 182
Collins, Paul, 157, 264
colour prejudice, 166–7
"Coming In on a Wing and a Prayer," 203–4, 207
Commercial Cable Company, 105

commercialism, 258
compensation, residents and, 44–6, 52–3, 61–2, 68
"Complaints Regarding the Conduct of Canadians," 172
Conception Bay, 49, 72, 116, 156
Concordia University, Centre for Oral History and Digital Storytelling, 271n9
consumer culture, 191–3, 202
Conway, Charlie, 7
Cook, June, 163, 172
corvettes, 57–8, 85–7, 94, 96, 102, 157
Costello, Gertrude, 209
Cowan, Hattie, 238
Crane, Norman, 122, 139, 143, 147
crime, 197; differential treatment of Canadian and U.S. servicemen, 176, 266
Crow's Nest Officers' Club, 7, 103, *157*
Cuckold's Cove, 24
cultural conservatism, 218
cultural imagery, 252
cultural insensitivity, 258
Cumbo, "Chick," 207
Czechoslovakia, invasion of, 126

Daily News, 197, 201, 206, 209, 210, 216, 217
dancing, 192, 194, 199, 202, 206, 207
danger, geography of, 116–17, 148
Davies, F.R.: *Stand By for Music*, 211
Dawson Creek (British Columbia), 256
defence agreements, 27–30
Defensively Equipped Merchant Ship (DEMS) training, 101
Delisle, 276n62
"denaturing," 212
Denny, Harold, 12
destroyers, 87, 94, 96, 102
destroyers-for-bases deal, 3, 11, 29, 40–2, 84, 255; Newfoundland and, 40–1. *See also* Anglo-American Leased Bases Agreement (1940)
Dickinson, Ethel, 226
disturbance, compensation for, 44–6, 52–3, 61, 68
Dominion Steel and Coal Company (DOSCO), 25, 26
Dönitz, Karl, 102
Dorsey, Jimmy, 207
"Down That Old Texas Trail," 207
Doyal, Thomas, 145, 289n88, 291n142
Doyle, Gerald S., 204, 208, 218
drunk and disorderly behaviour, 171–9
"drunken Canadian," myth of, 154
Duggan, Mickey, 203
Duley, Margaret, 198–9, 293n42
Dunfield, Brian, 24, 106

Eastern Defence Command, 181
ecological implications, military activity and, 252
economic prosperity, 263–4
Edmonton (Alberta), 256, 268
Edmund B. Alexander, *153*; arrival of in St John's, 3–5, 7, 8, 46, 48, 51, 130, 131, 137, 151, 171, 187, 191, 217, 251; attire of U.S. servicemen on, 12, 182; as floating barracks, 170, 210
Edwards, David, 118, 124, 133, 134, 141, 143, 161, 202, 215
Ellis, Fraser, 157, 158, 166, 177, 183, 189
Emergency Powers (Defence) Act, 276n47
Emerson, L.E., 26–7, 42, 43, 50, 77, 84, 91, 176
employment, on bases, 15, 47, 72, 170, 187
ethnicity, 119
ethnic stereotypes, 214
Evening Telegram (St John's), 5, 6, 107, 121, 128, 132, 145, 147–9, 155, 160, 167, 168, 171, 179

Fairbanks (Alaska), 256
fathers, role of, 123, 124–5
Fiji, U.S. base in, 259, 261
fishery, 22, 153
FitzGerald, John Edward, 14, 151, 152, 223
Flatrock, 50, 280n130
Flower-class corvettes. *See* corvettes
Forcier, Donat J., 206
forestry industry, 22
Fort Amherst, 97; battery at, 33–4, 48, 76, *77*, 93, 276n62, 277n67; Canadian Army at, 8, 276n60; isolation of, 165; Port War Signal Station at, 63, 94
Fort Chain Rock, 35; battery at, 34, *75*, 76, 276n60; as restricted area, 37
Fort Pepperrell, U.S. base at, 8, *17*, 22, *49*, 50, 71, 194, *195*, *196*, *201*, 203, *205*, 211, 219, 255, 279n123, 283n5; building of, 43, 47–8, 53; civilian workers at, 188; clearing the way for, 44–6; female food handlers at, 181; as "five-star hotel," 179; number of employees at, 72; post-war use of, 76; radio station at, 127; reduction in size of, 75; reputation of, 202; social life at, 146, 170, 176, 200, 203, 207–8, 216
Fort Townshend, 27
Fort William Officers Mess, 104
France, fall of, 3, 10, 11, 54
Fraser, Stuart, 126, 131, 133, 141, 143, 150, 162–3, 176, 289n64
Frayne, Trent, 8
French-Canadian regiments, 166, 293n33
"friendly invasions": characteristics of, 263–8, 273n31; historiography of, 252–4; rethinking, 151–90
Frobisher Bay, 256
fur industry, 22
Fussell, Paul, 207, 208

Gallagher, R.J., 122, 127, 139, 170, 182, 203, 293n35
Galloway, Priscilla, 126
Gander: airport at, 11, 22, 24, 26–7, 29, 84, 255, 271n4, 274n4; Canadian hospital in, 230, 247; defences for, 54
"Gap, The." *See* "Pit, The"
"gatching," 132
gate keeping, institutions and, 191–219
gender, 13, 14, 123–4, 194, 219, 252, 273n32; childhood and, 116, 124; oral history and, 115; Wilson and, 224–5, 244–5
gendered spaces, 138–47
General Greene, 272n25
geographies, children's, 116, 117–25
German, Tony, 82
Germany, 26, 38, 258, 268; *Blitzkrieg*, 84; militarism in, 255; U-boats, 55, 57, 59, 81, 85–7, 97, 102, 108, 135, 156, *253*, 256, 275n24, 275n28, 276n62, 279n113, 286n78, 286n82
Gilbert, Sir Humphrey, 226
Gill, Carman, 184
Gilmour, Clyde, 204
Gilpatrick, J.E., 202
Girl Guides, 225
girls, wartime experiences of, 120, 138
Globe and Mail, The, 10, 209
Goodyear, Tom, 118
Goose Bay, air base at, 255, 267, 274n4
Goranson, Paul: *Posted to Newfie*, *174*
Gosling Memorial Library, 105
government jurisdictions, overlapping, 265–6
Gray, Ruth, 108
Great Bear Lake, 260

Great Britain: agreement with United States, 27; Atlantic trade war, 81; destroyers-for-bases deal, 41–2; disruption of exports from, 193; friendly invasion in, 252, 254, 259; race relations in, 265; radio content from, 210; relationships with U.S. servicemen, 264; responsible government in Newfoundland, 154
"Great Circle Route," 3, 97
Great Depression, 122, 194, 238, 254, 264
Great Plains, ecological catastrophe on, 255
Green, Gary, 7; *A Guide for Some of the Gun Shield Art ...*, *3, 21, 81, 113, 151, 191, 220, 251*
Green Lantern, 103
Greenslade, John W., 42–3, 58, 272n25
gun shield art, *3*, 7, *21*, *81*, *113*, *151*, *157*, *191*, *220*, *251*

Hadley, Michael, 81–2; *U-Boats against Canada*, 81
"Hail! Hail! The Gang's All Here," 191
Halifax, Lord, 285n44
Halifax (Nova Scotia), 82, 85; Bedford Basin, 94; VE Day riots in, 287n119
Halley, James J., 156, 179, 293n44
Harbour Grace, 99, 236
Harrington, Michael: *Newfoundland Tapestry*, 216
Harrison, G.A., 101
Haywood, Ruth, 294n64
Heavy [Anti-Aircraft] (HAA) Battery, 38, *39*
Herbert, Tish, 108
Herbertson, J.W., 275n31
Higgins, John, 213
Higgins, Justice W.J., 44, 61
High, Steven, 83, 192, 283n19
"High Frequency Direction Finding" (HF/DF), 93, 100, 285n62
Hill O'Chips, 38, *39*
Hiscock, Daisy, 156, 160, 165, 166
Hiscock, Philip, 193, 208
His Majesty's Canadian Dockyard, 60–2, *63*, *159*
Hitler, Adolf, 97, 258
HMCS *Agassiz*, 93
HMCS *Alberni*, 93
HMCS Avalon, 62–3, *64*, 76, 82–3, 100–1, 107–8
HMCS *Burlington*, *260*
HMCS *Chambly*, 93
HMCS *Cobalt*, 93
HMCS *Collingwood*, 93
HMCS *Dauphin*, *151*
HMCS *Dolphin*, *151*
HMCS *Matapedia*, *87*, *89*, *90*, *92*
HMCS *Moose Jaw*, *81*
HMCS *Orillia*, 93
HMCS *Saskatoon*, *69*, *113*
HMCS *Skeena*, *21*
HMCS Stadacona, 107
HMCS *Transcona*, 220
HMCS *Trillium*, *113*
HMCS *Valleyfield*, 108
HMCS *Wetaskiwin*, *3*, 7, 93
HMS *Burwell*, *191*
HMS *Courageous*, 284n29
HMS *Dianthus*, *66*, *251*
HMS *Firedrake*, 150
HMS *Greenwich*, 96
HMS *Trillium*, *66*
Holloway School, 158
Holy Cross School, 139
home front vs battle front, 5–6, 116, 155, 197, 219
Hong Kong, British base in, 258
Hope, Bob, 201
Hope, G.B., 189
Hopper, George D., 163, 184, 185
House of Peter McGregor, The, 126
Hutchens, Cecil, 3–5, 7, 151
Hutchinson, Caroline, 226

Iceland, 85, 94, 158, 181, 252, 259, 261
"I'll Be Seeing You," 203
illegitimate births, 179
Imperial Café, 107
Imperial Oil, 25, 35, 281n159; fire at, 281n192
India, 260
individuality, suppression of, 193–4
inflation, 16
Ingram, Darcy, 298n27
Inner Sanctum, The, 126
institutions, as gatekeepers, 191–219
International Red Cross, 298n14
"Is You Is, or Is You Ain't, My Baby," 204
It Pays to Be Ignorant, 215

James Baird Ltd, 199, 241
Jamieson, Don, 21, 204
Japan, 257, 258, 268; militarism in, 255. *See also* Pearl Harbor
Jefferson, Thomas, 3
Jervis Bay, 231, 272n25
Jim Crow segregation, 167
Job Brothers, 281n159
Johns Hopkins Hospital, 223
Johnson Family Foundation, 271n9
Johnston, Wayne, 151
Joint Services Cemetery, 76
Joseph, Gilbert M., 274n51
juvenile delinquency, 113, 121

Kearney, Margaret, 126, 131, 134, 137, 143, 146, 165, 172, 182, 202, 289n88
Kehoe, E.L., 180
Kenna's Hill, 55–6, 74
Kennedy, Frank, 146, 166, 201, 215
Kerr, Philip. *See* Lord Lothian
Kiegesmarine, 102
King, William Lyon Mackenzie, 26, 29, 86, 89–90
King George V Seamen's Institute, 226
King Malcolm, 276n62
Knights of Columbus, 226
Knights of Columbus hostel, 105, 133, 155, *167*, 168, 169, 206, 248, 298n18; fire in, 7, *9*, 13, *78*, 105–7, 135–7, 157, 229, 235; Red Cross and, 229, 234, 246
Korneski, Kurt, 218
Krumm, Maude, *245*, *247*

Ladies' Auxiliary of the Irish Benevolent Society, 226
Lake, Harold, *15*
Lamb, James, 82
Lambiase, Louise, 152, 156, 160, 163, 165, 170, 182, 185, 217
League of Nations, 254
Leased Bases Agreement. *See* Anglo-American Leased Bases Agreement
Leboeuf, Levis, *167*
Ledrew, George, 116, 127, 130, 157
LeMessurier, H.W., 204
Lester, Charles, 32
Lester's Field, 8, *30*, 31–2, 35, 74, 83, 84, 177, 276n53, 283n5
"life history" approach, 13
Light [Anti-Aircraft] (LAA) Battery, 38
Lincoln and Welland Regiment, 25
Logy Bay, 50
Lone Ranger, The, 215
Lorenzkowski, Barbara, 84
Lothian, Lord (Philip Kerr), 44
Louisiana, purchase of, 3

Lowenthal, David, 114
Lunn, Janet, 113
Lyons, Major, 60–1

MacArthur, Douglas, 259
McCarthy, Charlie, *196*, 201
McClure, Don, 132, 288n39
McCormack, C., 174
MacDonald, Malcolm, 101
McEachren, Clara F., 220
Macintyre, Donald: *U-Boat Killer*, 283n2
MacKenzie, David, 119, 192
MacLeod, Malcolm, 185
MacLeod, Robert, 204, 218
McMurdo's pharmacy, 200
MacPherson, Cluny, 298n14
Major, Kevin, 15, 17
Maltese Falcon, The, 202
Maori, treatment of, 265
Maple Leaf Clubs, 298n27
marriage, 120, 264; between U.S. servicemen and Newfoundland women, 152, 154, 155, 182–5, 264
Marshall, Gene, 210
Martin, Dorothy, *247*
Marvita, 93
mass media, 192, 202
material culture, exchanges of, 217
materialism, 265–7
Memorial University: Centre for Newfoundland Studies, 271n9; Folklore and Language Archives, 273n33
Memorial University College, 31; Art Students' Club, 216
men, women vs, 130, 145, 219
Merchant Marine, 9, 64, 139, 156
Merchant Seamen's Club, 229, 299n32
Meschino, Paul, 72
Messacar, Herbert A., 227
Middle Cove, 50
Mid-Ocean Escort Force (MOEF), 64–70, 73, 81, 97, 98
Mid-Ocean Meeting Point (MOMP), 94
militarism, 255
militarization, 8, 84, 267–8
Miller, Glenn, 200, 207
Milner, Marc, 6, 81–2; *North Atlantic Run*, 9, 81
minesweepers, 87
mining, 22
"Miss You," 207
modernization, 192, 218
Monthly Anti-Submarine Report, 100
morality, public, 128
moral panic, 179–82
Morine, Alfred B., 10–11
mothers, 123; as homemakers, 120–2; working, 121
Mount Cashel Orphanage, 44
Mount Kitheron, 276n62
Mount Pearl, 25, 94
Mount Pleasant Cemetery, *78*
movies, 194, 199, 202
Murray, Jean M., 164, 168
Murray, L.W., 93, 94, 96–7, 285n77
music, 192, 195–7, 199, 202–4, 206–8, 215, 217; church, 206; country-western, 216; folk, 208, 218; Newfoundland, 193, 208, 218; popular, 193, 216; swing, 193, 203
Musical Commandos, The, 207, 208, 210

Nasaw, David, 119
National Film Board: *Proudly She Marches*, 108; *Wings on Her Shoulders*, 108; *Yanks for Uncle Sam*, 185
nationalism, Newfoundland, 153–4, 292n6
National Research Council (NRC), 86
Native Americans, liberation of, 252
Naval Barracks Officers Mess, 104
Naval Guide Book, 105
Neary, Peter, 4, 5–6, 17, 83, 163, 168, 180, 190; *Newfoundland in the North Atlantic World*, 192
New Brunswick, 225
Newbury, A. Doug, 186–7, 293n34
New Caledonia, 261
New England, out-migration to, 153
"Newfies": use of term, 209
Newfoundland: adaptation to by U.S. servicemen, 213; agreement with Canada, 29; art of, 193, 216–17; attitude towards Canada, 70–1, 223; Canada's possession of land title in, 54; Commission of Government, 6, 21, 29, 37, 42, 89–90, 99, 156, 188, 274n10; culture of, views on, 204; decision to join Canada, 83, 153, 192; declaration of war by, 24, 255; destroyers-for-bases deal and, 41–2, 90; effect of American efficiency on, 192; employment of civilians on bases, 47; enlistment of men of, 9, 189; fortification of, 11; as "garrison country," 4; German raid on, fear of, 97; hesitancy about St John's base, 89–91; history and geography of, 21, 213–14; intellectual and artistic contacts, 216; modernization of, 17, 192, 218; music of, 193, 208; nationalism in, 153–4, 292n6; "natives," reaction to label of, 214; popular culture, 191–219; relationship with Canada, 26; responsible and elected government in, 77, 154; roadways in, 186; rural population, effect of American culture on, 193; size and location of, 11; social and political differences between U.S. and, 213; strategic value of, 11–12, 256; treatment of residents as second-class people, 214; volunteers in, 125; war, public remembrance of, 154; working-class men in, 171. *See also* St John's
Newfoundland Airport. *See* Gander
Newfoundland Base Command (NBC), 46, 183, 184, 197
Newfoundland Broadcasting Company, 24–5
Newfoundland Constabulary, 24, 26, 27, *162*, 173
Newfoundland Defence Force, 92
Newfoundland Defence Scheme (1936), 24, 57
Newfoundland Dockyard, 94, 98, 101, 102, 280n155
Newfoundland Escort Force (NEF), 57–8, 59, 81, 89, 96–7, 102, 238; amalgamation of with RN, 64; arrival of in St John's, 93–4, 129–30; establishment of, 82, 84, 87, 107
Newfoundland Forestry Unit, 24, 156, 247
Newfoundland Hotel, 55, 96, 104, 225, 238, *240*
Newfoundland Militia, 9, 24, 26, 70, 74, 275n42; 1st Coastal Defence Battery, 26; Shamrock Field and, 27, *28*, *29*
Newfoundland Outport Nursing and Industry Association (NONIA), 217
Newfoundland Railway, 22, 175, 208, 218, 279n123
Newfoundland Ranger Force, 274n9, 292n7
Newfoundland Red Cross Society, 248
Newfoundland Regiment, 9, 156; decimation of, 22. *See also* Newfoundland Militia
Newfoundland Studies, 181
Newfoundland Tourist Board, 272n28
Newfoundland Visiting Forces (British Commonwealth) Act, 275n42

"Newfyjohn," 6, 8, 57–9, 82; etymology of term, 280n141. *See also* St John's
New Guinea, 261
New York, 119
New York Times, 10, 11, 272n25
New Zealand: African-American servicemen in, 265; U.S. servicemen in, 252, 259
Noel, S.J.R., *Politics in Newfoundland*, 191
Norman Wells (Northwest Territories), 256
Northern Ranger, 237
Northwest Staging Route, 256
NSHQ. *See* Canadian Naval Service Headquarters

Oakley, Gilbert, 122, 126, 135, 137, 141, 144, 145, 156, 158, 159, 215, 293n34
Ogdensburg Agreement, 29, 90
Old Colony Club, 103, 107
Omrac Sewing Club, 226
O'Neil, Frankie, 119
O'Neill, Paul, 6, 83, 114, 123, 126, 130, 132, 136, 137, 140, 141, 145, 162, 170, 175, 176
oral history interviewing, 13, 115, 119, 155, 156, 254
Otis Fensom Elevator Company, 277n66
Outerbridge, Colonel, 160
Outer Cove, 50
overseas forestry unit, 9
Overton, James, 292n7, 299n56

Page, L.F., 30, 38–40, 173
Palliser, Hugh, 213–14
Panama, 260, 261
Panama Canal, 3
Pasaro, Michael, 210
patriotism, 156
Pearl Harbor, 57, 72–3, 75, 96, 137, 255, 256, 259
Penney, Brad, 185
Pensolver, 276n62
Penson, J.H., 42, 91
Pepperrell, William, 279n103
Perlin, Albert, 197, 297n104
Permanent Joint Board of Defence (PJBD), 11, 29, 54, 90, 275n44
Philippines, 259
Philips, Lanier, 293n36
"Phoney War," 84
"pickups," 180
Pierson, Ruth Roach, 290n127, 294n62
Pike, Freddy, 148
"Pit, The," 85, 94
Placentia, 167
play, children's, 131, 138, 142–3, 147–50
Pleasantville, 8, 44, 45, 75, 177
Poland, invasion of, 126
Pollux, 166
popular culture: American, 193, 196, 218–19, 252, 258, 266–7; British vs American, 219; Newfoundland, 191–219
Port aux Basques, 279n123
Porter, Helen, 117, 119, 120, 123, 126, 128, 129, 130, 131, 135, 136, 137, 150, 156, 166, 169, 182, 289n78; *Below the Bridge*, 143
Port War Signal Stations, *33*, 34, 63, 93, 94, 276n60
Poulter, Gillian, 158
poverty, 119, 239–40, 292n7, 299n56
"poverty myth," 154
Powel, Harford, 211–12, 215
Power, C.G., 29–30, 272n20, 275n44
Powers, Frank, 171
pregnancy, unwanted, 199
Prentice, J.D. "Chummy," 93
Prim, Joe, 118, 121, 130, 139, 143, 147, 154, 157, 171, 175, 189, 289n88
Prince Edward Island, Mona Wilson and, 221–2, 223, 225, 237
Prince of Wales, 95
Prince Rupert (British Columbia), 268
private vs public, 142
Project Crimson, 256
property acquisition, military construction and, 35, 37–41, 52–3, 60–2, 66, 68
prostitution, 179–82
protectionism, 254
Prowse, D.W.: *History of Newfoundland*, 213–14
public space, reformulation of, 116, 147
Puddester, John, 163
Purity Factories, 74

Queen's Own Rifles, 275n45
Queen Tavern, 103
Quidi Vidi Lake, *17, 22–3*, 24, 43, 44, 47

race, 155, 166–7, 183
race relations, 265
racial mixing, 185
racial segregation, 212, 252
racism, 252, 258; attitudes towards, 265
radar, 100
radio, 125–7, 156, 191, 192, 197, 207–8, 210–16; orientation programs, 212–15
railway, speed of, 208–9
Ralston, J.E., 89
Ransom, Bernard, 6, 83, 178
rationing, 163, 240
Red Cross. *See* Canadian Red Cross
Red Triangle, 105, 107, 155, 168, 293n43, 298n18
Reeves, William, 218
regional cultures, re-militarization of, 267
religion, 13; childhood and, 116, 117–19; oral history and, 115
re-militarization, 267
Rennie's River, 76
residents, conflicts between military and, 35, 37–41, 52–3, 60–2
Reykjavik (Iceland), 259, 268
Rice, Bud, 210–11, 212
Riddell, Surgeon Lieutenant, *65*
Roosevelt, Franklin D., 3, 29, 41–2, 90, 95, 97, 255, 260, 278n89, 285n44; Presidential Library of, 188
Rose, Sonya, 13
Rosenberg, Neil, 208
Rotundo, E. Anthony, 138
Royal Air Force (Great Britain), 9, 156
Royal Artillery, 156
Royal Canadian Air Force (RCAF), 8, 22, 70, 73, 76, 85, *144*, 177, 206; arrival of in St John's, 54–7; No. 1 Group, Eastern Air Command, 55–6; RCN and, 94; Women's Division, *154*
Royal Canadian Artillery, 26; "Q" Battery, 33; 25th and 26th Anti-Aircraft Regiments, 277n67
Royal Canadian Mounted Police (RCMP), 274n9
Royal Canadian Navy (RCN), 8, 9, 22, 56, 73, 76, 129, 177, 220, 280n144; age of men in, 102; arrival of in St John's, 57–9; attacks in the Atlantic, 100; behaviour of service personnel, 107; building of base for, 58–9; "C" escort groups, 100; development of transatlantic base in St John's, 81–108; expansion of in St John's, 60–70; facilities for personnel, 102–5; hospitals, 63, *65*, 68–9, 74, 94; HX convoys, 95, 285n73; magazine exchange, 105; Mobile Anti-Submarine Training Unit No. 11, 101; RCAF and, 94; religion and, 105; Royal Navy and, 89; SC convoys, 95, 285n73, 286n101

Royal Canadian Navy Volunteer Reserve (RCNVR), 102
Royal Navy (Great Britain), 9, 10, 24, 64, 85, 86, 94, 100, 156, 189, 280n144
Royal Oak, 284n29
Royal Rifles of Canada, 166
Royal Stores, 241
Russia, 258
Rusted, Nigel, 160, 177, 293n44
"Ryans and the Pittmans," 204

St Bonaventure's College, 27
St John's: African-American servicemen in, 265; American materialism in, 267; arrival of American forces in, 42–4, 46–53, 193, 251; arrival of Canadian forces in, 30–46, 152, 252; arrival of RCAF in, 54–7; arrival of RCN in, 57–9; businessmen in, 61–2; Canadian hospital in, 230, 247; Canadian investment in base, 101; categorization of, 6; central role in Battle of the Atlantic, 82; City Council, 23, 32, 40, 70; civil defence organization, 159; Commission of Enquiry into Housing and Town Planning, 16, 239; coping with the occupation, 70–3; cosmopolitan nature of, 210; cost of establishing base, 91; cost of living in, 16, 189, 240–1; docking facilities in, 98–9, 101–2; eating and drinking in, 103–4, 241; economic prosperity in, 264; enlistment by men of, 128–9; as epicentre of tripartite militarization, 268; explosions in, 97; first World War II military encampment in, 27; as garrison town, 21, 171; as "Gibraltar of the West," 21; harbour, 5, *6*, *10*, *14*, 18, 21, *22*, *28*, 30, 33, 43, 48, 58, *60*, *61*, 64, *67*, 71, 79, 81–108, *114*, 117, *127*, 130–2, 155, 157–9, *221*, *224*, 276n62; hostels in, 105, 167–70; housing in, 16, 72–3, 239–40; inflation in, 240; initial defence arrangements in, 23–7; legacy in landscape of, 76–9; leisure activities and facilities in, 194; as main escort base, 82; memories of city at war, 125–38, 155–64; new aerodrome in, 54–5; number of military personnel in, 22, 274n5; occupation of in global perspective, 251–69; overcrowding in, 16, 189; overlapping government jurisdictions in, 266; as port of refuge for damaged ships, 158; post-war situation in, 73–5; poverty in, 239–40; property acquisition in, 35, 37–41, 52–3, 60–2, 66, 68; recreation programs in, 102–3; redefinition of urban spaces in, 263; religion in, 105; re-militarization in, 267; rent inflation in, 72; residents of as rubes, 209–10; as safe haven for survivors, 98, 158; shopping in, 105, 241; social clubs in, 73; social relations, 265; strained infrastructure of, 197; Tactical Training Centre (TTC), 101; taxes, levying of, 70; as town with limited recreational facilities, 197; traffic in, 147–9; transition of to transatlantic base, 81–108, 157; transportation in, 104–5; tuberculosis mortality rate in, 239; unemployment in, 238; water and sewer services, 70; Wilson's impressions of, 238–46. *See also* "Newfyjohn"
St John's Ambulance, 225, 230
St John's Housing Corporation, 78
St John's War Services Committee, 226
"Saint Louis Blues," 207
St Louis Post-Dispatch, 12
Salvation Army, 73, 206, 226, 298n18
Sarty, Roger, 284n33
Scammel-Reynolds, Elizabeth, 186
Scammell, Art, 208, 218
scarecrows, 55, 280n133
Scher, Ira, 207
Schnorkel, 102
Schull, Joseph, 82; *The Far Distant Ships*, 283n3
Schwerdt, C.M.R., 92–3, 284n33, 285n61
Seagoing Officers' Club. *See* Crow's Nest Officers' Club
Seal, E.A., 94, 100
searchlights, 162
secularization, 202
sex, 179–82; extramarital, 197
sexual double standard, 181
sexually transmitted diseases. *See* venereal disease
Shadow, The, 215
Shamrock Field, *40*; Newfoundland Militia and, 27, *28*, *29*, 70, 74
Sharpe, Chris, 83, 263
Shawyer, Jo, 83, 263
Shectman, Irving, 208
"sheepdog" navy, 8
Sheppard, Reginald, 215–17
Show Boat, 169, 204
Shulamite, 93
Signal Hill, 48–9, *51*, *52*
Silvers, Phil, 201
Sinatra, Frank, 201
Singapore, British base in, 258
Sky Nights, 203
Smith, Betty, *247*
Smith's Dock, 86
smoking, 144–5
social history, 5, 113; vs military history, 5
social relations, 264–5
social spaces, 116; men's and women's, 145
Solomon Islands, 261
SONAR. *See* ASDIC
Song of Bernadette, The, 202
Southern Pride, 86
Spencer College, 138
sports, 73, 102–3, 194, 202, 205, 212
steel industry, 25, 84
Stephens, G.L., 94, 99, 101
Stephenville, U.S. base in, 17, 43, 151, 188, 255, 279n123
Sterling Restaurant, *120*
Stewart, Ian M., 192–3
stock market crash, 255
sulfadiazine, 235–6
Superman, 126
Surinam, U.S. base in, 258
Sutherland, Neil, 115, 122, 287n6
Sydney, 25, 283n12

Tait, R.H.: *Newfoundland*, 213
"Tangerine," 207
Teakwood, 96
Terra Nova, 276n62
Terra Nova Club, 103, 298n18
Thule (Greenland), 203
Tonga, 18, 258, 259
Torbay, 8; aerodrome at, 40, 50, 56, 74, 133, 177, 255, 280n134
Torbay Bight, 50
Torch landings, North Africa, 98
Toronto Daily Star, 11
traffic, children and, 116, 147–9
trains: behaviour on, 173–5; speed of, 208–9
Trinidad, 18
Truxton, 166, 293n36
Tucker, Gilbert, 82; *The Naval Service of Canada*, 92, 283n3
Tuttle, William, Jr, 135, 138

U-boats. *See* Germany
U.K. Dominions Office, 24

unemployment, 263
United Service Organization (USO) club, 104, 168, 180, 192, 197, 200, 208, 293n43; army hostesses, 206; concerts, 203, 206–8; *Prepare for Action* radio program, 210–11
United States: agreements with Canada and Great Britain, 27; Army, 8, 15, 16, 181, 183; Army Nursing Corps, 223; Army Orchestra, 208; Army Supply Dock, 52–3; arrival of military in St John's, 46–53, 193; Atlantic trade war, 81; as belligerent, 97; choice of bases, 42–4; conscription in, 193; defence of, 3; defence of continent by, 12, 256; dependence of on Great Britain, 10; destroyers-for-bases deal and, 41–2; expansionism of, 251, 252, 257–62; "general powers," 91; involvement in World War II, inevitability of, 256; isolationism in, 260; leisure activities of servicemen, 193–4, 197; Lend-Lease Bill, 90, 92, 255; military expansion of, 252, 257–62; Navy, 15, 16, 87, 95, 99, 280n144; neutrality acts, 255; number of overseas troops, 261, 262; overseas mobilization of military, 257–9; policy on marriage with Newfoundland women, 183–5; post-war actions of, 261; protectionism of, 254; radio content from, 210; rate of VD infection among servicemen, 181; responsibilities in western Atlantic, 96; securing of Newfoundland by, 4; security of, 32; servicemen of, 13–16, 22, 84, 131–2, 151, 182–5; social and political differences between Newfoundland and, 213; social life in before war, 202; strategic control of Northwest Atlantic, 88; unemployment in, 255; vs Canada, views of, 152–5, 166, 175–6, 178–9; view of Newfoundland by, 21; as world's most important military and political power, 268
urban spaces, redefinition of, 263
USS *St Louis*, 42, 272n25

Valentine, Gill, 148, 150
venereal disease, 179–82, 183, 199, 294n71
Victoria Order of Nurses, 225
Victoria Rifles, 30–1
violence, 197
VLR (Very Long Range) aircraft, 284n26
VOCM radio, 106, 203, 215; *Army Night*, 211
"Voice of Newfoundland" (VONF), 127, 156, 191, 208, 210, 215
"Voice of the United States" (VOUS), 127, 192, 197, 211–12, 215–16
volunteers, 24, 73, 84, 125, 155, 156, 168–9, 225, 228, 230–3, 235–6

Wabana mines, 25–6
wages, 187–9
Walkowitz, Judith, 294n71
Walsh, James, 124, 125, 135, 136, 139, 143, 144–5, 149, 158, 160, 171, 179, 187, 289n62
Walwyn, Lady Eileen, 225–6, 246
Walwyn, Humphrey, 13, 16, 24, 26, 44, 58, 84, 91, 246
Wanderers Club, 299n29
War Assets Corporation, 75
war brides, 264–5
war effort, contributions to, 163–4
war savings certificates, 189
Waterford Hall Home for Infants, 294n64
Way, Ruth, 296n65
Welles, Orson, 204
Western Approaches Command, 91
Western Local Escort Force (WLEF), 94
Western Ocean Meeting Point (WESTOMP), 94
"Wet Ass Queen." *See* HMCS *Wetaskiwin*
"W" Force. *See* Canada, army of
Wheaton, Carla, 193
Wheler, Eleanor, 225
"When We Sing 'America,'" 208
White, Bill, *15*
White, Charles J., 208
Whitehorse (Yukon), 256, 263, 267
Williams, Andrew, 283n1
Williams, Kathleen, 136, 145, 169
Wilson, Mona, 18, 84, 117, 131, 158, 220–48; arrival of in St John's, 225; awards given to, 223; becoming assistant Red Cross commissioner of Newfoundland, 221; birth of, 223; as Canadian, 244; Caribou Hut and, 226–8, 246; education of, 223; experience of, 221–4; gender roles and, 224–5, 244–5; impressions of Newfoundland, 236–7; overseas experience of, 223; rank of, 244; relationship of with workers, 225; sense of privilege of, 225; sewing committees and, 230–2; social background of, 246; survivors, caring for, 230–6, 247; as volunteer, 234; wartime narrative of, 224
Wilson, Patricia, 134
Wilson, Woodrow, 254
Windsor Lake, 24
Winsor, Patricia, 118, 122, 123, 126, 128–9, 144, 147, 161, 165
Winter, H.A., 77, 273n47, 297n109
Witless Bay, 72
women, 142, 145–7; access of to entertainment on bases, 201; in childhood, 116; disorderly behaviour and, 171; in domestic service, 121; marriage with U.S. servicemen, 152, 154, 155, 182–5; memories of Canadian servicemen, 167–70; moral standing of, 181; as primary carriers of VD, 180; as promiscuous, 179, 182, 273n32; relationships with U.S. servicemen, 169–70, 198–9; safety of, 146–7, 172; sexual vulnerability of, 182; vs men, 130, 145, 201, 219; in war effort, 107–8
Women's Patriotic Association (WPA), 163, 168, 225, 247–8
Woods, Wilfrid, 38, 43, 70, 72, 101, 173
workmen's compensation, 188
world history, 253
World War I, 23, 86, 124, 156, 225, 254, 255, 267
WRCNS (Women's Royal Canadian Naval Service), 62, 107–8
Wrens, 107–8

YMCA, 73, 105, 169, 204, 226, 234, 248
York Theatre, *164*
Young, Harold, 207, 210
"youth problem," 113
Yukon, 18
YWCA, 73